THE POETICS OF NATIONAL AND RACIAL IDENTITY IN NINETEENTH-CENTURY AMERICAN LITERATURE

John D. Kerkering's study examines the literary history of racial and national identity in nineteenth-century America. Kerkering argues that writers such as Du Bois, Lanier, Simms, and Scott used poetic effects to assert the distinctiveness of certain groups in a diffuse social landscape. Kerkering explores poetry's formal properties, its sound effects, as they intersect with the issues of race and nation. He shows how formal effects, ranging from meter and rhythm to alliteration and melody, provide these writers with evidence of a collective identity, whether national or racial. Because of this shared reliance on formal literary effects, national and racial identities, Kerkering shows, are related elements of a single literary history. This is the story of how poetic effects helped to define national identities in Anglo-America as a step toward helping to define racial identities within the United States. This highly original study will command a wide audience of Americanists.

John D. Kerkering is Assistant Professor of English at Loyola University Chicago.

Recent books in this series

138. MICHELE BIRNBAUM
Race, Work and Desire in American Literature, 1860–1930

137. RICHARD GTUSIN
Culture, Technology and the Creation of America's National Parks

136. RALPH BAUER
The Cultural Geography of Colonial American Literatures: Empire, Travel, Modernity

135. MARY ESTEVE
The Aesthetics and Politics of the Crowd in American Literature

134. PETER STONELEY
Consumerism and American Girl's Literature, 1860–1940

133. ERIC HARALSON
Henry James and Queer Modernity

132. WILLIAM R. HANDLEY
Marriage, Violence, and the Nation in the American Literary West

131. WILLIAM SOLOMON
Literature, Amusement and Technology in the Great Depression

130. PAUL DOWNES
Democracy, Revolution and Monarchism in Early Modern American Literature

129. ANDREW TAYLOR
Henry James and the Father Question

128. GREGG D. CRANE
Race, Citizenship, and Law in American Literature

127. PETER GIBIAN
Oliver Wendell Holmes and the Culture of Conversation

THE POETICS OF NATIONAL AND RACIAL IDENTITY IN NINETEENTH-CENTURY AMERICAN LITERATURE

JOHN D. KERKERING

Loyola University Chicago

PUBLISHED BY THE PRESS SYNDICATE OF THE UNIVERSITY OF CAMBRIDGE
The Pitt Building, Trumpington Street, Cambridge, United Kingdom

CAMBRIDGE UNIVERSITY PRESS
The Edinburgh Building, Cambridge, CB2 2RU, UK
40 West 20th Street, New York, NY 10011–4211, USA
477 Williamstown Road, Port Melbourne, VIC 3207, Australia
Ruiz de Alarcón 13, 28014 Madrid, Spain
Dock House, The Waterfront, Cape Town 8001, South Africa

http://www.cambridge.org

First published 2003

Printed in the United Kingdom at the University Press, Cambridge

Typeface Adobe Garamond 11/12.5 pt. *System* LaTeX 2ε [TB]

A catalogue record for this book is available from the British Library

Library of Congress cataloging in publication data
Kerkering, John D.
The poetics of national and racial identity in nineteenth-century American literature /
John D. Kerkering.
p. cm. – (Cambridge studies in American literature and culture ; 139)
Includes bibliographical references (pp. 315–42) and index.
ISBN 0 521 83114 8
1. American literature – 19th century – History and criticism. 2. National characteristics, American, in literature. 3. Nationalism and literature – United States – History – 19th century. 4. United States – Race relations – History – 19th century. 5. Nationalism – United States – History – 19th century. 6. Group identity in literature. 7. Race in literature.
I. Title. II. Series.
PS217.N38K47 2003
810.9′358 – dc21 2003046081

ISBN 0 521 83114 8 hardback

For my mother and father

Contents

Illustrations

Acknowledgments

I am pleased to acknowledge the many generous institutions and individuals who provided support and assistance to me throughout my work on this project. It began as a dissertation for the English department at The Johns Hopkins University, which granted me generous fellowship support. That project was directed by Jerome Christensen and Walter Been Michaels, two challenging mentors whose critical responses to early drafts helped shape the key issues that remain the defining concerns of this project. I am particularly indebted to Walter Benn Michaels, who both demonstrated and demanded an analytical clarity that I have sought to emulate in this project. The initial dissertation project has undergone substantial revisions. The early stages of revision were made possible by three summers of generous funding provided by an H. G. Barnard Faculty Fellowship at Trinity University. I am grateful to my chair at Trinity, Peter Balbert, for his support throughout this period, and to my Trinity colleagues Caroline Levander, Willis Salomon, and Heather Sullivan for their thoughtful critical responses to my work. I was able to complete my revisions of this project with the support of a Du Bois-Mandela-Rodney Postdoctoral Fellowship from the Center for Afro-American and African Studies at the University of Michigan. In Ann Arbor I enjoyed not only time to write but also a dynamic intellectual environment, which included helpful conversations with Juanita De Barros, Julius Scott, and Arlene Keizer. Jennifer Ashton, Chris Castiglia, Susan Manning, and Priscilla Wald gave me useful comments on specific sections of the manuscript, and Carina Pasquesi was a valuable partner in preparing the index. Two anonymous readers from Cambridge University Press provided helpful comments on an earlier draft, and I am grateful to Cambridge editors Ross Posnock and Ray Ryan for their efforts to guide the manuscript toward publication. From its early drafts through its multiple stages of revision this project has benefited from the tireless feedback of several colleagues, each of whom has contributed insightful suggestions and criticisms that have enabled this project to attain its present form; my sincere thanks go out to Amy Hungerford, Chris Lukasik, Jane Thrailkill, and especially Steve Newman.

A shorter version of Chapter 1 was previously published under the same title in *Studies in Romanticism*, Volume 40, No. 1 (Spring 2001), pp. 85–98. I would like to thank the Trustees of Boston University for permission to reprint it here. A shorter version of Chapter 3 was published under the title "'Of Me and Of Mine': The Music of Racial Identity in Whitman and Lanier, Dvořák and Du Bois," in *American Literature*, 73: 1 (2001), 147–84 (Copyright 2001, Duke University Press). I am grateful to Duke University Press for permission to reprint that essay as part of this book.

I would also like to thank the many friends and family members who supported me during my work on this project. I am grateful to Paul Johnson, Darrel Tidaback, and Paul Keller for sharing their knowledge of music with me, and I would like to recognize Mark Canuel, Rachel Cole, Joan Burton, and Willis Salomon, with whom I enjoyed valuable musical partnerships during my work on this project. Several of my friends have remained steadfast despite geographic distance, including Jennifer Cox, Michael Dardik, Amy Hungerford, Caroline Levander, Mike Nakamaye, and Steve Newman. I am particularly grateful to my grandparents, John H. Kerkering and Marie H. Kerkering (1914–2003), who for many years provided me with a home away from home. Lastly, I am most grateful to my parents, Carol J. Murphy and John C. Kerkering, for their loving support.

JACK KERKERING

Abbreviations

B	Richard Wagner, *Beethoven*
BANP	James Weldon Johnson, *The Book of American Negro Poetry*
"BB"	Sidney Lanier, "From Bacon to Beethoven"
"CC"	Sidney Lanier, "The Centennial Cantata"
"CMC"	Sidney Lanier, "The Centennial Meditation of Columbia"
"CR"	W. E. B. Du Bois, "The Conservation of Races"
DA	*Dvořák in America*
J	Walter Scott, *The Journal of Sir Walter Scott*
"LII"	Sidney Lanier, "Lecture II" of *The English Novel*
LG	Walt Whitman, *Leaves of Grass*
LGL	William Dwight Whitney, *The Life and Growth of Language*
MHR	Houston Baker, *Modernism and the Harlem Renaissance*
PPO	Sidney Lanier, *Poems and Poem Outlines*
PW	Walt Whitman, *Prose Works*
R	Eric Foner, *Reconstruction*
SBF	W. E. B. Du Bois, *The Souls of Black Folk*
SEV	Sidney Lanier, *The Science of English Verse*
"SEV"	Sidney Lanier, *"The Science of English Verse" and Essays on Music*
SJS	J. B. T. Marsh, *The Story of the Jubilee Singers*
V&R	William Gilmore Simms, *Views and Reviews in American Literature, History and Fiction*
W&C	William Gilmore Simms, *The Wigwam and the Cabin*

Introduction: the poetics of identity

> I have wanted always to develop a way of writing that was irrevocably black. I don't have the resources of a musician but I thought that if it was truly black literature, it would not be black because I was, it would not even be black because of its subject matter. It would be something intrinsic, indigenous, something in the way it was put together – the sentences, the structure, texture and tone – so that anyone who read it would realize. I use the analogy of the music because you can range all over the world and it's still black . . . I don't imitate it, but I am informed by it. Sometimes I hear blues, sometimes spirituals or jazz and I've appropriated it. I've tried to reconstruct the texture of it in my writing. . . .
>
> – Toni Morrison[1]

> I had an instinct that [the invitation to translate *Beowulf*] should not be let go. An understanding I had worked out for myself concerning my own linguistic and literary origins made me reluctant to abandon the task. I had noticed, for example, that without any conscious intent on my part certain lines in the first poem in my first book conformed to the requirements of Anglo-Saxon metrics. These lines were made up of two balancing halves, each half containing two stressed syllables – "The spade sinks into gravelly ground: / My father digging. I look down . . ." – and in the case of the second line there was alliteration linking "digging" and "down" across the caesura. Part of me, in other words, had been writing Anglo-Saxon from the start.
>
> – Seamus Heaney[2]

The two passages quoted above exemplify this book's central concern, the work of writers who employ formal literary effects in order to establish the identity of a people. When Toni Morrison speaks of "a way of writing" that is "irrevocably black" and Seamus Heaney describes himself as "writing Anglo-Saxon," they each link their writing to a particular people, the "black" and "Anglo-Saxon" races. In these examples, what determines the race of the writing is not, as one might expect, the race of the writer or even the writing's race-specific themes. Morrison, for instance, hopes that her writing will be black "not . . . because I was" and "not even . . . because of its subject matter," and Heaney asserts that, "without any conscious intent," he was "writing Anglo-Saxon from the start." What ultimately makes writing racial, for both Morrison and Heaney, is the presence within it of certain race-specific effects. Morrison concerns herself with music, seeking "to reconstruct the texture of it in my writing," and Heaney finds evidence of race in his writing's "Anglo-Saxon metrics," specifically its "stressed syllables" and "alliteration." These alliterative stresses, as Heaney interprets them, do not reinforce the line's meaning – for instance, by reproducing the sounds and rhythms associated with the action of digging – but rather testify to the racial identity of the line itself. Similarly, Morrison seeks a style of writing whose "texture and tone" convey not sense but race. For both of these writers, then, the racial identity of certain literary effects is responsible for conferring racial identity on a larger piece of writing. The common language in which Morrison and Heaney each write – English – can in this way be assigned distinct racial identities as "black" or "Anglo-Saxon."

Even as Morrison and Heaney advance this account of their writing, they offer what seems to be a different account of themselves, linking their own group identities not to literary effects but to the circumstances and choices that led each of them to affiliate with a group. Morrison, for instance, was born into a family subject to the racism endemic to American society, and she has chosen to continue her solidarity with those who, like her, have been marginalized due to their color.[3] Heaney was born into a Catholic family, part of a minority long subject to discrimination in the North of Ireland, and has persisted with this affiliation as his own group identity.[4] And to a certain extent both Morrison and Heaney see their personal environments and the decisions they have made as explanations not only of their group affiliations but also of their writing styles. Morrison, for instance, acknowledges debts to a variety of influences, particularly James Baldwin: "I had been thinking his thoughts for so long I thought they were mine. . . . He gave me a language to dwell in" ("Living Memory," 180). Heaney, for his part, asserts that "poets' biographies are present in the sounds they make" ("Introduction," xxiii–xxiv), and the biographical influence present in his own work, he observes, is the alliterative verse of Gerard Manley Hopkins (xxiii). Yet even as they each tie their work to the environments they have known and the choices they have made, they also, as we've seen, characterize their writing in terms that subordinate authorial biographies to racial categories – describing it as either "black" or "Anglo-Saxon." Whatever Morrison may have learned from predecessors like Baldwin, the writing to which she aspires would not be irrevocably Baldwinian but instead, as she says of music, "irrevocably black." And however Heaney's ear may have been shaped by Hopkins, he finally chooses to describe his own early metrics as "Anglo-Saxon" – and not Hopkinsian – "from the start."

By characterizing their work in these terms, as "black" or "Anglo-Saxon," Morrison and Heaney each participate in a pattern of thinking that links writing to a people ("blacks" or "Anglo-Saxons") by first locating in that writing a people's distinctive literary effects (the "texture" of "blues" and "spirituals" or "stressed syllables" and "alliteration"). This pattern of thinking is not unique to these two Nobel laureates, for it has also figured prominently in the work of many literary critics. A point similar to Morrison's, for instance, has been advanced by Henry Louis Gates, Jr., who argues that "Blackness exists, but only as a function of its signifiers"; with the signifiers of dialect, for instance, there is "a musicality inherent in the form itself," a musicality Gates links with "black speech and black music (especially the spirituals)."[5] Gates's concern here is consistent with the work of Houston Baker, who argues of W. E. B. Du Bois's *The Souls of Black Folk* that "Du Bois . . . transmutes his text into the FOLK's singing . . . . offer[ing] a singing book" in which the "spirituals . . . [are] masterful repositories of African cultural spirit."[6] According to Baker, then, Du Bois effectively achieves what Morrison identified as her own goal, producing text informed by black music. Just as these critics have supported Morrison's project of making blackness "intrinsic" to writing, other critics have endorsed Heaney's account of writing that is racially "Anglo-Saxon." For instance Ted Hughes, to whose memory Heaney's translation of *Beowulf* is dedicated, has argued that "the tradition inherent in the natural sprung rhythms of English speech" is "the music of *Gawain*'s . . . meter" – the meter of *Sir Gawain and the Green Knight*, a work whose meter is based on a "two-part, alliterative accentual line."[7] Hughes here repeats a view prominent in Anglo-American criticism since Northrop Frye's influential assertion that "A four-stress line seems to be inherent in the structure of the English language," a structure dating back to "Old English."[8] An even earlier example of this analysis appears in a recently reprinted essay by Sculley Bradley, who suggests that when Walt Whitman abandoned "syllable-counting in his lines" he replaced it with a "rhythmical principle. . . . rooted in the very nature of English speech . . . since the Old English period," a rhythmical principle Bradley describes as "the most primitive and persistent characteristic of English poetic rhythm" and associates with a typical line from *Beowulf*.[9] These critical accounts suggest that Morrison and Heaney have internalized, and practice upon their own works, a mode of criticism more broadly available in contemporary literary culture: a race is asserted to be inherent in a formal effect, which is itself embedded within a piece of writing, making race itself intrinsic to that writing.

It is this shared understanding of how texts embody a people – by incorporating the formal effects specific to that people – that will be my focus in this book. In the chapters that follow I will argue that the account of texts presented here by Morrison and Heaney, and supported by these literary critics, has a history dating back to the early nineteenth century. During this period formal literary effects contributed to the efforts of many writers who sought to establish the collective identity of a people. In the early part of the nineteenth century, I will show, formal effects of literary texts were used to assert the collective identities of nations, including Scotland and the Southern Confederacy. In the latter half of the century writers continued their focus on formal effects but shifted their concern from national to racial peoples, specifically "Negroes" and "Anglo-Saxons," the races that would later, as we've seen, be the concern of Morrison and Heaney. As these examples from Morrison and Heaney suggest, my concern with formal effects will lead me to address a variety of writings beyond poems, writings that will include fictional as well as non-fictional prose texts, some of which will discuss these formal effects and others of which will employ them. Across these varying textual sources I will demonstrate a persistent pattern of thinking to be at work: like their present-day successors, nineteenth-century writers use formal literary effects as a vehicle for establishing the existence of distinct peoples, first nations and then races. This pattern of thinking about literary effects is shared, moreover, among a variety of writers who – like Morrison and Heaney – do not consider themselves to be part of the same "people." Yet the same basic premises are involved whether the people in question is "black" or "Anglo-Saxon," or even when that people is not a race at all but instead – as I will show – a nation. So when Morrison and Heaney use poetic effects to demonstrate the autonomy of a people, the two of them are ultimately thinking alike, drawing upon a pattern of thinking generally available not just to them but also to earlier writers like Walter Scott and William Gilmore Simms, writers who employed it to imagine national rather than racial identity.

NATION AND RACE

By associating national and racial identity in this sequential manner, with national identities of the early nineteenth century succeeded by racial identities in the late nineteenth century, I treat these two categories of identity in a way that differs significantly from other recent discussions. First, unlike those critics who assign each form of identity a discrete history,[10] I associate these two categories of identity as linked elements within a continuous historical narrative. And in the account I present, national and racial identity are linked in a different manner than has been suggested by still other critics, who link them as contemporary and antagonistic concepts.[11] Instead, in the account I present, national and racial identity are sequential and compatible notions – national identity is succeeded by racial identity, both of which are organized according to a common pattern of thinking. Thus unlike these existing critical accounts, this book's analysis will demonstrate national and racial identity to be linked in historical sequence with early nineteenth-century national identities succeeded by late nineteenth-century racial identities.

By way of contrast to my argument, consider Benedict Anderson's recent analysis, in which he presents racial identity as national identity's successor but sees it as logically *in*compatible with its predecessor.[12] Beginning with what he calls "nineteenth-century nationalist projects" (319), Anderson argues that the commitments central to this "age of classical nationalism" (325) have been undercut by "the 'ethnicization' process" (326).[13] This process "draw[s] a sharp line between the political nation and a putative original ethnos" (326), ultimately leading to a "transnational ethnicity" (325) that, for Anderson, is synonymous with racial identity.[14] According to Anderson, drawing such a line – dividing nations along racial or ethnic lines and thereby "unraveling the classical nineteenth-century nationalist project" (324) – is a recent impulse that stems from the "effects of post-industrial capitalism" (322). For Anderson, then, the "putative original ethnos" is a relatively new development that provides an alternative to classical nationalism. In contrast, I will argue that this "ethnos" is neither new nor, strictly speaking, an alternative to national identity. Instead of viewing it as new, I will argue that this "putative original ethnos" is not only a post-industrial concern but was also an early nineteenth-century concern, a concern advanced by writers like Walter Scott and William Gilmore Simms. Scott and Simms each sought to conceptualize a "people" in terms of just such a "putative original ethnos," and they did so, I will show, by arguing that the original ethnos of the people could be located within formal effects. What is more, Scott and Simms described these peoples not as ethnicities or races but as "nations" – the nations of Scotland (for Scott) and the Southern Confederacy (for Simms). During the nineteenth century, then, this account of nation – the one that locates a putative original ethnos in literary effects – coexisted with the very different classical nationalism that is Anderson's focus, the imagined communities of print-capitalism. The difference between these two accounts of nation was apparent, we will see, in conflicts that Anderson does not examine, conflicts pitting Scott's Scottish nation against the British Union and Simms's Confederate nation against the United States Union.[15] In these nineteenth-century conflicts between differing accounts of nation – between the nations of literary effects and the nations of Anderson's classical nationalism – we see a much earlier version of the more recent conflict Anderson observes, the conflict between classical nationalism and "ethnicity" (which, again, he equates with racial identity). Once these more recent "ethnicities" or races are likewise understood in terms of poetic effects – as they are in the above passages from Morrison and Heaney – we can then align them with the earlier nations of Scott and Simms. What this alignment suggests is that that the "peoples" posing a challenge to Anderson's classical nationalism are not just a recent phenomenon but are in fact part of a longer history: both nineteenth-century nations (as formulated by Scott and Simms) and the more recent "ethnicities" or races (as formulated by Morrison and Heaney) have relied on literary effects in order to assert an identity that is distinct from Anderson's classical nation. Once we identify the consistent pattern of thinking aligning these earlier accounts of national identity with more recent accounts of racial identity, we can see more clearly my literary-historical point: national and racial peoples are linked by a history not of competition but of continuity, a continuity rooted in a shared commitment to treating literary effects as a basis for collective identity, whether national or racial.

In presenting this analysis of national and racial identity, I am advancing an account that is related – both conceptually and historically – to the argument that Walter Benn Michaels has recently advanced regarding a different pair of identity categories, racial and cultural identity. Arguing that a crucial achievement of "the great American modernist texts of the '20s. . . . was the perfection . . . of what would come to be called cultural identity," Michaels asserts that this notion of cultural identity was inseparable from a prior notion of racial identity: "Culture, put forward as a way of preserving the primacy of identity while avoiding the embarrassments of blood, would turn out to be . . . a way of reconceptualizing and thereby preserving the essential contours of racial identity."[16] If, for Michaels, "the essential contours of racial identity" are preserved in a later account of cultural identity, in the account I propose the essential contours – what I am calling a pattern of thinking – behind national identity are preserved in a later account of racial identity. Thus like Michaels, I am arguing that the essential contours of an earlier account of identity (national identity) persist within a later, seemingly different account of identity (racial identity). But in addition to sharing this conceptual structure with Michaels's argument, my argument is also linked to his argument historically, as its chronological predecessor: the point of departure in Michaels's argument, racial identity, is my argument's destination. By placing my earlier historical account alongside his later one I propose an even longer narrative scope reaching back to the nineteenth century: Michaels's notion of cultural identity can be traced back not only, as he argues, to earlier accounts racial identity but also, I am arguing, through those earlier accounts of racial identity to even earlier nineteenth-century accounts of national identity. Or, to run the chronology forward, this book argues that early nineteenth-century accounts of national identity have persisted through accounts of racial identity to provide a basis for the still later pattern of thinking that Michaels calls cultural identity. The ongoing commitment to the notion of cultural identity is evident in the above passages from Morrison and Heaney, and their views, I am arguing, have conceptual antecedents in the works of the nineteenth-century writers featured in this book. To the extent that Morrison and Heaney are asserting "Black" and "Anglo-Saxon" as cultural rather than racial identities, they demonstrate Michaels's point, the effort to replace racial identities with cultural identities; but to the extent that they advance these accounts of identity by reference to formal textual effects, they participate in this earlier, nineteenth-century pattern of thinking, a pattern I will trace to the efforts of early nineteenth-century writers to conceptualize national identities.

But as this statement suggests, in order to extend Michaels's argument in this way – in order to trace contemporary accounts of cultural identity back not only to earlier accounts of racial identity but even further back to still earlier accounts of national identity – I must also diverge from that argument in a key respect: while Michaels argues that the link between racial and cultural identity is a shared commitment to identity inhering in bodies, and thus a shared commitment to racial biology (even as proponents of the latter, cultural identity, strive to deny that commitment), I am arguing that what links these accounts of identity – national, racial, and, ultimately, cultural – is a commitment not to racial biology but to identity inhering in formal literary effects. Thus while I acknowledge that many of the writers I address were convinced of the notion that racial identity inheres in bodies, I will argue that they made sense of this notion not through any knowledge or study of biology but rather by imagining the body (whose biology they understood rather poorly) as analogous to literary works (whose textuality they had, as we shall see, quite elaborately theorized). These writers, then, were drawing upon an existing account of literary texts – an account that racialized the formal features of those texts – in order to ground their quite speculative account of racial bodies. For these writers, bodies could be racialized insofar as texts were anthropomorphized and corporealized; put another way, bodies were examined not as objects of biological knowledge but as extensions of textual knowledge, and were thus treated as screens upon which an existing understanding of literary texts was heuristically and opportunistically projected. Once we see that this commitment to racial bodies was not only a flawed account of biology but was also a displaced understanding of textuality, we can see that this commitment to racial bodies has antecedents in prior discussions of textuality and identity, discussions I trace to earlier nineteenth-century writers who were committed to the concept of national identity. It is not enough, then, to describe the commitment to racial biology (as Michaels does) as a "mistake"[17] (which it most certainly was), for it is a mistake with a literary history, a mistake that arose from an ultimately misguided (and some might argue disastrous) effort to think about bodies by analogy to literary texts. So for the writers I address, who thought carefully (and quite erroneously) about the racial body, their commitment to thinking of the body in terms of racial biology was ultimately a displaced version of a commitment they already held regarding literary texts: the race in the "blood" of bodies was for them an analogical extension of the race in the formal effects of texts.

By proceeding in this manner, transferring to persons their understanding of texts and textual effects, nineteenth-century writers confirmed Allen Grossman's assertion of the close association between persons and poems: "Discourse about poetry," Grossman has observed, "is displaced discourse about persons."[18] Recasting Grossman's statement, I will argue that, for the nineteenth-century writers featured in this book, discourse about persons is displaced discourse about poetry. That is, having established an account of collective identity that was rooted in texts, nineteenth-century writers would then displace that textual account onto persons, using it as a conceptual template to guide their emerging efforts to imagine collective identity in those persons. Walter Scott, for instance, experiments with an allegorical form of this displacement, imagining that the Scottish national meter embedded within an English language poem corresponds to Scottish national habits embedded within an English-speaking subject. In the later work of William Gilmore Simms the literary effect of a Confederate people – the *genius loci* – remains tied to the landscape, so instead of imagining bodies as a version of this landscape, Simms imagines the landscape itself as a body, figuring the Appalachian Mountains – with their many instances of the *genius loci* – as the "backbone" of his southern nation, "Apalachia." A still later writer like W.E.B. Du Bois, however, will move in the other direction, imagining that the southern *genius loci* of particular concern to him, the "Sorrow Songs" of the slaves, is contained not only by the boundaries of a corporealized landscape (as in Simms) but also within the body itself, as one aspect of what he calls "double consciousness." Du Bois's notion of double consciousness, I will argue, exemplifies an increasingly prominent manner of displacing discourse about poetry onto persons: formal effects confer racial identity not only upon the texts and landscapes that contain them but also upon the persons who produce them. According to this displacement, the bodily production of these formal effects is increasingly understood as a symptom of that body's racial "instincts" and thus as a disclosure of that body's racial "blood." Once textualized in this manner, bodies could at least seem to operate in the same manner as texts, and thus the persons associated with these formal effects could, like the writings in which these effects appeared, be assigned a racial identity. Rooted in a prior understanding of texts, this account of the racial identities of persons' bodies reveals conceptual antecedents in prior accounts of literature, giving corporeal accounts of racial identity a nineteenth-century literary history.

By characterizing this account of racial identity as a displacement from texts to bodies I make it possible to advance two separate points. The first is the logical point that that, as Walter Benn Michaels argues, a commitment to racial identities entails a mistaken commitment to racial biology; the second is the historical point that a commitment to racial identities constitutes an extension to bodies of what had been a textual account of identity. Understood as a projection of textual thinking upon bodies, this notion of racial identity does not become any less a mistake about biology since, as we now know, biological processes ultimately operate in a manner quite different from textual ones; so in this sense Michaels's critique is quite correct. Indeed, my discussion helps explain why the notion of racial identity could be so mistaken about bodies: its expectations regarding bodies were shaped by its understanding of quite different material, literary texts. But in addition to prompting mistaken accounts of bodies, the nineteenth-century extension of literary analysis from texts to bodies was also, I am arguing, an astoundingly expansive projection of a text-based pattern of thinking from a literary-critical into a socio-political domain. Thus while viewing this projection in the former way, as a mistake about biology, rightly sees it as a problematic reliance on empirical commitments that the biological sciences cannot support, viewing it in the latter light, as an extension to bodies of a pattern of thinking initially focused upon texts, permits us to see the enabling role played by literary history in the formation of these seemingly non-literary – i.e. supposedly biological and corporeal rather than textual – accounts of collective identity. By proceeding in this manner – by, in effect, subsuming thinking that is supposedly biological within thinking that I am arguing was actually textual – my account permits a more extended historical narrative of identity to be told: from the early nineteenth century to the close of the twentieth, a variety of writers (leading up to and including Toni Morrison and Seamus Heaney) have derived accounts of national as well as racial identity from a shared pattern of thinking, one that roots collective identities in the formal effects of literary texts.[19]

In offering this specifically literary history of racial identity, this book proceeds in accordance with the recent observations of historian Thomas Holt. "The idea that race is socially constructed," Holt observes, "implies also that it can and must be constructed differently at different historical moments and in different social contexts."[20] Race, Holt continues, "attaches itself to and draws sustenance from other social phenomena" (21), and among these phenomena, I will argue, is the formal analysis of literary texts. But in order to tell such a history effectively, Holt observes, critics of race must "adopt a conception of historical transformation, in which we recognize that a new historical construct is never entirely new and the old is never entirely supplanted by the new. Rather the new is grafted onto the old" (20). As I will show, in the late nineteenth century a new understanding of racial identity in bodies was grafted onto an older idea of racial identity in literary texts, and that account had itself been grafted onto a still older idea, an early nineteenth-century understanding of literary texts as bearers of a specifically national identity. While this book will be predominantly concerned with tracing this literary history in the work of nineteenth-century writers, it will also seek to establish the implications of this literary history for the recent moment, a moment, as I've already suggested, in which writers like Toni Morrison and Seamus Heaney join literary critics in advancing this pattern of thought. As we shall see, the contribution of Morrison and Heaney to this long-standing pattern of thinking has been to infuse it with renewed vitality and prestige, extending the literary history of racial identity into the current moment and establishing it as an essential feature of the literary and critical present.

IDENTITY AND PASSING

By tracing current accounts of racial identity to literary history – and particularly to the history of formal effects – this book's understanding of race and racial identity differs in important ways from other critical accounts that tie racial identity to the discourse of the natural sciences. According to that line of analysis, racial thinking involves – as Michael Banton's *Racial Theories* observes – "people assigned to groups and categories on the basis of their physical characteristics."[21] Such categorizing of persons, however, was rarely, if ever, a neutral description. Instead, it almost invariably served as a supposedly "natural" pretext for invidious political and social distinctions, distinctions in which physical characteristics were taken as markers of "inner" differences in behavioral disposition, moral character, or intellectual capacity.[22] Just such a hierarchical ranking is starkly evident in the work of William Gilmore Simms, a writer I will discuss at length in Chapter 2. Responding to the abolitionist message of Harriet Beecher Stowe's *Uncle Tom's Cabin* (1851), Simms insists on the South's "perfect right to the labor of their slaves . . . so long as they remain the inferior beings which we find them now, and which they seem to have been from the beginning."[23] Even after the institution of slavery had, following the Civil War, come to an end, views like Simms's persisted, receiving ever-growing sanction from an emerging field of biological science.[24] This association of race not with literary history but with the evaluative hierarchies sanctioned by the natural sciences is perhaps the most broadly familiar account of racial identity in contemporary discussions of the topic.

This more familiar account of race has had such a broad cultural impact that it has prompted many literary critics to examine its influence on literary practice. Thus as Julia Stern observes, for all its effectiveness as an anti-slavery text, Stowe's *Uncle Tom's Cabin* exacerbated racial divisions by promoting the view that slaves, once freed, should be deported to Africa.[25] Addressing later realist texts, Kenneth Warren likewise demonstrates that Realism indirectly advanced the argument in favor of Jim Crow segregation.[26] While these and other critics reveal the complicity of literary texts in the social dissemination of racial hierarchies, still other critics have identified literary works that meet these hierarchies with open resistance. Thus if Simms's 1852 pro-slavery essay belittles the character and capacities of African-Americans, Frederick Douglass's 1855 autobiography *My Bondage and My Freedom* is notable, Eric Sundquist argues, for its "refusal to capitulate to the coercion of proslavery thought."[27] Speaking generally about such autobiographical writings, Henry Louis Gates, Jr., has observed, "[b]lacks were most commonly represented on the [great] chain [of being] either as the lowest of the human races or as first cousin to the ape. . . . Simply by publishing autobiographies, they indicted the received order of Western culture, of which slavery was to them the most salient sign."[28]

As recent literary criticism has explored such authorial resistance to biological racial hierarchies, it has directed particular attention to a subgenre of literary texts, narratives of racial passing. Prominent in the post-Reconstruction era, racial passing narratives typically presented characters whose appearance and conduct would permit them, despite their origins in the black community, to "cross" the color line and live among whites, thus escaping the restrictions imposed on African-Americans by Jim Crow segregation.[29] In her introduction to a recent anthology of critical essays on the literature of passing, Elaine K. Ginsberg identifies these crossings of the color line as the source of critical interest in passing narratives: "race passing threatens . . . the certainties of identity categories and boundaries."[30] That is, by featuring characters whose race is difficult to determine with certainty – characters whom observers might just as readily assign to one category (white) as to another (black) – these narratives suggest that the race of a person is a function not of the person's physical body itself but of the less certain matter of how that body is interpreted. Ginsberg's focus on the vagaries of interpretation implies an analogy between the assignment of race to bodies and the assignment of meaning to texts. As with the interpretation of literary texts, where readers frequently assign a variety of incompatible meanings to a text without having a way to decide among them with certainty, the racial passer would seem to produce a similar interpretive impasse – capable of being assigned an identity as either white or black, the passer threatens the observer's sense of certainty in interpreting the race of bodies. And just as the failure to achieve certainty about the actual meaning of a text has led critics to conclude that there is no actual or intrinsic meaning to be found in texts, so the failure to achieve certainty about the passer's racial identity suggests to critics that there is no actual or intrinsic race to be found in bodies. Race, these critics conclude, is as external to bodies as meaning is to writing.[31] By dramatizing an interpretive impasse, narratives of passing would seem to borrow a strategy of resistance supposedly intrinsic to writing itself, employing that strategy against racial oppression. This account of passing narratives has led literary critics to view them as a forceful challenge to the corporeal basis of all racial categories, "a challenge," Ginsberg argues, "that . . . discloses the truth that identities are not singularly true or false but multiple and contingent" (4). Other recent studies of racial passing narratives have drawn similar conclusions, leading critics to characterize the writers of racial passing narratives as strategically employing the supposed indeterminacy of literary signification in order to resist their society's dominant assumptions about race.[32]

But do passing narratives always involve such resistance? Many critics have argued that they do not, and my own argument will underscore these claims by offering a literary history that links the racial identity of the passer to the racial identity of literary texts, texts whose racial formal effects were imagined to reinforce rather than resist the commitment to racial identity. By providing a conceptual template for accounts of racial identity, including the racial identity of the passer, literary texts, I will argue, reveal passing to be complicit in, rather than resistant to, dominant assumptions about race. Consider, for instance, the case of Golden Gray, a character in Toni Morrison's novel *Jazz* (1992). The child of a white woman and a plantation slave, Golden Gray is "a beautiful young man whose name, for obvious reasons, was Golden. . . . because after the pink birth-skin disappeared along with the down on his head, his flesh was radiantly golden, and floppy yellow curls covered his head and the lobes of his ears."[33] These "obvious reasons" for naming him "Golden" stem, then, from his visual appearance as a "blond baby" (142) – "Completely golden!" (148), as his mother, Vera Louise Gray, exclaims. This visual assessment persists into Golden's adulthood, when his black father, meeting Golden for the first time, says, "You thought you was white, didn't you?. . . . I swear I'd think it too" (172). Golden not only looks like other whites, but he also acts like them: raised in the city so that he would "experience a more sophisticated way of living" (139), he is "dressed . . . like the Prince of Wales" (140), he shows "cavalierlike courage" (142–43), and he speaks in a manner that leaves those who hear him "convinced" (156) that he is a "whiteman" (155). Given this description of his appearance and behavior, one would conclude that Morrison's Golden Gray is not challenging the criteria for being white so much as satisfying those criteria.

But if, in satisfying these criteria, Golden is able to grow up believing he is white, soon after his eighteenth birthday his mother reveals to him that "his father was a black-skinned nigger" (143). The implication of this disclosure is that, as much as he might look and act like other whites, Golden's racial identity is not what he had believed it to be – it is not that of his white mother but rather that of his black father, Henry LesTroy, and of his mother's black servant, True Bell: "[Golden] had always thought there was only one kind – True Bell's kind. Black and nothing. Like Henry LesTroy. . . . But there was another kind – like himself" (149). Golden "himself" can be another "kind" of black person because there is another criterion at work here for being black, a criterion separable from judgments about his appearance and behavior, one that involves "the blood that beat beneath" Golden's "skin" (160). What Golden encounters here is thus not, as Ginsberg argues of passing narratives generally, a threat to the certainties of identity categories. Had Morrison intended to challenge these certainties, she could easily have made Golden a more difficult case, for instance giving him a more ambiguous physical appearance or making his ancestry unknown. But what she in fact presents is quite the opposite, a remarkable ease in applying each criterion: everyone who simply sees Golden is quite certain that he is white (he is named Golden for "obvious reasons"), while Golden himself has no doubt that his father is LesTroy and that his father's blood makes him black.[34] So rather than staging a dilemma about how to apply a given set of criteria with "certainty," Morrison's novel stages a dilemma about which of these two criteria to apply, the criteria of appearance and behavior or the (in this case) independent criterion of racial ancestry or "blood."

The dilemma Morrison stages was an overt part of the historical moment in which this portion of her novel is set, a dilemma effectively resolved by the US Supreme Court's 1896 decision in *Plessy v. Ferguson* to make the "one drop rule" – which had already gained considerable sway in many parts of the United States – the law of the land.[35] Set in the decade prior to this court decision, this section of Morrison's *Jazz* ascribes the Court's view to Golden himself: convinced that he has been passing all along, Golden displaces the criteria by which he had been deemed with certainty to be white – his outward appearance and sophisticated behavior – and imposes a new criterion by which he is deemed with certainty to be black – racial blood. The criteria that had made Golden certain that he and his father belonged to different races are thus supplanted by a criterion that makes him certain that he and his father share the same race. It is only an appeal to this new criterion, Golden's blood ties to his "black" father, that can transform his life as a white man into a deception by a black man.[36] Arguing more generally about racial passing narratives, Werner Sollors has observed that they did not challenge but in fact reinforced the one drop rule's commitment to making race inherent in the blood:

> the world of "passing" suggests, against first appearances, an unchangeable hold of at least one origin and "community." One may therefore say that the term "passing" is a misnomer because it is used to describe those people who are *not* presumed to be able to pass legitimately from one class to another, but who are believed to remain identified by a part of their ancestry throughout their own lives and that – no matter whom they marry – they bequeath this identification to their descendants. Ironically, the language speaks only of those persons as "passing" who, it is believed, cannot really "pass," because they are assumed to have a firm and immutable identity.[37]

Given this analysis, we should revise Ginsberg's claim that "both the process and the discourse of passing challenge the essentialism that is often the foundation of identity politics" (4). Instead of challenging that foundation, narratives of passing in fact install that foundation, making identity at once separable from the body (since the black Golden can look and act white) and inextricable from that body (since Golden's blood gives blackness an "unchangeable hold" on him).[38] It is this account of racial identity, where the work of identity is accomplished by a supposedly discrete but nevertheless inextricable feature of the body, that I will show to have a particularly literary history. For the writers I address, racial blood is ultimately understood in literary and indeed poetic terms rather than in terms of medicine or science, so instead of characterizing racial identity as a mistake about human biology, I want to treat it as an extension and adaptation of literary discourse, specifically the discourse surrounding formal textual effects.[39]

In order to draw this link between textual effects and racial bodies I will consider formal effects in a very specific sense: the "form" I have in mind is not the poem's visible, external appearance (for instance, its resemblance to the standard forms of a ballad, a sonnet, or a villanelle) but rather the set of formal effects that become apparent only after the performance of a text gets underway. It is only by entering within a text that we can disclose formal effects of this sort. Indeed, formal features of the kind I have in mind are often – like the racial "blood" that can go unseen in Golden's outward appearance while remaining inextricable from his body – overlooked in a first reading of a poem. As Heaney observes regarding the "Anglo-Saxon metrics" of his poem "Digging," he was unaware of this meter when he first wrote his poem, much as Morrison's Golden was unaware of his "black blood" until his mother revealed it to him. And just as this disclosure establishes that Golden had been black all along, so the discovery of his poem's meter demonstrates to Heaney that he has been producing Anglo-Saxon writing "from the start." By relying on meter to discern the racial identity of his poem, Heaney employs scansion in a manner similar to that described by John Hollander: "To analyze the meter of a poem is not so much to scan it as to show with what other poems its less significant (linguistically speaking) formal elements associate it; to chart out its mode; to trace its family tree by appeal to those resemblances which connect it, in some ways with one, in some ways with another kind of poem that may, historically, precede or follow it."[40] Interested in those "resemblances" that persist "historically" across a metrical "family tree," Heaney construes that "Anglo-Saxon" family – like Golden Gray's "black" family – in specifically racial terms.[41] His poem is tied by its meter to an Anglo-Saxon family, and thus to the Anglo-Saxon race, much as Golden is tied by his blood to a black family, and thus to the black race. What this parallel between Golden's body and Heaney's poem suggests is that meter does the same work for Heaney's poem that Golden's blood does for his body, providing it with a racial identity. It is this link between racial poetic effects and racial blood – the first giving racial identity to poems, the second giving racial identity to bodies – that I wish to explore in the chapters that follow. I will argue that behind this association between literary effects and blood there is an extensive literary history traceable to a variety of nineteenth-century writers. Early nineteenth-century writers used textual effects to locate national identity within literary texts, and later nineteenth-century writers, replacing national formal effects with racial ones, claimed that the identity within literary texts was racial. Other late nineteenth-century writers adapted this account of texts to their discussions of persons, leading them to extend the textual notion of racial identity to a new site, the body. Understood on the model of writing that contained racial formal effects, bodies could be imagined to contain racial blood. Establishing that these parallel but seemingly distinct ideas – the racial identities of literary texts and of bodies – share a common literary history is a central goal of this book.

IDENTITIES AND INDICES

But if Heaney's poem contains Anglo-Saxon meter, how does the meter itself contain Anglo-Saxonness? For that matter, how is it that – as Morrison asserts – blackness is to be found in jazz, blues, and the spirituals? One way of responding to these questions would be to view sound effect and racial identities to be associated with each other in accordance with the conventions of a symbolic code.[42] Such a symbolic code would consist of stipulated associations between sounds like blues and alliteration and races like "blacks" and "Anglo-Saxons," in much the same way that a social convention stipulates the associations between colors like red and green and commands like "stop" and "go." In such a symbolic code, the associations that are stipulated between the elements in the code – between green and "go" or between the blues and black – are broadly accepted but are ultimately arbitrary, arising out of social conventions that are culturally and historically contingent. If they were understood to function in this manner, sound effects like those singled out by Morrison and Heaney would coincide with the other semantic elements of a particular language's vocabulary. Such an arbitrary and contingent form of association ultimately differs, however, from the more forceful connection between race and sound effects that we have seen Morrison and Heaney drawing in the above passages. Specifically referencing the above passage from Morrison, Paul Gilroy addresses this more forceful association of race and sound effects, describing it as an account in which "music is thought to be emblematic and constitutive of racial difference rather than just associated with it."[43] Gilroy adds that from this perspective, which he assigns to Morrison and which I have extended to include Heaney's Anglo-Saxon metrics, "a style, genre, or particular performance of music is identified as being expressive of the absolute essence of the group that produced it" (75). While Gilroy acknowledges "a new analytic orthodoxy" (80) in which such accounts of music – "as being expressive of the absolute essence of the group" – are "dismissed as essentialism" (80), he declines to join this orthodoxy's ranks (81).[44] Other critics, however, have chosen to participate in the "analytic orthodoxy" Gilroy resists, and have thus offered sharp critiques of the musical essentialism he identifies. Voicing this analytic orthodoxy in the pages of *Poetics*, Keith Negus and Patria Román Velázquez have recently asked what they call "a significant and obvious question: what gives a *music* (a style or individual piece) its identity label (what makes a music Irish, Latin, Parisian, Chinese, bourgeois, African, or gay)? Are there enduring qualities shared by all music that is labelled in the same way and which enable them to be recognised from the *sound* alone?"[45] Their response to this second question is in the negative, a response that challenges the essentialisms to which musical identities must be committed: "there are two essentialisms here that fuse the idea that individuals, collectivities, and places possess certain essential characteristics and then link these to a further assumption that these can be found *expressed* in particular practices and cultural forms associated with those people. Yet . . . as soon as we start listening to music, we find that it continually subverts our assumptions about a relationship between 'cultural position and cultural feeling.' There is, in short," they conclude, "no such essential connection between a musical sound and a social identity" (136). What this argument suggests is that in taking the position mentioned by Gilroy – viewing formal effects as expressions of an essential identity rather than as semantic symbols of that identity – writers like Morrison and Heaney stand on theoretically shaky ground.

Yet simply to accept this theoretical critique – that, as Negus and Velázquez put it, "Music is surely something else besides or other than identities, and identities are something more (or less) than music" (140) – is to risk overlooking both the fact and the influence of statements like those made by Morrison and Heaney. And when identities and musical sounds are linked to each other in the way Gilroy describes, they acquire the capacity – as we have seen in the passages from Morrison and Heaney above – to accomplish substantial work for the writers asserting that link. In order to ensure that the work being accomplished by these associations of identities and musical sounds does not evade critical scrutiny, a different pair of critics, Ronald Radano and Philip V. Bohlman, has urged that efforts to associate music with the "absolute essence" of a group not be so readily dismissed.[46] On the one hand, then, Radano and Bohlman resist the "analytic orthodoxy" shunned by Gilroy and exemplified by Negus and Velázquez: "For many," they acknowledge, referring to those in this anti-essentialist "analytic orthodoxy," "it may seem that making a case for music's culpability in the reproduction of racial stereotypes is empirically unsound because music is music, not race. Music is, one might argue, no more than a non-signifying, free-floating, essentialized object. But. . . . to dismiss music as non-signifying is possible," they argue, "only when one ignores the power that accrues to musical practice" (43).[47] Yet even as they acknowledge this power, Radano and Bohlman resist accounting for that power in a manner that, as they observe of "ethnomusicology," "constructs its ontologies of music by accepting – and celebrating – differences as if they were givens" (9), an account, they observe, that has "reified forms of difference in ways no longer consistent with comprehensions of subjectivity and culture" (10). The notion of music's racial difference, then, is not one of the "givens" of "ontologies of music" but is rather a "power that *accrues* to musical practice."

Thus in the debate over music's essence – a debate in which an analytic orthodoxy claims that music's essence excludes race and the ethnomusicologists (including, according to Radano and Bohlman, Gilroy himself[48]) claim that its essence includes race – Radano and Bohlman embrace neither position, since both claims have had the effect of deflecting critical attention from its proper object of scrutiny, the social circumstances in which such claims circulate and accrue power. Arguing that "it is in music that the racial resonates most vividly, with greatest affect and power" (39), they urge critical attention to the social contexts in which "musical and racial experience" (6) come together to produce "the imagination of racial difference" (6): "At individual, group, and broader social levels alike, few deny that one type of music can be possessed and claimed as one's own, while there are other musics that belong to someone else. The music of this variously constructed Self is different from the music of the Other, therefore making it possible to articulate and even conceptualize the most basic differences through our musical choices" (6). Given this historically- and contextually-oriented account of music and identity, an effective practice of musicology, Radano and Bohlman argue, must attend to the social circumstances in which these fundamentally imaginative views take shape.[49] Accordingly, the musicology they "propose is one that begins with the revelations of the racial in order to foster interpretive procedures that reveal the ideological underpinnings of our enduring disciplinary color line" (39). In the mode of analysis they advance, music and identity are neither coincident with each other nor segregated from each other, but are instead contextualized in a manner that reveals how the two have historically been deployed in conjunction with each other, thereby revealing the goals and consequences of such context-specific deployments.[50]

The explicit focus of Radano and Bohlman's discussion is the discipline of musicology, but the critical approach they propose lends itself as well to the subject matter of this book, which addresses the seemingly quite different disciplinary domain of literary texts and their formal effects. The disciplinary differences between musicology and literary criticism, however, are more apparent, I want to argue, than they are real. For instance, while Morrison's concern in the above passage – the "texture" of "black music" – may seem to focus more on music than writing, it is Morrison's explicit goal that those musical textures should become, like Heaney's alliteration, a discernible feature of writing – "so that anyone who read it would realize." Rather than dwell upon the question of when or indeed whether certain formal effects stop being musical and start to be textual, I will instead concern myself with the context-specific decisions of particular writers to treat formal effects as not only incorporated into their writing but also as expressions of a particular people's identity.

In order to specify more precisely how formal effects might be imagined to perform this function of expressing a people's identity, I will draw upon C. S. Peirce's notion of an "index." For Peirce, an index is a kind of sign that he distinguishes from two others, the "symbol" and "icon."[51] What makes the index unique, according to Peirce, is that it "is a sign which refers to the Object that it denotes by virtue of being really affected by that Object."[52] Peirce mentions several examples of indexical signs, including a weathervane as an index of the wind, a bullet hole as an index of a bullet, a footprint as an index of the walker, and smoke as an index of fire.[53] As Floyd Merrill has observed of indices, they "are distinguished from other signs insofar as they have no significant resemblance to their semiotic objects; they direct attention to them through association by contiguity, or some natural or causal connection."[54] This characteristic of the index – association by contiguity with the semiotic object that it denotes – is apparent in the formal effects that writers like Morrison and Heaney associate with racial identities. An index is not, as Merrill observes, related to its semiotic object by "significant resemblance," so it is not, strictly speaking, onomatopoetic; as we have seen, Heaney does not claim that his alliterative verse sounds like digging, and Morrison does not seek to have her writing sound like jazz ("I don't imitate it"). Instead of resembling another sound (as in onomatopoeia), their writing is imagined as if it were (like smoke to fire) an index of a specific people, an effect that this people has caused. Toni Morrison, for instance, prefers an indexical to a symbolic account of racial music, asserting that "you can range all over the world and it's still black." Unlike symbolic systems, which vary all over the world according to local conventions, Morrison sees black music as a world-wide constant, everywhere attributable to blackness much as a weathervane's motion is everywhere attributable to the wind and a footprint is everywhere assignable to the person who made it. And while social conventions are imposed, and are thus subject to revocation, the "irrevocably black" writing to which Morrison aspires – like the music it emulates – would carry an indexical force, "so that anyone who read it would realize." That is, readers will reason from textual effect to racial cause, from formal index to its racial source, and thus conclude that the writing itself is not just textured like jazz or the blues but is, like that music, contiguous with (and thus expressive of) that texture's source, blackness. A similar pattern of thinking is evident in the passage from Seamus Heaney: when he encounters alliterative lines in his poems, he concludes that he is glimpsing the smoke of an Anglo-Saxon fire.

This discussion of the index – with a formal effect indexing the race that caused it – emphasizes a specifically causal form of contiguity, but Peirce's account of the index does not require a causal link in order for contiguity to be achieved. For instance, Peirce mentions the Bunker Hill Monument, which indexes the historic Revolutionary War battle not because it was caused by the battle itself but because it is located upon – and thus points to – the location where the battle took place.[55] This form of indexicality (which Peirce describes using his technical term "designations"[56] and which I will link with Geoffrey Hartman's notion of poetic "inscriptions") will be apparent in my discussion of the southern writer William Gilmore Simms, who most often treats poems as similar sorts of monuments, which point indexically to historically significant locations on the southern landscape. Occasionally, however, Simms will also treat the landscape as if it were populated by songs quite different from his own poems, songs that, as he imagines them, are the voice of the *genius loci* and are thus lingering effects of a given location's consequential history (as if one could, while visiting the Bunker Hill Monument, hear residual cries from the soldiers who once fought there). Viewed as such, these songs are contiguous with the locale's history in a specifically causal sense, and thus constitute a different form of index from the monument (a form of index that Peirce describes using the technical term "reagents"[57]). For Simms, these two forms of the index – the poems he writes, which point to historical locales, and the songs he hears there, which are the residual voice of that local history – will not fully converge. Other writers, however, will incorporate within their poems the second, specifically causal notion of indexical contiguity that Simms reserves for the landscape itself: as we've seen in Morrison and Heaney, literary texts are imagined not simply to point to a racial identity existing apart from them (in black music's Africa or Beowulf's Denmark) but instead to contain within them formal effects that are an index of the race that produced those effects; the texts are imagined, in effect, to be, themselves, consequences of race. But if they incorporate these indexical formal effects into their writings, Morrison and Heaney do not explicitly extend this account of racial identity from writings to bodies: while formal effects provide an index of textual race, they do not provide an index of biological or corporeal race. Morrison and Heaney are not, in other words, making the explicit claim that it is the racial "blood" of bodies that causes the racial formal effects of their writing.

For several earlier writers, however, this notion that race could be a causal force would bolster their commitment to thinking in just such corporeal and biological terms. According to these nineteenth-century writers, textual indices like those that Morrison and Heaney describe were thought to be imposed upon bodies from within – caused by the racial "blood" within the bodies that produced them. For these writers, the best way to explain how race exerted such a causal force within bodies was through research in the medical sciences, research that promised to expose the physical basis of a race's distinctive instincts and behaviors. Indeed, Peirce's discussion of the index coincides directly with a medical vocabulary of bodily symptoms: "what," Peirce asks, "is an index, or true symptom? It is something which, without any rational necessitation, is forced by blind fact to correspond to its object."[58] Thus when providing examples of indices, Peirce includes medical symptoms: "such is the occurrence of a symptom of a disease."[59] Imagined in these terms, as symptoms corresponding to the body's racial "blood," race-specific formal effects could be understood as providing diagnostic means for a body's racial "blood" to "tell."

But as I will show, many late nineteenth-century physicians – despite their most conscientious efforts – were unable to locate in the body any physical structures or processes that might be implicated as race's causal source: the causal work attributed to racial "blood" could not be meaningfully attributed to actual blood. As a result, the search for racial causality was forced to shift from the domain of medical biology to a quite different domain, that of supernatural agency – to an understanding of bodies, that is, in which the causal force of racial blood operated as a form of demoniacal or voodoo possession. It is this account of causality, I will argue, and not any coherent biological science, that ultimately lies behind the notion that formal effects could provide an index to the racial "blood" in bodies. Moreover, I will argue that, in its ultimate reliance on this supernatural understanding of causality, this seemingly biological understanding of formal textual effects employs the same account of indexicality as the other writers I address – not just the early nineteenth-century writers concerned with national identity but also the more recent writings of Toni Morrison and Seamus Heaney. However plausible one finds such supernatural accounts of causal agency to be, my point will be less to challenge these accounts of agency than to disclose them as the shared commitment permitting these various writers to advance a common account of indexicality, with writers from the early nineteenth century to the present viewing formal effects as an index of the "people" that caused them. It is this shared pattern of thinking within both the medical and the literary discussions – this shared commitment, that is, to treating formal effects as indices of the identitarian agency that supposedly caused them – that enables me to subsume a seemingly biological discussion within a larger literary history. Whether it has been attributed to a supernatural or biological agency, and whether it has been focused on a geographical, textual, or corporeal site, this consistently indexical approach to formal textual effects has remained a central feature of efforts to imagine collective identities of peoples.[60] Thus if writers like Morrison and Heaney seek to distance their work from one site where this pattern of thinking has recently been projected, the supposedly racial biology of the human body, and if they thereby seek to advance "Black" and "Anglo-Saxon" identities as cultural rather than racial identities and as textual rather than corporeal identities, they do so, I have suggested, by affiliating their work with another site where this pattern of thinking had earlier been applied, the nineteenth-century written text. In doing so Morrison and Heaney do not advance an alternative to racial bodies so much as they return to an earlier site – the literary texts – upon which this same pattern of thinking was exercised and from which a subsequent account of racial bodies drew its sustaining premises. Thus given the broader historical context that I am addressing, we can see Morrison and Heaney's accounts of "Black" and "Anglo-Saxon" identity restoring and revitalizing a set of nineteenth-century literary views: their apparent progress beyond biological accounts of racial corporeality is inseparable from an unacknowledged nostalgia for nineteenth-century accounts of literary textuality.

In the pages that follow I will devote the bulk of my analysis to those nineteenth-century writers who accepted and disseminated the notion that formal literary effects provided an index of a people's identity. Turning first to the early nineteenth century, I will consider the writings of Walter Scott and William Gilmore Simms, each of whom sought to demonstrate national identity by invoking the formal effects of literary texts. In Chapter 1 I discuss Walter Scott's effort to distinguish the Scottish nation from the larger British Empire, an effort that involved claiming poetic meter to be a distinctive form of the Scottish people. In Chapter 2 I move from the Scotland of Walter Scott to the Southern United States of William Gilmore Simms, a move that is based not on the substantial immigration from Scotland to the South, nor on Scotland's considerable intellectual influence on the Southern United States, nor even on Walter Scott's formative authorial influence on Southern writers like Simms.[61] Instead, I move from Scott to Simms on the basis of the similar manner in which they both came to conceptualize national identity, each of them tying it to the formal effects of literary texts. My account of Simms will demonstrate that he differentiated his southern Confederacy from the northern Union by imagining a landscape haunted by the songs of the *genius loci*, songs he characterized as the Confederate people's distinctive literary effects and expected would one day cease to stand alone on the landscape but would instead be accompanied by writing, thus forming a Southern national literature. While it was national peoples that concerned Scott and Simms, Sidney Lanier and W. E. B. Du Bois proposed formal features as an index of a seemingly different kind of "people" – a race. Thus as I show in Chapter 3, Lanier treated the characteristic rhythm of Anglo-Saxon poetry as evidence of an enduring race of "Anglo-Saxons," and Du Bois featured the "Sorrow Songs" in *The Souls of Black Folk* in order to assert the distinctness of another race, "Negroes." This racial division of literary effects extends, I will argue, into the musical score composed by Joseph Carl Breil for the silent film *The Birth of a Nation*, a score that presents musical themes as if they could serve as an index of race. In Chapter 4 I examine how this racial understanding of formal effects lent support to a medical understanding of racial bodies: like literary critics who viewed formal effects as an index of racial identity in texts, physicians viewed patients' symptoms as an index of racial instincts in bodies. Included among the "symptoms" was the supposed bodily disposition to produce these same formal effects, so as a result, the very effects that had indexed race in writing came to serve as symptoms of race in bodies. Understood in these medical terms – as diagnostic symptoms of a body's racial instincts – formal effects coincided with and lent credence to an emerging medical account of biological racial instinct, an account, I will show, that would later inform the Harlem Renaissance writings of James Weldon Johnson.

As nineteenth-century writers formulated this view of formal effects they engaged in implicit and often explicit debate with contemporary writers whose views on formal effects and collective identity diverged from their own. These dissenting views and the efforts to overcome them will figure prominently in the chapters that follow. In Chapter 1, opposition to Scott will be apparent in the writings of William Wordsworth, who interpreted the same metrical effects – and indeed, the same poems – in a different manner from Scott, viewing them not as an index of Scottish national identity but as the foundation for an international collectivity, a poetic "empire." As Chapter 2 will show, the resistance to Simms was explicit in the work of Nathaniel Hawthorne, whose earlier writings endorsed Simms's account of the *genius loci* but whose later writings repudiated that notion as well as its apparent product, a distinct national identity for the Confederacy. Hawthorne's ultimate repudiation of Simms helps explain the endorsement of Hawthorne's works by Henry James, who, as Chapter 2 also will show, favors Hawthorne's literary cosmopolitanism over Simms's literary nationalism. The prominent literary legacy of Hawthorne and James demonstrates their considerable success in resisting this early nineteenth-century effort to advance national identities via literary effects. The resistance was less effective, however, when the identities in question were not national but racial. Thus Chapter 3 will demonstrate that while national identity remains the central concern in the post-bellum writings of Walt Whitman and Antonín Dvořák, their views compete with the writings of Lanier and Du Bois, who divide American writing into the racial categories of "Anglo-Saxon" and "Negro." As this racialist account of texts was appropriated by medical discourse, it met resistance, as I will show in Chapter 4, from a variety of physicians who tried, to little effect, to refute the notion that bodily symptoms could be attributed to racial instincts. A more influential form of resistance, however, involved writers who sought not to repudiate racial instincts but to valorize them. This mode of resistance, which Anthony Appiah has called a "classic dialectic,"[62] led writers like James Weldon Johnson to treat racial instinct as the source of a distinctively black poetry. As Johnson's poetry of the Harlem Renaissance celebrates the "New

Negro," it relies for that celebration on an account of formal effects that presents them as literary indices of race precisely because they are bodily indices of racial instinct. In this sense, Johnson's response to this pattern of thinking is not so much to resist it as to institutionalize it in a modified, seemingly less damaging form. Having traced this literary history of racial identity up to the Harlem Renaissance, I will then return to the contemporary context in the Conclusion, where I will demonstrate in greater detail the links between these earlier accounts of identity and those advanced in the recent work of Toni Morrison and Seamus Heaney. My goal will be to illustrate the broad scope of this pattern of thinking so as to invite consideration of its possible limitations.

IMAGINED COMMUNITIES AND AUTHENTIC IDENTITIES

In order to register these potential limitations I must emphasize that the account of identity I will be documenting in these pages, whether national or racial, differs in important respects from the version of identity set out in the influential work of Benedict Anderson. In his *Imagined Communities* Anderson argues that national communities are "imagined" in a very specific sense, a sense he distinguishes from "'fabrication' and 'falsity,'" each of which, he argues, would "impl[y] that 'true' communities exist which can be advantageously juxtaposed to nations."[63] Instead of juxtaposing a "true" community to a "fabrication," Anderson wishes to convey the very different sense of "'imagining' and 'creation'" (6): "Communities are to be distinguished, not by their falsity/genuineness, but by the style in which they are imagined" (6). Understanding all nations to be such imaginative creations, creations distinguished not by their genuineness or authenticity but by their style, Anderson replaces the opposition "falsity/genuineness" with a different opposition, abstention/participation. That is, people either abstain from creating a nation or they participate in that creation, their participation yielding a range of stylistically distinct outcomes. For those individuals who participate in this creative process, their contributions to producing this national style confer upon them a national identity. While individuals may be more or less committed to a given national style, and may thus be more or less sincere as they participate in its creation, assessing this degree of commitment or sincerity is not Anderson's goal. Instead, he focuses on the evidence of participation, seeking to characterize the stylistic variety stemming from these creative acts of imagination. Although Anderson has, as I have already observed, cast this account of national identity as an historical antagonist of racial identity, a number of theorists have adapted Anderson's specifically national imagined community as a way of accounting, as well, for racial identity. For these theorists, racial identity, like national identity, arises as individuals participate in a creative style of imagining their racial community. For instance, Hazel V. Carby has recently addressed "the ambitious attempt of *The Souls of Black Folk* to create a genealogy of what Benedict Anderson has called an '*imagined community* among a specific assemblage of fellow readers.' Through its representations of individuals, Du Bois's book," Carby argues, "aims to bring into being a community. Imaginatively, he forges a people."[64] A racial identity is thus, according to Carby, another style, along with national identity, according to which a community can be imagined.

In contrast to such accounts, which present both national and racial identities as products of participation in a particular culture's stylistic repertoire of creative and imaginative behaviors, this book features writers who understand identity in quite different terms. For the writers central to this book, the notion that Anderson explicitly sets aside – the opposition of "falsity/genuineness" or, alternatively put, the question of authenticity – will be an important consideration. The issue of authenticity arises because the writers I address are concerned not with creative styles of imagining identity but with indexical modes of representing it. As we have seen, an index's relation to its object involves dynamic contiguity, not creative imagination. Smoke, for instance, is fire's physical consequence, not its imaginative creation, which is why smoke provides a specifically indexical way of representing fire. If smoke is a genuine or authentic index, it is contiguous with fire, but if it is a false or inauthentic index, it will not be accompanied by fire – indeed, it will seem not to be smoke at all, but a mere imitation of it. We can extend this opposition of genuine and false indices to the earlier examples from Morrison and Heaney: for these writers, just as smoke is an index of fire, formal effects and racial ancestry provide an index of identity. In Morrison's novel *Jazz*, for instance, she presents Golden Gray's blackness as independent of his creative participation in a style of imagining. Indeed, Golden actively participates in creating something quite different, whiteness, but Morrison presents that imaginative act as inauthentic – it is overruled, against his will ("I don't want to be a free nigger; I want to be a free man" [173]), by the one drop rule. The blackness of Golden's body corresponds to Morrison's claim about black writing, where blackness would involve "something intrinsic, indigenous, something in the way it was put together." Such writing, like Golden's ancestry, will provide an index of blackness – "so that anyone who read it would realize." Similarly, regarding Seamus Heaney's poem, Heaney wrote it without intending to create a work in the Anglo-Saxon metrical style, but despite this absence of intention, he later takes note of the way it was put together, construing the poem's meter as an index of Anglo-Saxonness. In each of these examples, the imaginative creation central to Anderson's analysis of identity is either overridden or ignored. Instead of participating actively in the imaginative creation of a style of group identity, novelistic characters and literary texts are involuntarily subsumed within the identity to which, respectively, their ancestry or their formal effects serve as an index.

One might seek to reintroduce Anderson's notion of imaginative creativity into this analysis by arguing that the imaginative creation taking place here is the very idea that these identities might be indexical. For instance, the notion that ancestry provides an index of racial identity could be seen as an imaginative creation stemming from fictional works like, among others, Morrison's *Jazz*. Or the notion that formal effects provide an index of a text's racial identity could be described as an imaginative creation stemming from literary criticism of the kind that Morrison and Heaney each provide. Such imaginative creations, one might argue, gradually gain widespread acceptance, leading ancestry and formal literary effects to be treated as if they were genuine indices of race. This process is in fact implicit in Morrison's statement that "I have wanted always to develop a way of writing that was irrevocably black." The notion that she would "develop" this style suggests that it is her own imaginative creation, but when she suggests that the style's blackness would be "irrevocable" she immediately elides her creative role, making an invention seem like a discovery and thus recasting her own imagination's creativity as her writing's intrinsic indexicality. Viewed in this light, writing claims a blackness apart from the author's imagination – as with black music, "you can range all over the world and it's still black." Such a recasting of an author's imaginative creation as if it were the writing's genuine indexicality would serve to explain what we saw above, the apparent restrictions placed on the imagination of novelistic characters like Morrison's Golden Gray (who actively participates in the style of imagining associated with whiteness but who nevertheless cannot help but be black) or authors like Morrison (whose writing will be "irrevocably black" not if she imagines it as such but only if it should succeed in emulating "black music") and Heaney (whose writing is "Anglo-Saxon" not because he imagines it as such but because, without having intended to, he has written lines that exemplify "Anglo-Saxon metrics"). It is only by viewing these restrictions on the imagination as, themselves, *products of* the imagination that one can view them in Anderson's terms, as one among many possible styles of imagining, a style that figures like Morrison and Heaney have in fact helped to "develop."

But to characterize these indices of race in such terms – as imaginative creations in whose development Morrison and Heaney each participate – is to emphasize Morrison's word "develop" at the expense of her word "irrevocably," an emphasis that blunts her explicit goal of producing writing that would be "irrevocably black" (and likewise undercuts Heaney's claim to have been "writing Anglo-Saxon from the start"). Morrison hopes to incorporate into her writing an indexicality that she believes is genuinely achieved elsewhere, in black music. In contradiction of this explicit goal, the Anderson notion of creative imagination would insist that, although Morrison's writing may represent blackness symbolically, it does not do so indexically. In other words, Morrison's ambition to produce writing that is an index of race may well, from the Anderson perspective, exemplify a distinctive style of imagining, but it also constitutes a mistake – just as it would be a mistake to view the word "smoke" as if it were, like actual smoke, a reason to call the fire department or evacuate a building. From Anderson's perspective, then, Morrison's pursuit of writing that is irrevocably black is the racial equivalent of a false alarm. Indeed, to concern oneself, as Anderson does, with the many styles in which identity is imagined, and not with the falsity/genuineness of the communities thus represented, is necessarily to concern oneself with representations that are symbolic, not indexical. The same declaration of a racial false alarm would likewise apply to Heaney's claim that his poem's metrics are an index of Anglo-Saxon identity. Thus if one is rigorously committed to Benedict Anderson's notion of community identities as stylistically varied imaginative creations, one would then conclude that both Morrison's ambition for "irrevocably black" writing and Heaney's claim to be "writing Anglo-Saxon" are racial false alarms.

Of course, there are other reasons for labeling these claims as racial false alarms besides a commitment to Anderson's terms of analysis: one may believe, for instance, that a genuine index of race can be found, but that it must be located someplace other than writing style – for example, only in dancing or painting but not in writing, or only in the body's genes, not in its cultural practices. Or one might offer an even stronger reason to consider Morrison and Heaney mistaken, because one believes there is no such thing as race at all, and hence that, when it comes to race, there can only be false alarms: just as unicorns leave no footprints, and thus can be represented only imaginatively, not indexically, there likewise can be no such thing as an index of race, whether in writing styles, music, genes, or anywhere else.[65]

This strong skepticism about racial indices – the view not only that formal effects fail to provide an index of race, but that there are, in fact, no such races to be indexed – is a view that I share with recent writers who have criticized the notion of authentic racial identities.[66] Even so, my aim in the pages that follow will not be to convince my readers of this point – indeed, readers of this book could remain committed to exactly the opposite view, continuing to treat formal effects as an index of race, while nevertheless being swayed by my literary-historical argument. That argument places literary history at the heart of racial identity by demonstrating that the writers I address were committed (mistakenly, I would argue) to viewing identity as a causal force whose indexical presence was registered by the formal effects of literary texts. This commitment was well established among early nineteenth-century writers concerned with national identity, it gained acceptance among late nineteenth-century writers concerned with racial identity, and it informed the efforts of later writers to imagine bodies as if they, like texts, had racial identities. Thus whether readers of this book ultimately agree or disagree with this commitment to viewing formal literary effects as indexical of an identity (national or racial, textual or corporeal), they can nevertheless register in the chapters that follow a literary history in which literary texts helped disseminate and enforce this commitment. For some readers, then, this will be the history of a good idea, a prescient insight into the deep sources of cultural difference, and for other readers it will be the history of a bad idea, a constraining endorsement of identity determinism. Either way, the literary history offered in the following chapters will demonstrate to both groups of readers that the commitment to such an indexical account of formal effects has had profound historical consequences.

Yet to observe, as this book will, that the commitment to literary indices of identity has proven historically consequential is not to concede that these literary effects are, in fact, indexical of either nation or race. They did not have to be indexical in order for the belief in their indexicality to be consequential; even a false alarm has consequences. And consequential as this belief may have been, its consequences could not extend so far as to make itself true, to transform an apparent index into an actual one. In other words, if this indexical account of formal literary effects is indeed accurate, it was accurate before the commitment to it became widespread; it was not rendered so by the dissemination of that commitment. Similarly, if this indexical account of formal literary effects is (as I would argue) a false alarm, then the widespread sounding of that alarm, and the widespread failure to see that alarm as false, did not make that alarm any less false. Put another way, indexicality is not, like the historical commitment to it, a social construct – it is either accurate or mistaken. Thus while the consequences of such a commitment are themselves historical constructs, and as such are subject to change, the concept of racial indices that, through its widespread acceptance, is responsible for producing these consequences is not, itself, an historical construct – it is either accurate or a mistake.[67] It is a commitment to the accuracy of this view that will be consistently apparent in the writers featured in the chapters that follow. Whether or not we agree with their commitments, we can recognize the contextual and historical consequences of those commitments, consequences magnified by the role literary effects played in disseminating them.

My point in distinguishing this commitment from Anderson's imagined community should now be clear: the point is not simply that to view these supposed indices as products of Anderson's style of imagining is necessarily to disagree with those who treat them as indices. My point is, more importantly, that the opposite claim holds as well: if one views these indices as in fact genuine, as do the writers featured in this book, then one rejects Anderson's account of identity. That is, one does not consider oneself to be participating in a community of the kind Anderson describes, a community that engages in one of many possible styles of imagining. Instead, one thinks one is simply correct, that one's writing is indeed an index of race.[68] From such a perspective, it makes sense to claim that a certain writing style could be "irrevocably black" or that one could be "writing Anglo-Saxon from the start." And it makes sense, from such a perspective, to argue that one could no more revoke the association of race and formal literary effects than one could revoke the causality and contiguity associating fire with smoke. Indeed, extending this analogy to smoke, one might argue, for instance, that one's creative acts are not merely smoke *signals* but are, instead, *smoke* signals – that one's creative actions, in other words, are generated by a certain kind of authentic flame, and that they are important not just for the message conveyed by those signals but for the medium itself, a medium that is, like smoke indexing fire, an index of one's racial identity. From such a perspective one must either conceal the smoke of this distinctive flame (thus presenting one's creative acts, such as writing, in a false or racially inauthentic light) or reveal the smoke from this flame (thus presenting one's creative acts in a genuine or racially authentic light, as Morrison aspires to do and as Heaney discovers he has done). Such a perspective, which cannot be subsumed within Anderson's notion of creative styles of imagination, leads not only to the textual consequences I've mentioned – for instance, literary characters like Golden Gray, whose imagination of his own identity is defeated by the indexical force of his racial ancestry, or authors like Morrison and Heaney, whose imaginations of racial writing are supervened by the indexical force of racial formal effects. It also leads to far more substantial social consequences, including entire populations imagined on the model of such characters and authors, populations whose lives and opportunities are routinely shaped by the conviction that there is such a thing as race and that there exist – for instance, in literary texts – genuine indices of it. It is literary history's contribution to these highly consequential outcomes, through its long-standing treatment of formal effects as if they might serve as indices of collective identities, that I will examine in detail in the chapters that follow.

PART I

The poetics of national identity

CHAPTER ONE

"We are five-and-forty": meter and national identity in Sir Walter Scott

While composing the second of his *Letters of Malachi Malagrowther* (1826), Sir Walter Scott paused long enough to record the following remarks in his *Journal*:

> Spent the morning and till dinner on *Malachi's Second Epistle to the Athenians.* It is difficult to steer betwixt the natural impulse of one's National feelings setting in one direction and the prudent regard to the interests of the empire and its internal peace and quiet recommending less vehement expression. I will endeavour to keep sight of both. But were my own interest alone concern[e]d, d – n me but I wa'd give it them hot.[1]

The tension between "National feelings" and "the interests of the empire" points to a problem that, as we shall see, runs throughout the *Letters of Malachi Malagrowther*, the problem of sustaining Scotland's national integrity under the imperial jurisdiction of Great Britain, but in this *Journal* entry the immediate concern is somewhat different. Here Scott wonders whether he asserts Scottish autonomy too forcefully – whether his tone is too "hot."

Scott's concern was justified. The Scottish Lord Melville was moved to "condemning . . . the inflammatory tendency of his letters," arguing that "popular inflammation . . . is seldom resorted to by those who really wish well to their country." The imputation of disloyalty was made more explicit when John Croker, in the government's official response to Scott's *Letters*, asserted that "the *loyalty* which could be shaken, as yours seems to have been . . . was, like your plaids, loosely worn, and easily cast off." Croker's response was both invoked and reiterated in Parliament, with one member of the Commons noting, "if not rebellion, there was certainly a very marked seditious spirit manifested in the appeal," and if this language is deliberately hyperbolic, the hyperbole nevertheless registers genuine concern for the integrity of the Union.[2]

Such concern seems misplaced given Scott's commitment, in the above *Journal* entry, to a "prudent regard to the interests of the empire." I want to suggest that these respondents cast Scott's *Letters* as a source of separatist politics because they fail to see Scott's Unionist poetics. Viewed in terms of this poetics, what is important about the *Letters* is not their inflammatory language but their national meter, and meter is national, according to Scott, insofar as it functions as a "summons" to Scottish national identity: meter's formal effects assemble the Scottish people as a people and thereby demonstrate Scotland's ongoing integrity as an autonomous nation. While this poetics escaped the notice of Melville and Croker, I will show it to be present not only in these *Letters* but also in Scott's other writings of the period, writings in which poetic meter is Scott's vehicle for imagining an identity for Scotland that is neither hostile to Britain nor threatened by it, an identity that would allow him to "keep sight of both" his "National feelings" and "the interests of the empire." As he adapts meter to this account of nation, Scott appropriates to his cause the prosody of contemporary poets, including Wordsworth and Coleridge, projecting upon their works his own view of meter and thus recasting those works as illustrations of his claim that meter serves as a national summons.

As recent scholarship has shown, there is something implausible in treating the meter of a poem – whether it comes from Wordsworth, Coleridge, or Scott himself – as intrinsically national.[3] Thus as I reconstruct the logic of Scott's metrical summons my aim is to emphasize not its suitability as a general account of poetics but its functionality as a vehicle for Scott's very particular politics – his defense of Scottish national autonomy within Britain. As we will see, Scott imagines national identity and national subjectivity in a manner that differs significantly from important accounts of national identity recently advanced by critics like Katie Trumpener, Homi Bhabha, and Benedict Anderson. Scott's account is more than merely idiosyncratic, however, for as I will show, in deviating from these critics' discussions, Scott exemplifies a pattern of thinking that will become quite prominent, the view that metrical form can serve as the foundation for the identity of a people.

NATIONAL IMPRESS

Scott was drawn into a public defense of Scottish national autonomy after the British Parliament responded to the 1825 financial panic with an 1826 currency reform: small bank notes would henceforth be replaced by specie throughout Great Britain.[4] In Scotland, opponents of the reform claimed that economic prosperity depended on these small bank notes, and while Scott's *Letters of Malachi Malagrowther* also spoke of them as "nearly indispensable to . . . carrying on business of almost any kind in Scotland," his contribution to the debate involved not so much an elucidation of currency theory as the creation of a persona, Malachi Malagrowther, the speaker in this series of three letters to the editor of the *Edinburgh Weekly Journal*.[5] Occupying the position of antiquarian cultural nationalism (Scott's *Journal* describes him as "an uncompromising right forward Scot of the Old School" [*J*, 99]), Malagrowther condemns the currency reform as much for its blatant "national insult" (735) as for its flawed monetary policy. In the discussion that follows I will be concerned not with Scott's (admittedly substantial) role in defeating the currency reform,[6] nor with his (frankly inconsequential) contribution to currency theory,[7] but rather with the larger question of how his engagement with this issue led him to "keep sight of both" nation and empire by formulating their relation in an unusual way, one that draws its underlying logic from discussions of poetic meter.

As he argues against the currency reform, Scott's Malagrowther asserts that "ministers see no reason why any law adopted on this subject [i.e. note issues] should not be imperative over all his Majesty's dominions, including Scotland, *for uniformity's sake*" (730). This pursuit of "uniformity" as an end in itself (728) overlooks the "three separate nations" that make up the "one empire" (749) of Britain, thus betraying the ministers' larger ambition to "assimilate" (726) Scotland within Britain's one "general system" (730). Such a goal threatens "to annul and dissolve all the distinctions and peculiarities" (748–49) that make Scotland Scotland. In response, Malagrowther asserts,

> For God's sake, sir, let us remain as Nature made us, Englishmen, Irishmen, and Scotchmen, with something like the impress of our several countries upon each! We would not become better subjects, or more valuable members of the common empire, if we all resembled each other like so many smooth shillings. . . . The degree of national diversity between different countries is but an instance of that general variety which Nature seems to have adopted as a principle through all her works, as anxious, apparently, to avoid, as modern statesmen to enforce, any thing like an approach to absolute "uniformity." (749)

Here Malagrowther invokes currency not as a theoretical issue but as a rhetorical device, one that counters enforced uniformity by asserting a distinction between value, on the one hand, and identity on the other. Shillings are "not . . . more valuable" even when worn "smooth" since their value to the empire stems from the quantity of silver they contain (1 / 20 £.) rather than the inscription they bear; smooth shillings, after all, continue to circulate throughout the "common empire" as silver bullion, a barter commodity that contributes to the empire's vast material resources.[8] What is true of shillings also applies to "subjects," for according to Malagrowther, imperial subjects are "like" smooth shillings insofar as they all "resembled each other" – subjects are likewise a uniform natural resource contributing their value to the common empire. While resemblance among smooth shillings or uniform subjects does not diminish the value of each to the empire, it does have an effect on national identity: just as an "impress" gives an identity to silver bullion (making it into shillings), so "Nature" adds its own mint mark to subjects, imparting the "distinctions and peculiarities" that, far from "empty forms,"[9] are the basis of a particular national identity as "Englishmen, Irishmen, and Scotchmen." According to Malagrowther, part of the impress that marks Scotsmen as Scotsmen is the long-standing practice of issuing small bank bills; the plan to end that practice, then, brings Scottish national identity that much closer to smooth imperial uniformity, a change that will not affect the *value* of British subjects (any more than the smoothness of a shilling affects its value as silver bullion), but that undermines the *identity* of Scotland itself, placing at risk "the well-being, nay, the very being, of our ancient kingdom" (737).[10]

Protecting the national "variety" of Scotland, then, requires protecting its national impress, and one of Malagrowther's strategies for such protection is to argue that Parliament can no more legislate circulation of specie over paper than it can legislate crops of wheat over oats (730), but this appeal to Scottish soil is undermined when Malagrowther goes on to embrace shared banking practices among Scotland, Ireland, and England (739, 726).[11] As an alternative protection of Scotland's national impress, Malagrowther argues that if civic institutions like banking *can* transfer to a different national soil, then whether they *may* do so is, according to the Treaty of Union, a decision for Scotsmen alone to make (731). Again, however, Malagrowther acknowledges that this is so only if England, the stronger party to the treaty, agrees to be bound by it, and this caveat places Scottish national identity at the mercy of "the national honour of Old England" (732).[12] Finally, Malagrowther seeks to protect Scotland's national impress by suggesting that ministers' aim of "*uniformity* of civil institutions" is "descended from . . . Conformity in religious doctrine" (734). The English become "Rabbies" and "Law Monks" who "are devoted to their own Rule, and admit of no question of its infallibility" (726), so conformity involves not a dispute within Christianity (i.e. disagreements between Scottish Presbyterians and English Episcopalians) but a fear that the English will "treat us as the Spaniards treated the Indians, whom they massacred for worshipping the image of the sun, while they themselves bowed down to that of the Virgin Mary. . ." (727).

By rewriting civil uniformity as religious conformity Malagrowther does not so much protect Scotland's national impress as re-describe its peril: the impress will be worn smooth as a result of conversion.[13] The problem, then, is not that the English are "devoted to their own religion" but that, as with the Spanish treatment of the Indians, such devotion is "monopoliz[ed]" (726): "these English Monks will not tolerate in their lay-brethren of the North the slightest pretence to a similar feeling" (726) – the English mistake, that is, is a "proselytism" (726) that is blind to "the feelings of dissenters" (726), of the Scots who feel a similar "devotion" to their own "ancient jurisdiction" (727). For Malagrowther, moreover, the danger is less that Scots will (like the Indians) resist such proselytism and be "massacred" but that the same result, the end of a distinct people, is already underway as Scots greet imperial uniformity with "submissive acquiescence" (735). After decades of commercial prosperity, a state of "repletion" (735) is causing national sentiment to wane. Rare exceptions include Malagrowther's grandfather who, after reading the clause in the Treaty of Union that guarantees Scottish autonomy, then (as Malagrowther relates) "exclaimed, '*Nemo me impune lacesset*!'[14] which I presume, are words belonging to the black art, since there is no one in the Modern Athens conjuror enough to understand their meaning, or at least to comprehend the spirit of the sentiment which my grandfather thought they conveyed" (731). Under this "Modern" condition of widespread indifference to Scotland's national autonomy the national motto is virtually unrecognized, and Malagrowther expects that the Treaty of Union itself will soon be "voted obsolete," with only "the old parchment . . . preserved . . . in the Museum of the Antiquaries, where, with . . . other antiquated documents once held in reverence, it might silently contract dust, yet remain to bear witness that such things had been" (732). As the "sentiment" for independence dies out and national documents gather "dust," Scotland's national impress starts to look like it needs protection as much from present-day Scots as from the imperial Parliament in England.

As a way of countering this threat – both internal and external – to Scotland's national impress, Malagrowther invokes a somewhat different motto from his grandfather's Latin phrase, a "verse from an old song" (739) that serves as a "motto" for the second of his *Letters*:

When the pipes begin to play
Tutti taittie to the drum,
Out claymore, and down wi' gun,
And to the rogues again.
(739 n.)[15]

Describing himself as "desirous, by every effort in my power, to awaken [my countrymen] to a sense of their national danger" (739), Malagrowther sees this song verse as one means to that end, for it is "the summons which my countrymen have been best accustomed to obey" (739). As a "summons" addressed to "my countrymen," the motto is intended to awaken the Scottish people to vigilant protection of their national impress. But even as it seems to protect the national impress of Scots, it seems also to endanger neighboring Englishmen, the "rogues" under attack. Aware of this potential reading of the motto, Malagrowther hopes to allay any concerns: "The motto of my epistle may sound a little warlike. . . . But it is not a hostile signal towards you [i.e. England] . . . To my countrymen I speak in the language of many recollections, certain they are not likely to be excited beyond the bounds of temperate and constitutional remonstrance" (739). Despite these assurances, the song verse generated such alarm among English readers that a later edition relegated it to a footnote, "some cautious friends," the note explains, "thinking it liable to misinterpretation" (739n.).

To interpret the song as "hostile" and "warlike" seems almost inevitable given the military circumstance it depicts. But such a literal reading of the song envisions victory for only one side, so it fails to "keep sight of both" nation and empire. If this warlike reading amounts to a *mis*interpretation, then what manner of interpretation would permit the motto to function, as Malagrowther imagines, as a gesture that both protects Scotland's national impress and avoids hostility toward England? One possibility is to read the story the song tells not as a literal call for violence but as an allegory for the currency reform. In such an interpretation the Highlanders' preference for claymores over guns ("Out claymore, and down wi' gun") might correspond to contemporary Scotsmen's preference for old banking methods over English reforms: out small notes and down with coins. This allegorical interpretation moves on the terrain of economics, where the aim is not a "warlike" revolt but a continuity of effective monetary policy, and this continuity of banknotes – Scotland's national impress – protects Scottish identity while avoiding "warlike" hostility toward England.

Such a reading may avoid misinterpreting the song as "warlike," but it nevertheless does not seem to be the reading Malagrowther has in mind.

Far from imagining that Scotsmen will have to interpret the motto as an allegory of their historical present, Malagrowther is confident that they will respond to it immediately and directly:

The motto of my epistle may sound a little warlike; but, in using it, I have only employed the summons which my countrymen have been best accustomed to obey. . . . The drums beat to *arms* and the trumpets sound *Heraus*, as well when the soldiers are called out for a peaceful as for a military object. And, which is more to the purpose, the last time the celebrated Fiery Cross was circulated in the Highlands . . . the clansmen were called forth not to fight an enemy, but to stop the progress of a dreadful conflagration. (739)

Scotsmen are "called forth" by the summons first and foremost to be a people, and only then to designate and carry out their common "object," whether it be "peaceful" or "military." By separating these various objects (i.e. charging with claymores, fighting a fire, paying with banknotes) from the summons that calls forth a group who might perform them, Malagrowther is not so much drawing an *analogy* among a sequence of distinct "objects" as asserting an *identity* among those who perform them: what directly identifies Scotsmen of 1745 with those of 1826 is their common response to the summons, regardless of what the assembled group is subsequently asked to do (and indeed whether they actually do it). So instead of urging Scotsmen to draw lessons from historical analogies – a history, after all, whose lessons would be available to Scots and non-Scots alike – Malagrowther urges them to identify directly with that past, and such direct identification is possible only if analogous but distinct aims (i.e. fighting with claymores or paying with banknotes) are subsumed under a common Scottish identity shared across time. The motto, by this account, is neither a literal incitement to violence nor an allegorical lesson from history; rather, it is a "summons" by which the Scottish people – whether of 1745 or 1826 – can be "called forth."

Treating the motto as a summons distinguishes it not only from its thematic account of "warlike" claymores but also from another thematic element of the song, the bagpipe signal. In the song, the sound of the bagpipes, or "*Tutti taittie*," is designated as the signal to charge. As with signals generally, this sound is stipulated as a cue for action. But since this cue can be stipulated to a group only after that group has been assembled, the summoning of that group must occur at an earlier moment. It is this earlier summons that matters to Malagrowther: his concern is not that an assembled group might be taught to interpret the bagpipe as a signal to charge but that such a group – a Scottish people – could be assembled in the first place. Thus for the purposes of the summons, the bagpipe and the action it cues are just as incidental as the claymore. Indeed, as a summons, the song is reducible to none of its thematic elements: since, as we have seen, it does not require an "enemy," even the "rogues" (i.e. the English) are irrelevant to its function as a summons. The summoning the motto accomplishes is ultimately distinct from the story the motto tells.

Once these thematic elements are set aside, the remaining feature of the motto that plausibly accounts for its summoning function is its formal status as a song, a metered set of lines. But if it is this form, and not the motto's content, that accounts for its function as a summons, then how does form alone accomplish this? That is, how can mere sound effects, as distinct from the meanings they convey, have this effect of summoning forth Scots as a people?

One way of answering this question is by reference to the motto's second line, which features the phrase "*Tutti taittie.*" Now from one perspective, this phrase is simultaneously a sound effect and a semantic sign – indeed, by embodying what it represents (the sound of the bagpipe), it is an onomatopoetic sign.[16] As with all instances of onomatopoeia, the medium is not merely transparent but also opaque, so it asserts itself in a manner that accentuates the meaning being conveyed – here, even as it *represents* the sound of the bagpipe, "*Tutti taittie*" also *embodies* that sound. Only the phrase "*Tutti taittie*" functions in this way; while all the lines of the motto share the metrical regularity of this phrase, only here are those metrical effects brought to the fore to work in partnership with the semantic content. But as we have seen, in imagining the motto as a summons, Malagrowther views its form as *distinct from* its content, not in *partnership with* its content: while the words are representing warlike conflict, the form is summoning Scots as Scots. Setting content aside in this way has two consequences for the discussion of "*Tutti taittie.*" First, in losing its partnership with thematic content, "*Tutti taittie*" loses the context that had identified what sound its sounds embody: if the phrase "*Tutti taittie*" is no longer *representing* the sound of the bagpipe, there is no longer any reason to think of its sounds as *embodying* the sound of the bagpipe.[17] Instead of being bagpipe sounds, it would seem to be nothing more than metered syllables. Second, without a thematic partner, these few syllables look no different from the metrical form in the remainder of the line and, indeed, the rest of the motto. From this perspective, the assertion of sound effects that had seemed to occur only locally – only within the onomatopoetic phrase "*Tutti taittie*" – reveals itself to be a pervasive feature of the motto. It is this pervasive metrical form – as distinct from the semantic content of "claymore," "rogues," and even "*Tutti taittie*," – that Malagrowther wishes to assert as the basis for his summons.

But if "*Tutti taittie*" and the rest of the motto's meter are not the sound of bagpipes, what are they the sound *of* such that they can assemble Scots as a people? Malagrowther's implicit answer comes by way of analogy to onomatopoeia: just as the sounds of "*Tutti taittie*" could embody the sound of the bagpipe, so the sounds of the motto as a whole are more than mere metrical effects – they embody Scottishness. Implicit here, this notion is explicit in Scott's later account of popular poetry in Scotland. There he observes that "the language of Scotland, most commonly spoken, began to be that of their neighbors, the English," but "the music continued to be Celtic in its general measure," so if "the Scottish people . . . adopted . . . the Saxon language" (542), they nevertheless remained true to the "aboriginal race, – a race passionately addicted to music, . . . preserving . . . to this day a style and character of music peculiar to their own country" (541).[18] The peculiarity of Scottish musical measure is embodied in the metrical features of the motto (itself a song verse), so just as Scottish music can remain distinct from English words, so too the motto's Scottish meter can remain distinct from its English language content. While the words may have meaning in English, the meter embodies Scottishness. This suggests a new way of thinking about "*Tutti taittie*": instead of bagpipe sounds working in partnership with the semantic meaning, it is an eruption of Scottish meter amidst English words. While this is most conspicuous in "*Tutti taittie*" (where sound effects are foregrounded), the motto as a whole is pervaded by these Scottish sounds. Two nationalities exist side-by-side, sorted according to form and theme.

But if this analysis helps clarify what is at stake for Malagrowther as he isolates the motto's form from its thematic content, our earlier question remains unanswered: once separated from the meanings they convey, how do these Scottish sounds summon Scots? As we saw, the English "misinterpretation" stems from reading the song's warlike words and ignoring the effect of its sound, a national sound that, according to Malagrowther, is recognizably Scottish. Stripped of thematic content and reduced to a peculiarly Scottish metrical form, the song does not have a semantic meaning so much as a national identity – it is not read so much as recognized. Recognizing the Scottishness of the motto's meter concerns a point prior to consent, when those "called forth" have not yet been told what they will be asked to do and thus have not been given a chance to comply or refuse. Instead of inviting listeners to make a choice, the summons induces them to assemble, and it does so by triggering shared experience of shared memories:

"To my countrymen I speak in the language of many recollections" (739). Those who are summoned both perceive the song and experience their recollections of it, the perception immediately triggering the recollection. Since this experience of the summons involves not choosing but remembering, it circumvents deliberation.[19] This is why the summons is something "which my countrymen have been best accustomed to *obey*" (739; emphasis added), and while the very notion of obedience would seem to imply the possibility of disobedience, Malagrowther rewrites a failure to obey as a failure to be: "If there is . . . a mean-spirited Scotsman, who prefers the orders of the [English] minister to the unanimous voice of his country . . . , let England keep him to herself. . . . he cannot be a Scottish man in spirit . . . . he is not of us" (737). Those who experience the summons as a summons – who, upon hearing it, also recollect it – confirm the presence within them of those memories, of that Scottish spirit. Just as viewing the motto as a summons brings to the fore its national meter, subordinating its meaningful words to its Scottish sounds, so summoned Scotsmen bring to the fore their national recollections, subordinating their status as deliberating imperial subjects to their underlying national memory and, thus, national identity. Scotland's national impress, then, consists not in Scotsmen's devotion to their own laws (a devotion that can be rubbed smooth by conversion) but in their more durable ability to be summoned forth, as a people, by "the language of many recollections," the metrical form of a poem. It is this status as the language of many recollections that allows meter to become more than a *figure* for nation and to function, more forcefully, as an *agency* of national continuity.

THE "LANGUAGE OF MANY RECOLLECTIONS"

Once Malagrowther relocates Scotland's national impress from civil institutions like currency to the "language of many recollections," it makes sense to ask how Scots of 1826 could have had these recollections impressed upon them. Given the decades of commercial prosperity that, as Malagrowther observes, have largely aligned the experiences of Scots with those of Englishmen, how could Scots of 1826, those younger than Malagrowther's grandfather, have experienced national difference in a way that would permit such "recollections"? According to Malagrowther, these recollections do not in fact stem from actual experience, and in trying to account for such non-experiential recollections among Scots, he draws an analogy between Scots and aristocrats: a vote against the currency reform is something

Scotland demands . . . from the small, but honourable portion of the Upper House, who draw their honours from her ancient domains. Their ancestors have led her armies, concluded her treaties, managed her government, served her with hand and heart, sword and pen; and by such honourable merit with their country, have obtained the titles and distinctions which they have transmitted to the present race, by whom, we are well assured, they will be maintained with untarnished honour. (737)

This appeal rehearses the paradoxical logic of aristocratic standing, a standing that is both absolute and subject to maintenance: the "ancestors" of today's "peers" performed acts of "honourable merit" by which they "obtained titles and distinctions," and those titles have in turn been "transmitted to the present race" along lines of descent.[20] But if these titles have devolved intact, it is nevertheless hoped that they will be "maintained" through "the present race['s]" similar acts of "honourable merit" on behalf of "her ancient domains"; it is hoped, more particularly, that peers will live up to the standing conferred upon them and resist the national affront of the currency reform: "whom among them could we suspect of deserting the Parent of his Honours, at the very moment when she is calling upon him for his filial aid?" (737). Such an act of maintenance wouldn't *earn* a title (since ancestors did that) and it wouldn't *confer* one (since "Scotland" initially did that, and descent or ancestry subsequently does so); rather, it *confirms* the inheritance of the title, serving as a representation of the otherwise invisible standing. The act of maintenance, then, is not only a political action but also a gesture of self-representation, and an act can have this double status only when there is an inherited title to represent; otherwise the deed would just be an isolated act, aid and not "filial aid," a gesture of patriotic sentiment rather than a representation of honourable (i.e. aristocratic) standing.[21]

Malagrowther not only makes this appeal to Scotland's peers, hoping to prompt votes against the reform, he also broadens the scope of his appeal to include the entire Scottish nation. Personifying Scotland as "Saunders" (just as England is "John Bull" and Ireland is "Paddy"), Malagrowther links his logic of aristocratic standing to his account of summoning: "in using it [the motto], I have only employed the summons which my countrymen have been best accustomed to obey. Saunders, if it please your honours [i.e. England], has been so long unused to stand erect in your honours' presence, that, if I would have him behave like a man, I must . . . slap him on the shoulder, and throw a word in every now and then about his *honour*" (739). Much as peers were challenged to maintain their aristocratic honor, so Saunders – who functions here both as a peer and as "my countrymen" – is challenged to respond to the summons, so the implication of Saunders (i.e. a Scottish peer) in the logic of aristocratic standing is just like the implication of Saunders (i.e. "my countrymen") in the logic of the summons: if peers have inherited titles (i.e. credit for ancestors' political actions), then "my countrymen" have inherited recollections (i.e. memories of ancestors' cultural practices). Thus while peers represent their inherited standing through actions that confirm a title, "my countrymen" represent their inherited recollection through recognition that confirms recollections – through, that is, obedience to the summons. In this analogy, inherited *merit* for ancestral service to the nation-as-state is aligned with inherited *memory* of ancestral participation in the nation-as-culture, and the need, in the first case, for *political actions* that confirm aristocratic standing matches a need, in the second case, for *cultural recollections* that confirm national identity. Scotland becomes a "birthright" (735) in and of itself, and *all* Scots – "a Scotsman, and especially a Scottish nobleman" (737) – can recognize "the unanimous voice of his country, imploring the protection of her children" (737) because they are all included among that nation's "children," the inheritors of its national memory. Class difference (between peers and commoners) is replaced by national identity, and filial aid to the "Parent of his Honours" (by aristocrats) becomes filial aid to the Parent of his Memories (by Scotsmen generally), the transmission of aristocratic titles giving way to the transmission of the language of many recollections.

This notion of inherited recollections lies behind Malagrowther's next example of the summons, an example in which he specifies how he would voice a rejoinder to English encroachments:

> England – were it mine to prescribe the forms, my native country ought to address nearly in the words of her own Mason, mangled, I fear, in my recollection –
>
> "Sister, to thee no ruder spell
> Will Scotland use, than those that dwell
> In soft Persuasion's notes, and lie
> Twined with the links of *Harmony*."
>
> Let us, therefore, my countrymen, make a proper and liberal allowance for the motives of the Ministers and their friends on this occasion. (739)

In this passage the poem occupies a space of apostrophe, for the first prose section describes the poem as an "address" to England and the second one suggests that it also speaks to "my countrymen," or Scotsmen. Viewed from the first perspective, this poem's words reflect the desired posture toward England: the notions of "*Harmony*" and "soft Persuasion" point to the "proper and liberal allowance" Malagrowther wishes to make for the Ministers' good motives. But if these conciliatory words are directed at England, the metrical form itself is drawn from and refers to the more reliable collective memory of Scotland: the native country speaks the verse form of William Mason, one of "her own" native sons. Thus the metrical form of the poem acts as a summons to "my countrymen" even as the words act as an address to "England." Such a split between form and content is itself thematized in the poem, where the "spell" is said to "dwell / in" or be "Twined with" "*Harmony*" and "soft Persuasion's notes." The "spell," then, figures the metrical summons to "my countrymen" that coexists with these words. English words might be a uniform institution across the British empire, but they are accompanied by a Scottish form that is irreducible to this institutional practice and that announces Scottishness even in the midst of that imperial sway. Indeed, once meter is invested with the force of a national summons, the words that accompany it become merely incidental: they can be "mangled" in one's recollection without affecting the underlying national form.[22]

Viewed along with the motto, Mason's poem and its metrical summoning force reveals a shift that has occurred in Malagrowther's approach to representing the persistence of national "variety" against pressures toward imperial "uniformity": abandoning coins as his figure for the nation's relation to empire, he no longer needs to protect a "national impress" from being worn smooth. Focusing instead on poems, he can now conduct literary analyses that reveal, lurking alongside uniform imperial words, the ongoing presence of a peculiar national meter, and he can expect that Scots (those who have inherited "the language of many recollections") will experience this meter as a summons. Embodied in metrical form and recollected by all Scots, such a national impress is in no danger of falling prey to imperial uniformity. Unlike the national slogan "*Nemo me impune lacesset*," which, when spoken by Malagrowther's grandfather, was mistaken for "the black art" because the sounds of its Latin words left contemporary Scots unable to "understand their meaning" (731), the motto avoids this problem by abandoning all meaning, its rhythmic sounds alone functioning as a summons to Scottish national identity.

Malagrowther's notion that Scotland's national "variety" could be embodied in metrical variety runs counter to the influential metrical principles set out in Samuel Johnson's *Dictionary of the English Language* (1755), which had called for uniformity of both words *and* prosody.[23] But as critics have often noted, the close of the eighteenth century saw a general retreat from Johnson's metrical principles as many poets, including Scott himself, cultivated a greater variety in their prosody. Doing so led to a tension between the uniformity demanded of word usage, on the one hand, and the variety embraced in metrical practice, on the other.[24] In his *Letters of Malachi*

Malagrowther, I am arguing, Scott is not only aware of this tension within poetry, but he also invests that tension with the political conflicts of imperial dominion: for Scott, the tension between uniform words and varying prosody comes to serve as a figure for the tension between the uniformity of the empire and the variety of its constituent nations, so English words are not just uniform but also imperial while meter – for instance, the meter of the motto or of Mason's poem – not only figures variety, but the variety it figures is, Scott claims, distinctly national – in this case, Scottish.[25] By perpetuating national identity in tandem with the institutions of empire, the metrical summons advances Scott's goal to "keep sight of both." More than just a figure for national variety, however, we have seen that meter – as the "language of many recollections" – is also the *agency* for asserting this national variety. As we will see, this metrical summons provides a referent for Malagrowther's notion that the "Parent of his Honours" is calling upon Scots for their "filial aid."

MALAGROWTHER'S NATION AND WORDSWORTH'S EMPIRE

Just before he quotes the Mason poem, Malagrowther asserts the tense coexistence of imperial words and national meter by way of a more familiar poetic reference, in this case invoking "the sweet little rustic girl in a poem which it is almost a sin to parody" (736), the girl in Wordsworth's "We are Seven" (1798). Wordsworth is an apt choice for exploring the relation between word and meter, for exploiting possible tensions between words and "superadded" meter is a prominent aspect of his poetry.[26] This particular poem exploits such a tension to an unusual degree, for even though its typical line is made up of seven iambic feet (four followed by three in the split-up septenarius), the poem's first line is missing two feet ("A simple child, – /That lightly draws its breath"[27]), so scanning it raises the question whether it consists of five or seven metrical feet. This formal choice between five and seven feet corresponds, of course, to the thematic debate between the poem's two main figures, the rustic girl and the traveler: counting according to the metrical form (in spite of the missing words) is consistent with the rustic girl, who counts seven siblings even though two have died; counting only the ostensible words is consistent with the traveler, who insists, "If two are in the church-yard laid,/ Then ye are only five" (84).[28]

Malagrowther adapts this debate about fives and sevens, words and meter, to his own agenda of defending Scottish national autonomy: this relation of traveler (words) to rustic girl (meter) repeats the relation of words to meter that we saw in Mason's poem, so for Malagrowther, the traveler stands in for the English Ministers and the rustic girl speaks for Scotland (736). Scottish national autonomy has, like the rustic girl's siblings, receded into the remote past, and the tendency of a "preemptory Minister" to act as if Scotland had "altogether los[t] consideration" (735) matches the traveler's impulse to give diminished consideration to the rustic girl's family – to count five instead of seven siblings. But if Scottish representatives would only treat their national past the way the rustic girl treats her deceased siblings and the way scansion treats the meter of the poem's first line, as a felt presence despite physical absence, then they could continue to assert their autonomous nationhood:

> our representatives must stand firm. I would advise that, to all such intimations as are usually circulated, bearing, "That your presence is earnestly requested on such an evening of the debate, as such or such a public measure is coming on," the concise answer should be returned, "*We are five-and-forty*;" and that no Scottish members do on such occasions attend. (737)

Instead of obeying an imperial summons, the forty-five Scottish Ministers should obey this national one. The refrain "*We are five-and-forty*" replaces the rustic girl's "We are seven," but the point remains the same: one must insist that an aspect of the remote past, Scottish national autonomy, still has bearing in the present. In this case, as with the rustic girl, meter marks the absence of, and thereby enables the persistence of, a superseded point of history, a point when words filled out a metered line, when siblings were still living, when the nation enjoyed independence. In appropriating the rustic girl's voice, Malagrowther urges that her persistent attachment to deceased siblings serve as a model for Scotsmen's persistent attachment to national autonomy, and like Wordsworth, he makes this point by subordinating traveler to rustic girl and words to metrical form.[29]

If Wordsworth's poem lends itself well to Malagrowther's project, a project of using the formal features of poems to imagine how the Scottish people might sustain their autonomy within Britain, this use of it nevertheless deviates considerably from Wordsworth's own poetic aims. In associating meter with the rustic girl's memories of deceased siblings, Wordsworth seeks to show how the girl fondly remembers habitual features of her personal past, and not, as Malagrowther would have it, how she is imperiously summoned to obedient recognition of her national past. Scott's deviation from Wordsworth's aims becomes apparent when we examine the context in which "We are Seven" first appeared, the 1798 collection of *Lyrical Ballads*.

In Wordsworth's "Preface" (1802) to this collection he describes the poet's aim as one not of enforcing obedience to a national metrical summons but of displaying the pleasurable relation people bear to the habits they have gradually acquired through their regular interactions with the surrounding empirical world, a world in which meter is just one of many sources of sensation:

> We have no knowledge, that is, no general principles drawn from the contemplation of particular facts, but what has been built up by pleasure, and exists in us by pleasure alone. . . . What then does the Poet? He considers man and the objects that surround him as acting and re-acting upon each other, so as to produce an infinite complexity of pain and pleasure; he considers man in his own nature and in his ordinary life as contemplating this with a certain quantity of immediate knowledge, with certain convictions, intuitions, and deductions which by habit become of the nature of intuitions; he considers him as looking upon this complex scene of ideas and sensations, and finding every where objects that immediately excite in him sympathies which, from the necessities of his nature, are accompanied by an overbalance of enjoyment. To this knowledge which all men carry about with them, and to these sympathies in which without any other discipline than that of our daily life we are fitted to take delight, the Poet principally directs his attention. He considers man and nature as essentially adapted to each other . . . (605–06)

The burden of this passage is to explain how it is that "objects . . . immediately excite . . . sympathies." They do so not because people obey a summons but because in the "ordinary" course of their "daily life" people interact with the objects that surround them, eventually becoming so "adapted" or "fitted" to those objects that experiencing them prompts an accompanying "enjoyment." This is not the pleasure of sensory stimulation from the object itself but, rather, an acquired and persistent *disposition* to take pleasure, so it stems from within, from the "habits" that sensation has gradually established, the "built up" "knowledge which all men carry about with them."[30] Once one's interactions with the empirical world have "by habit become of the nature of intuition," this enjoyment then becomes one of "the necessities of his nature" – i.e. it becomes second nature.[31] And if people have this pleasurable, habit-based relation to objects, the poet in turn has a relation to this relation: the poet "considers man . . . as contemplating . . ." or "he considers him as looking . . ." – "He considers," that is, the "essentially adapted" relation of sensory habituation that can develop between "man and nature."

Bearing in mind these statements from the "Preface," we can better understand Wordsworth's aim in "We are Seven." In counting to seven the rustic girl registers the presence not of siblings but of her habit-based attachment to them, an attachment that developed as they lived and persists (as her second nature) after their death, thus disposing her to continue to enjoy her habitual relation to them – eating and singing with them – even in their absence. It is not the siblings' summoning jurisdiction over her but her own "built up," pleasurable knowledge of them that the girl displays in her conversation with the traveler. Himself a stranger in the region, the traveler has not interacted with the objects that consistently surround the girl, so he cannot share her intuitive pleasure in them. For his part, Wordsworth takes the poet's role: he considers the little girl as contemplating her siblings in this intuitive or habit-based way, and his object is her habitual (and thus pleasurable) relation to these objects. We see, then, that the debate Wordsworth stages is not between nation and empire but between a person who carries around with her this empirically derived disposition to take pleasure in (now absent) objects and a person who, in the absence of these objects, cannot experience them at all.

If Wordsworth here treats siblings as objects which one can learn to delight in, he takes the same view toward poetic meter. When he speaks of the "feelings of pleasure which the Reader has been accustomed to connect with meter in general" (610), he attributes to readers an acquired delight in meter much like the rustic girl's acquired delight in her siblings.[32] If they are "essentially adapted" to take pleasure in meter, readers should be able to count out the missing metrical feet in the same way that the girl counts her absent siblings; they should have acquired an intuitive sense of how to complete the split-up septanarius just as she has acquired an intuitive sense of how to think of her siblings as ever present. When Wordsworth worries that readers might, like the traveler, not possess this intuitive disposition to take pleasure, he suggests an education program through which they can gradually develop it: "an *accurate* taste in poetry . . . is an *acquired* talent, which can only be produced by thought, and a long continued intercourse with the best models of composition" (614). This acquired (or at least acquirable) delight in poetic meter is not specific to any one group of people, for his notion of the "general power of numbers" (609) suggests that anyone could attain it.

One can attain such a relation to more than siblings and meter, for Wordsworth asserts this as an available relation to all objects of sense, even the new ones that science might disclose: "The remotest discoveries of the Chemist, the Botanist, or Mineralogist, will be as proper objects of the Poet's art as any upon which it can be employed, if the time should ever come when these things shall be familiar to us, and the relations under which they are contemplated by the followers of these respective Sciences shall be manifestly and palpably material to us as enjoying and suffering beings" (607). Across this diversity of sense objects, what is common is "the relations under which they are contemplated," and it is the poet's attention to these relations, to these habits, that permits him to look beyond the habit of cherishing a particular object and toward this general disposition to have such pleasurable knowledge:

> In spite of difference of soil and climate, of language and manners, of laws and customs, in spite of things silently gone out of mind and things violently destroyed, the Poet binds together by passion and knowledge the vast empire of human society, as it is spread over the whole earth, and over all time. The objects of the Poet's thoughts are every where; though the eyes and senses of man are, it is true, his favorite guides, yet he will follow wheresoever he can an atmosphere of sensation in which to move his wings. (606)

The notions of "soil," "manners," "language," and "laws" often served contemporaries (including, as we have seen, Scott's Malagrowther) as arguments for national distinctiveness, so Wordsworth's notion that "the Poet binds together . . . human society" despite such differences points to an explicitly anti-national stance. Instead of underwriting national particularity, Wordsworth seeks to put on display a human-wide "empire" of "passion and knowledge," finding "every where" habit-objects sufficient to inspire it. The "charm" he associates with meter, then, is not Scott's nationally specific summons but an international habit, "the charm which, by the consent of all nations, is acknowledged to exist in metrical language" (609). If Scott uses meter to secure a bounded national identity, Wordsworth uses it to anticipate an ever-expanding human empire of pleasurable knowledge. If Scott treats meter as an imperious summons that commands obedience from Scotsmen, Wordsworth sees it as an object of sense which "long continued intercourse" has rendered a source of delight. And if Scott suggests that a prior generation's habit of recognizing the metrical summons can be transmitted intact to subsequent Scotsmen (thus enabling "recollection" of the summons even among those "unused" to it), Wordsworth localizes habits within the empirical life of the individual – this habitual recognition, for Wordsworth, is acquired by empirical experience, not descent. Scott's invocation of the rustic girl as a spokesperson for national identity, then, obscures the difference between Scott's and Wordsworth's treatments of meter, a difference between habitual delight and obedient recognition, between built-up knowledge (second nature) and transmitted experience, between personal memory and national memory, between personal identity and national identity.

THE HIGHLAND WIDOW

A few months after appropriating Wordsworth's meter to the national aims of his *Letters of Malachi Malagrowther*, Scott continues to project the force of a national summons on the poetry of his contemporaries, this time the work of Samuel Taylor Coleridge. This becomes apparent in the fiction Scott wrote immediately following the currency crisis, fiction in which Coleridge's *Christabel* plays a prominent role. Coleridge wrote *Christabel* at a time when he was himself directing sustained attention to the topic of poetic meter,[33] and this disposition to experiment helps explain why, as Coleridge puts it, "the meter of Christabel is . . . founded on a new principle."[34] Coleridge's metrical innovations initially inspired Scott's own best-selling verse romances,[35] and some twenty years later, immediately following the 1826 currency crisis, Christabel was again on Scott's mind, for it supplies a (misquoted) epigraph to *The Highland Widow*, one of several stories collected in Scott's *Chronicles of the Canongate* (1827):

> It wound° as near as near could† be, °moaned, †can
> But what it is she cannot tell;
> On the other side it seemed to be,
> Of the huge broad-breasted old oak-tree.[36]

In Coleridge's poem these lines introduce the uncanny Geraldine, and Scott folds them into his own prose when he introduces his own "not canny" (98) character, Elspat MacTavish, who is discovered (paraphrasing Coleridge) "by the side of the great broad-breasted oak, in the direction opposed to that in which we had hitherto seen it" (99). Appropriating Geraldine for his own story gives Scott a model who not only has a magical power to coerce obedience, or "forced unconscious sympathy" (l. 609) – "In the touch of [Geraldine's] bosom there worketh a spell, / Which is lord of thy utterance, Christabel!" (ll. 267–68) – but who also, in Scott's view, functions as a figure for metrical form.[37] Thus not only does Elspat have "an unusual acquaintance with the songs of ancient bards" (125), but the "style of her rhetoric was poetical" (138), and she employs "the words of a Gaelic poet" as her own speech (143). Furthermore, she is seen "speaking to herself in a language which will endure no translation" (139), a description Scott elsewhere associates with poetic form.[38] Indeed, Scott's misquotation of Coleridge moves the epigraph further in the direction of an allegory for meter: substituting "wound" for "moaned" envisions Geraldine "wound as near as near could be" about Christabel (a circumstance that in fact occurs in the poem[39]), and we can see how "wound" parallels meter's "superadded" relation to words: the two are intensely proximate, but the one always remains irreducible to the other.[40]

If Scott invokes Geraldine as a basis for his own allegory of meter, he also deviates from Coleridge's example in ways that endow Elspat MacTavish with distinctly national features absent from Geraldine. While Geraldine's magic had involved serpentine evil, Scott removes Elspat's magic from the Christian context, aligning it instead with indigenous Druidical sacrifice (159–60). Moreover, if Geraldine's role in *Christabel* is to exploit a rift between Sir Leoline and Lord Roland, Elspat exploits a gap between Scotland and the empire: she is "seated by the stem of the oak, with her head drooping, her hands clasped, and a dark-colored mantle drawn over her head, exactly as Judah is represented in the Syrian medals as seated under her palm-tree" (99). This is a reference, John Barrell notes, to "a Roman coin which . . . depicts Judaea – the Roman province – in the form of a veiled woman, sitting under a palm-tree, weeping."[41] Malagrowther had warned that imperial encroachments threatened to reduce Scotland to "provincial" status (725), and Elspat, "the Woman of the Tree" (100), allegorically figures this once-autonomous entity – the Scottish nation.[42] Thus while Coleridge had asserted that "the meter of Christabel is . . . founded on a new principle," Scott's allegory of meter associates it with the much older principle of Scottish national independence. Bringing together the metrical power of Coleridge's Geraldine and the national independence of Scotland, Elspat MacTavish is thus poised to operate, like meter, as a metrical summons to national identity.

Elspat's exertion of this summoning force provides the main action of *The Highland Widow*. The object of her summons is her son, Hamish, who, just an infant at the time of his father's death in the 1745 uprising, has now joined the British army to fight for imperial conquest "against the French in America" (118). His mother, still loyal to her husband's anti-British stance, violently objects to Hamish's enlistment (120–21). The story's climactic scene underscores these tensions with the spatial orientation of the characters: Elspat stands within her hut, just behind Hamish, who stands on the "threshold" (149) with a gun leveled at his approaching military companions. Although clad in Highland tartans, these companions have been effectively assimilated within the British imperial structure,[43] for they "marched regularly and in files, according to the rules of military discipline" (146), something that authentic Highlanders were generally described as unwilling or unable to do.[44] Poised, then, between the metrical-national figure of Elspat MacTavish and the uniform and assimilating (indeed, converting) force of the British empire, Hamish's position reproduces the tension between nation and empire that, as we saw above, Scott projected onto the meter and words of Malagrowther's motto, Mason's poem, and Wordsworth's "We are Seven." But if these poems had served to cast this tension as a built-in feature of the poetic artifact, Scott's narrative version is necessarily dynamic, proceeding on to the catastrophe: Elspat demands that Hamish "Step back within the hut, my son, and shoot" (146) while the British commander, Cameron, instructs him to "lay down your arms and surrender" (147). Hamish refuses to make a choice (145), and into this vacuum of deliberation steps Elspat, who draws Hamish firmly to the side of nation by exacting forced unconscious sympathy – by demanding, that is, obedience to her summons to national identity:

[Officer Cameron] rushed forward, extending his arm as if to push aside the young man's levelled firelock. Elspat exclaimed, "Now, spare not your father's blood to defend your father's hearth!" Hamish fired his piece, and Cameron dropped dead. – All these things happened, it might be said, in the same moment of time. (147)

The story underscores Elspat's agency in this encounter by noting "how little [Hamish's] heart was accessary to the crime which his hand unhappily committed" (153); "no one doubted that in one way or other she had been the cause of the catastrophe; and Hamish Bean was considered . . . rather as the instrument than as the accomplice of his mother" (151).[45]

By labeling Elspat as the "cause of the catastrophe" the story underscores her function as a metrical summons to national identity: with Elspat as the actual agent, Hamish becomes a mere "instrument" of her power. As such he presents an example of a subjectivity that "one way or other" is susceptible to Elspat's metrical agency. What sort of subjectivity is this? We can account for this view of subjectivity if we first turn to the discussions of subjectivity according to which Scott himself was educated, those of the Scottish Common Sense philosophers. According to this school's leading figure, Thomas Reid, a person's "principles of action" can be either "*rational*" or "*mechanical*" (545), and "Mechanical principles of action produce their effect without any will or intention on our part" (579). Included among these mechanical principles of action is "the force of habits": "I conceive it to be a part of our constitution, that what we have been accustomed to do, we acquire, not only a facility, but a proneness to do on like occasions; so that it requires a particular will and effort to forebear it, but to do it, requires very often no will at all. We are carried by habit as by a stream in swimming, if we make no resistance" (550).[46] This account suggests "our constitution" involves a state of "double consciousness,"[47] where some actions are intentional and others are habitual, and in the latter case – where "the habit will operate without intention" (550) – it would make sense to describe the otherwise willing self as the "instrument" of his / her habits. Thus in Scott's story, as Hamish stands irresolute on the hut's threshold his lack of deliberate purpose allows habit to assert its force.

The problem with this account, of course, is that in the story Hamish is not the instrument of his habits but the "instrument . . . of his mother," so if Scott is in fact imagining Hamish's instrumentality on the model of someone subject to the force of habit, he must be conflating habit with Elspat. Such an alignment between Elspat and habit is supported not only by Scott's association of her with a "stream" that sweeps people away (158), but also by his description of the salient feature of "her imagination, anticipating the future from recollections of the past" (114), a description that virtually repeats David Hume's definition of "habits" as "the *reasons* which determine us to make the past a standard for the future."[48] Indeed, Scott's description of the shooting – "All these things happened, it might be said, in the same moment of time" – repeats Hume's own sense of how habits (or "customs") function: "The custom operates before we have time for reflexion . . . . we interpose not a moment's delay" (*Treatise*, 104). Scott's conflation of Elspat and habit is apparent not just in the story's language, but also in its narrative structure: when Hamish fires his gun at Cameron, his action is choreographed as a direct repetition of his father's actions in 1745, an event that Hamish himself was too young to register but that "Elspat witnessed and survived" (104), so instead of reflecting Hamish's own will or even his father's (his father's ghost, after all, endorses his desire to end the Highland way of life and join the British regiment [128]), firing the gun repeats an event from his mother's memories, a repetition that shows Elspat's memory asserting itself as Hamish's present acts. In this way Hamish is reduced to his mother's habits, his mother's memories, his actions becoming a re-enactment of those memories. From this perspective Hamish's act is remarkable not so much as an act of violence than as an instance of repetition: he is not resisting the British so much as providing the stage on which Elspat's recollections of such resistance act themselves out. This suggests a different gloss on Hamish's gunfire, a gloss more consistent with viewing Elspat as its cause: it is not that Elspat, as Hamish's *mother*, has a strong influence on his decision-making, but that she, as his *habits*, entirely circumvents his decision-making to exert herself as a mechanical principle of action, and once she has been cast in this way, she determines his actions in the same manner as would habits in the conventional sense of Hume and Reid.

But there remains something odd about referring to Elspat as Hamish's habits: as Reid and Hume describe them, habits typically reside within an *individual*'s psychology, so in order for Elspat to operate as *Hamish*'s habits she must, "one way or other," traverse the gap between them.[49] Scott's story accounts for how this might happen in terms consistent with his later work, his *Letters on Demonology and Witchcraft* (1831).[50] There Scott speaks not only of "the Hebrew witch" (55), a "medicator of poisons" (65) whose powers resemble Elspat's sleeping potion (129–30), but also of "a different class of persons, accused of a very different species of crime" (54), and when Elspat moves beyond sleeping potions to co-opt her son's agency she enters this later category, "that peculiar class of fiends who were permitted to vex mortals by the alienation of their minds, and the abuse of their persons, in the cases of what is called Demoniacal possession" (68). This appeal to witchcraft, and in particular to its capacity to overcome the gap between individual selves, helps account for something so odd as Elspat functioning as Hamish's habits: if an overpowering of the will occurring *within a single person* is attributable to the psychological force of habits, then an overpowering of the will occurring *between two different persons* is attributable to the magical force (what Coleridge called "forced unconscious sympathy") of demoniacal possession. What Scott tries to do in *The Highland Widow*, then, is to link these two accounts of how a subject's will might be overpowered, harnessing witchcraft's magical operation *between* persons to habit's mechanical operation *within* a person in order to suggest how Elspat – an external set of national memories and experiences – might function like habit, determining Hamish's actions from within. Thus when subject to demoniacal possession by Elspat's national memories – i.e. "his" national habits – even a youth like Hamish can, against his own will, be the "instrument" of what Scott, in his *Journal*, had called "the natural impulse of one's National feelings."

Although Scott's invocation of Coleridge's *Christabel* helps him cast Elspat as a metrical summons, this question about the "one way or other" in which she might be the "cause" of Hamish's actions has led to an additional description of her: she figures not only the summons acting from without, but also the recollection of that summons acting from within. She not only speaks the language of many recollections, she also exerts the force of recollection. In this sense, the story's two characters are best understood not as separate selves but as distinct aspects of a complex subjectivity. This combined status is most apparent when the story places both characters within the same hut, their spatial proximity implying a single self with double consciousness – a doubling, though, that involves not individual will and *personal* habit (the version of habit in Hume and Reid, as well as in Wordsworth's rustic girl) but individual will (Hamish) and *national* habits (Elspat). Occupied by these two characters, the hut figures the kind of subjectivity toward which Scott's Malagrowther had directed his summons: the youth and inexperience of Hamish represent an imperial subject who, never having known Scotland as an autonomous nation, might well decide to serve the empire; but the habits contributed by Elspat represent the national impress of someone who is accustomed to obey the language of many recollections. Viewed in this light, Scott's story becomes a context for pushing beyond contemporary descriptions of individual psychology and imagining, instead, a model of subjectivity whose factored elements can keep sight of both the nation and the empire. Experiencing their national history as an inherited habit, as a mechanical principle of action, Scots, on this model, retain a constitutive link to the national past even though they have been British subjects all their lives, and Scotland thereby retains its national integrity even after its absorption within the uniform empire.

In imagining such a subjectivity Scott has built directly from his prior account of poems: just as Malagrowther's metrical summons had paired imperial words with national meter, so too Hamish's will to align himself with imperial uniformity is paired with Elspat's national habits of repeating the past. Just as the meter wells up within the poem to assert Scottishness (as we have seen, "*Tutti taittie*" is more conspicuous for its Scottish sound than its English meaning), so too Elspat wells up from within the hut to assert Scottish national identity in her son. Like the motto stripped of its thematic content and reduced to its metrical form, Hamish is stripped of his independent will and reduced to his mother's memories. Such a composite self – experiencing the nation's history as one's own recollections, one's own habits, one's own mechanical principles of action – demonstrates Scott's reliance on poetry as the basis for his emerging vision of what it means to have Scottish national identity.

METER AND NATIONAL IDENTITY

As the previous section shows, *The Highland Widow* both rehearses and extends the logic that Scott had set out four months earlier in the *Letters of Malachi Malagrowther*; it rehearses that logic by casting Elspat as a metrical summons to Scottish national identity, and it extends that logic by exploring the kind of subjectivity that would be susceptible to the summons, a subjectivity in which inherited recollections (Elspat) exert the force of national habit against the will (Hamish) of an imperial subject. Throughout these writings Scott has consistently turned to metrical form in order to imagine, first, how the imperial subject might recollect the national past with the force of a habit, and second, how the Scottish nation might thereby resist absorption within the uniform empire. This consistent recourse to meter sets Scott's account of nation and national identity apart from the current critical discussion of how literary texts construct the category of nation. Some participants in this discussion take a thematic emphasis, focusing on how the idea of nation depends on a text's fictional content. For instance, although Katie Trumpener's *Bardic Nationalism*[51] invokes "literary form" (4), her discussion of "bardic poetry" is concerned less with a work's poetic effects than "its content and its historical information" (6). Thus her assertions about bardic poetry apply as well to "national tales," which likewise aim at "constructing an alternative picture" (142) of a given society: taking as its "setting or subject" (150) an "unchanging" (142) set of "national characteristics, conventions and experiences" (150), the national tale "sets out to describe a long-colonized country 'as it really is,'" thereby "attacking the tradition of imperial description . . . and constructing an alternative picture" (142). Such an emphasis on "setting or subject" is, as we have seen, far from Scott's concern, for he aligns nation not with a poem's thematic content but with its national metrical form, so his concern is less a text's ability to construct an alternative picture than its ability to summon Scots forth as a people. Thus while Trumpener references Scott's goal of "keeping sight of both" nation and empire when she proposes to show how "cultural nationalism (as long as it separates cultural expression from political sovereignty) can be contained within an imperial framework" (xiii), her discussion accounts neither for Scott's alignment of meter with nation nor for the subjectivity (i.e. the habits of inherited recollection) that Scott associates with the metrical summons's proper functioning.

Scott's metrically based account of Scottishness stands apart not only from Trumpener's thematic discussion, but also from more formal accounts of national identity. In one such account, Homi Bhabha argues[52] that since signs (as Derrida describes them) never achieve closure or totality, and since it is these very "contingent and arbitrary signs and symbols that signify the affective life of the national culture" (293), then the national entity is itself subject to the same partiality or fragmentation as the signs that constitute it – it, too, is undercut by "the alienating and iterative time of the sign" (309). Thus the "cultural construction of nationness" (292) proceeds through textual narratives in which "the alienating time of the arbitrary sign" (311) leads to an "incommensurable gap in the midst of storytelling"

(311). As a result, narrated nations must "alienate the holism" (318) they seek and are thus "always less than one nation" (318).[53] As we have seen, however, Scott's nation is not narrated but metered: his method of linking literary texts to national identity concedes the terrain of words, or arbitrary signs, entirely to the empire, retaining for itself the terrain meter. And if arbitrary signs, according to Bhabha and Derrida, must fail to be what they represent, meter, in Scott's view, suffers from no such limitation – Scott treats meter as a natural and sufficient embodiment of Scotland. By exempting meter from the limitations of arbitrary signs and then placing it at the center of his formal account of nation, Scott articulates a logic that achieves the national wholeness Bhabha would undercut. While this claim for a non-arbitrary (hence "natural") national meter may ultimately be impossible to defend,[54] Scott's commitment to such an account is what underwrites his claim that inherited recollections of this national meter permit Scots to be summoned forth as a people. Far from "alienating the holism" of the Scottish nation, meter, for Scott, enables the national whole.

A somewhat different formal account of national identity comes from Benedict Anderson, who emphasizes not the arbitrariness of the linguistic sign but the circulation of literary genres.[55] In his discussion of "print-capitalism" Anderson focuses on "the basic structure of two forms of imagining . . .: the novel and the newspaper," arguing that "these forms provided the technical means for 're-presenting' the *kind* of imagined community that is the nation" (24–25). With the newspaper, for instance, the "technical means" are "incessantly repeated" even as the specific "news" stories (the content) changes, and this persistent form enables a "mass ceremony" of "consumption" that collects "thousands (or millions) of others" into one community (35). The aggregating potential of novels and newspapers is something Anderson extends to include songs: in his discussion of "national anthems" (145) Anderson subordinates both "banal . . . words and mediocre . . . tunes" to the "experience of simultaneity" in singing (145), so just like novels and newspapers, songs provide another mass ceremony of consumption that gathers people into a single community. On Anderson's account, Scott's motto, a song that appeared in an English language newspaper, should enable mass consumption sufficient to unite Scotland and England as one nation.[56] But what Anderson is calling a "nation" has all the uniformity of what Scott would call the "empire," so while Anderson's account may well explain how the "British nation" achieves uniformity among the peoples it internally colonizes, Scott is concerned with how Scotland can resist this uniformity and sustain a distinct national identity within such a "British empire." Scott's focus on metrical form as a summons casts the motto not as an occasion for mass imperial (i.e. British) consumption of "print-capitalism" but as a spur to selective national (i.e. Scottish) recollection of national meter: only those with inherited recollections will experience the song as a summons, and once these Scots have been summoned forth as a distinct people, Scotland itself will demonstrate its ongoing integrity as a nation.

At once more formal than the "subject-matter" of Trumpener's "national tale," more stable than the "contingent and arbitrary signs" of Bhabha's "cultural construction of nationness," and more restrictive than the "print-capitalism" of Anderson's "imagined communities," the metrical summons provides Scott with a way of imagining Scotland as a distinct national entity within Britain. The emphasis, however, should be on "within": since Scott's aim is to "keep sight of both" national feelings and the interests of the empire, he envisions Scotland not as entirely separate from Britain but rather as a component of it, much as meter is a component of a poem. Scott made this point clear a few weeks into the currency debate when, in a letter to Croker, his accidental antagonist in the controversy, he denies any hostility to Britain and asserts, on the contrary, his ultimate motive of reinforcing Scotland's ties to the Union:

> But Scotland, completely liberalized, as she is in a fair way of being, will be the most dangerous neighbour to England that she has been since 1639. There is yet time to make a stand, for there is yet a great deal of good and genuine feeling left in the country. But if you *unscotch* us you will find us damned mischievous Englishmen. The restless and yet laborious and constantly watchful character of the people, their desire for speculation in politics or any thing else, only restrained by some proud feelings about their own country, now become antiquated and which late measures will tend much to destroy, will make them, under a wrong direction, the most formidable revolutionists who ever took the field of innovation.[57]

Those living north of the Tweed are a fundamentally "restless" people who might easily become "mischievous" "revolutionists," but once they are induced to hold "proud feelings" about national identity, a kind of identity Scott is effectively inventing in these writings, then imperial deference to that identity (as in the 1822 visit to Edinburgh by a Hanoverian monarch clad in Highland tartans) will cause them to be effectively "restrained" into the role of obedient imperial subjects. Scott seeks to counter the "restless . . . *character* of the people" by ascribing to them a more orderly national *identity*.

But just how orderly can such an identity be if it involves, as *The Highland Widow* shows, a re-enactment of the 1745 uprising? While poems permit

Scott to imagine identity in a way that contains political tension (since the poem unites both national meter and imperial words within a static literary artifact), his story unleashes that political tension by recasting the poem's conjoined elements – its national meter and imperial words – as antagonists in a dynamic narrative. When Elspat's habits cause Hamish to fire his gun at British soldiers – to, as Scott's *Journal* puts it, "give it them hot" – such an act seems impossible to reconcile with Tory unionism, and if what follows is Hamish's "immediate execution" (152), a "sentence, which required blood for blood" (156), it makes sense to see this zero sum game as undermining Scott's goal in his *Journal* to "keep sight of both." If Scots bear a national identity like Hamish's, how can they be anything other than a "dangerous neighbour" to England?

The answer to this question lies in Scott's decision to situate this dynamic scene of rebellion within a larger narrative frame. The frame narrator in *Chronicles of the Canongate*, Crystal Croftangry, relates Elspat's story to readers after obtaining it from Mrs. Bethune Baliol, who herself heard it from a guide on a "highland tour" (91). The relationship between Croftangry and Mrs. Baliol receives detailed development, and Scott's goal, it becomes clear, is to align the frame's relationship between Croftangry and Baliol with the central story's relationship between Hamish and Elspat: Mrs. Baliol is (Croftangry asserts) "old enough to have been the companion of my mother" (73), she and Croftangry are "blood relatives in the Scottish sense" (69), she has "juvenile recollections [that] stretched backwards till before the eventful year 1745" (74), and, as "the most valuable depositary of Scottish traditions that was probably now to be found" (85), she conveys knowledge of Scotland's national independence to the younger Croftangry, a Scotsman who, like Hamish, has known only the empire. Thus Croftangry receives from Mrs. Baliol almost exactly what Hamish received from Elspat. Yet despite these and other clear parallels, we nevertheless see that the characters in the external frame interact according to a very different dynamic: Croftangry receives from Mrs. Baliol not memories but a "memorandum" (91), and this material is conveyed not through hereditary recollections or demoniacal possession but by "bequeathing the materials in the shape of a legacy" (85), a packet of "manuscripts" "in her own handwriting" (70) that he receives only "after the excellent lady's death" (90). Croftangry, then, is not a passive "instrument" of Mrs. Baliol's living memories so much as an active "artist" (89) deliberately gathering her "vanishing" (66) "materials" (70), so unlike Hamish, who is forced by "his" habits (i.e. his mother's memories) to be a "hot" re-enactment of the national past, Croftangry is nothing more than a harmless and idiosyncratic "antiquary" (66).

What these differences show is that, instead of merely repeating the central story, the frame modifies that story – it is a translation of that story, one that, like a translation of a poem, lacks the original's volatile metrical effects.

What is gained in this translation is a certain distance from Hamish's violent act: unlike Hamish's habits, which re-enact Elspat's metrical-national memories, Croftangry's antiquarianism can be assimilated to harmless commerce (66–67). What is lost in this translation from story to frame is direct access to Elspat: mediated by the frame structure, she is available to Croftangry and his readers not as she was to Hamish, as inherited habits that overwhelm him, but instead as something that is reported to exist but that remains beyond immediate experience.[58] In this sense the frame narrative's distancing of Elspat's metrical memory reproduces the experience, as Peter Murphy describes it, of reading MacPherson's "translations" of Ossian: the prior metrical form (i.e. Elspat) is insisted upon but is so thoroughly mediated that it is ultimately unavailable to be experienced as actual poetic effects.[59] But if such alienation from meter strikes Murphy as a loss for Highlanders, since it inflicts on them "the extinction of a culture,"[60] Scott sees the Highlanders' loss as the Scotsman's gain: *alienation* from meter is also alienation *from* meter, so just as a translation of a poem traces itself to a metered original, so too Scots within Britain can view the Scottish nation as "their" source even though they, as imperial subjects, no longer (indeed, never did) participate in its vitality – it is only by seeing themselves as such a translation that their condition of never having been a Scot can be re-imagined as no longer being a Scot.[61] Understood on the model of a translated poem, both the Scottish nation and the Scottish national subject participate in the current imperial context while expressing an interest in "their" prior metrical-national circumstance – as Croftangry asserts, "I am glad to be a writer or a reader in 1826, but I would be most interested in reading or relating what happened from half a century to a century before. We have the best of it. Scenes in which our ancestors thought deeply, acted fiercely, and died desperately, are to us tales to divert the tedium of a winter's evening" (70). Unlike Hamish, who was obedient to "his" national habits, Croftangry is merely "interested" in "our ancestors" and so remains obedient to the empire.

Cultivating this double orientation, including its embrace of imperial rule ("We have the best of it"), is consistent with Scott's letter to Croker: Scots will be deterred from becoming "formidable revolutionists" if they are "restrained by some proud feelings about their own country" – what Croftangry calls "*our* ancestors." A general strategy starts to become apparent here: if Britain would describe its imperial subjects as translations from national originals, those subjects would, like Croftangry, celebrate "their" history instead of challenging imperial rule. Croker's and Melville's misinterpretations notwithstanding, Scott here demonstrates himself to be pursuing a Unionist politics by way of an equally Unionist poetics: having set aside banking practices as too weak (since this "national impress" can be easily rubbed smooth), and now setting aside poems as perhaps too strong (since their "hot" national meter can – like "*Tutti taittie*" in the motto or Elspat in the hut – overthrow imperial codes), Scott turns here to a national identity modeled on a translated poem, a text whose simultaneous alienation from and deference to its metered source effectively captures his effort to "steer betwixt" his "National feelings" and "the interests of the empire."[62] Throughout these various formulations of Scottish national identity Scott has been governed by a consistent strategy: whether he presents Malagrowther's motto and Hamish's habits (where meter is a potentially volatile presence) or Croftangry's antiquarianism (where one's status as a translation underscores meter's absence), Scott's effort to keep sight of both nation and empire consistently grounds national identity in metrical effects.

LITTLE CROFTANGRY

Scott's efforts to summon forth his fellow countrymen had a cultural impact beyond his immediate goal of overturning the 1826 currency reforms. As James K. Chandler has observed, "the continuing power of Scott in early twentieth-century southern literary culture" is evident in the novel *The Clansman* (1905) by the American Southerner Thomas Dixon.[63] Dixon's novel provides a fictional account of Ku Klux Klan activity in the post-Reconstruction South, and Dixon's Klan is summoned forth in a manner derived directly from Scott.[64] As we saw above, Scott's *Letters of Malachi Malagrowther* assert that "the last time the celebrated Fiery Cross was circulated in the Highlands . . . the clansmen were called forth not to fight an enemy, but to stop the progress of a dreadful conflagration" (739). Dixon draws upon this same fiery cross, making sure to note its old-world origins: "In olden times when the Chieftain of our people summoned the clan on an errand of life and death, the fiery Cross, extinguished in sacrificial blood, was sent by swift courier from village to village. This call was never made in vain, nor will it be to-night in the new world."[65] Just as Scott was confident that his fellow Scots would obey his metrical summons, so Dixon is confident that "our people" will assemble around his fiery cross.

And like Scott, who used the summons to resist the encroachments of an imperial British Union, Dixon imagines that his summoned group of "whites" would resist the encroachments of an imperial American Union. If Scott associates his summons with a kind of demoniacal possession by recollections of Highlanders like Elspat McTavish, Dixon imagines a similar demoniacal possession when he describes the Klan as "the reincarnated souls of the Clansmen of Old Scotland" (2).

But if Dixon appropriates the example of Walter Scott, he also deviates from Scott's example in an important way: while Dixon's concern with "the reincarnated souls of the Clansmen" resembles Scott's effort to build trans-generational recollections into the meter of poems, Dixon is ultimately much more committed than Scott to locating those recollections within the body.[66] Thus in his *Letters of Malachi Malagrowther* Scott speaks skeptically about the emerging science of "phrenology," which "has turned the system of Ethics out of doors, and discovers, on the exterior of the skull, the passions of which we used to look for the source within. . . . But should such a philosopher propose," Malagrowther continues, "to saw off or file away any of the bumps on my skull, by way of improving the moral sense, I am afraid I should demur to the motion" (755). Unwilling to embrace phrenology's commitment to casting the body's *exterior* as a marker of character, Scott is likewise committed to viewing the body's *interior* in the universalist terms of medical anatomy. During the early nineteenth century Scott's Edinburgh was a center of developments in anatomical science, a discipline whose central premise was that bodies shared anatomical features despite differences in national identity or culture.[67] This commonality of bodies across national and cultural borders provides a key narrative premise to Scott's story *The Surgeon's Daughter*, which is published along with *The Highland Widow* in *Chronicles of the Canongate*. In *The Surgeon's Daughter* two Edinburgh-trained doctors are able to move to India and pursue their medical practices precisely because their anatomical training readily transfers from Scotland to Madras.[68] The account of the body to which Scott subscribes, then, sees neither its exterior nor its interior as specific to a given people or as capable of containing that people's recollections.

As an alternative to associating recollections with bodies, Scott prefers to associate them instead with other locations – as we have seen, he associates them with the meter in poems, but he also associates them with the Scottish landscape. The relationship between landscape and recollections was a matter of ongoing attention for Scott, who in an 1802 letter makes the following comments about "locality":

A very commonplace and obvious epithet, when applied to a scene which we have been accustomed to view with pleasure, recalls to us not merely the local scenery, but a thousand little nameless associations which we are unable to separate or to define. In some verses of that eccentric but admirable poet, Coleridge, he talks of

An old rude tale that suited well
The ruins wild and hoary.

I think there are few who have not been in some degree touched with this local sympathy . . . . We are often charmed by the effect of local description, and sometimes impute that effect to the poet, which is produced by the recollections and associations which his verses excite.[69]

As we have seen, Scott continues to rely on this observation in his *Letters of Malachi Malagrowther*, where he likewise draws upon the verses of poets – not just Coleridge but also Wordsworth – in order to excite recollections about the national locality of Scotland. Indeed, Scott's Malagrowther asserts of "the Highlanders" that "their land is to them a land of many recollections" (754). This association of Scottish recollections with the Scottish landscape is likewise evident in *The Highland Widow*, where Elspat MacTavish, the figure for Scottish meter and the national recollections embodied within it, is also presented as one of several stops on a tour of the Scottish Highlands. Upon her death, Elspat vanishes, becoming a kind of *genius loci* haunting the location of her hut (163–64). Thus for Scott the recollections associated with meter are also ascribed to the landscape of Scotland.

This association between recollections and locality is evident not only in *The Highland Widow* but also in the surrounding frame narrative of *Chronicles of the Canongate*. The Canongate of the work's title is "an asylum for civil debt" (17) where Scott's frame narrator, Crystal Croftangry, spends time in refuge from his creditors – something Scott himself thought he might be forced to do in the wake of his own bankruptcy in 1826.[70] Managing to repay his creditors but losing his aristocratic family home in the process, Croftangry returns to the Canongate to build a new home, Little Croftangry, directly straddling the border separating the city of Edinburgh from the grounds of the Canongate sanctuary. Croftangry speaks favorably about his new home's location, a location that poises him on the dividing line between Edinburgh and the Canongate:

I think even the local situation of Little Croftangry may be considered as favourable to my undertaking. A nobler contrast there can hardly exist than that of the huge city [Edinburgh], dark with the smoke of ages, and groaning with the various sounds of active industry or idle revel, and the lofty and craggy hill, silent and solitary as the grave. . . . I have, as it were, the two extremities of the moral world at my threshold. From the front door, a few minutes' walk brings me into the heart of a wealthy and populous city; as many paces from my opposite entrance, places me in . . . solitude. (67–68)

Croftangry finds this "solitude" in the Canongate's "lofty rocks, called Salisbury Crags" (78), which are notable for "having been the sites of druidical temples" (202 n. 15). Associated in this way with the indigenous druidical past of Scotland, the Canongate sanctuary comes to resemble Scottish meter or Elspat McTavish as a summons to Scottish recollections. By taking up residence in Little Croftangry, then, Scott's frame narrator finds yet another way to "keep sight of both" nation and empire, his house straddling the line between the national sanctuary of an indigenous Scottish past and the imperial commerce of Edinburgh's city streets. Having lost his standing as a wealthy aristocrat, Croftangry – like the financially ruined Walter Scott – reconstructs an alternative version of identity, Scottish national identity. As we will see in the next chapter, this approach to national identity – its association not only with poetic effects but also with indigenous recollections located on the landscape – is the pattern of thinking expressed in the writings of the United States Southerner, William Gilmore Simms.

CHAPTER TWO

"Our sacred Union," "our beloved Apalachia": nation and genius loci *in Hawthorne and Simms*

> People have always had a strong sense of place. The Romans spoke of the *genius loci*, the "spirit of a place," and we can understand their meaning readily today, even if the spirit for us is a feeling rather than a deity.
>
> – *American Places: Encounters with History*[1]

Just five years after Walter Scott vowed to "keep sight of both" Scottish national identity and the British Union's integrity, William Gilmore Simms found himself engaged in a similar controversy over Union jurisdiction – in Simms's case, the jurisdiction of the US federal Union over his home town of Charleston, South Carolina. As Editor of the Charleston *City Gazette* in 1831, Simms published a July 4 paper featuring his poem "Union and Freedom," a work that aligns the revolutionary liberation from British colonial rule with the continued sovereignty of the American Union:

> And dear be the freedom they won for our nation,
>   And firm be the Union that freedom secures;
> Let no parricide hand seek to pluck from its station,
>   The flag that streams forth in its pride from our shores;
>   May no son of our soil,
>   In inglorious toil,
> Assail the bright emblem that floats on our view;
>   Let not that standard quail,
>   Let not those stripes grow pale,
> Take not one star from our banner of blue.[2]

This poem's call for solidarity with the Union is more than obligatory Fourth of July rhetoric, for it deliberately counters Simms's fellow South Carolinian, John C. Calhoun, a "son of our soil" who was at this very moment assailing the "banner of blue" through his doctrine of nullification.[3]

Calhoun's nullification doctrine was intended to eliminate the so-called "tariff of abominations" and, more generally, to secure greater state autonomy from Union legislation, but it met resistance from Charlestonians like

Simms who feared it would prompt federal retaliation. Speculating on the form this retaliation might take, Simms worries that South Carolina might see "her name & star place, blotted out, and her territory divided among the contiguous & more loyal states."[4] To imagine retaliation of this sort – the wholesale elimination of the state as a state – is to view South Carolina as entirely an artifact of the federal government, its "star place" referencing a nominal administrative unit that might as readily be eliminated by federal sovereignty as it had been imposed by that sovereignty. Thus unlike Walter Scott, who insisted on Scotland's autonomy within the British Union even as he struggled for a way to represent it (ultimately choosing, as we saw, to confer upon it an identity indexed by poetic effects), Simms here accords no autonomy to South Carolina apart from Union decree. Doubtful of popular support for his Unionist views, Simms anticipates victory for Calhoun and imagines that "we [union men] shall have to emigrate *en masse* to a territory which I doubt not the Government will assign us for a new state and leave this . . . to be over run by the U[nited] states" (47). Reluctant to leave, Simms anticipates that a veritable civil war – "strife – neighbour with neighbour – brother with brother . . . and hand to hand" (48) – may be necessary in order to maintain his state's star place on the banner of blue.

Having sided with the Union in this near civil war in Charleston, Simms would go on to formulate a very different relation to Calhoun, Charleston, and the Union when, twenty-five years later, he had grown more sympathetic to calls for southern autonomy.[5] This change is evident in Simms's essay "Charleston, The Palmetto City," published in 1857 in the northern journal, *Harper's New Monthly Magazine*. Organized as a guided tour, the essay conducts its northern readers to various sites in Charleston, culminating with a planned monument to the now deceased US Senator Calhoun.[6] In lieu of the anticipated monument Simms presents his "Calhoun – Ode," a poem that describes the former US Senator as "the genius, lost too soon" (22), Charleston's *genius loci*:

> Nations themselves are but the monuments
> Of deathless men . . .
> . . . .
> We rear our humble column to the name
> Of one who led our power and won us fame!
>
> (22)

Unlike Simms's Unionist newspaper poem, "Union and Freedom," which expressed anxiety about the precariousness of stars on banner of blue, this ode asserts the permanence of deathless men like Calhoun in the city of

Charleston. Memorializing Calhoun's life, however, is not the same thing as accepting his nullification policies, so Simms's invocation of Calhoun as *genius loci* is intended to shift the terms of the debate over southern autonomy: the question is not how to allocate legal sovereignty, whether primarily to the states (as Calhoun's nullification had argued) or primarily to the federal government (as Simms's early Unionism had argued); rather, the question is how to understand regional identity, whether in terms of federally imposed state boundaries (as Simms asserted earlier) or in terms of local genii permanently haunting the landscape (as Simms asserts here). Thus instead of invoking Calhoun as a constitutional theorist,[7] Simms's poem invokes him as a regional landmark, a deathless man whose ghost haunts the local landscape of Charleston. By transforming the question of sovereignty into an assertion of identity, Simms's poem accords Charleston a kind of haunting, ghostly permanence that no sovereign power – whether state or Union – can presume to undo. Northern readers of this tour could expect that, whenever they might travel to Charleston, Calhoun's *genius loci* would be waiting to greet them.[8]

In presenting Calhoun as Charleston's *genius loci*, this later work adapts to Simms's own ends the representational strategy that the last chapter showed to be at work in the writings of Walter Scott. Just as Scott's *The Highland Widow* discovers Elspat MacTavish on a guided tour of the Highlands, so too is Calhoun presented as a destination on this guided tour of Charleston. And just as Elspat MacTavish's lingering poetic presence enabled Scott to buttress claims of Scottish autonomy under the British Union, so too John C. Calhoun – understood as a *genius loci* – permits Simms to buttress claims of southern regional autonomy under the perceived encroachments of the US federal Union. Further, just as Elspat is associated with poems, and particularly poetic effects, we will see that Simms likewise associates local genii like Calhoun with poetry, poetry that does not itself contain the required effects (as we saw in Scott's Scottish meter) but that serves, instead, to guide readers to the place on the landscape where those poetic effects can be found. Indeed, as we will see, it is not just Charleston but the whole South that, in Simms's view, derives its autonomous identity from these poems on the landscape. So if Simms's early commitment to Union sovereignty had involved keeping his state's star visible on the flag, his later commitment to southern autonomy involves making a local genius visible on the map through guided tours to the poetic effects on the landscape.[9] And just like Walter Scott, who imagined that this particularly poetic way of asserting autonomy could serve as an alternative to warlike rebellion, so too Simms's tours of the *genius loci* – up to and including this 1857 tour of

Charleston – are intended to stop short of insurrection. This conciliatory intent is evident if we consider the contrast between this guided tour of Charleston and the decidedly warlike actions that Charleston would soon take toward the North: as the capital of South Carolina, Charleston initiated the 1861 secession of southern states, and soon thereafter it served as the launching point for an attack on nearby Fort Sumpter, the first shots fired in the Civil War.

But if Simms initially sought to avoid such hostilities through the *genius loci*, he ultimately supported southern secession and the formation of an independent nation, the Confederacy. In doing so, however, he retained his commitment to the *genius loci*. He could do so because the *genius loci* is a representational strategy that allows for a substantial degree of flexibility: if it permitted his writings of the 1850s to preserve southern *sectional* autonomy *within* the Union, it permitted his writings of the Civil War period to assert southern *national* autonomy *outside* the Union – as the Confederacy. As I will show, Simms's shifting positions toward the United States – initially supporting Union sovereignty, then articulating southern sectional autonomy within the Union, and ultimately advocating southern national identity outside the Union – reflect a gradually increasing commitment to the *genius loci* as a strategy for representing collective identity. This increasing commitment to local traditions stands in direct contrast, I will show, to the change that would take place in the views of Simms's contemporary, Nathaniel Hawthorne. Hawthorne's views would, over the same period, shift in nearly the opposite direction – from asserting local identity to advocating Union sovereignty. As with the late Simms, Hawthorne's early assertions of local identity feature sites haunted by local traditions, by genii like Calhoun. But for Hawthorne, we will see, the *genius loci* serves a more atomizing function than it does for Simms: in his writings of the 1830s Hawthorne features persistent local traditions that, in underwriting local identity, consequently undermine a larger American national identity. Seemingly ambivalent about this conflict in his early writings, Hawthorne grows more sympathetic to federal structures after serving as an employee of the federal government in the mid-1840s, and he consequently begins to repudiate the local traditions that his earlier writings had set against the larger American nation. Thus at the same time that Simms was beginning to embrace the *genius loci* as a basis for southernness (southern sectional identity), Hawthorne was beginning to repudiate it as an impediment to Union (American national identity). Gradually increasing his involvement with the American Union, Hawthorne ultimately advances a position similar to Simms's early opposition to Calhoun and nullification, a position favoring de-localized federal sovereignty as the only viable method for integrating diverse places into the larger American Union.[10] By the time, then, that hostilities commence between North and South, when Simms had fully embraced the *genius loci* as a basis for Confederate national identity, Hawthorne had come to predicate the success of the Union on the suppression of the *genius loci* and the local identities it helped underwrite.

In repudiating the *genius loci* as a way of retaining all the stars on the banner of blue, Hawthorne is more than simply Simms's opponent in the Civil War. As I will show, beneath this disagreement about secession lies a deeper agreement about the power of local poems – the *genius loci* – to constitute a people: harnessing that power underwrites Simms's southern nation while resisting that power underwrites Hawthorne's federal Union. With the victory of the Union army Hawthorne's account of nation triumphs over Simms's, solidifying a federal Union rooted in de-localized laws rather than local poems. But as this chapter will suggest, and as the subsequent chapters will demonstrate, Simms's nation may have been defeated but his account of identity was not. Instead of vanishing with the Confederacy it re-emerges, I will argue, in a new form: the poetic effects of place that underwrite Simms's account of national identity prepare the way, we will see, for the poetic effects of race that underwrite W. E. B. Du Bois's account of racial identity.

JOCASSÉE AND THE SOUTH

Long before making Calhoun the presiding genius of Charleston, Simms had featured other sites as part of his effort to imagine an autonomous South. Chief among these was the Jocassée River, a stream descending from the Appalachian Mountains in western South Carolina. So small is the Jocassée River that Simms's early writings treat it as essentially irrelevant to any discussion of the state of South Carolina. His *History of South Carolina* (1840) makes no mention of the Jocassée, and even his subsequent *Geography of South Carolina: Being a Companion to the History of that State* (1843) likewise ignores the river, the accompanying map excluding the Jocassée entirely.[11] When Simms does feature the Jocassée River – in his 1836 story "Jocassée" – it is to tell the Cherokee legend associated with the site. The Jocassée River matters to Simms, then, as a place where one can find a certain kind of story, one of "those thousand little traditions of the local genius."[12] These little traditions "give life to rocks and valleys, and people earth with the beautiful colours and creatures of the imagination" (*W&C*, 209–10), so the Jocassée legend imparts to the place the status of personification: "the grove had a moral existence . . . and all the waters around breathed and were instinct with poetry" (*W&C*, 210). Personified by the local genius, the place matters not for its role in South Carolina's history or geography but for its ability to bear a proper name: the Jocassée River is "named sweetly after the Cherokee maiden, who threw herself into its bosom" (*W&C*, 210). Excluded from Simms's *History* and *Geography* of the state, the river nevertheless sponsors a local tradition, and in doing so it reflects Simms's larger interest in personified places, places that – as we saw with Calhoun in Charleston – have been invested with a "moral presence" by one of those thousand little traditions of the local genius.[13]

Such a "belief in spirit of place, in a genius loci," is, according to Geoffrey Hartman, "one of the most persistent" of poetry's "founding superstitions," and he goes on to suggest close ties between the *genius loci* and personification.[14] Hartman's observation arises in reference not to Simms but to a long line of Britain's pre-Romantic poets: "Between the time of Milton and Gray," Hartman asserts,

> a formula arose which . . . . suggested that the demonic, or more than rational, energy of imagination might be tempered by its settlement in Britain – its naturalization, as it were, on British soil. This conversion of the demon meant that the poetical genius would coincide with the genius loci of England; and this meant, in practice, a meditation on English landscape as alma mater – where landscape is storied England, its legends, history, and rural-reflective spirit. (319)

Hartman associates this "formula" with a particular genre of poem called the "inscription," which "was in theory, and often in fact, a dependent form of poetry, in the same sense in which the statues of churches are dependent on their architectural setting or partly conceived in function of it. The inscription was anything conscious of the place on which it was written."[15] This consciousness of place is important because the genre of poetic inscription involves a "call from a monument in the landscape or from the landscape itself, which deepens the consciousness of the poet and makes him feel he is on significant ground" (211), ground inhabited by what Simms calls a "moral presence," and what Hartman calls a "sense for a life (in nature)" (210). While he associates the inscription with pre-Romantic poetry, Hartman also argues for the centrality of this genre to the poetry of William Wordsworth: "Wordsworth's belief in spirit of place determines . . . . the form of the poem, and perhaps the very possibility of Wordsworth's kind of poetry. Formally, it is the genius loci who exhorts reader or passerby; and the same spirit moves the poet to be its interpreter – which can only happen if, 'nurs'd by genius,' he respects nature's impulses and gives them voice in a reciprocating and basically poetic act" (225–26). Hartman associates this formal structure with Wordsworth's poems "Michael" and "Tintern Abbey" (223), works Simms would certainly have known.

If Hartman invokes this genre of "inscription" to align Wordsworth with his predecessors, he also seeks to differentiate Wordsworth from those poets by indicating "Wordsworth's refinement of the belief in spirit of place" (225). This refinement involves loosening the bonds that tie poetic inscriptions to the places upon which they had previously been inscribed: "Wordsworth was able to liberate the genre from its dependent status of tourist guide and antiquarian signpost: he made the nature-inscription into a free-standing poem, able to commemorate any feeling for nature or the spot that had aroused this feeling" (208). To achieve this end, Hartman observes, Wordsworth sought to displace the *genius loci* from the soil and transfer it to himself. Although "his [Wordsworth's] poems remain an encounter with English spirit of place" (329), nevertheless, Hartman asserts, "There are no ghosts, no giant forms, no genii in the mature Wordsworth. He is haunted by a 'Presence . . . ,' but" instead of "a specter," this is "an intensely local and numinous self-awareness" (330). Once the *genius loci* gets rewritten in this way, as "local . . . *self*-awareness," then the relevant place becomes the poet himself and the relevant genius his own mind; the resulting poetry is "deeply reflective, journeying constantly to the sources of consciousness" (330).[16] What Wordsworth's refinements of the inscription ultimately produce, then, is "less a geographical event than a development within the individual consciousness" (330). The speaker in a poem like Wordsworth's "The Vale of Esthwaite" (1786–88) may appear to be searching the valley for a *genius loci*, but what interests him, according to Hartman, "are not necessarily points on a map" (330), for he is really "a quester in search of a leading genius – his own identity" (328).[17]

If Wordsworth pursues romantic self-consciousness by dislodging the *genius loci* from points on a map and appropriating it to his own identity, we have already seen Simms expressing an interest in an actual point on a map, the Jocassée River. Simms, then, is concerned less with his own identity than with the identity of that place, less with a "second self" (333) than a separate self, the "moral presence" of the locale.[18] In 1836 the locale's identity is specifically Cherokee: written in the wake of federal efforts to expel the Cherokee nation from Georgia and the Carolinas, Simms's story asserts that the Cherokees continue – if only in spirit – to occupy this site.[19] If the actual people are being removed, their moral presence will persist through their ongoing local traditions.[20] Much later in Simms's career, however, Jocassée's presiding genius will serve a purpose similar to the one he accomplishes through Calhoun, the presiding genius of Charleston: it will come to matter less that this personification is Cherokee and more that it is local, a *genius loci* whose location is the South, an autonomous region within the Union. That is, a personification that initially marked the absence of the Cherokee nation comes, in Simms's later writings, to mark the identity of a specific people, Southerners.

Thus in 1850 Simms observes that northern abolitionism has led many Southerners to forsake travel in the North in favor of places "at home," i.e. in the South; he laments, however, that their "numerous points of assemblage had scarcely ever been indicated on the maps,"[21] so he provides a list, giving special notice to "The Vale of Jocassée" (55). Six years later Simms again sets out to claim the Jocassée legend for the South, this time in a lecture he prepares for his northern speaking tour.[22] The lecture begins by asking Northerners to "Fly with me then to the South" (5), where he would show them "The valley of Jocassée. And who was Jocassée? A Cherokee Princess . . . . Her name is linked with that of the beautiful valley upon which we are about to enter, and with the lovely stream" (153). Like the following year's tour of Charleston, this tour of Simms's home region is a vehicle of sectional conciliation between North and South – "I would have you know us better. . . . If we knew each other better, there would be no strife" (5). To achieve this sectional pluralism, Simms uses his guided tour to convey to his northern audience knowledge of something distinct, a separate southern region. To know these personified places, he suggests, is to know the South. The South not only has such places, it *is* the South as a function of those places, places like the Jocassée River.[23]

By approaching the question of southern autonomy in this manner, Simms sets himself apart from the more common language of his contemporaries, the language of states' rights and secessionism. While a confederation is made up of states, the South he imagines here is a whole whose parts are personified locales. And while states surrender sovereignty to become part of a Union, legendary locales lose nothing – are no less themselves – for being part of the South.[24] Thus in 1856 Simms observes that "At the head of the Jocassée river are two cataracts, one of which belongs to South, the other to North Carolina. The division line of the States, very unnaturally, cuts them in twain. But it is not for man to put asunder, what God hath joined together, and the stream is one for eternity" (155). If Simms had earlier excluded the Jocassée from his discussions of state geography and history, he is now excluding states from his discussion of the Jocassée and the South. As the 1850s advance and southern autonomy becomes more important to him, Simms shows less interest in separate states than in distinct places; he shows less concern for the negotiations through which states assemble as confederations or unions than he does for the collections through which personified places are gathered as parts of a national whole. Such a focus raises questions not of power but of presence, not of jurisdiction but of *genius loci*, not of sovereignty but of identity; inhabited by their own local genius and assembled through the mechanism of the guided tour, places like the Jocassée River and the Calhoun monument in Charleston underwrite the identity of an independent South.[25]

GENIUS LOCI AND AMERICA

In using the *genius loci* as a basis for southern autonomy, Simms sets himself apart from his contemporary, Nathaniel Hawthorne, who likewise employs this literary topos, but who does so in a manner that is distinct from Simms, a manner that undercuts rather than underwrites regional identity. This becomes apparent if we consider one of Hawthorne's earliest surviving stories, "An Old Woman's Tale" (1830), which was published just one year before Simms would speak out against nullification. The story's internal narrator is an "old toothless woman" whose "sole amusement" it was "to tell . . . stories at any time from morning till night."[26] Since her stories are consistently linked to a geographic site, "her birth-place, a village in the Valley of the Connecticut" (25), they resemble the poetic genre that Hartman calls the "inscription," which has a "dependent status of tourist guide or antiquarian signpost" (208). Although it is often the case, Hartman observes, that "the inscription calls to the passer by in the voice of the genius loci or spirit of the place" (212), and thus "allows landscape to speak directly" (213), inscriptions can also "assume the bardic and officious voice of the interpreter instead of letting the genius loci speak directly to us" (214). The "Old Woman" of Hawthorne's story serves as just such an interpreter: "Her personal memory included the better part of a hundred years, and she had strangely jumbled her own experience and observation with those of many old people who died in her young days; so that she might have been taken for a contemporary of Queen Elizabeth" (25). Although she speaks in her own "mumbling, toothless voice" (25), her "narratives possessed an excellence attributable neither to herself, nor to any single individual" (25), so she serves less as the source of these narratives than as their medium. Having heard her tales as a young boy, Hawthorne's narrator claims now to have "a thousand of her traditions lurking in the corners and by-places of my mind" (25). The narrator's memories, as described, are of course no more his than they were hers, and they only begin to function as memories several years later, when he visits the site for the first time: "I cannot describe the sort of pleasure with which, two summers since, I rode through the little town in question, while one object after another rose familiarly to my eye" (25–26). He can experience the town as familiar – as remembered instead of newly encountered – because the local tales have made the town's historical past part of his own personal biography. As with the old woman, his personal life is now "jumbled" with that of the town, so his arrival on the site seems to him like a return to a familiar place: he has become, like her, a local. Thus in this early tale Hawthorne takes a stance similar to the one we have seen in the later Simms, treating local traditions as productive of shared identity, but for Hawthorne the identity they construct is local – specific to a town – rather than regional or national.

While "An Old Woman's Tale" works on behalf of local identity, a series of stories Hawthorne wrote eight years later seems at first to suggest that, as Simms had asserted, the *genius loci* might perform a similar service on behalf of national identity. In *Legends of the Province-House* (1838–39) Hawthorne's frame narrator finds in Boston's Province-House the equivalent of his Old Woman – an "old legendary guest " (640), a man who, "between memory and tradition . . . . was really possessed of some very pleasant gossip about the Province-House" (629). This "old tradition-monger" (641) serves as "the ingenious tale-teller, and I," Hawthorne's narrator adds, am "the humble note-taker of his narratives" (652), "hoping to deserve well of my country by snatching from oblivion some else unheard-of fact of history" (640). The notion that he serves his "country" by recording these tales suggests that these local legends might also play the role of national legends. Indeed, the Province-House is the site of overthrown colonial rule, so its legends are bound up with the political conflicts that gave rise to American national independence. Given, moreover, that these tales were first commissioned to appear in the *Democratic Review*, whose declared mission was to promote America's cultural independence from Britain,[27] one might plausibly take them to pursue a distinctly national agenda.[28]

Such a view runs into difficulties, however, with the final story of the series, "Old Esther Dudley" (1839). As the last British resident of the Province-House, Esther Dudley was "still faithful to her king, who, so long as the venerable dame yet held her post, might be said to retain one true subject in New England, and one spot of the empire that had been wrested from him" (672). The story climaxes when John Hancock, "the people's chosen Governor of Massachusetts" (676), completes the Revolution by claiming from Esther Dudley her remaining "spot": "you are a symbol of the past,"

Hancock tells her, "And I, and these around me – we represent a new race of men, living no longer in the past, scarcely in the present – but projecting our lives forward into the future. Ceasing to model ourselves on ancestral superstitions, it is our faith and principle to press onward, onward!" (676). Refusing to be influenced by her legends, Hancock builds his new nation on the death of "ancestral superstitions" the expulsion of the *genius loci*. Critics have long debated whether Hawthorne supports or opposes an American nation modeled on Hancock's "new race of men."[29] For my purposes, however, the important question is not where Hawthorne's sympathies lie – with Esther Dudley or John Hancock – but, rather, the logic of exclusivity implied by this confrontation: the choice between Esther Dudley and John Hancock, I want to observe, suggests an ultimate incompatibility between local legend and nation.

The divide becomes clear when we see that, more than a mere loyalist, Esther Dudley is in fact a figure for the Province-House's colonial past, "the symbol of a departed system embodying a history in her person" (671). Identical with the Province-House's history, she performs the function of its *genius loci*: "old Esther Dudley . . . had dwelt almost immemorial years in this mansion, until her presence seemed as inseparable from it as the recollections of its history" (668). This explains why, once Hancock has re-claimed the Province-House, the frame narrator announces the end of the building's historic associations: "the glory of the ancient system vanished from the Province-House, when the spirit of old Esther Dudley took its flight" (677). Expelling local legend – exorcising the spirit of Esther Dudley – is what enables Hancock to assemble a "new race of men," so Hawthorne's Hancock suggests that an American nation exists only at the expense of the *genius loci*. According to Hancock's view, a Province-House with historic associations is an obstacle to, rather than an avenue toward, an American nation.

When Hancock expels Esther Dudley, however, he eliminates more than the traditions, for her departure also marks Hancock's hostility to the role of storytelling guide. We see Esther Dudley herself serving as such a guide when, just like the old woman in "An Old Woman's Tale" (1830), she recounts traditions to "the children of the town":

> she tempted their sunny sportiveness beneath the gloomy portal of the Province-House . . . . And when these little boys and girls stole forth again from the dark mysterious mansion, they went bewildered, full of old feelings that graver people had long ago forgotten, rubbing their eyes at the world around them as if they had gone astray into ancient times, and become children of the past. (672–73)[30]

This effect of storytelling – making "children of the past" – is precisely what Hancock seeks to terminate: "We will follow [Esther Dudley] reverently to the tomb of her ancestors; and then, my fellow-citizens, onward – onward! We are no longer children of the Past!" (677). Sealing ghosts in their tombs permits an onward march that leaves legends behind.[31] When Hancock expels Esther Dudley, then, he attacks not loyalist sympathies but a disposition of openness to the local past; that is, he attacks all local tradition, British or otherwise, taking legend as such to be inconsistent with America. Thus if Hawthorne seemed at first to align the legendary Province-House with an American nation, we see that he ultimately takes the opposite step, treating its local legends as incompatible with a post-colonial America governed by Hancock's commercial priorities.[32] Whatever choice Hawthorne prefers, persistent local genii or a nation that expels them, he demonstrates that legend and nation are irreconcilable options between which one is forced to choose.

Insofar as his Esther Dudley sets local traditions against nations, Hawthorne contradicts the stance we have associated with the later writings of Simms, which use the *genius loci* on behalf of a separate nation, the South. But even prior to the sectional tensions of the 1850s Simms had already invoked the *genius loci* on behalf of the South, his writings of the 1840s treating the South not yet as a separate entity outside America but as a distinct region within it. In 1842, for instance, just two years after Hawthorne's *Legends*, Simms wrote "Sectional Literature," an essay in the periodical *The Magnolia*, in which he advances a "seeming contradiction which it will not be hard to reconcile": "The truth is, there never was a national literature yet, that was not made up of the literature of distinct sections."[33] What Hawthorne's *Legends of the Province-House* presents as an actual contradiction Simms, here, presents as only a "seeming" one. Thus "the magazines of the North," with their "very unmeaning phrase" "Republic of letters" (252), are necessarily "untrue to the national character, by excluding . . . certain of its constituents" (251), and as one of these constituents, the South has a responsibility to the larger nation to write about itself as a distinct section:

> The truth is, that this feeling of place – this influence of the *Genius loci*, – is one of the strongest impelling forces, in the mind . . . . It . . . achieves, in a ten mile province, a mighty monumental work, which crowns and overlooks an entire nation. If there be not a sectional literature, there will be none national! (251–52)

The Magnolia, then, must accept the responsibility of promoting this "feeling of place" among its readership: "[I]f we succeed in forcing into exercise and industry one minstrel, like any one of the hundred of Great Britain; – who, with the eye of a son, shall survey our great monumental places, and honor, by fitting song, the genii thereof, his performance, though sectional, will be found to be nobly national" (252). Here the *genius loci* of the southern region is entirely compatible with, and indeed constitutive of, a larger American nation. America is not a republic of letters but a landscape of monumental places, each – like Hawthorne's Province-House – haunted by a *genius loci* who – like Hawthorne's Esther Dudley – makes children of the past.

The prevalence of such monumental places and their importance for *American* national identity are points Simms came increasingly to stress, the high point being his 1846 collection of essays entitled *Views and Reviews.*[34] Americans may not know about these places – "We look at the waste map from Passamaquoddy to the Sabine, and ask, – where are *our* treasures, – our jewels of song and story . . .?" (*V&R*, 48) – but, Simms insists, these supposed "waste" areas of the map are, like the Jocassée River, in fact rich with legendary lore. Florida, for instance, is where Ponce de Leon searched for "the fountain of youth and eternal beauty" (*V&R*, 88), and "It is from such fancies that the poet plucks his richest chaplets of romance and song. His mines of legendary lore are there . . . . and there they still lie awaiting his spells to unveil, awaiting his hand to gather . . . along the melancholy shores of Florida" (*V&R*, 89). Also awaiting the poet's gathering hand are the stories of Daniel Boone, Benedict Arnold, Pocahontas, and not least, the "wild fragmentary traditions" of "the American aboriginals" (*V&R*, 131). Like the Jocassée legend, such Native American traditions will "yield to the gleaner the living sweetness of some touching song . . . . We shall . . . gather . . . from the lips of tradition, some of those better histories . . . . which shall gather our children together, in sweet suspense and tearful expectation, around the family altar-place" (*V&R*, 124–25). Assembling these legends, then, is a preliminary step toward Simms's 1840s ambition, an ambition that matches the practice of Esther Dudley: telling tales that make children of the past. Gathered from America's many "kindred republics" (*V&R*, 126), these tales work in tandem toward a national end, for they point to the monumental locales that together constitute an American nation.

Consistent with this notion, Simms envisions a future poet-guide who leads children to important southern places and recounts the traditions specific to each: "What would be the homage of our children," Simms asks, to that inspired bard, who shall conduct them to the high places of our glory – who shall lead them to, and designate, by a song and by a sign, the old fields of Eutaw and Saratoga – who shall say . . . – "there, even beside yon hillock, fell the veteran De Kalb, and here – possibly on the very spot over which we stand – the death wound was given to the intrepid Jasper and Pulaski." (*V&R*, 55)

The figures named here died in revolutionary war battles fought in the southern colonies (South Carolina and Georgia, respectively), so Simms treats the Revolution itself as something brought about by many local actions performed at a variety of places.[35] Children are conducted to these local sites and told of local events, and it is only in this indirect manner that they learn of the larger national revolution to which those local events contributed. Unlike Hawthorne's Province-House, which produced a choice between Esther Dudley and John Hancock, Simms's "spots" are associated simultaneously with local tradition and America's revolutionary cause; unlike Hawthorne, Simms can have a local past as well as an American nation, for he gathers that local past on behalf of that nation. At the same time, however, the spots pointed out to these children are all southern spots, so they mark the gap between the nation and its constituent sections, the non-identity between part and whole. Simms's anticipated guide performs Esther Dudley's work of making children of the past, but he makes them children of a particularly sectional past by stressing the southernness of those legendary sites. For Hawthorne's Hancock, Esther Dudley had to be expelled to make way for an American nation, but Simms's American nation eagerly searches for a southern Esther Dudley, a sectional minstrel who, once found, will enable the South to contribute its regional part to the literary construction of an American nation.

SALEM, HILLSBOROUGH, AND CHARLESTON

Simms's search for a guide who will gather and convey the South's local traditions drew a critical response from Hawthorne. In an 1846 review of *Views and Reviews* Hawthorne shows little enthusiasm for Simms's claim that the map from Passamaquoddy to the Sabine is full of traditions just waiting to be gathered: "The themes suggested by [Simms], viewed as he views them, would produce nothing but historical novels, cast in the same worn out mould that has been in use these thirty years, and which it is time to break up and fling away."[36] Simms, Hawthorne complains, cannot see beyond Sir Walter Scott's example of historical novels devoted to recounting local traditions.[37] In mounting this critique of Simms, Hawthorne implies a transformation in his own practice: while *Legends of the Province-House* left us uncertain whether Hawthorne favors Esther Dudley or John Hancock, this 1846 review is more decisive, clearly rejecting the local traditions associated with Esther Dudley and Simms. Moreover, while the alternative to Esther Dudley had once been John Hancock, merchant and politician, the alternative now becomes a newly emerging profession in American culture, that of authorship. As Geoffrey Hartman observes of this period, "genius as individual talent separates off from the genius loci," and Hawthorne's separation of himself from Simms takes precisely this form.[38] Denying authorial status to Simms himself ("Mr. Simms is . . . not . . . a man of genius" [285]), Hawthorne suggests that the role of author provides an alternative to Simms's emphasis on local genii: "Mr Simms . . . possesses nothing of the magic touch that should cause new intellectual and moral shapes to spring up in the reader's mind, peopling with varied life what had hitherto been a barren waste" (286). Focused on this "barren waste" that is "the reader's mind," Hawthorne is no longer content to lead tours of haunted points on a map. Reacting against Simms, Hawthorne presents a glimpse of authorship's alternative to conducting tours of the local genius: instead of dwelling at places on a map, stories now emerge directly from an authorial source, inhabiting the works themselves and, in turn, readers' minds.

Hawthorne's call to "break up and fling away" Simms's "old mould" is not so decisive as it sounds, however, for just a year later, in a "Review of Whittier's *The Supernaturalism of New England*" (1847), Hawthorne comments, "There are many legends still to be gathered, especially along the sea-board of New England – and those, too, we think, more original, and more susceptible of poetic illustration, than these rural superstitions."[39] Hawthorne's complaint here is that Whittier has omitted stories, and has thus proven inadequate as a bard of the *genius loci.* Given this apparent advocacy of the Simms program, we might wonder whether Hawthorne truly manages to "fling [it] away" when, two years later, he writes *The Scarlet Letter.* Indeed, several aspects of "The Custom-House" introduction to *The Scarlet Letter* suggest the continued force of Simms's program.[40] Much as Esther Dudley embodied the persistence of the local past, Hawthorne presents himself as Salem's *genius loci*: "The new inhabitant . . . has little claim to be called a Salemite; he has no conception of the oyster-like tenacity with which an old settler, over whom his third century is creeping, clings to the spot."[41] Imagining his life as entering its "third century," Hawthorne casts himself as an ongoing extension of the local past, much as Esther Dudley embodied the persistence of British colonial rule. "This long connection of a family with one spot, as its place of birth and burial, creates a kindred between the human being and the locality" (1,253). Hawthorne's tie to the place seemed confirmed by his return to Salem as "chief executive officer of the Custom-House" (1,254): "My doom was on me. . . . Salem [was] for me the inevitable centre of the universe" (1,254). Moreover, by casting himself as the compiler of materials conveyed to him by a "local antiquarian" (1,265), his "official ancestor" (1,266) Surveyor Pue, he implies the same kind of narrative frame we see when Esther Dudley uses local stories to make "children of the past" or when Simms's "inspired bard" serves as a mere conduit for transmitting local legend. It is this status as mere conduit that prompts Hawthorne, at the close of "The Custom-House," to voice the "transporting and triumphant thought! – that the great-grandchildren of the present race may sometimes think kindly of . . . [him] when the antiquary of days to come, among the sites memorable in the town's history, shall point out the locality of THE TOWN-PUMP!" (1,273). Imagining himself a local attraction exhibited to future children of the past, Hawthorne identifies with the narrator of his 1835 story "A Rill from the Town-Pump." Like Hawthorne's other story, "An Old Woman's Tale," this story is an "inscription" that tells the history of the locale. As such, it exemplifies Hawthorne's early participation in the Simms program. By invoking that story here, Hawthorne implies that his participation in that program will be the basis for his enduring fame.

But if all of this seems to suggest that "The Custom-House" might extend rather than repudiate the Simms program, Hawthorne's tone, for one thing, tells us otherwise. The supposedly "transporting and triumphant thought!" (1,273) that he might be known as Salem's Town-Pump is of course made in jest, and the invocation of Pue shows only mock deference to antiquarian practices. As Hawthorne has discovered, the best way to escape this doom, and to separate himself from Salem once and for all, is to return there as a federal official. Although his service in Salem's Custom-House introduces a "wretched numbness" to his "intellectual effort" (1,267), this effect is merely "transitory," for he remains "conscious that it lay at my own option to recall" the "faculty" that "was suspended an inanimate within me" (1,262). If this numbness will pass, the permanent – and quite welcome – effect of the Custom-House is to release him from the "spell" or "doom" (1,254) that until then had repeatedly returned him to Salem: "the connection, which has become an unhealthy one, should at last be severed. . . . My children have had other birthplaces, and, so far as their fortunes may be within my control, shall strike their roots into unaccustomed earth" (1,254). By 1850, then, Hawthorne has fully internalized his earlier critique of Simms by directing it at Salem itself. Rejecting the role of Esther Dudley and her practice of making "children of the past," Hawthorne favors the "unaccustomed earth" of the Custom House to the local legends haunting the Province-House. "Custom" now refers not to Salem's local legends but to the federal authority whose jurisdiction is marked by its emblems and officers.

As Salem's "Surveyor of the Customs" (1,269), Hawthorne holds an "office" (1,252) in "Uncle Sam's government" (1,250), so when standing within Salem itself, he nevertheless works in "Uncle Sam's brick edifice" (1,254) and under "the banner of the republic" (1,250). Such a relation to Salem does not really count as a return, for federal duties now mediate his relation to the place, effectively alienating him from his home town – while Salem continues to be Salem, it has ceased to be an inescapable locale and has become, instead, a national place. Seen from his federal vantage point, Salem no longer imposes its past upon him: "Henceforth, it ceases to be a reality of my life. I am a citizen of somewhere else" (1,273). In this way the federal Custom-House exactly reverses the effect of the Old Woman's tale: while her stories had made locals out of strangers, the Custom-House makes strangers – or, more accurately, American citizens – out of locals. American citizenship, for Hawthorne, is predicated upon estrangement from place. Thus when the election of Zachary Taylor shifts federal authority to the Whigs, Hawthorne's dismissal from his political office ("My own head was the first that fell!" [1,271]) demonstrates a point Simms had made during the nullification controversy, that federal power can cause a state's "name & star place" to be "blotted out" – that the federal government can render a site a barren waste and people it with new shapes, new appointees. In using the "Custom-House" to mount a critique of the Province-House, Hawthorne not only demonstrates his diminished interest in local tradition, he also embarks upon a path of increasing involvement with federal authority.[42]

Just as his federal office releases Hawthorne from the role of Salem's *genius loci*, so Hawthorne goes on to release his subsequent novel, *The Scarlet Letter*, from the conventions of the Simms program. This release is evident in Hawthorne's treatment of Hester Prynne. Hester's body is fitted with a marker, the scarlet letter A, that serves as a reminder to all of her adulterous history. But this monument to the past receives considerable resistance not only from Hester, who refuses to tell this story (1,284), but also from the narrative itself, which, as is so often noticed, never uses the word adultery. Indeed, for many townspeople the A stops referring backward to the adulterous act and starts to mean "Able" (1,333), referring to Hester's "helpfulness" (1,333) in the present. Both the locale – Hester's body – and its historical marker – the A – gradually lose their status as tradition's site and record. This process is of course too slow and partial for Hester, who is eager to fling away entirely both the A and the history it still occasions to be told. It is in this spirit that she urges Dimmesdale to "Begin all anew!": "Leave this wreck and ruin here where it hath happened! Meddle no more with it! . . . The future is yet full of trial and success. . . . Let us not look back . . . . The past is gone! Wherefore should we linger upon it now?" (1,352, 1,354). This willingness to abandon the locale and dismiss its past makes Hester Prynne look less like Esther Dudley, who made children of the past, and more like John Hancock, who guided tradition to its grave as he set out to lead a new race of men.

This refusal to serve as a guide to local traditions continues once Hester returns "of her own free will" (1,385) and resumes wearing the A. Although Hester haunts the old site, as Esther Dudley did the Province House or Hawthorne himself did Salem, she is not Simms's "inspired bard" and does not go about making children of the past. Quite the contrary, "as one who had herself gone through a mighty trouble" (1,386), but whose scarlet letter had "ceased to be a stigma" and become, instead, an object of "reverence" (1,385), she can provide an audience for other people's "sorrows and perplexities" (1,385) and help them look toward "some brighter period, when . . . a new truth would be revealed" (1,386). Hester's goal is not to gather local legends but to direct these interlocutors' thoughts away from stories about their troubled pasts and toward the promise of a better future. In this sense the Hester of novel's end resembles the Hawthorne of "The Custom-House," for each gains some relief from the constraints of local history by supporting, of their own free will, a presiding legal authority – Hester's "A" and Hawthorne's federal citizenship. This legal authority is not grounded in the retelling of local legends and is thus capable of progressing – like Hester's A or Hawthorne's citizenship – beyond the need to collect and preserve the *genius loci*. Thus if the novel's final scene of a burial plot might seem to invite the Simms perspective of looking backward to local tradition and becoming children of Salem's past, Hawthorne intends us to look forward to the institutional progress that he takes to characterize his present moment's valorized evolution beyond that past.[43]

A more decisive rupture from the Simms program is apparent in the writings Hawthorne produced subsequent to *The Scarlet Letter*. Hawthorne obtained the office of customs inspector through the influence of his college friend, Franklin Pierce, and in 1852 Pierce sought a return favor from Hawthorne, a biography to support his presidential campaign. Pierce's candidacy was part of a Democratic Party plan to increase its national support by downplaying sectional conflicts, and Hawthorne's *Life of Franklin Pierce* (1852) adheres to this strategy when it asserts of the nominee that "it was impossible for him not to take his stand as the unshaken advocate of Union."[44] What makes it "impossible," Hawthorne claims, is Pierce's own upbringing. After college, for instance, Pierce returned to his home town of Hillsborough, New Hampshire, where the "inhabitants" offered him their "recollections" and "reminiscences" (19). Yet unlike Hawthorne, who had returned from college to the stories of Salem's *genius loci*, Pierce encounters Hillsborough residents who are less ghosts of a local past than sources of the federal present: "reviving the old sentiments of . . . seventy-six" (19), several "survivors of the revolution" recall how their commitment to Union alienated them from the place – how they were "prepared . . . at the first tap of the shrouded drum, to move and join their beloved Washington" (19). "A scene like this," Hawthorne asserts, gave Pierce "a stronger sense, than most of us can attain, of the value of that Union which these old heroes had risked so much to consolidate – of that common country which they had sacrificed every thing to create" (20). Powerful as it was, this episode is just one of many that recurred "through the whole of his early life" (20), for Pierce's father was not only "one of the earliest settlers in the town of Hillsborough" (7) but also "present at the battle of Bunker Hill" (8), so stories about Hillsborough's past went back no farther than Pierce's own father, and the stories his father told were stories about creating the Union: "His sense of the value of the Union . . . had been taught him at the fireside, from earliest infancy, by the stories of patriotic valor that he there heard . . . . It is this youthful sentiment of Americanism . . . that we see operating through all his public life, and making him as tender of what he considers due to the south, as of the rights of his own land of hills" (32–33). Pierce's fireside education came not from an Old Woman or an Old Esther Dudley but from his father the Union general, so there could be no discrepancy between Hillsborough's local past and the principles of the American Union. While Hawthorne had to repudiate Salem's past to gain his federal "office," Pierce's hometown of Hillsborough was identical to the Union, so he need repudiate nothing in his run for the Presidency: by living in Hillsborough, he had always lived in the Union. We can thus see the logic of Hawthorne's claim that for Pierce, anything other than allegiance to the federal government is "impossible."

But if his past in Hillsborough is a Union past, without competition from other local genii, what really sets Pierce apart from his Whig opponent, General Winfield Scott, is the way in which having this local past of unionism exempts him from a national past of sectionalism (32). "The two great parties of the nation," Hawthorne observes of the Whigs and Democrats, "have nearly merged into one another" (137), and in occupying the same political space, they have declared a common political agenda: "Both parties . . . are united in one common purpose – that of preserving our sacred Union" (137). Although these parties may "preserve the attitude of political antagonism," this is "rather through the effect of their old organizations, than because any great and radical principles are at present in dispute between them" (137), and their old organizations are based, ultimately, in the "prominent statesmen, so long identified with those measures" (137), figures like "Calhoun, Webster, and Clay" (33). But since these old statesmen "will henceforth relinquish their controlling influence over public affairs" (137), the election comes down to a question of which candidate, Scott or Pierce, can best succeed them as the leader of this emerging unionist consensus. It is with this question that Hawthorne concludes the Pierce biography:

> It remains for the citizens of this great country to decide, within the next few weeks, whether they will retard the steps of human progress by placing at its head an illustrious soldier [i.e. Scott], indeed, a patriot, and one indelibly stamped into the history of the past, but who has already done his work, and has not in him the spirit of the present or of the coming time, – or whether they will put their trust in a new man, whom a life of energy and various activity has tested, but not worn out, and advance with him into the auspicious epoch upon which we are about to enter. (137–38)

Hawthorne casts the choice between Scott and Pierce as identical to the choice between Esther Dudley and John Hancock. Although running on a platform of compromise, the Whigs' General Scott is, like Esther Dudley, "indelibly stamped into the history of the past," so he will tend to perpetuate that past, i.e. make children of that past, and since this past has been divisively sectional, Scott will perpetuate the current obstacles to compromise. Pierce, however, is "a new man," like Hancock, and what Hancock did under the sign of commerce Pierce will do under the sign of politics: treating the American Union as Hancock did the Province-House (or as Hawthorne himself did Salem), Pierce will expel its *genius loci*, its history of sectional conflict. Without its sectional past, America will look less like Salem and more like Hillsborough, less like a place whose history sets it at odds with the Union and more like a place whose history derives directly from that Union. If Pierce should come to occupy the presidency, he will wield this federal authority in a manner consistent with the political goal shared by Whigs and Democrats alike: having "in him the spirit of the present or of the coming time," Pierce will usher in a new consensus and a renewed American Union.

The *Life of Franklin Pierce* not only restates Hawthorne's conviction that *genius loci* and Union are incompatible, it also reaffirms Hawthorne's preference for the latter, the American Union. In Simms, however, we have already seen a very different idea: a fundamental compatibility between the *genius loci* and America. A shift in Simms's thinking begins to appear, though, in the aftermath of the Mexican War: at that point Simms begins to suggest that southern traditions, instead of contributing to a larger America, in fact work against that America – like Calhoun and Jocassée, local traditions contribute to the formation of a separate South. An early indication of this shift comes in Simms's 1849 book, *Father Abbot, or, The Home Tourist*. A mouthpiece for Simms himself, Father Abbot advocates a strong attachment to a given region:

> There is nothing so sectional, so exclusive as genius. . . . Our affections and sympathies are of little use, scattered over all the dominions of mankind. We better prove our sympathies with the rest, when we attach ourselves to one of its sections, and expend our strength, our art, our affection upon that. Let the *Genius Loci* do thus always, and what region will remain without its tutelary god and crowning altars![45]

At first glance this looks compatible with Simms's earlier discussion of an American nation: by attaching our affections to this exclusive sectional genius we "prove our sympathies with the rest," i.e. we contribute to the collective effort of making an American nation. But unlike the earlier formulation, this "exclusive" stance casts one region not as a partner with other "kindred republics" but as an alternative to them, so what had once been one of America's constituent sections now stands alone as an autonomous and independent object of attachment.[46]

This tendency becomes even more explicit the following year when Simms encourages an exclusively southern itinerary by advocating travel "through the length and breadth of the land, in the several States of Virginia, the two Carolinas, Georgia, and even Florida."[47] The reason for visiting these places remains the "*genius loci*" (65), but the region where one finds it – the South – is no longer just one among many American sections, for it has become, instead, a preferred alternative to those other sections. While Simms had initially appeared to be intensifying his focus on a region within America, it turns out that he is limiting his attention to the South itself, replacing the earlier concern with the American nation with this more restricted focus on the South as a separate entity. It was with this idea in mind that Simms undertook his ill-fated 1856 lecture tour to the North, for in one of his planned lectures, "Idylls of the Apalachian," he casts himself as a guide to explicitly southern locales: "I am one of the Birds of the South and would conduct you to retreats which your eyes have never seen. . . . Fly with me then to the South. . . . I will be your medium, to use the language of the Spiritualists, and will put you *en rapport* with the *genius loci* in the wild abodes of the Apalachian."[48] Here the *genius loci* has fully shifted its affiliation away from places in America and to places in the South: local traditions that had once made America America now make the South the South. At the same time, then, that Hawthorne was serving the American Union as President Pierce's consul in Liverpool, Simms was acting as the South's emissary to the North: as a guide to legendary locales, Simms portrays the South as a distinct entity, an entity whose identity is rooted in these personified places of the *genius loci*.

It was in the following year that Simms published his guided tour of Charleston, so that text's culminating gesture – casting Calhoun as Charleston's presiding genius – participates in this same effort to construct an autonomous South. Twenty-five years earlier, during the 1832 nullification crisis, such a view of Charleston was far from Simms's mind, for at that time, when his Unionist cause faced impending defeat, Simms had "determined on expatriation" (47), envisioning the "mournful . . . spectacle" of Union loyalists "leaving in sad & solemn procession, from the homes of their birth & growth, carrying with them their domestic goods & gods to other regions."[49] At that time Charleston's domestic gods were portable, so Simms was willing to follow the model of Aeneas, relocating to another site and resuming his American citizenship there instead. By 1857, however, Charleston has become a place of untransportable gods, genii rooted in specific sites. Thus when his tour of Charleston arrives at the "Custom-House" (7) Simms notes that the "building itself has quite a history" (8): since it is "associated with so much that is grateful to patriotism, the Charlestonians will hardly suffer [it] to be pulled down" (8). As a history-laden site, Charleston's Custom-House not only resembles Hawthorne's Province-House, the Boston building haunted by Esther Dudley, it also stands against Salem's Custom-House, the federal site that eventually severed Hawthorne's local attachments and made him a citizen of somewhere else – no longer a Salemite but an American. Simms casts Charleston's Custom-House as a site of local history while Hawthorne casts Salem's Custom-House as a federal alternative to local history. Thus Hawthorne, after ending his early attachment to Salem's local past, can describe that attachment as something that had alienated him from the larger nation: "Few of my countrymen can know what it is" (1,252). For Simms, however, attachment to a place's lingering past, far from alienating him from his "countrymen," is what gives him a country in the first place: in order to imagine an independent South, Simms needs those local genii – ghosts like Calhoun or Jocassée – that constitute the South as a distinct entity.

YANKEES, GREEKS, AND SOUTHERNERS

Hawthorne's resistance to the pull of Salem – his hope, expressed in "The Custom-House," that soon "my old native town will loom upon me . . . as if it were no portion of the real earth, but an overgrown village in cloud land" (1273) – extends into his subsequent writings, including the novel he wrote in the following year, *The House of the Seven Gables* (1851). In this novel's well-known preface Hawthorne again privileges "cloud land" over "real earth," asserting that "the book may be read strictly as a Romance, having a great deal more to do with the clouds overhead, than with any portion of the actual soil of the County of Essex."[50] It is a romance, then, not only insofar as it *embraces* "latitude" (1) – i.e. it differs from the novel, which displays "a very minute fidelity, not merely to the possible, but to the probable and ordinary course of man's experience" (1) – but also insofar as it *repudiates* latitude and longitude, or points on a map. Hawthorne's first sense of latitude coincides with Simms's own effort to distinguish the romance from the novel (Simms uses the word "extravagance" [24] instead of "latitude"),[51] but Hawthorne's second criterion, placelessness, would exclude Simms's most popular work, *The Yemassee*, whose subtitle – *A Romance of Carolina* – underscores Simms's investment in local history.[52] It is this commitment to placelessness, then, that sets Hawthorne's definition of romance apart from that of Simms. "The Reader may perhaps choose," Hawthorne concedes, "to assign an actual locality to the imaginary events of this narrative," but since "the Author would very willingly have avoided" all suggestions of an actual place, he urges readers to view him, ultimately, as someone "building a house, of materials long in use for constructing castles in the air" (3).

In the following year, Hawthorne finds an even better way to avoid all suggestion of place: unlike *The House of the Seven Gables*, in which he must resist the suggestion of a location carried by the specific "house," his *A Wonder Book for Girls and Boys* (1852) focuses on "the classical myths," noting that "they are marvellously independent of all temporary modes and circumstances."[53] So autonomous are they from place that, as Hawthorne's narrator, Eustace Bright, puts it, to call these classical myths "Greek" is to make a fundamental mistake: "the Greeks, by taking possession of these legends (which were the immemorial birthright of mankind,) . . . have done all subsequent ages an incalculable injury" (1,255); "an old Greek," Eustace insists, "had no more exclusive right to them, than a modern Yankee has. They are the common property of the world, and of all time" (1,255). With this perspective, Eustace can "[tell] his stories to the children in various situations, – in the woods, on the shore of the lake, in the dell of Shadow Brook . . ." (1,311), etc., without risk of becoming an Esther Dudley. Although Hawthorne announces the location where each classical myth gets told, he makes no effort to link it with the place, so the myths are generically distinct from the "inscription," which Geoffrey Hartman, as we have seen, describes as dependent upon place. For Hawthorne, there is nothing local about the legends and nothing legendary about the locales.[54] The elderly female Esther Dudley, a place-bound *genius loci*, gets replaced here by the youthful, male, and mobile Eustace Bright, an apprentice to "the business of authorship" (1,312) whose tales are as appropriate to Tanglewood as they would be to Salem, Hillsborough, or Charleston.

Hawthorne goes out of his way to underscore this point: atop an unnamed mountain Eustace and the children can see the Catskills, the site, Eustace announces, "where an idle fellow, whose name was Rip Van Winkle, had fallen asleep, and slept twenty years at a stretch" (1,278). Whereas Simms surely would have seized upon the opportunity to tell this local legend, Hawthorne's Eustace invokes Irving's story only to dismiss it as unavailable, protected by the legal obstacle of copyright: "The children eagerly besought Eustace to tell them all about this wonderful affair. But the student replied, that the story had been told once already, and . . . nobody would have a right to alter a word of it, until it should have grown as old as . . . the rest of those miraculous legends" (1,278). With the "classical myths," however, "the forms . . . have been hallowed by an antiquity of two or three thousand years. No epoch of time can claim a copyright in these immortal fables. They seem never to have been made . . ." (1,163) – or, as Eustace puts it, subsequent tellers do not so much remake as revisit them: "The ancient poets re-modelled them at pleasure, and held them plastic in their hands; and why should they not be plastic in my hands as well?" (1,255; see also 1,168 and 1,311). Such modification is of little consequence since, as Hawthorne's own "Preface" concludes, the myths "remain essentially the same, after changes that would affect the identity of almost anything else" (1,163). Through these myths, then, Hawthorne discovers an avenue to the placelessness of romance that neither "Rip Van Winkle" nor even his *The House of the Seven Gables* could provide – a form like the stars on the flag, one that remains itself despite instances of local specificity. Leaving aside the Catskill Mountains and Irving's (legally static) legend, Eustace chooses, instead, the plastic classical myth of Pegasus, a myth that stands apart from the place – or, rather, that is appropriate to the place only in light of the (much weaker) thematic connection between a flying horse and this spot's high elevation: "of all places in the world, it ought certainly to be told upon a mountain-top!" (1,279).

If Hawthorne's Eustace insists that these myths are broadly classical, rather than specifically Greek, it is the Greekness of such stories – their capacity to underwrite a specifically Greek identity – that is of interest to Simms. Presiding Greek deities would be a persistent reference in "Charleston, The Palmetto City," and in texts of the early 1850s Simms asserts that just as Greece can boast of the Vale of Tempe, the place where the events of classical mythology supposedly took place,[55] so the South has comparable locales of its own, including, as we have seen, the "Vale of Jocassée": "The Vale of Tempe . . . may be allowed to speak for the past; our valley declares for the present and the future" ("Summer Travel," 55). Transcribing this same passage into his 1856 lecture, Simms asserts that "It was only in its divine arts and speaking statues that the vale of Tempe was superior. Here [i.e. in the Jocassée valley] nature works alone, unaided, is required to do every thing. It is for the future to bring art to her succour" (153). Thus even without a southern Homer to impart the "art" of poetic adornment, these legendary places are sufficient in and of their haunted selves to do for the South what the Vale of Tempe does for Greece, for it is in such "precincts" that one finds "the voice of the *genius loci*, speaking through scenes of eminent traditional and historical interest" ("Summer Travel," 52). While Hawthorne's Eustace subordinates such local tales to the pursuit of a "publisher" – thus he is more interested in "writing [the stories] out for the press" than he is in the "wreath" of "mountain-laurel" placed "on his brow" by a child in his audience (1,302) – Simms takes the place itself as already worthy of poetic laurels, itself a poem *avant la lettre*.

Simms features the South's local voices in a section of his 1853 volume, *Poems Descriptive, Dramatic, Legendary and Contemplative*, the section entitled "Tales and Traditions of the South."[56] In "The Syren of Tselica; A Tradition of the French Broad" (324), for instance, Simms's headnote explains that "Tselica is the Indian name of the river" in North Carolina otherwise known as the "French Broad," and a "tradition of the Cherokees asserts the existence of a Syren, in the French Broad, who implores the Hunter to the stream, and strangles him in her embrace" (324). "Enough that such [a tradition] exists, and that its locality is one of the most magnificent regions, for its scenery, in the known world." This headnote's emphasis on the locale becomes all the more striking if we set it alongside another headnote, that preceding Edgar Allen Poe's poem "The Raven" (1845): comparing the "resources of English rhythm for varieties of melody, measure, and sound" to "the classic tongues, especially the Greek," Poe observes that "Alliteration is nearly the only effect of that kind which the ancients had in common with us. It will be seen," he continues, "that much of the melody of 'The Raven' arises from alliteration, and the studious use of similar sounds in unusual places."[57] If sounds are to be found in unusual places, the places are within Poe's poem itself, and not in remote areas of the Appalachian Mountains.[58] For Simms, however, the important music is not in the poem but at a place on the map – it is the Syren song that matters, and the poem simply guides us to that river and recounts its story, making the locale available to visitors but its verse making no effort to rival that locale's song.

Local music upstages poetic artifacts in another poem in Simms's collection, "The Last Fields of the Biloxi; A Tradition of Louisiana."[59] The headnote of this poem points us to the "Bay of Pascagoula," "a lovely and retired spot, lying at nearly equal travelling distances between the cities of Mobile and New Orleans" (273). This "spot" is "remarkable" not just for its "beauties" but for a "superstition which pertains to it," the "Indian tradition" that attributes a "most spiritual kind of music . . . heard above and around its waters" to the songs of the vanished Biloxi, a "people" who "had attained a very high . . . civilization" and who, facing a choice between submitting to the "fiercer tribes" attacking them or drowning themselves in the sea, opted for the latter. They died while "singing their last song of death and defiance," and "The strange spiritual music of the Bay of Pascagoula is said to be the haunting echo of that last melancholy strain" (273). As was the case with the Syren song, the song to be found on this site is more important than the song within the poem itself; these poems are acting as ordinary guidebooks, telling us where to go to hear the song that really matters, the song that emanates from the place itself.[60]

Of the several other poems assembled in "Tales and Traditions of the South," the one that most forcefully illustrates Simms's post-1850 tendency to associate *genius loci* and poem more with place than with textual artifact is "The Cassique of Accabee; A Legend of Ashley River." This poem features several young people in a "boat drifting softly to the shore . . . / . . . within the shades of Accabee," a "farmstead, in the neighborhood of Charleston, on Ashley River" (209). The boat's arrival on shore leaves "Our spirits rapt, our souls no longer free" (209), for it is "sure the spot was haunted by a power / To fix the pulses in each youthful heart" (210). The source of this power is "the old Yemassee" (209), a "native chief" (211) whose "ghost still walks" (209) the site. He had granted the land to his white lover, but she soon ran off with a white "pedlar" (214) who "bargain'd for the sale of Accabee" (227), and although the chief later restored it to the woman, she herself then "sold / . . . the beautiful estate" (233). "The purchaser," however, finds that the land will not admit of sale: "But still the spot was haunted by a grief" (234). So heavy is the chief's presence there that subsequent attempts to settle the site – "A noble dwelling," "Fair statues," and "pleasant lakes" (233) – fail to displace him: "Whatever be the graft of foreign mood," "The native genius . . . / Maintains its ancient, sorrowful, aspect well; / Still reigns its gloomy lord" (234).

For our purposes, what is more remarkable than the Indian chief's persistent and posthumous refusal to sell is this site's forceful resistance to lyric speech. The poem begins by noting that a woman "Pour'd forth her own sweet song, / A lay of rapture not forgotten soon," but her "own song" is interrupted ("'Ah!' sudden cried the maid") by the group's arrival at this haunted site (209). A figure like Hawthorne's Eustace, the woman is invested in the beauty of her own artifacts, and she gets displaced in Simms's account, ceding the floor to "Our Hubert," a guide to this local tradition: "'Give us thy legend, Hubert;' cried the maid" (211). Once this "legend of our comrade" (211) has concluded, however, she fails to recover her lyric mode: ". . . but no more / Rose love's sweet ditty on our ears that night" (234). The haunted locale overpowers the lyric singer; genius is silenced by *genius loci*. In particular, what deprives her of lyric speech is the vivid experience of place that follows upon hearing the locale's legend:

> Silent the maid look'd back upon the shore,
> And thought of those dark groves,
> And that wild chieftan's loves,
> As they had been a truth her heart had felt of yore.
> (1: 234)

After hearing the legend, her reaction to the place – "a truth her heart had felt of yore" – resembles memory or déjà vu, and it is this same intuitive immediacy that Simms elsewhere describes as the response elicited by poems: "Whatever commends itself to our mind instantaneously, without process of reasoning, as a familiar observation . . . [or] true sentiment . . . is poetry."[61] The effect that makes poetry poetry is, for Simms, the effect produced by this haunted locale. Thus if the *genius loci*, after 1850, tends not to need textual rendering, or poetic diction, this is because traditional locales are sufficient in themselves to count as poetry; haunted places are not just independent of poems, they *are* poems. As Simms puts it in his 1856 lecture,

"Such is the effect of place. A single glance recalls the most wondrous dramas. The Imagination . . . brings on all the dramatis Personae" (8).[62] The maid stops her "lay" because, after Hubert's story, the haunted place's "Persona" speaks even more forcefully than she does; instead of her song, the product of an author, it is this personification, this *genius loci*, that ultimately asserts itself in this poem. Thus instead of abandoning the goal of a national literature, Simms's silencing of the lyric speaker indicates that such a literature is already present in legendary locales. Simms rewrites deficiency as sufficiency by asking places themselves, and place as such, to fill the role of a national literature. As he puts it at the end of "Summer Travel in the South," the Appalachian Mountains will become a place just like Greece, a place "which the future will as greatly love to tread, with a passionate veneration, such as we now feel when we wander along the banks of the Illissus, or muse upon the past beneath the mountain summits of Taygetus and Ægaleus" (65). Just as these tradition-laden places underwrite the identity of Greece, so he knows similar places that will – and indeed currently do, for those who visit them – underwrite the identity of the South.

"OUR BELOVED APALACHIA"

"The tempest rages, and the bloody banner of the foe goes down in its own blood. We are victors, and this time the route is complete." So run the shared thoughts of Wharncliffe and Stylus, two characters in Simms's 1863 novel *Paddy McGann; Or, The Demon of the Stump*.[63] Gazing upon South Carolina's Edisto River, these two southern landowners take stock of the Confederacy's recent military successes at Cold Harbor, Manassas, and Sharpsburg: "Our triumph is secure – our independence! and Peace, with her beautiful rainbow . . . spread . . . over . . . our beloved Apalachia, sends our gallant sons . . . home" (221). Yet even as these characters embrace "independence" from those "insolent invaders" (220), the "accursed Yankees" (221), they still face an open question about the "home" to which their victorious soldiers will return: what is "our beloved Apalachia"? In a footnote, Simms specifies what he takes this name to designate: "The Apalachian [*sic*] chain of mountains, stretching from Virginia to Georgia, through the two Carolina's [*sic*], and forming the backbone of the country, links together the whole South, the States equally, of the Atlantic and the Gulf. Apalachia," he continues, "should be the poetical name of the Confederacy. This native word, of the red man, cannot be surpassed in equal dignity and euphony" (221). This statement shows Simms practicing a bit of cartographic license, for his earlier writings had described the Appalachian range as extending well north of the Mason–Dixon line – in 1846, for instance, he had described "the blue summits of Apalachy" as stretching from "the hills of New Hampshire" to "the purple waters of the gulf" of Mexico (*V&R*, 126), and his point at that time was to treat these mountains as the backbone of America, with the South constituting just part of that whole.[64] Here, however, the Appalachians extend only as far as Virginia and include all southern states "equally," thus forming the backbone of the South. Simms still requires lines on a map, i.e. the Mason-Dixon line, to cordon off those places whose local genii contribute to the South, but the line has nothing to do with states and is something he tries, rather implausibly, to naturalize as a mountain range, as an extension of the local terrain. This redescription of the Appalachians, then, becomes a way of policing the Mason-Dixon line and reserving for the South all of that mountain range's personifications or local genii.

Yet if the open hostilities of 1863 led Simms to claim the Appalachian Mountains as the "backbone" of an "independent" South, his novel's characters openly debate whether there indeed exists a nation corresponding to this place: "We lack antiquity," Stylus complains to Wharncliffe; "our people have no past – no present memorials – which can excite; they have had no youth!" (223). The chief evidence of this, Stylus asserts, is to be found among the "uneducated people": "With . . . such glorious forests, overhanging such waters, forever murmuring their under-song to the sea . . . . our uneducated people should glow with wild and beautiful superstitions" (223). Wharncliffe agrees, finding the South to compare unfavorably with, for instance, nomadic Arab tribes: the Arabs can rely upon "the ancient of the tribe, who remembers far back, and can trace out the details of old adventures . . . . And so the traditions of the tribe are perpetuated. . . . The palm tree sheltered [the Arab's] great grandsire, Abou Hassan, three hundred years before . . . . and Abou . . . indicated it as under the special protection of a Djinn or presiding genius" (224–25). No such presiding genius, Wharncliffe and Stylus lament, is available to Southerners, for unlike the Arabs, Southerners are so transient that they "lose . . . what they had of old tradition" (225). Consequently, it would seem, "Apalachia" lacks a past – it is little more than a set of features to be recorded in a geography text.

Despite these concerns, Wharncliffe goes on to allay them by offering a different account of "our uneducated people," an account that affirms the presence of "wild superstitions" among them: "here . . . lies the reason why so little is known, among the higher or educated classes, of the prevalence of the superstition. The people say little about it . . . . There is a lurking dread of the wizard himself, who does not like to be spoken of too freely . . . . But the faith is present, is still active" (226–27). Traditions exist, but they remain ungathered, unpublicized, and to support this claim, Wharncliffe offers tangible proof: "Now . . . shall I be able to verify some of the things that I have been saying to you" (228).

The occasion of proof is the arrival of Paddy McGann, "one of the most uneducated of our people" (228). Escorted back to the plantation house, this sample of "our uneducated rustics" (238) tells "one of his own stories" (238). Not at all shy about declaring belief in superstitions, Paddy relates his general conviction that, "instead of one devil, there's a thousand . . . . and some [live] in the waters and rivers, and some in the air . . . and they're so made that, just as they live, according to the place, or element, so they have a perticklar nather [i.e. nature], for that same place or element" (259). Through this belief in these thousand local devils, or genii, Paddy is providing Wharncliffe and Stylus what "Abou Hassan" gave the Arabs, a tribal member who knows this local past. One of these thousand devils takes the form of a stump and disrupts Paddy's hunting, claiming to be guardian and protector of the local wildlife (314–16, 445). Even though Paddy escapes briefly to New York, the demonic stump is waiting for him when he returns.[65] By entertaining the gathering of planters with this story, Paddy assures them that "Apalachia" is not just a chain of mountains: more than a mere geographic site, it is haunted by a thousand traditions of the local genius. Just as Esther Dudley assembled children and made them children of the past, so Paddy McGann assembles these aristocratic planters to make them into denizens of "Apalachia," i.e. Southerners.[66] Having assured them that there indeed exists a nation to fight for, Paddy then leaves the group to join a Confederate regiment (492, 494). Just as Simms himself had affirmed southern identity on his lecture tour of the North, so Paddy, likewise a guide to the *genius loci*, sets out to wage war on behalf of this independent nation. Paddy's narrative, then, supplements the novel's earlier celebration of military victory with a clearer sense of the combatants and the cause: the guide to the *genius loci* fights on behalf of this haunted place, the southern nation, his "beloved Apalachia."

Just a few months before Simms published *Paddy McGann* Hawthorne, too, was writing about southern soldiers drawn from the ranks of "our uneducated rustics." Hawthorne had encountered several "rebel prisoners" while pursuing his "official duty" of inspecting the ongoing war effort, and the prisoners he describes are like Paddy McGann – "peasants, and of a very low order."[67] "Almost to a man," Hawthorne observes, "they were simple, bumpkin-like fellows," but unlike Simms's Paddy, "not a single bumpkin of them all . . . had the remotest comprehension of what they had been fighting for" (55). Far from seeing them as guides to – and defenders of – the *genius loci*, Hawthorne describes them as dupes of the South's social system: "they have a far greater stake on our success" in the war, he asserts, than do Northerners themselves (56), for "the present war . . . will free this class of Southern whites from a thraldom in which they scarcely begin to be responsible beings" (55).

If Hawthorne finds thoughts of the *genius loci* to be absent from the minds of these uneducated rebel prisoners, he nevertheless acknowledges the general force of such thoughts. When his official survey takes him to Fort Ellsworth, a military installation on the Potomac River, Hawthorne makes the following observation about the place:

> The fortifications . . . will serve to make our country dearer and more interesting to us, and afford fit soil for poetry to root itself in: for this is a plant which thrives best in spots where blood has been spilt long ago, and grows in abundant clusters in old ditches, such as the moat around Fort Ellsworth will be a century hence. It may seem to be paying dear for what many will reckon but a worthless weed; but the more historical associations we can link with our localities, the richer will be the daily life that feeds upon the past. (49)

Like Simms, Hawthorne assimilates poems to place: a century hence these localities will, like the Province-House, be linked with historical associations. But if such places are a welcome prospect since the poetry they inspire will make daily life richer (Simms's goal), it is the current existence of such places that makes "treason" (Simms's practice) " . . . so easy" (48). Hawthorne explains, "that sentiment of physical love for the soil" is sufficient to generate love for "the altar and the hearth" and even for "our own section" (48), but not for "our country," the whole United States, which is "too vast by far to be taken into one small human heart" (48). This means that a person's physical love for the soil comes into conflict with "the General Government," which "claims his devotion only to an airy mode of law, and has no symbol but a flag" (48). Local poetry (the seemingly "worthless weed" that will grow around Fort Ellsworth) competes with the airy law and its flag, producing an "exceedingly mischievous" "anomaly of two allegiances" (48). As we have seen in Hawthorne's earlier writings, he is sympathetic to this dilemma – "treason" is indeed "easy."[68] But however sympathetic he may be, he continues to see a logical incompatibility between these two allegiances and to assert the supremacy of "an airy mode of law" over any "physical love for the soil": "there seems to be no way but to go on winning victories, and establishing peace and a truer union in another generation" (61). Just as Hester Prynne had turned away from the local past to favor a better future, so Hawthorne resists immersion in local legend and chooses instead to embrace "our sacred Union and Constitution" (60). In the 1830s Simms had been the avid Unionist and Hawthorne the guide to haunted places, but by 1863 these two writers have virtually reversed their earlier positions. Arising from this reversal are not only two distinct versions of national identity, one based on the *genius loci* and the other on an airy mode of law, but also two opposed national commitments: in Simms, devotion to "our beloved Apalachia" and in Hawthorne, allegiance to "our sacred Union and Constitution" (60).

CAUSES WON AND LOST

On July 4, 1831, the same day that Simms published his poem "Union and Freedom" in the Charleston *City Gazette*, a Unionist rally at Charleston's First Presbyterian Church featured Simms as a guest speaker. Simms's contribution to the rally was a reading of another poem, "Our Union – A National Ode," the opening three lines of which are self-consciously drawn from Walter Scott:

> "*Breathes there a man with soul so dead,*
> *Who never to himself hath said,*
> *This is my own, my native land*" – [Scott
> Who, gazing on each valley round,
> Exults not in that daring hand,
> Which made it – consecrated ground![69]

What consecrated the ground is the Union's heroic victory in the Revolution of 1776, and the "daring hand" one exults will vary depending on the valley upon which one gazes. Treating heroic ground as the source of poetry, Simms asserts that "Each spot of land, in time, became / A theme for Freedom's choral song" (76). Although Simms emphasizes heroic acts that occurred in the South (77–78), he also mentions "Lexington" (75), and his Unionism becomes apparent in his concluding lines as he assembles all heroic acts of the Revolution as "the fruit, / From our proud Union's glorious root, – / The offspring of whatever state" (79). What Simms's poem makes available, then, is a form of local legend that is identical with the national history of the Revolution, and in doing so Simms's poem pursues the strategy Hawthorne would later employ in his 1852 biography of Franklin Pierce. In Simms's early Unionist poem, as in Hawthorne's later Unionist biography, the local *genius loci* is inseparable from the Union's revolutionary cause, the cause of the American nation.

Despite this convergence in Hawthorne's and Simms's rhetoric of nation, we have already seen how dramatically their accounts of nation would ultimately diverge, with Hawthorne's Unionism elevating federal jurisdiction over local history and Simms's secessionism elevating local history over federal jurisdiction. Hawthorne died in 1864, a year before the Confederate surrender at Appomattox, so he would never know a Union victory. Simms, however, died in 1870, so he lived to see his "Apalachia" go down to defeat. Although his own house and library were destroyed by Sherman's march to the sea, Simms continued to write and publish, and in 1867 he edited *War Poetry of the South*, a collection of poems inspired by the events of the war and "derived from all the States of the late Southern Confederacy."[70] Simms calls these poems "a contribution to the national literature" (v), but he only reluctantly concedes them to the Union, as one might concede the contraband of war: "this collection is essentially as much the property of the whole as are the captured cannon which were employed against it" (v). While the captured cannon are silent, these poems continue to speak, and Simms takes these poems to express "the genius and culture of the Southern people" (vi). The very first poem Simms includes is Henry Timrod's "Ethnogenesis," which celebrates "the meeting of the first Southern Congress, at Montgomery, February, 1861" (7). As we have already seen, however, Simms believed a southern identity to antedate such procedural actions: it was dispersed across the southern landscape awaiting poetic inscriptions to commemorate it. So if Simms's dedication speaks of "the cause which is lost" (iii), the political and military loss is only so much fodder for an identitarian gain: now that the war has concluded, the landscape is covered with what Hawthorne described as "fit soil for poetry to root itself in: for this is a plant which thrives best in spots where blood has been spilt long ago. . . . [T]he more historical associations we can link with our localities, the richer will be the daily life that feeds upon the past."[71] No longer relying on the local history of the Revolution, and setting aside as well the local history of politicians like Calhoun or Native Americans like Jocassée, Simms has now discovered a local history rooted in the lost cause, a history indigenous to his "beloved Apalachia." Thus if Simms's final collection finds him once again serving as a guide to the *genius loci*, he is no longer forced to anticipate the day when poetic inscriptions will capture the essence of the South's haunted locales. Bound to various places in the South, the poems featured in Simms's collection serve as textual monuments to the southern *genius loci*. As inscriptions, these poems hold what Hartman calls the "dependent status of tourist guide and antiquarian signpost" (208), and each poem will thus remain "conscious of the place on which it was written" (207). Monumentalizing the southern *genius loci* in this way, Simms ensures that despite vanquished armies and fallen institutions, southern identity itself will not be lost.

A SOUTHERN BOOK?

Hawthorne's and Simms's homes were on the itinerary of American expatriot Henry James when, in 1904, he cast himself as "an inquiring stranger" making a "visit to America," a visit later recounted in his *The American Scene* (1907).[72] On the surface of his account, James seems pleased with Salem: having encountered there "the very genius of the place," James declares "the making of his acquaintance alone worth the journey" (271). This *genius loci* "dropped straight from the hard sky for my benefit" (270), and as "a presence . . . old enough, native and intimate enough, to reach back and to understand" (270), this guide was "so completely master of his subject" (270) that he could, like Hawthorne's Town-Pump, conduct James to Salem's important sites. This guide, however, was no Hawthorne but rather an "American boy" (270) who "[fed] his small shrillness on the cold scraps of Hawthorne's leaving" (271). James's mock pleasure at finding this "spirit of the place" barely masks the derision of an expatriate author who dismisses his forsaken America as a nation where a mere pre-adolescent boy is sufficient to serve as guide to the local genius.

Ridiculing Salem's youthful *genius loci*, however, is part of James's larger strategy of rescuing Hawthorne from the city, and indeed from the entire American scene. With this boy as his guide to Salem, James encounters only cold scraps of Hawthorne, such as the house that had inspired *The House of the Seven Gables*: "The weak, vague domicilary presence at the end of the lane may have 'been' (in our poor parlance) the idea of the admirable book," but that actual house, James concludes, is something ultimately separable from Hawthorne, something Hawthorne had "repudiated like a ladder kicked back from the top of a wall" (271). James borrows this ladder figure from Hawthorne himself, who in his preface to *Tanglewood Tales For Girls and Boys; Being a Second Wonder Book* (1853) remarks with surprise that, after the previous volume's success, the frame narrator, Eustace Bright, has once again sought his editorial advice: "nor was [Eustace] by any means desirous, as most people are, of kicking away the ladder [i.e. Hawthorne] that had perhaps helped him to reach his present elevation."[73] Eustace has achieved the elevation of successful authorship, and Hawthorne is the ladder Eustace has climbed to get there. James revises this structure by figuring Hawthorne not as Eustace's ladder but as Eustace himself – an "author by profession" (1,312) – and thus privileging Hawthorne-as-author over Hawthorne-as-local: "Hawthorne's ladder at Salem, in fine, has now quite gone, and we but tread the air if we attempt to set our critical feet on its steps and its rounds, learning thus as we do . . . . how merely 'subjective' in us are our discoveries about genius" (271). Hawthorne's "genius" – "the idea that is the inner force of the admirable book" (271), *The House of the Seven Gables* – follows the opposite route of James's young "spirit of the place," for while this boy *genius loci* had "dropped straight from the hard sky" into Salem, Hawthorne's genius achieves an "elevation" that forces us – now without a ladder down to Salem – to "tread the air." In separating Hawthorne from Salem and America, James both seizes upon the ambition for delocalized authorship that I have identified in Hawthorne's later career and also expands that authorship's scope so that it merges with his own expatriot status – like James himself, Hawthorne is not only beyond the specificity of particular locales, he is also beyond the specificity of particular nations.[74] Hawthorne, then, can be assigned to an extra-national category of great authors; for James he is not a fellow American but a fellow artist.[75]

If James's visit to Hawthorne's home town confirms and indeed extends Hawthorne's ambition to disconnect from Salem, James's subsequent trip to Charleston, the hometown of Simms, complies with Simms's call for immersion in the locale. While in Charleston, James takes many of the suggestions Simms made to northern visitors in his 1857 guided tour, "Charleston: The Palmetto City."[76] Simms had urged visits to St. Michael's Church (11) and the Magnolia Cemetery (20), and James is led by his own local guide (410) to "several successive spots" including "St. Michael's Church" and "the old Cemetery" (415) – which, he adds, "distils an irresistible poetry" (419). And although James does not mention the Calhoun monument, he does match Simms's restaurant suggestion: Simms's choice could boast of "the presiding genius of Nickerson" (18), and James finds his own "genius of the place" presiding over the Charleston "luncheon-room" where he "fantastically feasted" (416). By immersing himself in these Charleston sites, and even undergoing, as Kenneth Warren has argued, a brief "transfer of . . . allegiances from North to South,"[77] James seems to reproduce the sympathetic identification with Charleston that Simms had thought his tours would engender in Northerners – "Fly with me then to the South. . . . I will be your medium, to use the language of the Spiritualists, and will put you *en rapport* with the *genius loci* in the wild abodes of the Apalachian."[78]

James's rapport with Charleston is only fleeting, however, for he is ultimately left with an impression quite different from the one Simms had intended to give northern visitors. James concludes that "the best word for the general effect of Charleston" is "vacancy": "It is the vacancy that is a thing by itself, a thing that makes us endlessly wonder. How, in an at all complex, a 'great political,' society, can *everything* so have gone? – assuming indeed that, under this aegis, very much ever had come. How can everything so have gone that the only 'Southern' book of any distinction published for many a year is *The Souls of Black Folk*, by that most accomplished of members of the negro race, Mr. W. E. B. Du Bois?" (418).

Having traveled to Charleston only to find a fundamental vacancy, James claims instead to have found a more substantive version of the South in Du Bois's 1903 book. To call *The Souls of Black Folk* a "'Southern'" book, however, is somewhat surprising given that Du Bois was, like James, a Northerner, born and raised in Great Barrington, Vermont. But the label becomes less surprising once we realize that, when listing exceptions to the cultural "vacancy" of Charleston and of the South generally, James singles out "the weird chants of the emancipated blacks" (387), the very "Sorrow Songs" that would be central to Du Bois's *The Souls of Black Folk*. And it turns out that Du Bois uses these songs in a way that coincides with the most "Southern" writings of Simms. As Robert Stepto has observed, "For Du Bois, expressions of *genius loci* . . . have manifested themselves in the lilt and imagery of the Sorrow Songs. Thus when they occur in *The Souls*, spatial expressions of *genius loci* bind spirit of song to spirit of place."[79] Du Bois's willingness to bind songs to places lends support to James's assertion that Du Bois writes a southern book, a latter-day version of Simms's *Southward Ho!*.[80] Indeed, Du Bois's book is itself in many ways a guidebook to these songs: much as Simms had sought to guide readers to encounter the songs of the Cherokee or the Biloxi, Du Bois depicts a voyage through "The Black Belt" and "Atlanta," "the ancient land of the Cherokees" and "the land of the Creek Indians," ultimately instructing readers how to discover not the Native American but the African-American Sorrow Songs on the landscape.[81] It is this guidebook dimension of *The Souls of Black Folk* that comes to the fore when Robert Stepto characterizes it as "a journey both to and into the South" (66): the book is "Du Bois's cultural immersion ritual" (66), and "the 'weary traveler's' perception of the *genius loci* is the goal of the immersion ritual" (70).[82]

This goal of immersion in the *genius loci* – as opposed to Hawthorne's goal of escape from it – brings to the fore additional similarities between Simms and Du Bois, similarities that further support James's characterization of *The Souls of Black Folk* as "a 'Southern' book." As we have seen, in his poem "The Last Fields of the Biloxi" (1853) Simms features a site in Louisiana where, according to "Indian tradition," the Biloxi tribe met their doom while "singing their last song of death and defiance. . . . The strange spiritual music of the Bay of Pascagoula is said to be the haunting echo of that last melancholy strain."[83] Du Bois likewise features the "haunting echo" of "strange" music, for he describes the "Sorrow Songs" as "a haunting echo of these weird old songs in which the soul of the black slave spoke to men" (204). Not only do they use similar language to characterize these songs, Simms and Du Bois also imagine similar encounters with these songs on the landscape. Thus in Simms's poem, which is set on the shores of Louisiana's Bay of Pascagoula, "The Poet is . . . a spectator of the scene" (274) and asks,

> – 'Tis sure a dream that stirs
> These sounds within my soul; or, do I hear
> A swell of song . . .
> . . . along the yellow sands! (280)

Like Ferdinand in Shakespeare's *The Tempest*, who hears Ariel singing of "these yellow sands" and wonders, "Where should this music be? – I'th' air or th'earth?," here too this song emanates not from within the speaker but from without.[84] So just as we saw in Simms's poem "The Cassique of Accabee; A Legend of Ashley River," the lyric speaker or "poet" is here subordinated to the song emanating from the site itself.

Du Bois would likewise feature songs that were apart from himself – songs that "came out of the South unknown to me" (204) – but the location he selects is not Louisiana's Bay of Pascagoula but rather Tennessee's Jubilee Hall: "To me Jubilee Hall seemed ever made of the songs themselves. . . . Out of them rose for me morning, noon, and night, bursts of wonderful melody, full of the voices of my brothers and sisters, full of the voices of the past" (204–05). Simms had made similar comments about the long-vanished Biloxi Indians: "Sweetest strain! – / Once more it rises into sounds, that grow / Human in strength" (287). Du Bois, we see, seizes upon the slaves in the same way that Simms did the Native Americans, preserving the vanished group – if only in song – as a basis for his own identity: the Native American songs of "Apalachian" folk like Simms become the slave songs of "black folk" like Du Bois. Indeed, just as Simms describes himself as "gifted with the faculty of the clairvoyant,"[85] so Du Bois claims that "the Negro is . . . gifted with second-sight" (5), and just as this "faculty" makes Simms uniquely qualified to guide northern readers across the Mason Dixon line, leading them into "Apalachia's mysterious regions" (5), so Du Bois's "second-sight" qualifies him to guide white readers across the color line, leading them "within the Veil, raising it that you may view faintly its deeper recesses" (1–2). It is this sense of Du Bois as such a guide to local songs that prompts Houston Baker to describe *The Souls of Black Folk* by – like Simms – invoking Shakespeare's *The Tempest*: although it is Ariel who actually sings the island's haunting music, Caliban at least knows where to find it and thus can – unlike the outsider Ferdinand – lead others to it.[86] Aligning Du Bois with Caliban, Baker casts Du Bois as the guide to the *genius loci*, thus reinforcing the parallel I am drawing between Du Bois and Simms.[87] Indeed, intensifying James's claim that Du Bois writes "a 'Southern' book," Baker has come to "regard *The Souls of Black Folk* as a profoundly southern book" (58).

This link between place and race in Du Bois is consistent with recent observations by Roberto Dainotto, who has argued that formulations of identity advanced by literary critics have come to place increasing emphasis on the literature of place, or region. "Critical Regionalism," Dainotto observes, ". . . believes in the possibility to return, in short, to a past idea of culture as *cultus*, of literature as the local crop of a regionalized *genius loci*."[88] One ambition of such thinking, Dainotto observes, is that "regionalism will decolonize the place of literature and recover residual forms of cultural identity ready to resurface" (5). This concern with recovering a residual identity is central to Dainotto's critique of such regionalism: "A 'region,' in fact, is the commonplace of an ethnic purity" (22), and thus regionalism expresses "an old desire for authentic identity" (21). One result of this desire, Dainotto observes, is a corresponding shift in the definition of the literary intellectual: "If the old modernist intellectual, fundamentally a *déraciné*, saw literature as a 'strategy of permanent exile' and fundamental displacement . . . the new intellectual rather likes to pose as a topologist: S/he speaks *from* one specific place of cultural production. . . . 'Positionality,'" Dainotto concludes, ". . . is the magic word, and you'd better take it literally" (3). As an example of this literary-critical concern with positionality, consider Houston Baker's recent claims, in *Turning South Again*, that "Modernism's emphasis falls on the locative – where one is located or placed," and that "the *framing* of black being toward anything suitably called 'modernity' has its primary locus south of Mason-Dixon."[89] The South's role in identity formation is not limited, according to Baker, to this "*framing* of black being": "From the inscribed beginnings of the American Republic to the present day, it is the mind of the South . . . that frames American being" (26). A unified "mind of the South" (18–26) provides coherence both to the American identity it spawns and to the African-American identity it excludes. What Baker here exemplifies is what Dainotto effectively criticizes, a logical dynamic in which "the old nationalistic dream of cultural unity . . . finds in the rural areas of regionalism its sole possibility to survive" (23). My claim is that this cultural unity of nation has survived through its relocation not only to the rural areas of regionalism but also to the corporeal areas of racialism. It is this corporeal relocation that I am claiming to be at work in Du Bois: the southern *genius loci* that had given Simms a national identity is the same location-bound pattern of thinking that, in turn, provides Du Bois with a "Negro" racial identity. It is this reliance on a location-bound account of identity that makes Du Bois's book seem "Southern."

But when James characterizes *The Souls of Black Folk* as "Southern," his decision to place the word in quotes registers his sense that there is a difference between Du Bois's book and the writings of a Southerner like Simms. One way of understanding that difference is evident in Robert Stepto's assertion that, "For Du Bois, expressions of *genius loci* are 'race-messages' . . . of Afro-Americans" (76). So if Du Bois is concerned, as Stepto asserts, with portraying "the inner spirit of a people" (58), this people is not Simms's southern nation but rather something entirely different, "a race" (66) that Du Bois calls "Negro." Du Bois may well follow Simms, as we have seen, in binding these "race-messages" to a geographic locale, but he also asserts that "the true Negro folk-song still lives . . . in the hearts of the Negro people" (206), a people he understands by reference not just to a common geography but also to a shared corporeality: "need I add that I who speak here am bone of the bone and flesh of the flesh of them that live within the Veil?" (2). Here Du Bois shifts the *genius loci*'s imagined location from landscape to bodies, from soil to flesh, and it is this shift that enables his move away from Simms, associating the *genius loci* not with nation but with race. Simms had invoked a metaphorical corporeality when he imagined the songs of the *genius loci* to be scattered across the Appalachian Mountains, the "backbone" of his southern nation. But Du Bois moves from a metaphorical skeleton on the landscape to the literal circulatory system in the body: "Negro blood has a message for the world" (5), a message told in the race-messages of the "Sorrow Songs." Relocating songs from landscape to bones and flesh, Du Bois transfers Simms's version of southern national identity onto the body as racial identity, his "beloved Apalachia" providing the prototype for Du Bois's "Negro."[90] Simms's southern national identity is the conceptual precursor of Du Bois's "Negro" racial identity, and the *genius loci* that made the South the South is here transported onto bodies, thereby situated to make the race the race.

This difference between Simms and Du Bois – the replacement of southern national identity with Negro racial identity – certainly serves to qualify James's assertion that *The Souls of Black Folk* is a "Southern" book, and this qualification is probably one Du Bois himself would endorse since he claims to be writing not about southern souls but about black souls, North and South. But apt as it is, this does not seem to be the qualification James himself had in mind when using quotes on the word "Southern." Indeed, James thought more in terms of differences in class than differences in race,[91] and the difference foremost on his mind at this point in his tour of the American Scene is the difference between America's two sections, North and South. So the real problem for James in calling *The Souls of Black Folk* a southern book (the problem registered in his quotes) seems to be that it is not just "a 'Southern' book" but also, like Hawthorne's *House of the Seven Gables*, a Union book. That is, not only is Du Bois, like Simms, immersed in the *genius loci* (serving as guide to the songs of "Negro" flesh rather than of the "Apalachian" terrain), he is also, like Hawthorne, a genius in his own right, one who aspires to ascend the ladder and dwell in the placeless and cosmopolitan space "above the Veil":

> I sit with Shakespeare and he winces not. Across the color line I move arm in arm with Balzac and Dumas, where smiling men and welcoming women glide in gilded halls. From out the caves of evening that swing between the strong-limbed earth and the tracery of the stars, I summon Aristotle and Aurelius and what soul I will, and they come all graciously with no scorn nor condescension. So, wed with Truth, I dwell above the Veil. (90)

What Hawthorne imagined via the Union's sacred Constitution, a cosmopolitan escape from the confining *genius loci* of Salem, Du Bois imagines via intellectual endeavor, a cosmopolitan escape from the *genius loci* of race.[92] So for all its "Southern" interest in immersion in "race-messages" "within the Veil," Du Bois's book is also interested in escaping those race-messages and the racial particularity they involve. Just as James's Hawthorne kicked back the ladder from atop the wall of Salem and forced us to "tread the air," so too Du Bois kicks back the ladder from atop the veil of the color line and invites us to "swing between the . . . earth and . . . the stars."

The double status of Du Bois's book as both a southern and a Union book – as both immersed, like Simms, in the *genius loci* of the southern landscape and simultaneously aspiring, like Hawthorne, to rise above the particularities of any given place – informs Du Bois's notion of "double consciousness." This becomes evident when we recall that during Hawthorne's own wartime visit to the South, he had identified an "exceedingly mischievous" "anomaly of two allegiances" that set the federal Union against particular locales, "the General Government" and its "airy mode of law" against "that sentiment of physical love for the soil."[93] Having replaced Hawthorne's notion of the physical love for the soil of the South with his own notion of love for the race-messages in the blood of "the Negro," Du Bois reproduces this mischievous anomaly of two allegiances, now consolidated in his "double self": like the Southerner Hawthorne envisions, whose "two allegiances" make him both a Southerner and an American, Du Bois is "both a Negro and an American" (5). Like Simms, Du Bois cherishes the *genius loci*, but like Hawthorne, he wishes not to be bound by it. Du Bois has thus retained both accounts of nation set out in Simms and Hawthorne, combining Simms's account of "our beloved Apalachia" with Hawthorne's account of "our sacred Union." And just as those accounts led to civil conflict, so their retention in Du Bois – consolidated in his "double self" – leads to an equally contentious personal conflict: "One ever feels his two-ness, – an American, a Negro; two souls, two thoughts, two unreconciled strivings; two warring ideals in one dark body, whose dogged strength alone keeps it from being torn asunder" (5). The warring ideals separating Hawthorne and Simms (American Union and southern Apalachia) have become the warring ideals within double consciousness (American and Negro), and the battlefield has changed from a geographical terrain to a corporeal one, a "dark body."[94] While a nation was torn asunder, leaving only Hawthorne's version of nation intact, Du Bois is not torn asunder, thus retaining both ideas at once. So instead of being simply "a 'Southern' book," *The Souls of Black Folk* is a Civil War book, one that converts the irreconcilable accounts of nation in Simms and Hawthorne into the equally irreconcilable sides of Du Bois's hyphenated identity, African-American.[95]

While critical discussions of *The Souls of Black Folk* have focused primarily on Du Bois's testimony about double consciousness, and particularly this civil war internal to raced subjects, my focus here is one side of this hyphenated identity, what James called the "'Southern'" side and what Du Bois himself called the "Negro" side. This focus permits us to see Du Bois as a pivot point in the analysis of national and racial identity that I am pursuing here. On the one hand, as I have tried to emphasize, Du Bois's notion of "the Negro," relying as it does on the "Sorrow Songs," reproduces the pattern of thinking present in earlier accounts of poetics and nation. Not only, as I have suggested, does it reproduce the logic of Simms's southern nation, but also, as I have argued, Simms's notion is itself reproducing the logic of Walter Scott's account of the Scottish nation. Thus we see a continuous pattern of thinking reaching back from Du Bois through Simms to Walter Scott. Indeed, Du Bois's resemblance to Walter Scott is all the more striking given his discussion of double consciousness. As we saw, Scott imagined Scottishness to be intrinsic to the poetic meter of his motto, and he insisted on that meter as evidence of a Scottishness that could resist assimilation within the uniform institutions of the British Union. Du Bois, too, asserts of "the Negro people" that "their destiny is *not* absorption by the white Americans."[96] For Scott, one way of keeping sight of both Scotland and Union involved poetic effects: he maps them onto poems, aligning words with British uniformity and meter with Scottish national particularity. Another way of keeping sight of both, we saw, was a spatial metaphor, the hut in *The Highland Widow*. Scott consolidates two emblematic characters, the cosmopolitan Hamish (who embodies imperial semantics in his wish to leave the Highlands and join the British army to fight the French in America) and the locally embedded Elspat (who embodies Scottish metrics and the associated traditions of Scottish national autonomy in the Highlands). When the hut combines these two figures, the architectural structure produces, we saw, a model for the kind of subjectivity Scott was attributing to Scots, a "double self" whose internal conflict – between Union and nation – replicates what we see in Du Bois – "an American, a Negro." And just as Du Bois experiences this doubleness as the exceedingly mischievous anomaly of two allegiances, so too does Scott, in depicting the hut where Elspat forces Hamish to fire on his comrades, try with great difficulty to "keep sight of both" nation and empire. Thus we can see a continuity moving backward from Du Bois through Simms to Scott, a continuity based on the same pattern of thinking, one that relies on formal literary effects to produce an account of collective identity.

But as we have seen, on the other hand, Du Bois also deviates from Scott and Simms, for the identity underwritten by his "Sorrow Songs" is racial, not national, and the location of that identity is a new place, not only poems (as in Scott) or the landscape (as in Scott and Simms) but also the racial body. The Mason-Dixon Line, which had separated the *genius loci* of the North from that of the South, gives way to the color line, which will separate the *genius loci* of blacks from that of whites. Demonstrating that this new, racial context relies on the same pattern of thinking involved in the earlier discussion of nation – a pattern in which formal literary effects provide an index for a collective identity – will be the focus of the second part of this book. Chapter 3 will discuss the debate through which literary effects came to be understood primarily as racial, rather than national. As we will see, Du Bois's approach to the "Sorrow Songs" joins with the writings of Sidney Lanier in recasting literary effects from a vocabulary of nation to one of race. Chapter 4 will document how these now racial literary effects come to be associated not just with poems but also with the body. This corporeal association is aided, I will show, by supposedly scientific developments in contemporary medical research into "racial instincts."

The same scientific community that, as we will see, would endorse Du Bois's specifically corporeal *genius loci* was, at the same time, "killing" Simms's geographic *genius loci*. As I have shown, Simms's poem "The Last Fields of the Biloxi" features the "musical sands" of Louisiana's Bay of Pascagoula. Having prompted Simms's to offer legendary explanations, these singing sands prompted subsequent writers to seek explanations in science. In writings from the early 1890s, several scientists published findings that attributed the apparent singing sound of these sands not to the voices of vanished Biloxi but to the friction of coarse surfaces. Cecil Carus-Wilson, for instance, proposed "a theory to account for the cause of musical sounds issuing from certain sands. . . . [T]he music from the sand was simply the result of the *rubbing together* of the surfaces of millions of perfectly clear grains of quartz."[97] Carus-Wilson came to this conclusion by inducing the sand to be "musical *off the patch*" (323) – that is, to produce the same sounds in his laboratory that it had on the beach. It is in this laboratory that an editor of *Chemical News* "had the pleasure of witnessing Mr. Carus-Wilson's experiments with musical sands – sands originally musical, musical sands which had been killed and then revived, and sands originally mute which had had the gift of music conferred on them."[98] In using words like "killed," "revived," "mute," etc., this editor matches Carus-Wilson's own anthropomorphic language (i.e. "emits notes 'under protest' only"; "'sulky' sand"; "musical sands are quickly 'killed' by constant striking"; "inclination to 'sing' under any of the 'coaxing' methods" [323]) and shows that, while it may be rather simple to delocalize Simms's *genius loci* from the beach to the laboratory, the impulse to personification remains strong.[99] This reluctance, even among scientists, to reduce sounds to mere physics, helps explain how such sounds could retain the force of personification even after being displaced onto the racial body of medical science. In this newly racialized account of formal effects, the "Apalachian" *genius loci* of Simms's "yellow sands" will be replaced by the "Sorrow Songs," the *genius loci* that Du Bois maps onto the "dark body" of the "Negro."

PART II

The poetics of racial identity

CHAPTER THREE

"Of me and of mine": the music of racial identity

With Reconstruction entering its tenth year in 1875, plans were underway in Philadelphia for a gala event to mark the following year's national centennial. Opening ceremonies would feature a choral cantata with music by Northerner Dudley Buck and words by Southerner and former Confederate soldier and poet Sidney Lanier (see Figure 3.1.).[1] This collaboration between North and South was intended to symbolize the national unity that Reconstruction had so far failed to restore.[2] Lanier's poem "The Centennial Meditation of Columbia" asserts national continuity by personifying America as a single entity, the goddess Columbia, whose declaration "I was: I am: and I shall be" asserts a national will to endure.[3] Lanier was not the only poet, however, to mark the centennial, for Walt Whitman's 1876 "Preface" also references "the Centennial at Philadelphia," describing *Leaves of Grass* as "my contribution and outpouring to celebrate . . . the first Centennial of our New World Nationality."[4] Both Lanier and Whitman, then, seize the centennial moment to look beyond civil war toward national unity.

In doing so, however, each poet provides a different account of the nation's history. Whitman invokes the Revolution of 1776 to celebrate a "New World Nationality" that coincides with "the Hundred Years' life of the Republic" (*LG*, 751). Figuring the Revolution as a national birth, he asserts: "[A]ll the hitherto experience of The States, their first Century, has been but preparation, adolescence – and . . . This Union is only now and henceforth (i.e., since the Secession war) to enter on its full Democratic career" (*LG*, 750). In contrast to this account of national maturation, Lanier's Columbia announces not progress but stasis. The line "I was: I am: and I shall be" echoes assertions of divine permanence in the Bible's Old and New Testaments,[5] and the poem itself supports such permanence by reaching back to a time well before the Revolution when "Jamestown" and "Plymouth" first struggled against "Famine" and "War" ("CMC," 61). Thus Whitman's narrative of maturation – the struggle of

1776—1876.

BY APPOINTMENT OF THE U. S. CENTENNIAL COMMISSION.

THE

CENTENNIAL

MEDITATION OF COLUMBIA.

A CANTATA

FOR

THE INAUGURAL CEREMONIES

AT

PHILADELPHIA, MAY 10, 1876.

POEM BY

SIDNEY LANIER,

OF GEORGIA.

MUSIC BY

DUDLEY BUCK,

OF CONNECTICUT.

NEW YORK:

G. SCHIRMER, 701 BROADWAY.

Figure 3.1 *Centennial Meditation of Columbia. A Cantata for the Inaugural Ceremonies at Philadelphia* (New York: G. Schirmer, 1876), title page.

American patriots to free themselves from the British and pursue a "Democratic career" – contrasts with Lanier's narrative of perpetuation, in which British settlers struggle to extend the ways of the Old World into the New.

Bound up with these different narratives of national history are different approaches to poetic form. "[M]y form," writes Whitman, "has strictly grown from my purports and facts, and is the analogy of them" – that is, free verse is the "analogy" of "a revolutionary age" (*LG*, 755). For Lanier, the form of "The Centennial Meditation of Columbia" involves "the short, sharp, vigorous Saxon words [that] broke, rather than fell, from the lips of the chorus"[6] – and these are not "analogies" of the Revolution but relics of a prior civilization: "[T]he author desiring to experiment upon the quality of tone given out by choral voices when enunciating Saxon words, as compared with that from smoother Latin derivatives, wrote his poem almost entirely in the former" ("CC," 272). Thus, while Whitman's centennial writings link poetic form to America's revolutionary origins ("Out of the Hundred Years just ending . . . my Poems too have found genesis" [*LG*, 756]), Lanier derives the formal features of his "Centennial Meditation of Columbia" from a source that predates both the Revolution and colonization – from the "abrupt vocables" of Anglo-Saxon ("CC," 273).

By insisting on Anglo-Saxon sounds in the text of his cantata, Lanier redirects the force of the line "I was: I am: and I shall be," for although spoken by the New World's goddess Columbia, these are Old World sounds. And it is this focus on sounds, I will argue, that underwrites Lanier's break from Whitman's "New World Nationality." Where Whitman asserts an "Indissoluble Union" (*LG*, 747), Lanier's concern is the sounds of Anglo-Saxon; where Whitman's poetic form underwrites an American nation, Lanier's embodies an Anglo-Saxon race. This difference between racial and national forms extends beyond these two writers and into the late-century work of Antonín Dvořák and W. E. B. Du Bois. Although the 1890s posed different challenges to the integrity of the nation's identity, replacing Reconstruction's problem of overcoming sectional division with the problem of assimilating newly arrived immigrants, Dvořák and Du Bois nevertheless consolidate a people by reproducing their predecessors' reliance on form: Dvořák repeats Whitman's emphasis on the forms of a New World nation and Du Bois follows Lanier's reliance on those of an Old World race – not the Anglo-Saxon but, to use Du Bois's term, the Negro race.

By linking Lanier's and Du Bois's commitments to racial forms, I will demonstrate that their categories of *Anglo-Saxon* and *Negro* are structurally identical, each relying on racialized sound. What this similarity suggests is that the commitment to race-specific sound was not just to what Houston Baker has called "African sound" and Eric Sundquist "a sound that is . . . Pan-African" – but it was also, and initially, to Pan-Anglo-Saxon sound.[7] Moreover, by questioning the plausibility of such panracial sound, whether Anglo-Saxon or Negro, I will show that relying on form to do the work of racial identity ultimately amounts to an act of arbitrary imposition, one that appropriates literary form to the project of underwriting the racial politics emerging in the postbellum United States. Finally, I will show that this racialist approach to sound substantially alters the cultural significance of poems, shifting the focus from the meanings they convey to the sounds – and thus the races – they embody.

FROM WORDS TO MUSIC

Lanier's interest in Anglo-Saxon sounds stands apart from other prominent discussions of Anglo-Saxon in the United States during the nineteenth century. The centrality of Anglo-Saxon to the curriculum at the University of Virginia (1819), for instance, reflected Thomas Jefferson's aim of inculcating solid citizenship in young Americans who, he writes, "will imbibe with the language their free principles of government."[8] By mid-century this educational goal had escalated into Manifest Destiny's geopolitical mission of imposing Anglo-Saxon institutions on "inferior" non-Americans.[9] A corollary to this expansionist Anglo-Saxonism was an insular nativist desire to protect New England's Anglo-Saxon elite from the influx of supposedly "degenerate" immigrants.[10] In a specifically southern version of this insularity, one presumably closer to Lanier's interests, defeated Confederates drew "a cultural analogy that aligned Southerners with Anglo-Saxons and Northerners with the Normans," an analogy that "provided comfort to Southerners who believed their region had been unjustly conquered by antidemocratic forces"; like the Anglo-Saxons before them, they too would preserve and perpetuate their indigenous values, embodied in the Confederate cause.[11] While this analogy may help explain an upsurge in Anglo-Saxon language instruction in the postwar South,[12] such nostalgia for the Confederacy runs counter not only to ideas Lanier put forth in "The Centennial Meditation of Columbia" but also to his other statements of support for sectional reconciliation. Lanier's interest in Anglo-Saxon sound was driven, then, not by lingering sectionalism but by a desire for national reunification, and he was able to turn it in that direction through his involvement with two emerging academic disciplines.

The first of these disciplines was scientific philology, which Lanier encountered at Johns Hopkins, a research university patterned after the German model and founded in Baltimore in 1876. Having moved to Baltimore in 1873 to play flute in a local orchestra, Lanier petitioned Daniel Coit Gilman, the university's first president, for an appointment in "Poetry and Music,"[13] and he later proposed a course "suitable to a student of philology who is pursuing Anglo-Saxon."[14] Gilman, however, was seeking a specialist in philology; although Lanier was eventually appointed Lecturer in English in 1879, in the meantime Gilman arranged visiting lectures by William Dwight Whitney, whose *The Life and Growth of Language* (1875) had set out the general aim of the new school of philologists.[15] Countering earlier romantic philologists who claimed that "words get themselves attributed to things by a kind of mysterious natural process, in which men have no part," Whitney describes language as made up of "signs which have no . . . natural and necessary connection with the conceptions they indicate . . . but are . . . arbitrary and conventional."[16] Language, for Whitney, is ultimately a human "institution" in which "the community as final tribunal . . . decides whether anything shall be language or not" (*LGL*, 280, 150). This commitment of the new philology to what Kenneth Cmiel calls a "social compact theory of language" figures prominently in Lanier's "From Bacon to Beethoven," an essay composed in 1876, the year of Whitney's lectures in Baltimore.[17] "A language," Lanier insists, "is a set of tones segregated from the great mass of musical sounds, and endowed, by agreement, with fixed meanings. The Anglo-Saxons have, for example, practically agreed that if the sound *man* is uttered, the intellects of all Anglo-Saxon hearers will act in a certain direction, and always in that direction for that sound."[18] Lanier's phrase "endowed, by agreement" echoes Whitney's "arbitrary and conventional" signs, demonstrating Lanier's embrace of the fundamental claims of the new philology.

In embracing these claims, however, Lanier ultimately aims to redirect attention away from scientific philology and toward his own, somewhat different, concern: pure sound. If a language is "a set of tones segregated from the great mass of musical sounds, and endowed, by agreement, with fixed meanings," then "in the case of music," he continues, "no such convention has been made" ("BB," 276). Musical tones do not start out as meaningful; on the contrary, as part of "the great mass of musical sounds," they are "wholly devoid of intellectual signification in themselves" ("BB," 277), acquiring meanings only when incorporated into the conventions of a given language. The mistake, then, according to Lanier, is to read the effects of this social process – the arbitrary assignment of meanings to sounds – back onto the original reservoir of musical sounds and assume that music itself is meaningful.[19] Thus Lanier urges readers "to abandon immediately the idea that music is a species of language, – which is not true, – and to substitute for that the converse idea that language is a species of music" ("BB," 276); language, then, is music with a difference – with conventional meanings attached. Moreover, although linked arbitrarily to a meaning, tones retain their initial independence from that meaning, and Lanier's aim is to focus attention on this ongoing musical dimension of a language, its status as an object not of linguistics but of "Acoustics."[20] Scientific philologists like Whitney, then, helped Lanier specify how linguists approach language, treating musical tones as arbitrary but meaningful signs, so that he could then set out his own quite separate desire to restore the tones of a language to their status as mere sound. Rescuing language's "musical sounds" from the procedures of linguistic analysis marks an important first step in Lanier's effort to imagine the Anglo-Saxon sounds of his "Centennial Meditation of Columbia" as a basis for sectional reconciliation.

Lanier not only separates a language's musical status from its semantic function, he also elevates the former over the latter; to do so, he draws from a second academic discipline, the opera theory of Richard Wagner. Wagner's *Beethoven* (1870) – which Lanier read and on which he commented[21] – describes the *Ninth Symphony* as a "choral cantata" (much like Lanier's "Centennial Meditation of Columbia") and asserts that "the music bears no relation to the verses other than it would bear to any 'vocal text'" – that is, the words to Schiller's "Ode to Joy" bear no special or privileged relation to Beethoven's music.[22] Thus the words matter to Beethoven's symphony not for the message Schiller asks them to convey but for the sounds Beethoven himself uses them to produce. "[I]n truth," writes Wagner, "it is not the sense of the words that takes hold of us when the human voice enters, but the *tone* of the human voice itself" (*B*, 70). Because Beethoven composes with the tones of human voices as well as those of violins and trumpets, this attention to tone over sense illustrates, for Wagner (and for Lanier), the general principle that "[a] union of music with poetry must . . . always result in . . . a subordination of the latter" (*B*, 74).[23] Having praised Beethoven for this innovation, Wagner goes on to compose his remaining operas according to this principle of subordinating libretto to score.[24]

What Wagner does for opera, Lanier's *The Science of English Verse* (1880) does for poetry, but while Wagner sees a hierarchy between the libretto and the score that subordinates words to music, Lanier finds it within the poem itself – that is, between its words understood as Whitney's arbitrary signs and its words understood as Wagner's musical sounds. Anglo-Saxons may well have "practically agreed that if the sound *man* is uttered, the intellects of all Anglo-Saxon hearers will act in a certain direction, and always in that direction for that sound," but this convention is effectively suspended when the sound "*man*" appears in a poem ("BB," 276). "In fine," writes Lanier, "when the term 'words' is used as describing the peculiar set of sounds used in verse, the reader must understand it merely as a convenient method of singling out that specialized set of musical sounds made by the musical instrument called 'the human speaking-voice.'"[25] And for Lanier, "[T]he tones of the human voice are in themselves as meaningless, intellectually, as the tones of all other reed-instruments" ("BB," 280). In the case of "formal poetry silently perused by the eye of a reader," the words on the page are not semantic symbols but sound-indicators: "[T]he characters of print or writing in which the words are embodied are simply signs of sounds" (*SEV*, 21). Ultimately, for Lanier, "formal poetry . . . impresses itself upon the ear as verse only by means of certain relations existing among its component words considered purely as sounds, without reference to their associated ideas" (*SEV*, 21).

By abandoning the philologist's concern with conventional meaning while retaining the medium of musical sound, the writer of poetry thus becomes a composer of music. This 1880 treatise helps clarify Lanier's 1876 cantata text. Unlike Beethoven's *Ninth Symphony*, in which the text of Schiller's "Ode to Joy" is, according to Wagner, subordinate to the music, Lanier's poem *is* music; Columbia's statement "I was: I am: and I shall be," then, does not produce meaning conventionally, for as a line of poetry, it is just sound, and as sound, it has no meaning. Properly construed, this "meaningless" line tells us nothing at all about the continuity of national identity in the United States; rather, it is just *being* music. Thus "The Centennial Meditation of Columbia" is not the union of a Southerner's text with a Northerner's music so much as a single, jointly-composed musical score; in that sense, it would seem to provide a more potent symbol of post-war reconciliation than a pairing of text and music ever could. Instead of reproducing the distinction between North and South in the difference between text and music, it replaces that distinction with an internally unified national artifact – one musical medium for one United States.

FROM MUSIC TO RACE

To describe "The Centennial Meditation of Columbia" as national music, however, is to overlook Lanier's concern with race, which emerges as he distances himself from contemporary debates on proper usage. Whitney, among others, used his philological findings to critique the notion, widely held among verbal critics, that "proper" language was the basis of an ideal cultural ethos. If all conventions of usage are intrinsically arbitrary, Whitney reasons, then no pattern of usage is more proper than another, and thus no speaker can legitimately invoke language practice to claim superior standing. This line of argument leads scientific philologists like Whitney to accept the shifting usage and slang so galling to verbal critics, for, as Whitney asserts, the ultimate justification of any usage, whether refined or slang, is necessarily circular: "'It was the usage'" (*LGL*, 141).[26] A similar turn from the goal of "proper" usage is evident in Lanier's 1879 Johns Hopkins lectures, but instead of merely dismissing usage as Whitney does, Lanier replaces the ethos of language users with the ethos of the language itself:

> You may have observed that I sometimes speak of the Anglo-Saxon tongue with that peculiar kind of veneration which we accord to a great hero who has fought his way into a lofty position through unspeakable checks and discouragements. English is indeed the Washington of languages; and when you shall have reviewed with me for a moment the astonishing vicissitudes and overwhelming oppressions through which our Anglo-Saxon tongue has managed not only to preserve its idioms but to conquer into its own forms all the alien elements which have often seemed to tyrannize over it, I feel sure your reverence for it will be as great as my own.[27]

While "reverence" is central here, it is reverence not for users of proper English but for English itself, as a *self*: by personifying Anglo-Saxon as an entity in its own right, as "the Washington of languages," Lanier makes explicit his impulse in "The Centennial Meditation of Columbia" to replace the heroic national figure Columbia with his real hero, "our Anglo-Saxon tongue." Like Whitney, Lanier has no "reverence" for high usage over low, but unlike Whitney, Lanier does have reverence for persistent identity over assimilation. Thus the ability of Anglo-Saxon "to conquer . . . alien elements" and to incorporate them into its "lofty position" is ultimately a tribute to its ability to "preserve its idioms [and] . . . its own forms" – to remain itself. Whitney takes for granted the fact that "[a]ll living language is in a condition of constant growth and change" and seeks a descriptive "classification of the kinds of linguistic change" (*LGL*, 33, 36), but Lanier personifies the language as an entity struggling to resist such change.[28] While philologists describe and verbal critics prescribe usage, Lanier sets usage aside altogether to focus on the identity inhering in the language itself: despite the changes that Whitney catalogues and verbal critics castigate, the language was, is, and ever shall be.

Lanier does more than praise the language's heroic self-preservation; his lecture also analyzes how it was achieved, addressing what he calls "poetic Form."[29] While Lanier admits that the language has undergone the very changes Whitney describes in grammar, pronunciation, and semantics, becoming almost unrecognizable to contemporary English speakers,[30] in poetic form, Anglo-Saxon remains, as he claims here of *Beowulf*, the same as it always was: "These words look strange and rugged enough to you at first; but on scanning them attentively, presently you will find one after another putting on a very familiar face and speaking to you with the voice of an old friend."[31] This familiarity stems from a "sense of rhythm which is well-nigh universal in our race," something "founded upon the rhythmic practices of the fathers" (*SEV*, 113, 146) – not founding fathers like Washington but Anglo-Saxon poets of a thousand years ago. Thus while Thomas Jefferson's Anglo-Saxonism focuses on the legal codes of tribal chiefs (leading him to propose two such chiefs, Hengist and Horsa, as central figures on the great seal of the United States),[32] Lanier's Anglo-Saxonism subordinates codes of conduct to scansion of poetic form, inspiring him to prepare two editions of ancient poetry to introduce children to Anglo-Saxon rhythms.[33] Lanier thus replaces Jefferson's reliance on Anglo-Saxon legal codes for instilling national character with a pattern of sound for perpetuating Anglo-Saxon racial identity.

Lanier's *The Science of English Verse* gets more specific about racial sounds when it identifies the formal features constituting the persistence of the Anglo-Saxon race over time: "From the beginning of English poetry . . . through all the wonderful list down to the present day, every long poem and nearly every important short poem in the English language has been written in some form of 3-rhythm" (*SEV*, 110). Focusing on an example from the tenth century (see Figure 3.2), Lanier proceeds "to arrange twenty-five lines . . . so that the general reader though wholly unacquainted with Anglo-Saxon may represent to himself with tolerable accuracy the swing and lilt of the original sounds." Setting the words beneath musical staves, with each staff containing the three primary beats of his "3-rhythm," he provides "directions" for "pronunciation" (*SEV*, 114). What results is a "musical map" for reproducing, even in the absence of comprehension, "the mighty rhythm which beats through all these songs" (*SEV*, 118, 112). Commenting on the result, he concludes: "[I]n truth I do not know where to look in English poetry, old or new, for a succession of words which make more manly music as mere sounds" (*SEV*, 119).[34]

Not only older poems display this race-specific sound; Lanier also finds "the most modern English verse tending into the very specific forms of

I wish now to arrange twenty-five lines from *The Battle of Maldon* so that the general reader though wholly unacquainted with Anglo-Saxon may represent to himself with tolerable accuracy the swing and lilt of the original sounds. For this purpose, the following simple directions will suffice to indicate the pronunciation, letters not given being sounded as in modern English.

a as a in "f*a*ther."
æ " " " "m*a*n."
ē " prolonged e in "m*e*rry."
e " e in "m*e*t."
i " i " "mach*i*ne."
y " i " "*i*t."
ea nearly as ea in "r*ea*r."
eo " " eo " "Leoville."

Pronounce all the *c*'s like *k;* and always make a syllable of *e* at the end of a word, as "stæthe" = *stath-eh,* "stithlice" = *stith-lik-eh,* "clipode" = *clip-o-deh.*

. . .

Figure 3.2 Sidney Lanier, *The Science of English Verse* (1880; New York: Charles Scribner's Sons, 1894), 146–48.

3-rhythm used by our earliest ancestral poets" (*SEV*, 137). Lanier describes Tennyson, his contemporary, as having "carried-on the ancient battle-rhythmus of the fathers," which "never varies from the beginning to the end of what we may call Anglo-Saxon poetry" (*SEV*, 142, 120). This continuity likewise applies to Lanier's own work. Having composed his "Centennial Meditation of Columbia" in the precise forms – the "abrupt vocables" – of these Anglo-Saxon fathers, his line "I was: I am: and I shall be" is not only, as we saw before, simply *being* music (rather than being *about* the United States), it is also *being* Anglo-Saxon. Lanier, it would seem, is less an American than an Anglo-Saxon poet, and his "Centennial Meditation of Columbia" is less a centennial celebration of the nation than a millennial celebration of what he calls "our race" (*SEV*, 113).

Yet, before accepting this replacement of an American Nation by an Anglo-Saxon race we should ask whether it makes sense to label the sounds of Lanier's "The Centennial Meditation of Columbia" as "Anglo-Saxon." If words, as poetry, cease to mean, and thus become pure sounds, why should the designation *Anglo-Saxon* still apply? If a poem's sound is just sound, with no institution of meanings behind it, then there is nothing necessarily Anglo-Saxon about it. Lanier himself effectively acknowledges this point when he suggests "the simple experiment of substituting for the words of a formal poem any other words which preserve the accentuation, alliteration, and rhyme, but which convey no ideas to the mind, – words of some foreign language not understood by the experimenter being the most effective for this purpose. Upon repeating aloud the poem thus treated," he says, "it will be found that the verse-structure has not been impaired" (*SEV*, 21). If the verse-structure remains intact, then the poem, which is nothing more than this verse-structure, remains itself. The words of a language like Anglo-Saxon are thus sufficient but not necessary to produce these sounds. But why, after separating these sounds from a given language's conventional codes, retain that language's name? If the label *Anglo-Saxon* serves to specify the institutionalized codes or conventions needed to decipher meanings but no meanings are present – if poems are music, not language – then why make reference to such codes?[35]

Yet it is precisely Lanier's assimilation of poetry to music that enables a poem's Anglo-Saxon identity. Standing aloof from changing conventions, a rhythmic pattern arbitrarily designated as the embodiment of a language's identity allows that language to appear to be one self – like "the Washington of languages." For Lanier, the heterogeneity of conventions is overcome by the continuity of sound, which is more than mere sound in its also being Anglo-Saxon sound. As such, it remains itself across time, from the tenth century through Tennyson. For Lanier, the arbitrariness of casting these forms as essentially racial presents no obstacle; race inheres in the formal features of archaic poetry, and the superintendents of racial continuity are people like himself, literary scholars empowered by their critical procedures to discern the racial identity intrinsic to a line. Poems become a repository for metrical effects that lie ready to be disclosed by formal analysis so that they can do the work of embodying the persistence of a race. While Lanier's application of musical notation to the study of poems has made only a marginal impact on prosody,[36] of far greater significance, we will see, has been this idea of reducing poems to racial music in order to assert the persistence of a race's identity.[37]

LANIER'S ANGLO-SAXON WHITMAN

Lanier's reduction of poems to music encounters the opposite claim in Whitman's "Eidólons," a poem first published in 1876 and collected in that year's edition of *Leaves of Grass*. The poem's speaker meets a "seer" who encourages him to "Put in thy chants . . . / . . . eidólons," which "Ever shall be, ever have been and are" (*LG*, 5, 7). Whitman's line virtually repeats Lanier's "I was: I am: and I shall be," but while Lanier's line consists not of words but sounds (sounds that do not refer but, rather, embody "the ancient battle-rhythmus of the fathers"), Whitman's line contains words that merely mean, describing without also embodying "[t]he entities of entities, eidólons" (*LG*, 7). Thus Whitman separates the poem itself from the eidólon, and his commitment to doing so stems from the poem's more general adherence to a Swedenborgian doctrine of correspondences.[38] That is, the poem aligns all physical objects with privileged metaphysical counterparts ("The true realities" [*LG*, 7]), as in the following correlation of the physical body with its more "permanent" eidólon:

> Thy body permanent,
> The body lurking there within thy body,
> The only purport of the form thou art, the real I myself,
> An image, an eidólon. (*LG*, 8)

By establishing a correspondence between the "body" and the "body permanent," the poem precludes a conflation of the two entities: "Thy very songs not in thy songs" (*LG*, 8). But if the poem cannot *be* its own eidólon, its "very song," it can at least be *about* such eidólons, and this is precisely the seer's advice. To "Put in thy chants . . . / . . . eidólons" is to make poems that sing "No more the puzzling hour nor day, nor segments, parts" but that, instead, sing about "The whole . . . summ'd, added up, / In its eidólon" (*LG*, 5, 6). To embrace the seer's advice, however, is to turn from Lanier's practice. For Whitman's speaker, poems are words instead of music, so they merely represent instead of embodying the eidólons that "Ever shall be, ever have been and are"; instead of embodying permanence (as does Lanier's line), they merely report it.

If Whitman differs from Lanier in distinguishing between the "very song" and the poem, he resembles him in equating these very songs with the identity of a people – not Anglo-Saxons but Americans. Just as material objects have eidólons, so do nations, and as the United States emerges materially as a nation, it releases corresponding national eidólons:

> The present now and here,
> America's busy, teeming, intricate whirl,
> Of aggregate and segregate for only thence releasing,
> To-day's eidólons. (*LG*, 6)

In the 1876 "Preface" to *Leaves of Grass*, Whitman quotes from "Eidólons" to specify the general project of all his poems: "The Prophet and the Bard / . . . Shall mediate to the Modern, to Democracy – interpret yet to them, / God and Eidólons" (*LG*, 755). Himself such a "Bard," Whitman writes poems that, as a group, seek to "mediate" the relation between Americans and the eidólons they release, helping them look past their selves to see their very selves: "I . . . now bequeath Poems and Essays as nutriment and influences . . . to furnish something toward what The States most need of all, . . . namely, to show them, or begin to show them, Themselves distinctively" (*LG*, 754). This ambition to "show" Americans their very selves makes Whitman the kind of poet the seer suggests, a witness ("as I have lived in fresh lands . . . in a revolutionary age, . . . I have felt to identify the points of that age" [*LG*, 755]) whose poems testify to the enduring significance of the United States as a nation. Thus while Lanier features poems that embody (and indeed perpetuate by embodying) the sounds of the Anglo-Saxon past, Whitman searches for poems that "show" the eidólons produced in an unfolding American present; thus, Lanier's and Whitman's poetry opposes racial embodiment in a poem's musical sound to national representation via a poem's mediating words.

Whitman's 1876 "Preface" describes his poems as "my recitatives" (*LG*, 755) in reference to the inspiration he drew from the opera ("But for the opera I could never have written *Leaves of Grass*"[39]), but his model was the libretto rather than the score, and in his 1881 essay "The Poetry of the Future" Whitman explicitly criticizes contemporary poetry's excessive focus on sound.[40] Assessing "our New World Progress," Whitman laments that "the prevailing flow of poetry . . . is (like the music) an expression of mere surface melody," which, while "perfectly satisfying to the demands of the ear," nevertheless "shrinks with aversion from the sturdy, the universal, the democratic" (*PW*, II:490, 481). Mere surface melody fails to mediate these New World "eidólons," and, like Lanier, Whitman associates this melodic impulse with a "current leading literary illustrator of Great Britain" (*PW*, II:485, 478) – Tennyson – whose "verbal melody" shows him to be a "feudalistic" "*attaché* of the throne" (*PW*, II:477, 479, 477). What Whitman seeks, instead, is the work of "future poets . . . referring not to a special class, but to the entire people," the people of "the great radical Republic with its . . . loud, ill-pitch'd voice, utterly regardless whether the verb agrees with the nominative" (*PW*, II:486, 478). This embrace of improper grammar not only invokes contemporary debates about proper usage (that is, the distinction between the proper language use of a "special class" and the improper language use of the "entire people"), it also superimposes on that distinction a further distinction between two nations, between the English (who speak properly) and the Americans (who do not).[41] Calling for writing that Tennyson "cannot stomach," Whitman hopes to encourage an "autochthonous national poetry," "a national poetry which was not English but American" (*PW*, II:478, 484, 481).

In a rebuttal explicitly targeted at this essay, Lanier equates Whitman's call for a "loud, ill-pitch'd voice" with the "crye" of an enemy attacking "English warriors": "And so the Poetry of the Future has advanced upon us . . . , relying upon its loud, ill-pitched voice."[42] In response to this assault, Lanier alters Whitman's terms: no longer a matter of improper American usage attacking proper English usage (a question of national difference), he sees in this confrontation Anglo-Saxon forms perpetuating themselves (a question of racial identity). Thus although Whitman "shouts . . . of a progress that claims to be winning freedom by substituting formlessness for form," Anglo-Saxon – "the Washington of languages" – nevertheless retains its essential forms: "Perhaps we may fairly say, gentlemen, it is five hundred years too late to attempt to capture Englishmen with a yell," for Whitman's strategy "never yet succeeded as against Anglo-Saxon people."[43] It is not that proper usage defeats improper usage (one nation defeats another) but that form preserves itself against formlessness (racial form remains itself, preserves its identity).

Indeed, this victory of formal persistence is not so much in spite of Whitman but because of him, for according to Lanier, Whitman – despite his effort to write in an English that embraces improper American usage – writes unwittingly in the rhythmic forms of Anglo-Saxon. To demonstrate, Lanier compares "Song of Myself" to the Anglo-Saxon poem in Figure 3.2 (see the final line), setting lines of each side-by-side in order to show

> that even the form of Whitman's poetry is not poetry of the future but tends constantly into the rhythm of
>
> Brimmanna boda abeod eft ongean,
>
> which is the earliest rhythm of our poetry . . . For example:
>
> I loaf and invite my soul;
> I lean and loaf at my ease, observing a spear of summer grass.
> . . .
> I doat on myself – there is that lot of me and all so luscious.
>
> ("LII," 54–55)

What Lanier finds in Whitman's lines are not brash claims but Anglo-Saxon forms, and he suggests that Whitman's best results come when he quits trying to pass as an American poet and instead embraces his poetry's essential Anglo-Saxonness: "[O]n the occasion when Whitman has abandoned his theory of formlessness and written in form he has made *My Captain, O My Captain* [*sic*] surely one of the most tender and beautiful poems in any language" (LII, 39).[44] Whitman claimed that his poems were written for Americans in order "to show them . . . Themselves distinctively," but Lanier's formal analysis is indifferent to showing and concerned instead with being, so he recasts revolutionary "formlessness" as persistent Anglo-Saxon sound. Properly construed, the American national poet is in fact – just like Tennyson – a poet of the Anglo-Saxon race.[45]

THE RACIAL ALTERNATIVE TO UNION

I emphasize these differences in the poetics of Whitman and Lanier to suggest that what is at stake in their disagreement is what one might describe as the emergence of a distinctly racialist poetics. Whitman could insist on the difference between patterns of usage in America and Great Britain because he thought differences in usage were consistent with differences in nationality. Lanier, however, equates the American and English languages, insisting both are Anglo-Saxon, because he considers their national differences entirely compatible with their racial identity; that is, he treats the difference between Great Britain and the United States (the difference between two nations and their conventions of usage) as separate from and subordinate to the continuity of Anglo-Saxon form. Indeed, for Lanier, differences in usage between two nations are as easily overcome as those between two periods in history – all are unified by the ongoing presence of racial rhythm. Lanier extends this Anglo-Saxon identity across national boundaries when he claims to find examples of pure Anglo-Saxon pronunciation not only among Americans – thus, "many words in Chaucer [are] spelled exactly as they are pronounced by a Georgia 'cracker' at this day"[46] – but also among Scotsmen: "[T]he Scotch dialect to the present day . . . presents us with many interesting old Anglo-Saxon words in the very forms used by our forefathers."[47] For Lanier, the Scots are, from the perspective of race, as Anglo-Saxon as the Americans.

This racialist poetics helps Lanier solve a problem he had posed in an earlier poem, "Civil Rights" (1874). Written in opposition to the Civil Rights Bill of 1874, this poem registers Lanier's more general disappointment with the legal measures through which Reconstruction sought to reunite the nation.[48] It features a southern speaker who, while conceding that "My way was clear to like 'em [the Yankees], and to treat 'em brotherlee," then complains about the racial equality imposed by "this Civil Rights":

> "Them Yanks had throwed us overboard from off the Ship of State.
> Yes, throwed us both – both black and white – into the ragin' sea,
> With but one rotten plank to hold; while they, all safe and free,
> Stands on the deck, and rams their hands into their pockets tight,
> And laughs to see we both must drown, or live by makin' fight!
> For, Jeems, what in this mortal world of trouble *kin* be done?
> They've made this Southern plank so rotten, it will not bear but one!
> . . . .
> *By God! ef they don't fling a rope, I'll push the nigger in!*"
>
> (*PPO*, 41–42)

The problem, according to this speaker, is that northern-backed legislation like the Civil Rights Bill places southern whites, many of whom were already denied civil status because of their rebel activities, in competition with newly enfranchised blacks.[49] The response this speaker envisions, to "*push the nigger in*," both offensively and succinctly captures the contemporary politics that Eric Foner describes: while the late 1860s saw a "New Departure" in which southern "Democrats . . . proclaimed their realism and moderation and promised to ease racial tensions," the period after the 1873 depression saw a change as "Democrats throughout the South were abandoning the centrist rhetoric of the New Departure in favor of a return to the open racism of early Reconstruction" (*R*, 412, 547). Assisted by Klan violence, this change ultimately led to a widespread sense of "Redemption" for whites, and their return to an exclusive hold on power.[50] More than merely a southern policy, Redemption enjoyed the tacit support of northern whites as well, for as Foner notes, by 1875, "Northern support for Reconstruction was on the wane" and "Congressional Republicans had little stomach for further intervention in Southern affairs" (*R*, 544, 556). They thus permitted a return to "home rule" (*R*, 581), the 1877 Hayes-Tilden compromise reflecting implicit acceptance of the Redeemers' white supremacist programs.[51] As the *Nation* remarked after the withdrawal of federal troops in 1877, "The negro will disappear from the field of national politics. Henceforth, the nation, as a nation, will have nothing more to do with him."[52] Lanier's speaker proves prophetic: it is now blacks, and no longer southern whites, who would be thrown overboard from the ship of state, and the remaining Northerners and Southerners would now stand together as whites – no longer as regional antagonists but as racial partners. Taking the initiative upon themselves, southern whites like Lanier would "*fling a rope*" to northern whites and replace the regional conflict of Reconstruction with the supposed racial unity of Redemption.

Lanier's "Civil Rights" anticipates Redemption not only thematically, in the proposal to "*push the nigger in*," but also formally, in its being "written in the dialect of the Georgia crackers,"[53] a medium, as we have seen, that Lanier treats as a repository for Anglo-Saxon sounds. Thus, when viewed from the perspective of Lanier's later racialist poetics, this poem's form solves the problem raised by its theme: its Anglo-Saxon sounds already embody the shared racial whiteness that would provide the basis of Redemption. Viewed in this way, "Civil Rights" anticipates the racial commitments of the following year's "The Centennial Meditation of Columbia." The chief difference between the two poems, then, is not formal (since both have Anglo-Saxon sounds) but thematic: "The Centennial Meditation of Columbia" replaces the threat of resistance that "Civil Rights" presents to northern legislation ("*I'll push the nigger in!*") with its own commitment to Anglo-Saxon racial identity ("I was: I am: and I shall be"). Placing the North's "Plymouth" in apposition – and not opposition – to the South's "Jamestown," "The Centennial Meditation of Columbia" gives each region a link to white colonial settlement while making no mention of the slave trade or the middle passage. By ignoring the connections of blacks to the Old World (of Africa, not Europe) and emphasizing instead each section's shared tie to Old World Anglo-Saxonism, Lanier directs the nation toward his own vision of postwar unity. We see, then, the political implications of Lanier's poetic break with Whitman: by emphasizing continuity with Britain over Whitman's New World Nationality, Lanier's "The Centennial Meditation of Columbia" does not so much restore the legal Union as it imposes a racial alternative to Union, and the celebration that results features a unity and continuity that are ultimately more racial than national.

DVOŘÁK'S AMERICAN MUSIC

Lanier's exclusion of African-Americans from the American centennial exemplifies the kind of treatment endured by the Fisk Jubilee Singers. Although, as W. E. B. Du Bois observes, the Fisk Jubilee Singers "sang the slave songs so deeply into the world's heart that it can never wholly forget them again,"[54] J. B. T. Marsh's history of the group registers the "odious and cruel caste-spirit" that confronted them during their 1870 performances. But Marsh goes on to emphasize that the group's music did much to "break down" such "prejudice against color" and to promote, instead, the cause of "social equality."[55] An 1872 concert in Boston, for instance, "was worth more than a Congressional enactment in bringing that audience to the true ground on the question of 'civil rights'" (*SJS*, 42). This openness proved even greater when the tour left the United States for Britain: at the same time that Lanier was writing the "cracker" dialect of his poem "Civil Rights," the Jubilee Singers were receiving a special reception in Scotland (*SJS*, 62), and soon after, while Lanier was proposing Anglo-Saxon sounds as the basis of his "The Centennial Meditation of Columbia," "the great Christian heart of England gave [the Jubilee Singers] a specially fraternal greeting" (*SJS*, 82). "After three months in London," observes one historian, "they invaded and conquered the rest of the British Isles."[56] Capturing Englishmen with a song, their performance succeeded where, according to Lanier, Whitman's "loud, ill-pitched voice" could not.[57]

The Jubilee Singers did not limit themselves to conquering the seat of Lanier's Anglo-Saxon language, for their success led them to ask the same question about their songs that Lanier had raised about poems: "Would the slave songs keep their power where the words lost their meaning?" The "where" in question was "on the Continent," and the answer proved to be a resounding yes (*SJS*, 86). As in England, where "that earnest, evangelistic element in the churches . . . prized their services of song as an effective ally in gospel effort," so too in Germany "the same class of Christian people . . . met them with the same fraternal heartiness, and rejoiced in this unique instrumentality for bringing gospel truth to the formalists and the materialists whom it was so difficult to reach" (*SJS*, 96). Thus the songs are an "instrumentality" for producing a "Christian people," one that is "the same" despite differences in language, nationality, and race – a people, in other words, that is neither racial nor national but ecumenical.[58]

Encouraged by their international success, the Jubilee Singers "decided to circumnavigate the globe," making stops in Australia, Japan, and India. While in India they sang at the Taj-Mahal, where "the tones of that beautiful slave song, 'Steal Away to Jesus,' . . . awoke the stillness of that most wonderful of temples" (*SJS*, 124, 146). By singing at the Taj-Mahal they effectively accomplished their own version of the passage to India confidently predicted in Whitman's poetry, for by establishing "the spiritual as a worldwide phenomenon,"[59] their songs became the "international poems" that Whitman had called for in "The Poetry of the Future."[60]

In 1890, "having made the circuit of the globe," the Jubilee Singers returned to America to find, as the group's leader put it, that they were "no longer free from that prejudice . . . which we had not met with in any other quarter of the globe" (*SJS*, 152–53). What distinguishes the United States from other nations of the world is its persistent racial prejudice toward African-Americans, even despite the achievements of the Jubilee Singers. The notion that the slave songs serve as a reproach to American nationality stands diametrically opposed to the claim Antonín Dvořák would make about them: "It is my opinion," he wrote in the *New York Herald* in May 1893, "that I find a sure foundation in the Negro melodies for a new national school of music . . . in America."[61] Instead of belonging anywhere but America, as the leader of the Jubilee Singers had suggested, the "Negro melodies," Dvořák claims, belong to America exclusively. To Dvořák, they are a unique instrumentality for bringing not gospel truth but national identity; the same songs whose international religious appeal had enabled the Jubilee Singers to overcome national difference serve Dvořák as a "foundation . . . for" it. For Dvořák, the songs are not ecumenical but national, consolidating not a Christian but an American people.

The question of American national identity became a matter of concern for Dvořák after he assumed the directorship of New York's National Conservatory of Music in September 1892. Immediately after his arrival he found himself drawn into ongoing debates about the prospect of an American national music. "I did not come to America to interpret Beethoven or Wagner for the public," he asserts. "This is not my work and I would not waste any time on it. I came to discover what young Americans had in them and to help them to express it."[62] As this search unfolded, however, Dvořák discovered that Americans themselves were increasingly unsure about how to describe their nationality, given the ever-expanding influx of foreign immigrants, and, in particular, the so-called "new immigration" from southern and eastern Europe.[63] Dvořák's experience in New York led him to recognize the perspective of those who would argue against an American national music: "Because the population of the United States is composed of many different races . . . and because . . . the music of all the world is quickly absorbed in this country, they argue that nothing specially original or national can come forth."[64] But while Dvořák acknowledges this account of a hopelessly heterogeneous nation, he nevertheless continues to search for a music that will give it unity:

All races have their distinctively national songs, which they at once recognize as their own, even if they have never hea[r]d them before. When a Tcech, a Pole, or a Magyar in this country suddenly hears one of his folk-songs or dances, no matter if it is for the first time in his life, his eyes light up at once, and his heart within him responds, and claims that music as his own. So it is with those of Teutonic or Celtic blood. . . . It is a proper question to ask, what songs, then, belong to the American and appeal more strongly to him than any others? What melody could stop him on the street if he were in a strange land and make the home feeling well up within him? (*DA*, 376)

As potential sources for this American music, Dvořák lists "the songs of the creoles, the red man's chant, or the plaintive ditties of the homesick German or Norwegian," but "according to my estimation," he concludes, the "most potent as well as the most beautiful among them . . . are certain of the so-called plantation melodies and slave songs" (*DA*, 377), the same music he had singled out early in his visit. Dvořák associates these songs not with Africa but with the Negro in the South,[65] and he casts them as the music of all Americans, regardless of race or region: "These beautiful and varied themes are the product of the soil. They are American. . . . The American musician understands these tunes and they move sentiment in him."[66] This sentiment is not racial (as with Lanier's "veneration" for the tones of the Anglo-Saxon tongue) or ecumenical (as with the "Christian song" of the Jubilee Singers) but national: "To read the right meaning the composer need not necessarily be of the same blood," Dvořák asserts, since "white composers" can write "touching Negro songs" that show a "sympathetic comprehension of the deep pathos of slave life."[67] Dvořák himself undertook such an effort in his symphonic arrangement of the spiritual "Old Folks at Home," and he described the resulting work as "purely national."[68]

Dvořák, then, envisions an America like Whitman's, a New World nation distinct from its European antecedents. Just as Whitman's poems advocate a "New World Nationality," so Dvořák has a similar ambition in his symphony *From the New World*: "My new symphony is . . . an endeavor to portray characteristics, such as are distinctly American."[69] In preparing it, Dvořák sought exposure to Negro melodies by asking Henry Burleigh, an

African-American student at the National Conservatory, to sing spirituals for him. "It was my privilege," Burleigh wrote, "to sing repeatedly some of the old plantation songs for him at his house, and one in particular, 'Swing Low, Sweet Chariot,' greatly pleased him, and part of this old spiritual will be found in the second theme of the first movement of the [symphony *From the New World*], first given out by the flute."[70]

The flute was Lanier's instrument – he played first chair in Baltimore's Peabody Orchestra – and had he not suffered an early death at age 39, the Baltimore premiere of Dvořák's symphony would no doubt have featured him on this solo. The scenario, although hypothetical, is worth considering: Lanier, a former Confederate soldier and ardent Anglo-Saxon, performing a Negro spiritual in Dvořák's all-American symphony. Lanier had turned to music to identify an Anglo-Saxon race, an alternative to Reconstruction's ongoing conflict between sections, but the hypothetical idea of his playing the "Swing Low" melody suggests that Dvořák's music produces an entirely different kind of identity, one that rises above the friction Lanier experienced between North and South and blacks and whites, or the conflict Dvořák observed between immigrants and natives. Dvořák's effort to transform cultural heterogeneity into US nationality aligns his project with Whitman's: both turn to songs – whether Whitman's recitatives or Dvořák's melodies – to establish a national people in the United States.

In describing these musical forms as national, Dvořák diverges from the description in the book distributed by the Jubilee Singers during their tours. That book's "Preface to the Music" casts the songs as resistant to national designations, like the international audience of the touring singers:

> It is a coincidence worthy of note that more than half the melodies . . . are in the same scale as that in which Scottish music is written; that is, with the fourth and seventh tones omitted. The fact that the music of the ancient Greeks is also said to have been written in this scale suggests an interesting inquiry as to whether it may not be a peculiar language of nature, or a simpler alphabet than the ordinary diatonic scale, in which the uncultivated mind finds its easiest expression.[71]

Here the songs Dvořák built into his symphony *From the New World* are the "peculiar language of nature," not of a nation – the mark of a primitive human, not a specific national, culture. In one sense Dvořák agreed, for in a newspaper interview he concedes the formal identity between the plantation melodies and the music of other nations: "I found that the music of the Negroes and of the Indians was practically identical,"[72] adding that "the music of the two races bore a remarkable similarity to the music of Scotland" (*DA*, 362): "[T]he Scotch scale, if I may so call it, has been used to impart a certain color to musical composition. . . . The device is a common one" – so common, he continues, that many composers have used it, including Mendelssohn, David, Verdi, and Dvořák himself. "In fact," he notes, "the scale in question is only a certain form of the ancient ecclesiastical modes" that "have been employed time and time again" (*DA*, 363) – a mode so common that musicologists continue to discuss it, labeling it Dorian,[73] which is itself, according to *Webster's Tenth*, the name of "an ancient Hellenic race."

To Dvořák, these plantation songs are as plausibly Scottish or Greek as they are Negro or Indian, yet acknowledging this point in no way diminishes his conviction that they are the basis for a music that is distinctively American. This problem of classification raises the same question about Dvořák's symphony that I asked about Lanier's Anglo-Saxon poem: as musical sounds devoid of conventional meanings, on what grounds should these expressive works bear the name of a specific social group? These sounds may be found in these cultures, but if these cultures impose none of their conventional meanings upon them, are these cultures – Scottish, Negro, US, Greek – in these sounds?[74]

A contemporary music critic, James Huneker, raises this very question in his review of Dvořák's symphony *From the New World*. Turning to the first movement's second theme (the version of "Swing Low Sweet Chariot" played by the flute), he describes it as "negro or oriental, just as you choose."[75] When Dvořák chooses, he calls it American, and while Huneker implies that such choices are purely arbitrary, Dvořák, openly acknowledging the formal identity among these scales, nevertheless insists that his designation is the right one. Lanier had taken the same approach to the "3-rhythm" of poems, insisting that it was intrinsically Anglo-Saxon. And just as sound's embodiment of a culture was an opportunity for Lanier, helping him unify the heterogeneity of Anglo-Saxon across time, so too it was an opportunity for Dvořák, a means for unifying the people of the United States despite an accelerating influx of diverse immigrant groups.

DU BOIS'S AFRICAN MUSIC

The orchestras Dvořák conducted figure prominently in another work from this period, W. E. B. Du Bois's *The Souls of Black Folk* (1903). In chapter 13, "Of the Coming of John," John attends a New York performance of Wagner's *Lohengrin*; as the orchestra plays he begins "to rise with that clear music out of the dirt and dust of that low life that held him prisoned and befouled" (*SBF*, 193). But no sooner has John's reverie begun than it is cut short. John's boyhood playmate, a white man, is also in the audience and is uncomfortable with John's presence; he requests that the color line be enforced, so the opera house and its liberating music are suddenly off limits to John. It was in 1895, the year of Dvořák's return to Prague, that the color line received its infamous sanction from Booker T. Washington: "In all things that are purely social we can be as separate as the fingers, yet one as the hand in all things essential to mutual progress."[76] For John, this separation affects him as much in Georgia as it had in New York, and the cumulative insult drives him to kill his boyhood playmate. Lingering by the body, he once again hears Wagner's music, his memory of it blending with the sound of an approaching lynch mob: "Hark! was it music, or the hurry and shouting of men? Yes, surely! Clear and high the faint sweet melody rose and fluttered like a living thing, so that the very earth trembled as with the tramp of horses and murmur of angry men" (*SBF*, 202). Wagner's white swan becomes indistinguishable from the "white-haired man" with his "coiling twisted rope" (*SBF*, 203). John had initially treated Wagner's music as a symbol of escape from the South and the color line – as a way to "dwell above the veil" (*SBF*, 90) – but here the music ultimately merges with the white oppressors and becomes, effectively, white.[77]

In his next chapter, Du Bois explicitly contrasts "the songs of white America" with what Dvořák calls "plantation melodies" and Du Bois himself "the Sorrow Songs" (*SBF*, 209, 204). Dvořák had predicted that Americans would embrace the Negro spirituals as their "distinctively national songs, which they [would] at once recognize as their own, even if they had never hea[r]d them before." Du Bois attributes to the Sorrow Songs the same autochthonous power: "[T]hese songs. . . . came out of the South unknown to me, one by one, and yet at once I knew them as of me and of mine" (*SBF*, 204). But there is an important difference in the positions of Du Bois and Dvořák, for while Dvořák imagines as "American" the person who "claims that music as his own," Du Bois's description of the Sorrow Songs as "of me and of mine" is meant to cast the listener not as an American among Americans but a Negro among Negroes. This is "primitive African music," he writes, "the voice of exile" in "the foster land" (*SBF*, 208, 209). Thus Du Bois's turn to the Sorrow Songs looks less like Dvořák's search for American national identity and more like Lanier's assertion of Anglo-Saxon racial continuity. Du Bois, in other words, treats these songs not as an alternative to racial distinctions but, like Lanier's Anglo-Saxon rhythm, as a basis for making them.[78] If Du Bois's Sorrow Songs are "of me and of mine," then others' songs – "the songs of white America" (*SBF*, 209) – must be of them and of theirs.

What Du Bois might have called white Sorrow Songs can be found in Lanier's *The Science of English Verse.* Here Lanier quotes a thousand-year-old Anglo-Saxon poem, "calling attention to a profound mournfulness and gentle dignity which breathe subtly out of the melodious movement of the verse. . . . Even those who understand no word of Anglo-Saxon must be deeply impressed with the tender sing [*sic*] which goes all along through the poem, when it is properly read aloud" (*SEV*, 123). Du Bois offers a remarkably similar account of the Negro Sorrow Songs: "My grandfather's grandmother was seized by an evil Dutch trader two centuries ago; and . . . she . . . often crooned a heathen melody [that] . . . we sing . . . to our children, knowing as little as our fathers what its words may mean, but knowing well the meaning of its music" (*SBF*, 207). Although "[w]ords and music have lost each other," Du Bois nonetheless knows that "these songs are the articulate message of the slave to the world" (*SBF*, 209, 207); loss of meanings, then, does not compromise the standing of the songs as the embodiment of a race. Agreeing with Lanier that words can be separated from music, Du Bois also agrees that these extralinguistic sounds are tied to a particular people. Just as Du Bois offers a catalog of the Sorrow Songs, singling out "Ten master songs . . . – songs of undoubted Negro origin . . . and . . . peculiarly characteristic of the slave" (*SBF*, 208), so Lanier provides his own race-based canon of song: "I have selected out of the body of English poetry five battle-songs, written at intervals of three centuries apart. . . . Surely no one can regard without interest this succession of manful songs, all moving in exactly the same verse-beat and carrying us on their rhythmic movement, by three-century leaps, through twelve centuries of English verse" (*SEV*, 137). Both Lanier and Du Bois place their respective Sorrow Songs on opposite sides of a musically-based color line.[79]

Included in Du Bois's list of "master songs" is "Swing Low, Sweet Chariot," which appears in musical notation as an epigraph to chapter 12 of *The Souls of Black Folk* (see Figure 3.3). This is the same song that Dvořák gives to the flute in his symphony *From the New World*, but while Dvořák wants to present it as American national music, Du Bois, we see, claims it as distinctively Negro – not of the New World but of the Old World (African, not European) that the slaves brought to America.[80] Above this song, Du Bois prints a passage from Tennyson. Tennyson had been the explicit object of Whitman's complaint about poetry that is British instead of American, but Lanier had praised Tennyson for having "carried-on the ancient battle-rhythmus of the fathers"; moreover, as we have seen, Lanier assimilated all poetry to music, even placing "the alphabet on exactly the same plane with the common European musical system of notation."[81]

Twelve

★

OF ALEXANDER CRUMMELL

Then from the Dawn it seemed there came, but faint
As from beyond the limit of the world,
Like the last echo born of a great cry,
Sounds, as if some fair city were one voice
Around a king returning from his wars.

TENNYSON

Figure 3.3 W. E. B. Du Bois, *The Souls of Black Folk* (1903; New York: Gramercy Books, 1994), 165.

Thus Lanier (if not Du Bois himself) would have viewed this epigraph from Tennyson as nothing more than musical notation for an Anglo-Saxon song. From Lanier's perspective, then, Du Bois's page presents us with two adjacent instances of sound notation; no words, only music. But they are not simply two songs; they are, according to Lanier and Du Bois, an Anglo-Saxon song and a Negro song.

While Du Bois may not have shared Lanier's investment in reducing Tennyson's poems to Anglo-Saxon sounds, he was deeply invested in the blackness of the Sorrow Songs: "We are that people whose subtle sense of song has given America its only American music," Du Bois wrote in "The Conservation of Races" (1897).[82] But this is not "American music" in the Dvořák sense, for while Dvořák had envisioned a single music for a unified New World nation, Du Bois asserts of "the Negro people" that "their destiny is *not* absorption by the white Americans" (" CR," 23). Seeking to avoid such racial "self-obliteration," Du Bois imagines "200,000,000 black hearts beating in one glad song of jubilee" ("CR," 24, 23). Race is conserved, then, through the racial identity inherent in these sounds, sounds that were, are, and ever shall be.[83] The question, then, is not whether the jubilee songs are intrinsically racial but whether the race they embody is one's own – whether they are "of me and of mine" – and whether one will choose to acknowledge them as such. On this point Du Bois's instruction is clear: "[I]t is our duty to conserve . . . our spiritual ideals; as a race we must strive" toward "that broader humanity" – that cultural pluralism – "which freely recognizes differences in men, but sternly deprecates inequality in their opportunities of development" (" CR," 25). Difference among races is something Du Bois "freely recognizes" so long as its effect on cultural resources is not to restrict access to them (such as excluding John from the Wagner concert) but to regulate how people identify with them. If no one is socially barred from hearing these songs, some are racially barred from identifying with them and others are racially required – "it is our duty" ("CR," 25) – to view them as "of me and of mine."

Du Bois opposed Booker T. Washington's call for "separation" in "all things purely social," but he does not eliminate the color line so much as displace it, transporting it from a social context to a literary one, making sounds – and, by extension, the people whose sounds they are – seem "as separate as the fingers" of a hand. In 1876 Whitman heralds an American nation emerging from civil war to embark upon its "full Democratic career," and in 1895 Dvořák proposes the musical forms on which such a "New World Nationality" will be based. Lanier and Du Bois, however, subordinate American national identity to racial identity, and their respective commitments to Anglo-Saxon and Negro music together inscribe within literary form what would become "the problem of the Twentieth Century," the problem of the color line (*SBF*, 1).

THE RACIAL SCORE

During the early years of the twentieth century the commitment to racial sound effects would extend beyond the "Battle Songs" and "Sorrow Songs" envisioned by Lanier and Du Bois and would begin to appear in another literary genre, the stage drama. One dramatic work that might at first seem to resist such a racialization of sound effects is Israel Zangwill's 1909 play *The Melting-Pot*.[84] After all, following its multiple performances throughout the country in 1908, Zangwill's play helped make the term "melting pot" synonymous with progressive assimilationism.[85] Central to this play's assimilationist plot is a musical work composed by the play's central character, David Quixano, a Russian Jew who, following the massacre of his family in a pogrom, has settled in the United States where he is writing "my American symphony" (33), a work aimed at capturing "what America means to me" (32): "America is God's Crucible, the great Melting-Pot where all the races of Europe are melting and re-forming!" (33). David premiers his symphony on "the Fourth of July" (142) at an immigrant settlement house, fulfilling his "dearest wish . . . to melt these simple souls with [his] music" (163). For Zangwill, David's "American symphony" would seem to be serving an end similar to the one Dvořák had imagined for his *New World Symphony*, the end of integrating immigrants into the New World nation. As David exclaims, "Germans and Frenchmen, Irishmen and Englishmen, Jews and Russians – into the Crucible with you all! God is making the American" (33).

Yet if David's melting-pot music follows Dvořák in its receptivity to immigrants from "all the races of Europe," it neglects the group Dvořák had singled out for special recognition, those forcibly transported from that other Old World, Africa. The virtual absence of blacks from Zangwill's play no doubt reflects a contemporary tendency to distinguish practices of Jim Crow segregation, on the one hand, from immigration policies, on the other, with Zangwill's play focusing on the latter. Yet Zangwill's *The Melting-Pot* explicitly breaches this distinction when, through the character Baron Revendal, it addresses the United States' systematic mistreatment of African-Americans. A Russian nobleman, who supervised the "Jew-massacres" (109) in Russia in which David's parents were killed, Baron Revendal is in the United States to visit his daughter, Vera. Revendal links "Jews and Blacks" (106) as undesirable social elements and then defends his past violence toward Jews (including the murder of David's family) by pointing out the United States's own attacks on blacks: "Don't you lynch and roast your niggers?" (111). Lynching was still prominent when the play was performed,[86] but while Zangwill registers this challenge to the melting-pot's assimilationist ideal, his play never overcomes it. In the closing scene of the play the "blood hatreds and rivalries" (33) of the old (European) world are effectively set aside as David plans to marry Vera, Baron Revendal's daughter. But if this marriage suggests how Old World conflicts can become New World bygones, the New World conflict between blacks and whites remains intact; despite David's claim to place "black and yellow" peoples together into God's "Crucible" (184), the play stages no marriages across the color line.[87] Predicting that "the real American . . . will be the fusion of all races," David had exclaimed, "Ah, what a glorious Finale for my symphony" (34), but the melting-pot symphony remains unfinished insofar as the fusion it envisions – a "fusion of all races" – excludes African-Americans.[88] Thus even as it casts "America" as a New World nation distinct from the Old World, the play's reliance on the races specific to that Old World – "all the races of Europe" – as its source for peoples to be melted by David's music has the effect of making race, and not nation, central. Americans may emerge from the performance of David's symphony, but it is only Europeans who are eligible to undergo the transformation the music supposedly effects.

As the curtain falls on Zangwill's play, the premier of David's symphony having just concluded, the designated background music is "My Country, 'tis of Thee" (185), a "national hymn" (27) whose tune is "God Save the King."[89] Born and raised in London, Zangwill would certainly have known this tune as the British national anthem, so in his closing "national hymn" the words that describe the United States are paired with a music of Old World origin.[90] Ultimately, then, Zangwill's focus on music – both this performed "national hymn" and the thematized "American symphony" – ends up using sound effects in a manner less like Dvořák and more like Lanier and Du Bois, as a way of demonstrating not separation from but rather continuity with an Old World. Like Lanier's "Centennial Meditation of Columbia," whose supposedly Anglo-Saxon sound effects replaced the conflict between Northerners and Southerners with racial unity among Anglo-Saxons North and South, this closing hymn of Zangwill's *The Melting-Pot* replaces conflict among European nations – the immigrants "at Ellis Island . . . in your fifty groups, with your fifty languages and histories, and your fifty blood hatreds and rivalries" (33) – with racial unity among Europeans. Once David's music has subtracted these "feuds and vendettas" (33), the residue that remains is a people that may be national in name – American – but is racial in substance – European.

As Zangwill's *The Melting-Pot* toured the United States, it shared the theater circuit with another popular drama, *The Clansman*, a 1906 stage adaptation of Thomas Dixon's 1905 novel of the same title.[91] While the exclusion of African-Americans is implicit in Zangwill's play, it is the explicit focus of *The Clansman*, which, based on the second novel in Dixon's *Trilogy of Reconstruction*, glorifies the Ku Klux Klan's efforts to replace the sectional policies of northern Reconstruction with the racial policies of white "Redemption," the return to white rule in the South.[92] Having been adapted as a stage drama, Dixon's novel was later presented as a "photo drama," D. W. Griffith's *The Birth of a Nation* (1915).[93] Although a silent film, *The Birth of a Nation* was – like many films of the period – accompanied by live instrumental music, but while directors of earlier silent films typically entrusted these musicians themselves with the choice of musical accompaniment, providing only instructions for the moods their selections should convey, *The Birth of a Nation* was among the first silent films to employ a "special score," a score in which specific musical passages – whether original compositions or selections drawn from the existing repertoire of popular and classical music – were designated to accompany individual scenes.[94] To prepare this special score, Griffith enlisted the services of composer Joseph Carl Breil, whose score is perhaps best remembered for the choice of Wagner's *Ride of the Valkyries* as musical accompaniment for the climactic scene near the movie's close, a scene in which hooded Klansmen "rescue" white Southerners under attack from black Union soldiers. Just as Du Bois had paired Wagner's opera *Lohengrin* with the white lynch mob in "Of The Coming of John," so too Briel's score associates Wagnerian opera with white attacks on blacks, attacks that, as *The Birth of a Nation* presents them, are responsible for overthrowing the rule of these black soldiers and thus initiating – with the end of Reconstruction and the return to white rule in 1877 – the "birth" of the American nation. Wagner himself had contributed to the United States's 1876 centennial celebration in Philadelphia by premiering a musical work specifically commissioned for the event, his *Centennial March*, which was performed a few minutes prior to Lanier's "The Centennial Meditation of Columbia."[95] But if Wagner himself had, like Walt Whitman, imagined 1876 to be the *centennial* of a national birth, a birth dating back to the 1776 Revolution (Wagner's march is subtitled as "Commemorative of the Declaration of Independence"[96]), Griffith and Breil use Wagner's music to advance a different account of the nation, one in which 1876 is not the *centennial* of national birth but rather 1877 is the *actual moment* of that birth.[97] As with Lanier, who, as we have seen, viewed the centennial as a moment when Anglo-Saxons, North and South, would replace sectional hostility with racial solidarity, *The Birth of a Nation* traces national nativity less to the revolutionary documents of the 1770s than to the Klan violence of the 1870s and the racial solidarity that this violence imposed.

Yet, just as Lanier had imagined racial solidarity to inhere in poetic sound effects, effects like those featured in his text for "The Centennial Meditation of Columbia" (and, we might add, in his 1870–71 poem "Them

Ku Klux"[98]), Griffith and Breil make a comparable use of sound effects in the score to *The Birth of a Nation.* As Breil recalls in his essay "On Motion Picture Music," his approach to the score for *The Birth of a Nation* was shaped by the same ideas that had so strongly influenced Sidney Lanier's poetry, the operatic conventions set out by Richard Wagner:

[Watching the film] it finally dawned upon me that the first half of the picture . . . was a most tragic romance, just such as every opera composer is looking for. And right there I decided that the film would be treated as an opera, without a libretto, of course. . . .There, too, it was decided that the principals should be invested with "leitmotifs"; and contrasting ideas, such as lofty love against drunkenness and lust, brutality against the manly determination of Southern gentlemen to protect womankind and their firesides, patriotism against rapacious ignorance – all these were to be contra-distinguished in the score by their own individual motifs.[99]

As Martin Miller Marks notes, Breil not only adopts Wagner's idea that a specific "leitmotif" should correspond to each of the story's different "principals," he also goes beyond Wagner to imagine a leitmotif corresponding to each of the film's "contrasting ideas."[100] The "ideas" that are "contra-distinguished" in the score – love against lust, patriotism against ignorance – are ultimately reducible, for Breil, to an opposition between races, an opposition setting the Klan against its black foe. For most of *The Birth of the Nation*'s viewers and even some of its actors, the leitmotif for the Klan would seem to be Wagner's *Ride of the Valkyries*, the music so vividly associated with the film's climax.[101] But Breil and Griffith associated the Klan with a different leitmotif, "The Ku Klux Clansmens' Call" that Breil (perhaps with help from Griffith) composed.[102] (See Figure 3.4.) This theme first appears toward the end of the film in association with a title that introduces "The Ku Klux Klan, the organization that saved the South from the anarchy of black rule."[103] Subsequent recurrences of this theme are likewise associated with images depicting the assembly of the Klan.[104] Understood as a "call" to the Clansmen, Breil's musical motif performs a function comparable to the Klan's "fiery cross," which the film describes as a "summons" to the members of the Klan.[105] Viewed as a summons, this musical motif sets out to accomplish what Zangwill's *The Melting-Pot* imagines will take place with David Quixano's symphony: it calls forth an otherwise diverse New World population to assemble in the name of their common race – what Zangwill had imagined as a shared Europeanness and what *The Birth of a Nation* calls an "Aryan birthright."[106]

Committed to "contrasting ideas" in his score, Breil sets this Aryan Klan against "the blacks,"[107] who are assigned their own racial leitmotif. In

Figure 3.4 Joseph Carl Breil, "The Ku Klux Clansmens' [*sic*] Call." In *Selection of Joseph Carl Breil's Themes from the Incidental Music to "The Birth of a Nation"* (New York: Chappell & Co., 1916).

composing this "Negro theme"[108] Breil again sought input from Griffith who, Breil recalls, "had spen[t] his boyhood days on a Kentucky plantation."[109] Having listened to Griffith "hum and chant some of the old croons of (the) mammies and (the) loose jointed young plantation negroes which he still remembered in a vague sort of way," Breil then composes "the theme which opens the film"[110] (see Figure 3.5.). By drawing upon these "plantation" songs, Breil derives his opening "Negro theme" from the same source consulted by both Dvořák and Du Bois: Dvořák had asked Henry Burleigh to sing for him songs like "Swing Low, Sweet Chariot," the spiritual that he would incorporate into his symphony *From the New World*, and Du Bois listened to the Jubilee Singers in order to become acquainted with the "Sorrow Songs" that "came out of the South unknown to me, one by one, and yet at once I knew them as of me and of mine" (*SBF*, 204). Although less thorough than the researches of Dvořák and Du Bois, Breil's consultation with Griffith was effective, for according to Martin Mill Marks, Breil's "Negro theme" is "reminiscent of a Negro spiritual."[111] As *The Birth of a Nation* opens, this theme accompanies, first, a caption reading "The bringing of the African to America planted the first seed of disunion," and next, an image of African captives arriving in the

Figure 3.5 Joseph Carl Breil, "The Motif of Barbarism." In *Selection of Joseph Carl Breil's Themes from the Incidental Music to "The Birth of a Nation"* (New York: Chappell & Co., 1916).

New World as slaves.[112] Following this opening association with African slaves, the musical theme is – as Breil puts it – "thereafter ever applied to the description of the primitive instincts of the blacks."[113] Associated in this way with black characters throughout the film, this "Negro theme" serves as a leitmotif not for a single character or "principal" – the precedent set by Wagner's opera theory – but rather, like the call to the Klan, as a leitmotif for a race. In the year following the film's release, both of these leitmotifs were published in an unprecedented anthology entitled *Selection of Joseph Carl Breil's Themes from the Incidental Music to "The Birth of a Nation,"* the "Negro theme" now bearing a new title, "The Motif of Barbarism."[114]

Noting this manner through which whites and blacks are "contradistinguished" in Breil's film score, Jane Gaines and Neil Lerner have argued that these themes, particularly the "Motif of Barbarism," are "musical signifiers" (256, 259) that are "rich in signifying potential" (256) and "would have been 'read' as carrying particular connotations" (256). Gaines and Lerner concede that "Breil would not think in terms of elementary semiotics in his own understanding of how he might have encoded his music to produce a particular meaning," arguing that, instead of employing "[t]his cultural studies approach," "Breil wants to think that his music works at the connotative rather than the denotative level – that is, it is added on top of the meanings exuded by Griffith's characterizations (and understanding that music seems only to work at the connotative level, as a second order signifying system)" (254). Setting aside denotation, Gaines and Lerner nevertheless retain connotation, and thus advance a view of Breil's score as a "signifying system" that produces "meanings." It is not entirely clear, however, that Breil himself viewed his racial themes in this manner, as "signifiers" for racial meanings. As James Chandler observes of *The Birth of a Nation*, the film's "fiery cross" is a "summons" modeled on the writings of Walter Scott.[115] But Scott's summons, as we saw in Chapter 1, involved not only this fiery cross but also poetic meter, sound effects like the ones at work in Breil's score. For Scott, the point about this metrical summons (the point that allowed the summons both to advance his goal of defending Scottish national identity and to threaten his goal of maintaining the British Union's integrity) was not simply that it *meant* Scottishness but that it *embodied* Scottishness: wherever the summons appeared, Scottishness would be made present. Much as contemporary critics may wish to re-characterize this historical commitment to identity as, in fact, nothing more than semantic encoding of meanings (whether first-order denotation or second-order connotation), and accurate as those critics may be in providing such a *theoretical* correction,[116] the *historical* fact remains that Scott's investment in the metrical summons stems from his conviction (mistaken as it may be) that the summons is not *meaning* Scottishness but is rather *being* Scottishness, providing not an alternate way to *signify* Scotland but rather a way to bring Scotland forth as a persistent identity. Scott, in other words, envisions meter not merely as a sign of Scottishness but as an index of Scottishness. As we have seen, Sidney Lanier is also thinking in these identitarian terms: familiar with the works of William Dwight Whitney and his linguistic notion of an arbitrary sign, Lanier nevertheless sets this linguistic view aside in order to isolate what genuinely concerns him – not the arbitrary and ephemeral linguistic conventions used by Anglo-Saxon's speakers but the persistent identity of Anglo-Saxon itself, an identity embodied in the three-rhythm of Anglo-Saxon poetry. Likewise at work in Du Bois's *The Souls of Black Folk*, particularly in his account of the "Sorrow Songs," this pattern of thinking, I am arguing, extends forward into the racially specific leitmotifs in Breil's score to *The Birth of a Nation*.[117] Concerned less with the "encoding" that would be "read" by his audience than with the racial identity supposedly inhering in the musical motifs themselves, Breil investigates not the musical codes familiar to the film-going public but rather the musical memories of a native informant – the memories of Griffith himself.

By employing this quasi-anthropological method of musical field work, Breil was conducting, on a much smaller scale, a version of the more extensive ethnomusicological inquiry undertaken the previous year by Henry Krehbiel, "dean" of American musical critics.[118] In his book *The Afro-American Folksongs: A Study in Racial and National Music* (1914),[119] Krehbiel characterizes "folksong" as "an adjunct to ethnology" (9), arguing that his book is "written with the purpose of bringing a species of folksong into the field of scientific observation" (v). Although he made first-hand observations of the Fisk Jubilee Singers – "It was their singing which interested me in the subject" (71) – Krehbiel admits that "I did not hear the songs sung in slavery" (71), so he bases his observations on, among others sources, "songs which were gathered for me by Miss Hill in Kentucky" (91), Griffith's native state. After consulting such sources, Krehbiel concludes of these songs' "intervallic, rhythmical and structural elements" that, "while their combination into songs took place in this country, the essential elements came from Africa" (ix). Krehbiel is certainly correct about this – and he is thus correct to "challenge . . . [the] statement that the songs of the American negroes are predominantly borrowings from European music" (13).[120] But as he acknowledges the African sources of this music's "essential elements," he also laments the limits of his ability to specify those sources beyond a monolithic notion of Africa:

> The slaves in the Southern States were an amalgamation of peoples when the songs came into existence. . . . Among the negroes of Africa the diversities of tribe are so great that over a score of different languages are spoken by them, to say nothing of dialects. . . . . It does not seem to be possible now to recall all the names of the tributary tribes – Congos, Agwas, Popos, Cotolies, Feedas, Socos, Awassas, Aridas, Fonds, Nagos; – who knows now how they differed one from another, what were their peculiarities of language and music which may have affected the song which they helped to create in their second home? We must, perforce, generalize when discussing the native capacity for music of the Africans. (56–57)

Noting the astonishing cultural variety across the African continent, Krehbiel only reluctantly agrees to "generalize" in the very same manner that had once been imposed by the slave traders – as he puts it, "All was fish that came to the slaver's net" (57). What results from this generalization is a melting pot similar to Zangwill's: the middle passage becomes a crucible of Africanization running parallel to Zangwill's crucible of Americanization, a crucible reserved specifically for immigrants from that other "Old World" (103) – by which Krehbiel means the African continent. Forced to accede to the slave-traders' generalization, Krehbiel then goes on to rationalize that generalization, arguing that "diversity of speech as well as of tribes and customs" (130) among these forced emigrants from Africa becomes less of a concern when one's focus is "not words, but musical cries" (36). While the interpretation of words is subject to the diversity of local linguistic practice, the interpretation of musical cries involves "unconscious, unvolitional human products" (3), products that are "at [music's] base" (3). Resting on this broader "base," "musical cries" permit a generalization comparable to the one motivating the Jubilee Singers on their world tour. But if the music of the Jubilee Singers rested on an ecumenical base that extended across the world, the music that Krehbiel treats rests on an ethnological base whose reach is restricted – as was the slaver's net – to the continent of Africa.

By shifting the base of this music from the ecumenical to the ethnological, Krehbiel sets up an analysis whose terms are quite similar to those of Sidney Lanier. Just as Lanier set aside the dramatic changes in Anglo-Saxon linguistic conventions in order to emphasize a continuity of Anglo-Saxon poetic effects – and thus of an Anglo-Saxon race – over a millennium, so Krehbiel sets aside the dramatic diversity in African linguistic practices in order to emphasize a continuity of African musical effects – and thus of a "Negro" race – across a continent. Moreover, Krehbiel likewise follows Lanier in extending this racial identity from the Old World into the New. As with Lanier, who asserts of Walt Whitman's poetry that it perpetuates an essentially Anglo-Saxon three-rhythm, Krehbiel asserts that "it was to have been expected that the black slaves would not only develop [rhythm and dance] in their new environment, but also *preserve* the rhythms of those primitive dances in the folksongs which they created here" (112; my italics). "Folksongs," Krehbiel insists, "are echoes of the heart-beats of the vast folk, and in them are *preserved* feelings, beliefs and habits of vast antiquity. Not only in the words, . . . but also in music, and perhaps more truthfully in the music than in the words" (3; my italics). Understood as music that "preserves" a generalized African "antiquity" rather than words that convey a particular speaker's meanings, the Afro-American folksong becomes, for Krehbiel, "a relic of the life of the negroes in their aboriginal home" (46).

In order to demonstrate that these monolithically "negro" relics have been preserved in the United States, Krehbiel employs a method now familiar from Lanier's analysis of Whitman, the side-by-side comparison of Old World and New World sound effects. In a visual display entitled "Specimens of African Music Disclosing Elements Found in the Songs of the Negro Slaves in America," Krehbiel places several examples of music drawn from across the African continent alongside the song "Round About the Mountain," a "funeral hymn from Boyle Co., Kentucky, taken from the singing of a former slave" (63) (see Figure 3.6). Just as Lanier had set Whitman's

African Music

No. 1. Drum Call from West Africa

No. 2. Tuning of a Zanze from South Africa

No. 3. Melody from the Ba-Ronga District

No. 4. A Melody of the Hottentots

No. 5. A Melody of the Kaffirs

...

No. 9. A Fantee Dirge

Andante
(Flutes)
p
(Drums, Gongs, etc.)
ff
(Flutes)
p
(Drums, etc.)
ff

...

Round about the Mountain

Moderato
Round a-bout the mountain, O round a-bout the val-leys, O
sempre arpeggiando
p
round a-bout the moun-tain, and she'll (he'll) rise in His arms.
Fine

Figure 3.6 Henry E. Krehbiel, *Afro-American Folksongs: A Study in Racial and National Music* (New York: G. Schirmer, 1914), 61–63.

"Song of Myself" alongside a line of Anglo-Saxon poetry, thereby seeming to demonstrate, through the formal features supposedly shared among these lines, that Whitman's poem was not American but rather Anglo-Saxon, so too Krehbiel sets this Kentucky song alongside musical fragments drawn from throughout the "Old World" of Africa, claiming that both the African music and the Kentucky song contain the same formal feature, a rhythmic "snap" or "syncopation" (vi, 92). The syncopation in the Kentucky song is consistent, Krehbiel argues, with these "African prototypes" (77) and thus, he concludes, the Kentucky song contains within it an "African relic" (40). Viewed in this light, as a hold-over from the Old World (Africa) rather than as something discrete to the New World, the song is not American in the sense that, as we have seen, Dvořák had earlier asserted. Instead of imagining these songs as unique to the New World, Krehbiel asserts a continuity of racial forms connecting the New World "Negro" to the supposed racial homogeneity in the Old World of Africa.[121] As we have seen, Krehbiel's methods are similar to those of Joseph Carl Breil: just as Krehbiel relies on "songs which were gathered for me by Miss Hill in Kentucky" (91) in order to convey the "singing of a former slave" (63), so Breil relies on D. W. Griffith, likewise of Kentucky, to recall the slave songs that would inform his score's "Negro theme." The theme that Breil composes contains the same rhythmic feature that Krehbiel had called an "African relic," a feature that Gaines and Lerner describe as "a mildly syncopated melody, a rhythmic effect (syncopation) created by the accenting of the weak part of the first beat in measure one" (257). Breil's small-scale version of Krehbiel's more extensive musical study not only reveals him to imagine of Africa (as Zangwill had of Europe) that the entire continent can be melted into a single race, but it also leads him to suggest that this "Negro" race and the "Aryan" Klan can be "contra-distinguished" through the musical themes of his film score.

Given Krehbiel's musical analysis, we can challenge the view of Gaines and Lerner that, in Breil's score, the "Negro" "motif draws on rhythms and melodies that are *meant to be read* as characteristically un-European" (Gaines and Lerner, "The Ochestration of Effect," 259–60; my italics). The "Negro theme" is un-European not because of how it is "meant" or "read" but rather, following Krehbiel's analysis, because of the race it embodies. As Krehbiel puts it, "the old dances and superstitious rites of African peoples have left an impress upon the music of their descendants in America" (37), and "the impress of African music is unmistakable and indelible" (83). Concerned more with the preservation of an indelible racial impress than with the communication of conventional authorial intention, and thus more concerned with racial identity than with authorial meaning, Krehbiel's analysis is committed not to a musical semantics but rather to a racial index.[122] Understood from this perspective, Breil's score to *The Birth of a Nation* reveals a desire to use music not to express racial meanings but to embody racial identities, an ambition likewise present in the work of earlier writers like Sidney Lanier and W. E. B. Du Bois. The racialization of sound in the writings of Lanier and Du Bois thus anticipates this central function of the score of *The Birth of a Nation*: as in Lanier's Anglo-Saxon "Battle Songs" and Du Bois's "Negro" "Sorrow Songs," sound effects in the film score are sorted according to a phonic color line that rigorously segregates "The Ku Klux Clansmens' Call" from the "Motif of Barbarism." Whether through the formal features of literary texts or through the special effects of film music, supposedly racial sounds are in each case employed in order to underwrite an unbridgeable distinction between races, black and white. Though its musical score, *The Birth of a Nation* reveals itself to be implicated in racialism on a level beyond its production of racially charged visual stereotypes.[123] As it extends from formal effects of literary texts to the sounds of the cinematic score, this pattern of thinking provides a specifically phonic avenue through which the twentieth century's emerging problem, the problem of the color line, infiltrates the twentieth century's emerging medium, the medium of the motion picture.

Just prior to the New York premier of *The Birth of a Nation*, James Weldon Johnson, then a columnist for the *New York Age*, urged that, in accordance with the advice of the city's Board of Censors, the production be prohibited.[124] Johnson's rationale was the immense harm that he anticipated would arise from a film version of Dixon's *The Clansman*:

> "The Clansman" did us much injury as a book. . . . It did us more injury as a play. . . . Made into a moving picture play it can do us incalculable harm. Every minute detail of the story is vividly portrayed before the eyes of the spectators. A big, degraded looking Negro is shown chasing a little golden-haired white girl for the purpose of outraging her; she, to escape him, goes to her death by hurling herself over a cliff. Can you imagine the effect of such a scene upon the millions who seldom read a book, who seldom witness a drama, but who constantly go to the "movies"? (12)

Johnson's focus here is the "eyes of the spectators," not the ears of the auditors, so his anticipations of harm are prompted by the film's visual elements, not its score. Indeed, as I will argue in the next chapter, Johnson emerges as a supporter of the pattern of thinking involved in the production of the film's score, a pattern of thinking in which formal sound effects are taken to be an index of racial identity. Johnson would go on to write additional editorials condemning *The Birth of a Nation* as a harmful film, and he would make great strides toward countering these harms as a leader of the NAACP.[125] Yet Johnson would also, as the next chapter will show, play a prominent role in advancing the pattern of thinking behind this film's score, a pattern of thinking that his writings would elevate to a position of prominence within the intellectual developments of the Harlem Renaissance.

CHAPTER FOUR

"Blood will tell": literary effects and the diagnosis of racial instinct

I went down to that St. James Infirmary,
And I saw some plasma there.
I ups and ask the doctor man,
"Now was the donor dark or fair?"
The doctor laughed a great big laugh
And he puffed it right in my face.
He said, "A molecule is a molecule, son,
And the damn thing has no race."
– Josh White, "Free and Equal Blues" (1945)[1]

In the 1880 "Introduction" to *Uncle Remus: His Songs and His Sayings*, Joel Chandler Harris acknowledges that his stories appear in many other locations throughout the world besides the southern United States.[2] What distinguishes his own versions of these stories, then, is "the medium" (39) – "the dialect of the cotton plantations, as used by Uncle Remus" (43). But once he turns his attention from the stories to Uncle Remus's songs, Harris describes them not in terms of their dialect but rather in terms of their "versification" (45). To explain this versification Harris invokes "Mr. Sidney Lanier, who is thoroughly familiar with the metrical peculiarities of negro songs" (46), as demonstrated by "his scholarly treatise, 'The Science of English Verse'" (46), which was published earlier that same year. In this treatise Lanier analyzes "a typical negro sermon" as a type of "musical recitative" and, as in Harris's discussion of "Negro songs," Lanier's central concern is not the sermon's dialect but its versification, or what he calls "poetic effects."[3] "[T]he half-chanted sermon of the negro" (215), Lanier asserts, has a "sing-song" (215) effect in which "tones are almost exactly reproducible in musical notation" (214). Lanier's presentation of the sermon (see Figure 4.1) provides not only the preacher's dialect ("Ef you don' make haste") but also the musical "tones" that accompany his speech. The sermon may – as with Harris's songs – employ dialect, but what matters most to both Harris and Lanier about "Negro" songs and sermons is not their

276 *Science of English Verse.*

I can now again point to the negro as exhibiting a most striking example of the transition-period from pure musical poetic recitative to the speech-tune, or more refined recitative. One who has ever heard a typical negro sermon will have observed how the preacher begins, in the ordinary tones of voice, announcing his text and gradually clearing the way to the personal appeal of the sermon : here he rises into a true poetic height, and always falls into what is an approach to musical recitative : "Yes, my bretherin and sisterin," (he will say) "ef you don' make haste and repent of all your sins and wásh yourself cléan in de rivér of life, de Lord will fling de lás' mán of you down into everlásting perdition."

The transition-nature of this, between musical recitative and the speech-tune, appears from the fact that its tones are almost exactly reproducible in musical notation. Every one who has heard it will readily recognize it in the following scheme :

Figure 4.1 Sidney Lanier, *The Science of English Verse* (New York: Charles Scribner's Sons, 1880), 276–77.

regional dialect ("of the cotton plantations") but their racial sound effects ("Negro" "versification" or "poetic effects").

This focus on "poetic effects" rather than dialect would likewise be the concern of James Weldon Johnson, whose "Preface" to *The Book of American Negro Poetry* (1922) asserts that the "colored poet. . . . needs a form that is freer and larger than dialect, but which will still hold the racial flavor."[4] A problem with dialect, for Johnson, is that it is too regional to be adequately racial: it may be suited to "a Negro in a log cabin" – the focus of Harris's *Uncle Remus* – but not to "a Negro in a Harlem flat" (*BANP*, 41). Five years later, in the "Preface" to his poem collection *God's Trombones* (1927), Johnson repeats this critique of dialect,[5] but he now offers an alternative, one consistent with what Harris calls "versification" and what Lanier calls "poetic effects." For Johnson, the "form that will express the racial spirit" (8) is to be found in the very same genre first analyzed by Lanier, the "folk sermons" (1) of the "Negro preacher" (5): "The old-time Negro preacher," Johnson asserts, ". . . . knew the secret of oratory, that at bottom it is a progression of rhythmic words more than it is anything else. Indeed, I have witnessed congregations moved to ecstasy by the rhythmic intoning of sheer incoherencies. . . . It was from memories of such preachers there grew the idea of this book of poems" (5).

Johnson's book of poems draws attention to this "rhythmic intoning of sheer incoherencies" through its title, *God's Trombones*, which associates the expressive range of the "Negro" preacher's voice less with speech than with a musical instrument: "he brought into play the full gamut of his wonderful voice, a voice – what shall I say? – not of an organ or a trumpet, but rather of a trombone" (6–7). By identifying the preacher's voice with a musical instrument, Johnson's account of the sermon resembles that of Lanier. For Lanier, the "negro sermon," as a "musical recitative," dramatizes "a struggle for independence . . . on the part of words as against pure musical tones" (208). Music will only achieve full independence, according to Lanier, "as soon as it has freed itself from the fetters of . . . conventional words, and has obtained a completely instrumental medium of expression" (210) – as soon, that is, as it achieves the "completely instrumental" character that Johnson finds in the voice of the "Negro preacher": "He often possessed a voice that was a marvelous instrument, a voice he could modulate from a sepulchral whisper to a crashing thunder clap" (5). Indeed while Johnson characterizes the "intoning" (10) of a preacher as "a rising and falling between plain speaking and wild chanting" (10), he emphasizes the latter through the onomatopoeia of his description: "He intoned, he moaned, he pleaded – he blared, he crashed, he thundered" (7). Johnson's onomatopoeia stretches his prose to the limit in order to convey the instrumental sound effects of the preacher's voice. "At such times," Johnson observes of this "wild chanting," "his language was not prose but poetry" (5).[6]

Johnson's distinction – "not prose but poetry" – would be put differently by Lanier: what Johnson calls "poetry" (the preacher's trombone-like voice) Lanier calls music, so for Lanier, the preacher's voice would be *not poetry but music.* For Lanier, distinguishing poetry from the specifically instrumental sounds of music permits him to address poetry itself, which involves the (in his view) entirely distinct set of sounds produced by the words of poems: "poetry . . . has tended to relieve itself from all dependence on, or association with, music, and to rely upon the more subtle and practicable tunes of the speaking-voice" (205).[7] Having distinguished these poetic sounds from the sounds specific to music, Lanier goes on to claim of English poetry that, in the period since the seventeenth century, when it managed "to split away from music and become a wholly separate art with wholly separate methods" (205), it has achieved "the highest delicacy of the cultivated speech-tune" (215). The implication for the "negro sermon" is quite pejorative: as a "musical recitative," it is "not exactly musical tune nor exactly speech tune" (208), so it "exhibit[s] a most striking example of the transition-period" (214) from the one to the other. For Lanier, the "negro sermon's" lingering affiliation with instrumental music is betrayed by its "sing-song" (215) effect, which his musical notation (in Figure 4.1) serves to illustrate. As an evolutionary precursor to the fully independent "speech tune" of English poetry, poetry whose independence from music has allowed it to become "delicate," "subtle," and "refined," the "negro sermon" is, according to Lanier, comparatively "primitive" and "crude" (214, 215). Lanier's criticism of the "negro sermon," then, stems not from its use of dialect rather than standard speech; indeed, as the previous chapter demonstrated, Lanier himself employs southern dialect as a way of rendering the speech tunes he considers to be characteristic of Anglo-Saxon poetry. Rather, Lanier's complaint is that the "negro sermon" employs the tunes of both poetic speech and music at once, rather than the tunes of poetic speech alone.

Lanier's pejorative account of the "negro sermon" is merely elided from Joel Chandler Harris's discussion of the Uncle Remus songs, but it is flatly contradicted in James Weldon Johnson's writings. While for Lanier, the lingering tie to instrumental music is what makes the "negro sermon" inferior to English poetry, for Johnson, this persistent tie to instrumental music permits him to seize upon the "Negro preacher's" trombone-like voice as an alternative to dialect, a "form that will express the racial spirit" (8).

Although dialect has the liability that the "Negro of the uplands of Georgia" and the "sea island Negro" can have "difficulty in understanding" each other (*BANP*, 46), the problem of "understanding" does not arise with the "Negro preacher's" instrumental voice. Indeed, it is precisely through its incomprehensible sounds – its "sheer incoherencies" (5) – that the Negro sermon achieves its most instrumental effects, effects rendered by Johnson through onomatopoetic words like "blared," "crashed," and "thundered" (7). So unlike dialect, which Johnson describes as a "mere mutilation of English spelling and pronunciation" (*BANP*, 41), the Negro sermon transcends English, whether dialect or standard, with its instrumental sounds.[8] As instrumental music, the "Negro" preacher's sermon recasts dialect's interregional liability – its failure to convey meaning outside a specific geographic area – as its own pan-racial asset: "It was through [the old-time "Negro" preacher] that the people of diverse languages and customs who were brought here from diverse parts of Africa and thrown into slavery were given their first sense of unity and solidarity" (2). Through unintelligible, instrumental sounds – sounds freed from the fetters of conventional meaning – the sermon overcomes the atomizing effect of local "diversity" with the unifying effect of racial "solidarity." Johnson has found a form suited both to "a Negro in a log cabin" and to "a Negro in a Harlem flat" (*BANP*, 41).

What this analysis suggests is that Johnson imagines racial "unity" through the specifically instrumental sound effects of his poems. By isolating these effects as the basis of his poems' "racial flavor" and "racial spirit," Johnson in effect racializes Lanier's distinction between poetry and instrumental music. As we saw in the previous chapter, Lanier had claimed the poems of Keats or Tennyson to contain a specifically Anglo-Saxon "speech tune," but in his corresponding selection of great musical composers, Haydn, Bach, and Beethoven (210), Lanier likewise features Europeans, thus relegating black music, as he does the "Negro sermon," to a comparatively inferior position.[9] Johnson, however, objects to the musical primacy Lanier accords to Europeans, asserting a distinctively black domain of musical achievement.[10] Indeed, Johnson wrote extensively about the "Negro's accomplishment" in producing the "noble music" of the spirituals (*BANP*, 17), and given this "vast mine of material" (*BANP*, 19), he could predict that "there will yet come great Negro composers who will take this music and voice through it not only the soul of their race, but the soul of America" (*BANP*, 20).[11] Claiming that infusions of this race-specific music could, as an alternative to dialect, give "Negro" poetry its "racial flavor," Johnson shows that he is just as willing to attribute racial specificity to musical sounds as Lanier was to attribute racial specificity to the sounds of poetic speech.

The relationship I am drawing between Johnson's racialized "musical tune" and Lanier's racialized "speech tune" in some respects resembles the one I presented in the previous chapter between Lanier and Du Bois: each viewed songs – Lanier's "Battle Songs" and Du Bois's "Sorrow Songs" – as embodying racial sounds, the sounds not of the British and American nations (as was proposed by Whitman and Dvořák) but, respectively, of the Anglo-Saxon and "Negro" races. Johnson was profoundly influenced by Du Bois's *The Souls of Black Folk*,[12] so it should come as no surprise that both Johnson and Du Bois bear a similar relation to Lanier. But the relationship I am drawing here between Lanier and Johnson, while likewise concerned with a color line in sounds, nevertheless extends this concern in an important respect. This extension is apparent in Johnson's suggestion that the distinctiveness of the "Negro" preachers' trombone-like voices might stem from "the innate grandiloquence of their old African tongues" (9). By describing this "grandiloquence" as "innate," Johnson implicates bodies, and not just poems (as in the previous chapter), as the source of racial sounds; "innate" to bodies, race is imagined to cause bodies to produce certain effects, including sound effects. In the pages that follow I will demonstrate that Johnson's impulse to attribute racial poetic effects to the "innate" instincts of racial bodies stems from an historical development arising between Lanier and Johnson, one that subsumes the literary "science" in Lanier's *The Science of English Verse* within an emerging medical "science" of "racial instincts." Through a careful examination of the medical literature of the time I will demonstrate that late nineteenth-century doctors posited "race" as an invisible cause for a variety of bodily effects, effects that ultimately stemmed from heredity or environment but that seemed, to these doctors, to be race-specific, attributable to an invisible racial agency somewhere "in the blood." Writing in 1896, the same year in which *Plessy v. Ferguson* invoked "racial instincts" as a justification for making the "one-drop rule" the law of the land, Dr. Rudolph Matas conceded, "The truth of the matter is, the comparative hæmatology of the races still awaits a pioneer investigator."[13] A genuinely scientific understanding of the body was thus never part of this discussion. In the absence of this biological data, what served to sustain the medical community's conviction that bodies are innately racial, I will show, was the mistaken belief among physicians that observable bodily effects were being caused by the remote, extra-corporeal agency of racial instincts, an agency doctors described as an "occult condition" exerting its force on bodies. Physicians imagined that by discerning its various effects on the body, they could disclose this otherwise invisible "occult condition" of racial instinct. Through these visible bodily manifestations, racial instinct, or "blood," could be made to "tell."

The bodily effects serving this racially indexical function were not only epidemiological and anatomical but also, I will show, poetical. That is, as the contemporary commitment to racial instincts extended outside the medical community, the range of bodily effects imagined to be capable of disclosing racial instincts expanded to include a variety of poetic effects, including the "innate" "racial flavor" Johnson associates with the poems of *God's Trombones*. Once they become subsumed within the discussion of racial bodies, and thus understood as an effect of these supposedly innate "racial instincts," poetic effects take on a function that they did not serve in the earlier discussion of Sidney Lanier and W. E. B. Du Bois: poetic effects provide diagnostic symptoms of a body's racial identity.[14] Not only for James Weldon Johnson but also, I will show, for novelist Benjamin Rush Davenport, poet Vachel Lindsay, and music critic Henry Krehbiel, the otherwise invisible racial instincts of bodies are imagined to become apparent through the poetic effects used by bodies – bodies like those of Johnson's "Negro preachers" and, by extension, Johnson himself. By casting poetic effects in this light, as diagnostic symptoms of bodily racial instincts, writers like Johnson lend credence to a supposedly "scientific" notion that bodies themselves stubbornly refused to confirm, the notion that racial instincts could be attributed to persons. Seeming to provide additional ways to discern racial instincts, this racial poetics becomes an accessory to the medical community's effort – today widely discredited as futile – to ground racial identities in bodies.[15]

Yet this racial poetics proves to be more than just an accessory to racial medicine. While poems were, like bodies, imagined to disclose racial instincts, the analysis of poems nevertheless retained a certain degree of disciplinary independence from the medical community's analysis of bodies. Instead of requiring a microscope or a scalpel, poems required the knowledge and tools of the literary critic in order for their race-specific effects to be disclosed. Thus poetic criticism developed its own, relatively autonomous discourse of racial diagnostics, the literary critical discourse evident in James Weldon Johnson's notion of "racial flavor." Given this relative independence of racial poetics from racial medicine, many challenges to racial medicine do not extend into the domain of racial poetics. Thus while corporeal effects such as race-specific differences in epidemiology or anatomy have gradually ceased to be attributed to racial instincts, poetic effects like the "racial flavor" of Johnson's *God's Trombones* have continued to be treated as diagnostic signs of racial instinct, as ways of making blood tell. As a result, the notion of racial instinct has persisted within literary criticism, and specifically, I will show, within accounts of James Weldon Johnson and the poetry of the Harlem Renaissance. Although this literary discourse of racial poetics has come to seem separable from medicine, it perpetuates, I argue, the impulse it once shared with late-nineteenth-century medicine, the impulse to identify diagnostic signs of racial instinct, signs that cause the body's racial "blood" to "tell."

RACIAL INSTINCTS

Looking back upon his *The Souls of Black Folk* (1903) in the year following its publication, W. E. B. Du Bois asserts that the book's "style is tropical – African. This needs no apology. The blood of my fathers spoke through me and cast off the English restraint of my training and surroundings."[16] Du Bois's "training and surroundings" – a Massachusetts upbringing and a Harvard education – closely resemble those of Walter Burton, the central character in Benjamin Rush Davenport's 1902 novel *Blood Will Tell* (1902).[17] Burton is a Harvard graduate who, having lived in Boston for fifteen years, marries into an old Anglo-Saxon family. Not long afterward, however, the "trace of negro blood" (6) in Burton's veins begins to assert itself, much as the "blood of my fathers spoke through" Du Bois as he wrote *Souls*. The parallel I am drawing between Du Bois and Davenport should not obscure the radically different attitudes of these writers toward African-Americans – a celebratory attitude in Du Bois's case and a derogatory one in Davenport's. Neither should we be blind to the profound ethical and historical differences in the positions of these two writers – Du Bois, struggling to come to terms with the legacy of slavery and enduring racism in the United States, Davenport seeking to perpetuate that very oppression.[18] Yet this difference in attitude, I want to emphasize, does not prevent Du Bois and Davenport from advancing a common stance, a commitment to racial instincts. Thus just as Du Bois is led, by the "blood of [his] fathers," to "cast off the English restraint of my training and surroundings," so too does Burton ultimately "stand forth stripped of the acquired veneering created by the culture of the white race" (247). And if Du Bois's "tropical – African" style "needs no apology," so too does Burton come to "rather enjoy the relapses into my natural self" (255), relapses that permit him to set aside "an artificial existence" (255) as a white man and embrace what he had long "repressed" (303) behind a "concealing veil" (130), "my nature as a negro" (251).

For Burton, this Negro "nature" reveals itself as "natural proclivities within me" (267): "movements, rhythmic but novel, fantastic, barbarous, jerked my limbs about in the measure of some savage dance" (127–28). This focus on "rhythmic . . . measure" as the basis for racial identity differs from the account we saw in Lanier in that these are rhythms in "limbs," not lines, persons, not poems. Lanier, we recall, understood the Anglo-Saxon rhythmic tradition in explicitly textual terms, as a literary lineage; thus in an essay on tenth-century Anglo-Saxon poetry he asserts, "Surely it is time our popular culture were *cited* into the presence of the Fathers."[19] Lanier goes on, through extensive quotations, to do precisely this, explaining that "our tongue [must] recur to the robust forms – and from these to the underlying and determining genius – of its Anglo-Saxon period" (296). Such literary citation is indeed all too rare for Lanier, who asks, "Why have we no nursery songs of Beowulf and Grendel? Why does not the serious education of every English-speaking boy commence, as a matter of course, with the Anglo-Saxon grammar? . . . For the absence of this primal Anglicism from our modern system goes . . . to the very root of culture" (292). Here the "root of culture" – of "primal Anglicism" – is not blood but *Beowulf*, and when educational programs neglect Anglo-Saxon texts in favor of the *Iliad*, the result is that "We do not bring with us out of our childhood the fibre of idiomatic English which our fathers bequeathed to us" (292).

For Davenport, by contrast, the method of bequeathing primal Negro rhythms is not this "literary lineage" but rather a biological one, so while Lanier issued several boys' editions of Anglo-Saxon poems to ensure their future availability and influence,[20] Davenport's Walter Burton needs no such textual mediation to accede to "those innate characteristics inherited by him from his ancestors" (266). In fact, the inevitable rhythmic expression of his biological inheritance leads Burton to conclude that texts like Lanier's are ultimately irrelevant to his racial identity: "The acquirement of the education, culture and refinement of the white race has made no change in my blood and inherent instincts. I am ever a negro" (250). Thus while Davenport describes Burton's link to the Negro people as "a scientific problem" (150), this is not the same science addressed in Lanier's *The Science of English Verse*, for Burton's "innate" (268) proclivity for Negro rhythm manifests itself at the "physical" (237) site of his body, not the textual site of a poem: "I saw clearly," Burton declares, "what produced the strange spells that for so long have mystified me. I am a negro. My blood and natural inclinations are those common to the descendants of Ham" (250). This tendency for the "things . . . inherent in Burton's blood" to "tell their story" (237) as the "strange spells" of rhythm is explained not through scansion but through "the science of ethnology" (142), so between Lanier's 1880 work and Davenport's 1902 novel a racialist corporeality replaces racialist textuality – Davenport's racial body replaces Lanier's racial poem.

This notion of racial instincts is evident not only in the writings of Du Bois and Davenport but also in the work of Nathaniel Southgate Shaler, professor of paleontology at Harvard University and, beginning in 1891, Dean of Harvard's Lawrence Scientific School. Throughout his career, Shaler worked to popularize emerging scientific knowledge, including the theory of race instincts.[21] Thus in his book *The Neighbor; a Natural History of Human Contacts* (1904),[22] published just one year after *Souls of Black Folk* and two years after *Blood Will Tell*, Shaler compares the "inorganic realm" (3) of "atoms" and "molecules" (2) with "living things" (3) in order to assert of the latter that they "inherit their experience with environment from their ancestors and are much affected by that experience" (4). This "previously inherited experience" is a "form of memory" (11) that, according to Shaler, constitutes "the ancient primal form of intelligence which acts without consciousness, and is blindly moved by the form of mental impulse we term instinctive" (19). Included among these instinctual memories are the cultural practices of specific tribal – and indeed racial – groups: "Within the tribal pale . . . . people . . . are certain to accumulate traditions. These take shape in literature, or in formulas of religion or other activities which may become the moral and intellectual life-blood of the folk, maintaining their life in its pristine quality . . . and making their extirpation almost impossible" (41). This Lamarkian stance allows Shaler to distinguish an individual's "acquired habit" (313) – the "English restraint" that Du Bois and Burton each cast aside – from "our inheritances of custom" (307) – the racial instincts that Du Bois and Burton each identify as their most natural self.[23]

The concept of "racial instincts" had already been endorsed in the Supreme Court's notorious ruling in *Plessy v. Ferguson* (1896),[24] and if this concept had come to seem acceptable to the court majority, to Du Bois, and to Davenport, this is due in no small measure to the earlier efforts of Shaler. As Joel Williamson observes, Shaler "wove the American race problem smoothly into the new science," a goal apparent in his 1884 *Atlantic Monthly* essay entitled "The Negro Problem."[25] There Shaler claims that those who promote racial equality see only an African-American's "outward aspect" but not "the inner man" (700) and thus "overlook the peculiarities of nature which belong to the negroes as a race. . . . The fundamental, or at least the most important, differences between them and our own race," Shaler asserts, "are in the proportions of the hereditary motives and the balance of native impulses within their minds" (700). By focusing on "motives and . . . impulses" transmitted by "the laws of inheritance" (697) Shaler posits racial instinct without offering any data to substantiate it. He would call for that data six years later when, again in the pages of *The Atlantic Monthly*, his essay "Science and the African Problem" (1890) raises "the question of the improvability of the lower races of mankind," a "question" that he hopes will occasion "systematic scientific effort" consistent with "the scientific method."[26] Accordingly, Shaler lists "certain very important lines of research. The first of these concerns the existing mental and physical condition of the negro race in this country, and a comparison of their state with that of their kindred who dwell in Africa" (40). To study "the negro race" regardless of geographic location, as a "kindred" entity whose integrity is preserved whether in Africa or America, is to posit not physical environment but race as the crux of the "problem,"and although Shaler's comparison ostensibly seeks "[a]ny evidence of real, deep-seated organic advance under his American condition" (41), he strongly doubts whether African-Americans can assimilate like other immigrant groups.[27] What he really seeks, then, is evidence of this failure to assimilate, and thus confirmation of African-Americans' ongoing connection to Africa. Gathering this evidence requires attention to the site and vehicle of inherited racial instincts, the racial body itself. Accordingly, Shaler gives a particularly medical focus to his research program: arguing that "the pathology of the race in different positions is a matter of great interest" (41), he urges attention to such areas as "anthropometry" (40) and "the matter of disease and longevity" (41).

Research in these two areas was already underway, but, as we will see, doctors who not only saw a correlation between race and "pathology" but also sought to explain that correlation faced a certain dilemma: the explanation they consistently invoked – racial instinct – was not itself a visible feature of the body. While they were confident about classifying bodies according to phenotypic differences and diagnosing those bodies' pathologies, they were unable to locate the agency causing race-specific pathologies. This should come as no surprise given that recent medical research increasingly explains the correlation between race and medical pathology by reference not to race instincts but to environmental factors. As one prominent medical researcher asserted in 1991, "ethnic and racial categories are among humanity's most dangerous inventions," so medical researchers ought to "ascribe[] cause-and-effect-relationships to factors that can actually be measured."[28] But for many doctors of the 1880s and 1890s, an inability to measure racial instinct in no way deterred their commitment to it as an explanation for race-specific health effects, thus demonstrating, as Nancy Kreiger has observed, that in a seemingly "neutral science" of empirical medicine, "politics . . . entered into the very practice, content, and even theory of the science itself."[29] To pursue their politics of racial segregation, these doctors advanced a medical model strikingly similar to another account of agency well-known at the time but seemingly at odds with these doctors' empiricist commitments, a model Davenport's novel describes as the "supernatural" (123) force of "Voo Doo" (83). As we will see, it is just such a remote racial force that doctors imagine to exert its sway over bodies, a force inducing those bodies to display the supposedly race-specific effects listed within Shaler's categories of "anthropometry" and "the matter of disease and longevity." It is this ultimately supernatural notion of racial instincts, I will argue, that comes to gain acceptance beyond the domain of medicine, permitting writers like Du Bois and particularly Davenport to follow the medical community's lead. Classifying not just a body's health and behavior but also its literary practice according to the racial instincts that supposedly caused them, Du Bois and Davenport treat poetic effects as – like "anthropometry" and "the matter of disease and longevity" – symptomatic of race's influence, allowing writing style to serve as diagnostic evidence that – as Du Bois asserts – the "blood of my fathers spoke through me."

"THIS MEDICAL MYSTERY OF THE NEGRO RACE"

A 1996 paper in a prominent medical journal poses the following question: "When we conduct analysis of the relationship between race and health status and find that one race group is at significantly greater risk for poor health, to what should we ascribe this finding?"[30] Still a genuine problem for today's medical researchers, this question was likewise of concern to those nineteenth-century doctors seeking to address what Shaler calls "the matter of disease and longevity."[31] As they notice the racial differentials in mortality statistics, medical researchers from both the late nineteenth and the late twentieth centuries begin to wonder whether this pattern can be explained by environmental factors or whether race itself is the cause. While more recent doctors have tended to favor environmental explanations and to dismiss "the fabrication of race,"[32] nineteenth-century doctors showed a greater willingness to consider race itself as a causal force. Thus in an 1875 issue of the *Virginia Medical Monthly* Dr. L. S. Joynes notes that "The greater liability of the negro to [tuberculosis], has attracted the special attention of medical men, many of whom have strongly insisted that such greater liability is to be referred to the influence of race – that the negro more frequently falls a victim to pulmonary consumption and other tubercular diseases, *because he is a negro*."[33] Over a decade later, in 1888, Dr. J. Wellington Byers raised this same issue in the *Medical and Surgical Journal*, showing no hesitation in attributing differential disease rates to a racial predisposition: "One important question associated with the statements set forth in the mortality tables of this paper, is how far the excessive mortality is due directly to the influence of racial characteristics, that is, to less actual vital capacity to resist disease and death, or to peculiar susceptibility to certain forms of disease. We are qualified to state that the observations here presented are sufficient to warrant the assertion that the high rate of mortality of this race is certainly due more to inherent weakness or physical degeneracy than to any special faults in the environment."[34] These and many other statements reveal that the influence of race as such, as distinct from environment, had become a focus of increasing medical attention.[35]

One of the most prominent nineteenth-century studies of these differential disease rates was conducted by Frederick L. Hoffman on behalf of life insurance companies, organizations who sought to adjust their premiums in accordance with race-specific mortality rates.[36] These insurance companies, however, were not responsible for treating disease, only for maximizing profit through accurate projections of its impact. But for many doctors the matter could not end there. Thus while they often, as we have seen, agreed with Hoffman's claim that "The effect of the conditions of life is . . . comparatively unimportant, while to the effect of race and heredity are largely due the existing differences in the mortality of the two races,"[37] they held that the "effect of race and heredity" was not simply to be predicted but must also be analyzed. Dr. Eugene R. Corson, for instance, undertakes "a study of the physical status of the race, their morbid tendencies, and their mortality compared with that of the whites," arguing that "the morbific tendencies which produce these racial differences come directly before the observing physician, and they soon become . . . evident. . . . I therefore purpose to show more plainly the sources of this greater mortality among the colored."[38] For doctors like Corson, a race's "morbific tendencies" were not just to be calculated but also to be traced to their "sources," and while he joined many physicians in a fundamental pessimism about the potential to mitigate these tendencies,[39] he nevertheless recognized that his role as a physician placed him in a particularly good position to clarify this corporeal aspect of the "Negro problem."

The physician's search for "sources" was made more complex by statistics which revealed the racial body to have a large variety of both immunities and predispositions to disease. As one journal article observed in 1890, "The negro is known to be less susceptible to malarial fevers and to scarlet fever than is his white brother, but more prone to strumous and scrofulous affections of all kinds."[40] Other writers sought to add to this list,[41] but as they did so they also puzzled over what J. Morrison Ray calls this pattern of "peculiar, indescribable immunity": "It appears inexplicable that such a disease as trachoma, the bacterial origin of which seems conclusively proved, and which observation teaches is undoubtedly contagious, should show an aversion for the conjunctiva in the negro. . . . [W]e see no reason why the negro should escape."[42] The problem with imagining a bacterial "aversion for the conjunctiva in the negro," according to Ray, is that this and other bacterial aversions are accompanied, paradoxically, by bacterial preferences: "the negro race is remarkably prone to certain forms of eye inflammation, and, on the other hand, presents an apparently complete immunity from certain others" (87). How can the tissues of African-Americans be both immune, and vulnerable – both strong and weak – at the same time?[43] Having ruled out environmental factors, these doctors now begin to suspect that racial bodies cannot be evaluated according to a common scale of strength and weakness (i.e. all whites uniformly stronger than blacks, or all blacks uniformly stronger than whites). Instead, a pluralist approach to racial bodies seems to be in order.

One step toward this pluralist approach to is to speak metaphorically, as in the work of Dr. Louis McLane Tiffany. Setting aside the question of how tissues are affected by bacteria, Tiffany thinks instead about how bacteria are affected by race, and he does this by describing races as distinct culture media for which certain types of bacteria have their own aversion or affinity:

> As in laboratory work it is a question of soil, as to whether potato, gelatin, or boullion is going to grow best certain infecting organisms of one kind or another; so can we learn by observation whether the white, dark, yellow, or red race is the best culture medium for certain infecting principles. The statistics which have been given are of a certain amount of interest, but this subject can only be studies by looking at the different individuals as so many laboratory culture media.[44]

According to this metaphor the bacteria still produce the disease and its symptoms, but the racial "soil" or "culture medium" regulates the disease rate, producing the bodily effects of immunity or predisposition according to whether it deters or encourages the growth of an infecting agent. By positing a medical multi-culture-ism, this metaphor seems to make the earlier "inexplicable" immunity more understandable: a disease like trachoma shows an "aversion for the conjunctiva in the negro" because African-Americans, as opposed to whites, offer the bacteria an inhospitable soil. It turns out that this soil metaphor was widespread among doctors seeking to understand how race might produce the simultaneous effects of disease susceptibility and immunity for a given race. For instance, Matas, speaking of tuberculosis, said that "this terrible plague has in the negro a most favorable soil for its development"; "he appears to be even a more favorable culture medium for the bacillus of tuberculosis than other races when placed under similar conditions of environment."[45] Another writer, Dr. Warwick M. Cowgill, likewise employs this figurative turn: "Why the negro does not have [trachoma] has been largely theorized on. Probably the explanation most largely entertained is that he is immune to this disease, that the conjunctiva of the negro does not present a soil suitable for the development of trachoma."[46]

Even as he acknowledges the widespread acceptance of this view, Cowgill seeks an alternative reason for this immunity, an "explanation that does not call for some unique quality of construction in the negro" (399). Cowgill's resistance highlights a problem with the turn to metaphor: the notion of race as a bacterial culture medium does not explain the observed immunities so much as it simply redescribes them, and doing so involves circular reasoning: bacteria are averse to African-Americans because they are averse to the African-American soil, i.e. to African-Americans. To avoid this circularity, the "soil" metaphor must come back to the body, and this returns us to the problem that occasioned the metaphor in the first place, the problem of identifying a "unique quality of construction in the negro" that might explain both resistance and susceptibility to bacterial disease.

Among those doctors who believed that a racial "soil" was producing the observed effects, there were a variety of speculations on its bodily foundation. For instance, a doctor writing in 1894 asserts that "there is something in the blood of the negro predisposing to the development of fibrous growths," concluding, "it may be laid down as a pathologic law, not heretofore enunciated, that there is some peculiarity in the dark-skinned races rendering them liable to growths of fibrous nature in a degree greatly exceeding that observed in the white race."[47] The focus here is not the growths themselves, but the force that encourages them, for their prevalence (as opposed to their mere presence) is symptomatic of race itself, providing diagnostic evidence that race – "something in the blood" – is exerting its influence at that bodily site. Similar formulations appear in the writings of Dr. William Benjamin Smith, who likewise attributes the racial regulation of disease to a force associated with but imperceptible in the body. Writing in 1905, he argues that the source of an apparently superior vitality in whites "need not reveal itself to any mass-measurements; it might hide away in the cells and the finest tissue; it might not be anatomic, but histotomic [i.e. cellular] only. . . . Black and White are sensibly the same."[48] The force that produces differences in disease susceptibility may not coincide with any visible "quality of construction" (hence "Black and White are sensibly the same"), so it is a supersensible force, Smith implies, that is responsible for differentials in disease susceptibility.

Even as he imagines a bodily correlate for his soil metaphor, this doctor's notion of a supersensible force "hid[den] away in the cells and the finest tissue" effectively directs attention away from the visible body. This implicit move from the sensible to the supersensible as an explanation for disease differentials is more explicit in the work of other contemporary doctors who assert that the racial force producing these effects on bodies is not itself reducible to those bodies. Thus in his 1890 article on African-American immunity to trachoma Dr. Swan M. Burnett argues that attention to the body's "pathological anatomy" – to "the changes in the conjunctival tissue as a result of the disease" – has only "obscured" the issue without producing successful treatments. But this failure did have "the negative value of causing us to look outside of the eye for the original cause of the affection." Once he looks "outside the eye" itself for an understanding of the disease, the doctor concludes that "The only factor that can be considered is that of race, with its powerful influence in predisposing to or giving immunity from the operation of morbid processes. The influence of race is marked, and I presume will not be doubted by anyone." Burnett concludes that "Trachoma must be something more than a local disease." This redirection of attention away from the eye, and from the "local" context of the body itself, carries great practical significance: "The influence of this view of the pathology of trachoma upon our therapeutics must, it seems to me, be radical. We should cease to treat merely the local manifestation of the disease and should turn our attention to the diathesis [i.e. constitutional predisposition] lying back of it."[49] This claim is indeed "radical": if the predisposition stems from the "influence of race," the proper object of medical attention is not bacterial interaction with eye tissue but rather the promotion of that interaction by something "outside the eye," the remote agency of race itself. This formulation not only moves beyond mere metaphor, transforming a figure for racial effects ("soil") into an actual agent ("race, with its powerful influence"), it also displaces that agent from its presumed location in the body's tissues.

The impulse to imagine race as a remote agency producing local effects on bodies is even more clearly present in an article by Dr. W. A. Dixon published first in 1892 in *Medical News* and reprinted the next year in *The Journal of the American Medical Association*. Dixon's concern is a supposed "constitutional" weakness among mulattos, and he holds that this weakness must be explained by looking "beyond the microbe or bacillus." Dixon thus speaks disparagingly of "the scientist with his microscope hunting for the enemy of life and health in the sputa, the excreta and the cell elements, when in fact the modification of the racial type, by the influence of some media not apparent in the cell elements themselves, altered in some way by the process of miscegenation, generates this virus – these microbes, these bacilli, which claim for their victims more than 25 per cent of the dying."[50] Here it is metaphorical microbes that are held responsible for higher than normal susceptibility to the ravages of actual microbes, and those metaphorical microbes are attributed to an agency quite distinct from either a bacillus or "the cell elements themselves," for they are "generate[d]" by "the cross of races," as if a "racial type" were resisting its modification. Dixon claims that physician scientists are wasting their time unless they recognize the "importance of looking back beyond the bacillus" to the force exerted by race in producing unusual susceptibility to disease.

As they "look back beyond the bacillus" for this unlocatable influence of race, some doctors even start describing it in distinctly supernatural terms. In an 1891 article from *The Alabama Medical and Surgical Age* a doctor observes that "Irregular hours, irregular living, exposure when illy clad, and meagerly fed, are necessarily also potent factors, but do not and cannot explain the specially great and increased mortality among the negroes of this section of the country. Some supreme law, far greater than the aggregate of all these latter, is doing its deadly work at a terrible rate."[51] An article appearing three years later repeats this notion of a "supreme law" distinct from the body but producing effects in the body. Focusing specifically on African-American convicts, it suggests, first, that "there is something in or about the negro . . . that prompts him to acts of crime" and that, second, "there is something in him that more greatly predisposes him to disease; or that aggravates the type of disease."[52] Leaving the violence-causing "something" to the attention of "the moralist," the author takes up the second, disease-causing "something" as "a problem of absorbing interest" "to those who are responsible for his health and life" (113). But later he returns to the violence-causing "something," calling it an "occult condition which we do not understand . . . that operates upon the mind in such a way as to suggest crime" (116). This "occult condition" then undoes his earlier distinction between violence and disease as it assumes responsibility for both: "is it not logical to conclude that this occult condition would affect, in some way, the physical condition also?" (116). Race itself becomes an "occult condition," the single source of both pathology and crime, a seemingly supernatural force lurking beyond the range of empirical investigation but producing observable effects on the body.

Anticipating these suggestions of an "occult condition" responsible for immunity and susceptibility to disease is an article appearing in the *New York Medical Journal* in 1886. The author, Dr. F. Tipton, considers the possibility that environment might be responsible for high African-American susceptibility to tuberculosis but then notes that the disease "finds its richest holocaust" in "the better class of these people," African-Americans whose living conditions resemble those of the less-susceptible whites. Thus Tipton is in search of something peculiar to "the soil" of African-Americans: "there is an undiscovered something still behind all this silently working . . . and this is why I opened this paragraph by the remark that no satisfactory reason had yet been offered to explain away this medical mystery of the negro race." Like the "supreme law," the "something in the blood," or the "occult condition which we do not understand," this "undiscovered something" remains a "mystery" even as it asserts a genuine force. A few paragraphs later the doctor registers an apparently unrelated complaint about his African-American patients, noting that they

> are still victims of superstition and "voodooism" to the last degree, and this often seriously interferes with the proper administration of remedies in sickness. . . . When any of them are "*conjured*" or "*kungered*," as they term being bewitched, no kind of treatment will benefit them till the charm is broken. . . . the "conjure-bag" must be found or he will die.[53]

This pejorative invocation of voodoo reflects a common tendency of the time to equate it with witchcraft or sorcery.[54] The point, however, is not Tipton's prejudice but his implication in what he condemns: the bewitching discussed here closely resembles the "medical mystery of the negro race" to which he earlier refers. Race, as he imagines it, acts just like this "conjure-bag," as "an undiscovered something still behind all this silently working" to produce the "charm" of race-specific susceptibility or immunity. Race, like the conjure-bag, is associated with the body of "the Negro" (who "must pass over" the bag before "he falls sick" [571]) but, like the "conjure-bag," race remains distinct from and not localizable in the body itself. By setting out to find the conjure bag of race, Tipton and the other doctors posit race as a remote agency producing local effects, and in doing so they participate in the very supernatural logic they denigrate. Intending to follow Shaler's call for "scientific" research into "the matter of disease and longevity," these doctors cling so tenaciously to the idea of racial difference that their effort to locate it takes them beyond empiricism into the realm of the supernatural.[55]

Having seen this turn to supernatural agency in the first category of Shaler's proposed research program, we will quickly see how his second category, what he calls "anthropometry," or measurements of anatomy, takes a similarly supernatural turn. The study of race-specific anthropometry struck Dr. Middleton Michel, writing in 1892, as a task particularly suited to the physician:

> The degree of interest now centered upon the negro in his social, political, and racial relations to the white man demands that he shall have his special history clearly established and written. To the medical scientist particularly we look for the supposed racial distinctions that are to individualize him. . . . Interest in this question, of course, centers in any determinate pathologic or anatomic peculiarity; in any fixed organic difference always to be recognized, classic and distinctive.[56]

An anatomical feature both necessary and sufficient to establish racial identity would be, Michel notes, "of the greatest moment in all ethnologic inquiries," for it would produce an identity between a physical trait and race as such, making the one reducible to the other.[57] Such a feature would be sufficient, in itself, to draw the color line. An 1894 article indicates just how much attention was given to this search for a "determinate . . . peculiarity," noting that "the Association of American Anatomists has taken this question in hand and has issued a circular asking that practical anatomists give their attention to it, and keep careful record of all variations and anomalies."[58] But even as Michel envisions this ideal, he must correct several "erroneous statements advanced respecting peculiarities supposed to distinguish the negro from the Caucasian," statements which "show great neglect of accurate research."[59] Other doctors engaged in this research likewise found erroneous claims for a "determinant peculiarity." Skin color is perhaps the most significant example, for it ultimately failed to function in this way.[60] Several other anatomical features, including eyes,[61] hymen,[62] muscles,[63] flat foot, chorea, and keloid,[64] were likewise proposed, each failing to become this definitive marker of race. In every instance, race fails to be reducible to a single anatomical feature.

But if not *reducible* to any one feature, race might nevertheless be *signaled* by those features, in much the same way – as we saw above – that the "occult condition" of race registered itself in the differential impact of disease. Viewed in this way, anatomical features could be understood as the effects of a racial cause. It is this idea that led anatomists to search the body not for a "determinant peculiarity" but for anatomical atavisms, features that could be read as the mark of race's ongoing potential to exert its influence upon the body. In 1896, for instance, Dr. D. K. Shute's "Racial Anatomical Peculiarities" asserts that ". . . it is important to note in the different races the . . . percentage of relapse into more primitive conditions," where these more primitive conditions are understood as physical coincidences with the earlier evolutionary ancestor, anthropoid apes.[65] Many doctors claimed to have found anatomical variations that suggested such relapses.[66] This notion of registering race in the body through its effects – through race's ability to induce atavisms – was central to the argument of William Lee Howard, whose 1904 article in *Medical News* asserts, "It is not necessary here to dwell on the main anatomical points of difference that are known to exist between the Caucasian and the African. These variations show conclusively to the student ineradicable racial traits. The phylogeny of the negro will exert itself under all conditions."[67] By ascribing anatomical differences to the exertions of "phylogeny," Howard demonstrates how the study of anthropometry begins to look beyond the body itself for the racial force responsible for producing that body's anatomy.

Anticipating Howard by some four years is a paper by Dr. Paul Barringer read before the Tri-State Medical Association of Virginia and the Carolinas.[68] Barringer's paper uses the term "phylogeny" not only to assert "the existence of the force we call 'heredity' in life" but also to cast that heredity force in specifically racial terms: "There is a short, crisp biological axiom which reads 'the ontogeny is the repetition of the phylogeny.' This axiom literally translated, means, 'the life history is the repetition of the race history'" (437). While exertions of this racial heredity, or racial instinct, are held responsible for producing the atavisms evident to anthropometry, Barringer extends phylogeny's force beyond mere anatomy into the domain of behavior: "The above axiom covers more than simple heredity, as we shall see," for "this tendency to repeat is not only structural, but physiological and psychic as well" (437). Just as phylogeny perpetuates racial ancestors' anatomy, so it perpetuates their customary activities, and for Barringer the salient activities customary to African-American phylogeny are "murder, lust and rape" (442). Barringer was not alone in expanding the range of racial phylogeny's effects to include such actions,[69] and we have already seen that doctors were inclined to hold the "occult condition" of race responsible not only for differential disease rates but also for crime. It appears, then, that these two branches of Shaler's research program are converging upon a single notion of racial instinct: not itself local to the body, it is an extra-corporeal "force" that produces in bodies a variety of race-specific effects, effects that for African-Americans supposedly include immunity from some bacterial infection, susceptibility to anatomical atavisms, and propensities for certain criminal behaviors. As these doctors respond to Shaler's call for scientific research, they seemingly confirm his presumptions of racial instincts, but doing so requires them to locate those instincts in a supernatural realm, well beyond the bacillus.

HAITIAN AND NEW ENGLAND VOODOO

A concern with this sort of supernatural agency was not unique to doctors of the period, for this kind of force likewise figures prominently in Davenport's novel *Blood Will Tell.* Walter Burton's ultimate embrace of "my nature as a negro" (251) results from the "relentless influence" (125) of his "inherent instincts" (250) driving him toward a "pure spirit of religion" (302), a condition the novel associates with "the worshipers of Voo Doo" (269). As we have seen, Shaler's *The Neighbor* includes the "formulas of religion" among the "traditions" that are passed along as a race's inherited instincts, instincts whose "extirpation [is] almost impossible" (41), and Burton's inclination to voodoo is presented in a similar light. He initially resists these inclinations, imagining them to be "foreign to my natural self" (50), a self he associates with the "refinement, culture and manners" (251) that he has acquired living among whites in Boston. But there soon ensues a "struggle in the dual nature of the man between the contending forces of the innate and the acquired" (268), and the acquired refinement that had once seemed so natural now strikes him as a "farce" (249): "I may have every outward and visible sign but the inward and spiritual grace of the white race is not and can never be mine. I am a wretched sham, fraud and libel upon the white race with my fair skin and affected manner" (250). Burton finally overthrows this imposture when he turns to the practices of his "great-grandmother" (267), Mother Sybella, the "High Priestess" of a "temple of Voo Doo" (83) on the island of Haiti. After a short period of watching her conduct a voodoo ceremony, he can no longer resist joining in as a "howling dancer" (276): "Yells of long pent-up savage fury rang through the dank night air, as Burton threw back his head and whooped in barbarous license" (276). Joining in the voodoo ceremony – as opposed to his earlier practice of singing German opera (58, 163) and dancing waltzes (61) – makes him a "reclaimed scion of the negro race" (277) and brings him in contact, finally, with "my own people" (264, 267), the black inhabitants of Haiti.

As one of Haiti's reclaimed sons, Burton rehearses at the site of his body a narrative that many contemporary writers were telling about the island nation of Haiti itself, a narrative, as Frederick Douglass summarizes it, in which "the Negro, left to himself, lapses into barbarism" (483).[70] Douglass invokes this narrative in his dedication speech for the Haitian Pavilion at the 1893 Chicago World's fair, and having recently completed two years of service (from 1889 to 1891) as the United States Minister-Resident and Consul-General to the Haitian Republic, he offers personal experience to counter the "argument as stated against Haiti, . . . that since her freedom . . . .voodooism, fetichism, serpent-worship and cannibalism are prevalent there; that little children are fatted for slaughter and offered as sacrifices to their voodoo deities" (480–81). Concurring with "[t]hose who have studied the history of civilization" in their "profound philosophical generalization . . . that men are governed by their antecedents" (487), Douglass attributes to Haiti a past which highlights "the Negro's courage . . . [and] intelligence" (486).[71] But if this version of the past portends "hope for Haiti" (487), many others see different antecedents and thus different prospects.[72] Among these is Shaler, whose early contributions to *The Atlantic Monthly* invoke this narrative of Haiti's "lapses into barbarism"[73] and whose *The Neighbor* extends this narrative to "the lamentable decade following the Civil War, the so-called period of reconstruction," describing it as a time when "the Negroes . . . were evidently possessed by the Haytian motive" (138), a condition in which, "immediately on attaining independence, the population began to return to the African condition" (137). It is this extension of the Haitian threat into the US that Davenport novelizes in *Blood Will Tell*: not only does Burton's blood cause him to "breed[] back to the type of a remote ancestor" (8), producing a child with "features of an apish cast" (216), but Burton himself is driven to commit the "nameless crime" of rape and murder (296). Encapsulating in his body the dominant narrative of Haitian degeneration, Walter Burton predicts the fate of all those like him in the US, whether in the South or North, whether visibly black or able – like Burton, with his 1/8 black blood – to pass as white. The warning is clear: when white New England women marry such men, their husbands, however "cultured" (42) they seem, however able to mimic the ways of whites, will inevitably repeat in their bodies the narrative of Haiti: "That granite cliff of Christianity whereon I builded my castle of morality, that bastion of education, those redoubts of refinement. . . . are trembling and toppling, undermined by the waves of that inexplicable, relentless influence" (125). Despite his embrace of New England Christianity, Burton is irresistibly drawn to Haitian voodoo.

But to cast voodoo simply in these terms – as an ancestral inheritance that, along with susceptibility to disease, affects those with even a drop of black blood – is to miss the force of the account of voodoo offered in the previous section. The point of showing medical journals deploying the supernatural logic of voodoo was to demonstrate that, instead of being one of the many racial instincts attributed specifically to blacks, voodoo provides doctors with the general logic explaining how anyone, whether white or black, could have a racial inheritance. My point about the role of voodoo in these texts, in other words, is not that, for those with black ancestors, it constitutes what they instinctively do, but that regardless of race, voodoo enables people to imagine what they do as properly their own, as an expression of their "natural self." In effect, if one's racial past asserts itself as a remote agency producing local bodily effects, effects ranging from disease immunity to an inclination to practice certain religious rites, then the influence to which one is subject is the race to which one belongs. Much as one may resist, this agency will have its way, and such a condition of subjection to a remote force amounts to a form of possession, something voodoo readily explains.[74] Shaler, we have seen, invokes the language of possession in *The Neighbor* when he speaks of Reconstruction as a time when blacks were "possessed by the Haytian motive" (138), and later in the same text he speaks of "the state designated of old as 'possession'" (302), describing it as a "hypnotic condition" brought about by "certain incantation-like modes of speech" (302), much like the "droning monotonous incantations" (271) of Mother Sybella's voodoo rite. But if the phrase "of old" seems to separate possession from Shaler's more modern science of racial instinct, we can nevertheless see the link between the two: regardless of how one may appear, one's race is determined by the set of racial instincts by which one is possessed. Thus if blacks and whites are possessed by different racial pasts, the one thing they do have in common is this condition of possession, so voodoo possession provides the universal mechanism, not merely the race-specific content, of racial inheritance. While Shaler attributes racial instincts to whites,[75] he, like the doctors discussed above, obscures white possession behind the euphemisms of scientific vocabulary. It is Davenport's novel *Blood Will Tell* that most explicitly articulates how voodoo possession provides both races, black and white, with the logic and agency necessary for the transmission of racial instincts.

Davenport's Walter Burton is convinced that "in the home of the Dunlaps," the Anglo-Saxon family into which he will soon marry, "enlightenment has dispelled prejudice" (52), so "the fact that my mother was a quadroon" is "trivial" (51): "The idea of blood making any difference! Men are neither hounds nor horses!" (52). But among the Dunlaps such "enlightenment" is more "affectation" (10) than conviction: "Social equality may be all right," one of the senior Dunlaps asserts, "but where it leads to the intermarriage of the races all the Aryan in me protests against it" (10). Unable to prevent Burton from marrying their daughter Lucy, the two senior J. Dunlaps (the twin brothers James and John [4]) watch in dismay as Burton tries with decreasing success to hide a sequence of troubling episodes, episodes during which "there seems to come a strange inexplicable spell over my spirit – a something that is beyond my control. A madness seems to possess my very soul" (50). Unable to recall "the feeling that possessed me" (123), Burton proves no more successful than the doctors of the period in his effort to identify the source: "Could I but hold that sensation that steals upon me, while my mental powers are yet unimpaired by its presence, I might make a diagnosis of the disease, analyze the cause and produce the remedy, but my attempts are always futile" (124). Burton's rational – indeed, medical – analysis is defeated as his few drops of blood, which had seemed to be a "scientific problem" (150), turn out to be a supernatural one: "Mother Sybella, who has proven herself my great-grandmother, ... seems to possess hypnotic power over my senses; she leads me by some magnetic influence that exerts control over the negro portion of my nature" (267). Using "incantations" (271) and a "drum upon which she beat at short intervals" (270), Mother Sybella is able to induce "Tu Konk, the Voo Doo divinity" (276) to become "re-incarnate" (274) in a serpent, and she affects Burton's body in the same way. As she projects her incantations across the distance separating herself (in Haiti) from Burton (in Boston) she renders Burton "powerless to control myself" (126): "Wild and ribald songs burst from my lips, hilarious and lascivious music poured from the instruments that I touched, movements, rhythmic but novel, fantastic, barbarous, jerked my limbs about in the measure of some savage dance" (127–28). These episodes escalate, as we have seen, into his full participation in the voodoo ceremony as a "howling dancer" (276), so if he had resisted the earlier comparison between himself and horses, he has now become a horse of another kind, the riderless horse of voodoo possession.[76] The notion set out here of a remote racial agency producing visible effects at the site of the body is logically consistent with the accounts of doctors trying to look beyond the bacillus to find a remote agent responsible for the racial body's immunity and susceptibility to disease. While the doctors didn't know where it was or what it should be called, Davenport has given it a local habitation (Haiti) and a name (Tu Konk).

As Davenport sets out this account of racial agency, he applies it to the cultural inheritance of Anglo-Saxons as well, so even as he consistently distinguishes blacks and Anglo-Saxons along lines of class, gender, and race, he nevertheless characterizes each according to a single logic in which racial identity involves susceptibility to ancestral possession. For instance, Mother Sybella and the house of J. Dunlap each react to disruptions in family continuity: when Walter Burton marries Lucy Dunlap, he not only removes himself from Sybella's "negro" tradition (as Sybella chants, "One drop left to me now gone to white cow" [85]) but he also prevents Lucy from marrying her cousin, the Anglo-Saxon Jack Dunlap, who would become the next "J. Dunlap." As each family – i.e. race – seeks to resolve this disruption, many other similarities become apparent: in Haiti, Sybella discusses her family's continuity while "the blaze of the burning fagots cast a glow over the grewsome interior of this temple of Voo Doo" (83); in Boston, the Dunlap elders discuss their family's future "before a large grate heaped high with blazing cannel coal" (4) within the private office of the J. Dunlap firm, "the *sanctum sanctorum* in this temple of trade" (4). Each of these flame-lit "temples," furthermore, has its own presiding official: Sybella is the "High Priestess" in the "temple of Voo Doo" (83), and Mr. Chapman, the Superintendent of the J. Dunlap firm, is effectively the house's head priest, treating the firm as "the chiefest idol of his religion and life" (37).[77] Each temple likewise has its presiding deity: the Haitian temple is a "lair where Tu Konk dwells" (83), and the Boston firm's "temple of trade" is presided over by identical "twins" (5), James and John Dunlap – "They are 'J. Dunlap'" (4). According to voodoo doctrine, identical twins are "*marassa*," a force even "more powerful than the *loa*,"[78] so instead of aligning New England Anglo-Saxons with Christianity, as against the voodoo of Haiti's "Negroes," Davenport aligns both races with voodoo, placing the *loa* Tu Konk on the side of the "Negroes" and the most powerful voodoo force – *marassa* – on the side of the Anglo-Saxons. In doing so, Davenport imagines the competition between "Negroes" and "Anglo-Saxons" in terms specific to voodoo.

Davenport extends these racial parallels into his description of the single heirs charged with restoring continuity to each racial family. Jack Dunlap, the only remaining male in the Dunlap line, initially refuses an invitation to join the J. Dunlap firm, telling his uncles that he is "a sailor by nature" and is thus "worthless in an office" (11). This initially seems like a problem for the Dunlap line since any change in the firm's founding name is deemed a "sacrilege" that "would surely have caused the rising in wrath of the long line of ghostly 'J. Dunaps' that had preceded" (4–5) (much as Sybella raised the wrath of Tu Konk to sabotage Burton's marriage to Lucy). But if Jack's refusal to join the firm seems like a departure from the family line, it is in fact the deepest form of continuity. The J. Dunlap firm traces its beginnings to the "early days of the Republic" (2) when it was founded by an "old trade pathfinder" who "had in a small way traded with the West Indian islands" (2), so Jack Dunlap's choice to engage in precisely these practices – "I am a sailor's son and have a sailor's soul" (70) – is not a departure from but, on the contrary, a deep continuity with the firm's ghostly founder: "'See that now!' exclaimed the listener. 'Blood will tell. The blood of some old Yankee sailor man named Dunlap spoke when our young kinsman made that reply. Breed back! Yes indeed we do'" (11) (just as Burton's blood breeds back to produce an ape-like child [216]). During his sailing exploits Jack encounters a foundering ship of Irish immigrants bound for Australia, and he risks his life to rescue a sick woman among them (118), a gesture that symbolically unites Americans, Irishmen, and Australians under the common banner of Anglo-Saxon. Upon hearing this story, one of the J. Dunlap elders observes that "the blood of a good old Yankee race . . . tells its story in noble deeds" (120) (much as the "things . . . inherent in Burton's blood . . . tell their story" [237] when he joins the voodoo ceremony). Indeed, Jack Dunlap's protective stance toward Anglo-Saxon women is not the only way in which Anglo-Saxon blood is imagined to tell. John Dunlap imagines that, if a member of his own family were raped he would, like his fellow Anglo-Saxons of the South, "forget about my calm theory of allowing the regular execution of justice . . . and be foremost in seeking quick revenge" through lynching (298). For both "Negroes" and "Anglo-Saxons," this novel imagines characters to be most forcefully themselves when they are subject to possession by their racially discrete ancestral pasts.

The account of possession that Davenport advances here, and that is suggested as well by physicians like Tipton and natural scientists like Shaler, differs in a variety of respects from the instances of possession that take place among actual practitioners of voodoo. Most notable among these differences is Davenport's requirement that possession be an event that causes "blood," or racially specific ancestry, to "tell." In most forms of voodoo practice, by contrast, the agents responsible for possession, the "*loa*" of the voodoo pantheon, are imagined as divine entities but, as Alfred Metreaux observes, they "are not always deified ancestors."[79] In those instances when the *loa* are imagined to be human predecessors, they are not restricted to possessing their lineal descendants; nor are they obliged to do so.[80] Thus within the ritual practice of voodoo, there need be no coincidence between the race of a given *loa* and the race of the body possessed by that *loa*.[81] For Davenport, however, this racial coincidence is precisely the point: the spirit by whom one is possessed is supposedly determined by one's "blood": racial "blood" makes one susceptible to possession by a racially specific ancestral past, and one's inevitable possession by that past serves, in turn, as a diagnostic sign that racial blood is present in one's body (causing even "one drop" of that "blood" – whether "Negro" or "Anglo-Saxon" – to "tell"). Given this emphasis on racial ancestry, Davenport's notion of possession thus looks less like voodoo and more like contemporary medical accounts of racial phylogeny or instinct. Davenport's goals become clear: hoping to buttress the account of racial instinct that medical research was failing to substantiate, Davenport, like Tipton and Shaler, appropriates the supernatural logic of voodoo in order to rewrite it as a way of diagnosing a body's racial instincts (and thus disclosing those who are genuinely "Anglo-Saxon" and those whose "Anglo-Saxonness" is "impure"). By imagining that voodoo possession adheres in this way to a color line, Davenport effectively deputizes the agents of possession as enforcers of racial segregation: by making "blood" tell, Davenport's *loa* prevent "Negroes" from passing as "Anglo-Saxons." This infiltration and appropriation of the voodoo pantheon, explicit in Davenport and implicit in writers like Shaler and Tipton, suggests that voodoo is not merely demonized but also adapted by those turn of the century United States writers, physicians, and scientists who are committed to making "blood" tell. In addition to these writers, we have seen another participant in this adapted logic of voodoo possession, the United States Supreme Court. When it asserts in *Plessy v. Ferguson* that "Legislation is powerless to eradicate racial instincts," the court defers to a power that contemporary writers like Davenport, Tipton, and Shaler were using voodoo to imagine: conceding that there are indeed "racial instincts," the court majority then claims to be "powerless" to exorcise these spirits from racial bodies. But in appearing merely to concede this supposedly scientific point about "racial instincts," the court in effect endorses the ultimately supernatural point about race-specific possession.[82] The seemingly "powerless" court thus makes quite a powerful move, not only instituting legal segregation in the United States but also, in the process, extending its jurisdiction outside the United States and into the voodoo pantheon in order to make racial segregation not just the law of the land but also the law of the *loa*.

ALLITERATION AND ONOMATOPOEIA

As he presents these instances of "Negro" and "Anglo-Saxon" possession, Davenport is careful to find evidence of racial possession within the realm of poetics, assigning to each race its own poetic effect that will serve as an expression of its racial instincts. The family of J. Dunlap, for instance, pays considerable attention to repeated first letters: "A maxim of the Dunlap family had been that there must always be a J. Dunlap, hence sons were ever christened John, James, Josiah, and such names only as furnished the everlasting J as the initial" (2). This interest in the "everlasting J" as the "initial" letter suggests that what connects family members (i.e. white Anglo-Saxons) over time is alliteration. Alliteration surfaces as well in the description of the J. Dunlap firm's accumulated capital: "There was not room on a single line in the Commercial Agency books to put A's enough to express the credit and financial resources of 'J. Dunlap' . . . . Absolutely beyond the s̲hoals and s̲hallows of the dangerous s̲hore of trade where small crafts f̲inancially are f̲orced to ply, 'J. Dunlap' sailed ever tranquil" (2–3; underlines added). Having described a long history of commercial credit as an alliterative sequences of "A's," the passage itself then exemplifies this poetic effect. Aligning alliteration with financial resources as part of the Dunlaps' family wealth suggests that the family also inherits a certain cultural capital, the alliterative verse that forms the core legacy of Anglo-Saxon poetry.[83] This legacy of alliteration is evident not only in the family's name and account books but also in the speech of other, fellow Anglo-Saxons. Thus an Anglo-Saxon character makes the following observation in response to a toast given by one of his friends: "I say! Tom, have you been studying up on alliteration? You rang in all the B's of the hive in that toast" (167). According to Tom, alliteration comes to him as a spontaneous and unconscious poetic impulse: "I don't require thought or study to become eloquent" (167).

Alliteration is also present in the speech of Walter Burton, appearing most prominently when his acquired Anglo-Saxonism initially seeks to resist the assertions of his innate "Negro" "natural self." Thus as he condemns his growing "Negro" inclinations, his words just happen – like those of the Anglo-Saxon Tom – to scan as alliterating lines of Anglo-Saxon poetry: "l̲ewdness, l̲asciviousness, b̲rutality, b̲eastliness and l̲icensed libidinousness lead to s̲avage s̲atiety" (128; underlines added). But since Burton's Anglo-Saxonism is ultimately not natural to him – since, that is, his civilized behavior results from "studying up" and is thus a "sham. . . . an artificial existence" (255) – his turn away from the acquired to the innate coincides with a turn away from this alliteration to another poetic effect, the sounds Davenport associates specifically with the "Negro," the sounds of "wild melody" (44). Burton is "a natural musician" (48) who produces sounds that, according to the classically trained ear of Chapman, are "musical screams of melodious frenzy, dying away in rhythmic cadence" (43), music that is "now wild and unbridled as the shriek of a panther, and then low, gentle and soothing as the murmuring of a peaceful brook" (44). Chapman's description, the narrator notes, "reproduced the sounds he sought to describe" (44). The words "shriek" and "murmuring," in other words, *are* the sounds they represent. As such, they constitute classic examples of onomatopoeia. Burton's "metamorphosis" (301) from seeming Anglo-Saxon to actual "Negro" is linked with a move from a "sham" use of alliteration to this new set of sounds that are natural to him, sounds that must be rendered onomatopoetically. Here we see the novel's racial logic mapped onto these two different textual effects, and doing so, for Davenport, extends into the domain of poetic effects the supernatural account of racial instinct that we have seen unfolding in the contemporary medical literature.

Why should Davenport turn to these sound effects, in particular, as diagnostic signs of racial instinct? The reason seems to be that these sounds lend themselves to the strict line of demarcation that Davenport wishes to draw between the "Negro" and the "Anglo-Saxon." One way of characterizing this difference between alliteration and onomatopoeia is to observe that each of these poetic effects appears to be concerned with a different moment in the formation of words. Onomatopoeia starts with sounds that are then introduced into language as words: the sounds of a shriek and a murmur are reproduced by phonically similar words, the onomatopoetic words "shriek" and "murmuring." Alliteration, by contrast, starts with words that, through their proximity, produce a residue of sound: in the phrase "back beyond the bacillus," for instance, the "b" sounds are generated from within language, arising as a consequence of the choice to place the *words* "back," "beyond," and "bacillus" in close proximity. In onomatopoeia, sounds *precede* words, a given sound's features dictating (or at least seeming to dictate) the kind of word by which the sound will be mimetically reproduced; in alliteration, by contrast, sounds are *occasioned by* words, the adjacent consonants and vowels of already-existing words serving to produce this supplemental sound effect.[84] As a phonic supplement to words, alliteration is nothing more than a secondary acoustic pattern that sometimes arises as sounds perform their primary semantic function as signs: the sounds stipulated to convey certain meanings (e.g. "back," "beyond," and "bacillus") also interact among themselves to produce a concurrent pattern of sounds. Alliteration, in other words, constitutes – to borrow a phrase from Robert Frost's poetics – the "sound of sense" (as opposed to the sounds of non-sense, the natural or musical sounds reproduced by onomatopoeia).[85] For some writers, alliteration's conjunction of words and their supplemental sound effects provides an opportunity for interaction, the words' sounds reinforcing their sense.[86] But for a writer like Davenport the association of these sound effects with a specific language, English, creates the opportunity for a different kind of interaction, where alliteration starts to look not like a parallel expression of the semantic sense but instead like an independent expression of the semantic system as such, English itself, and indeed like an embodiment of English's Anglo-Saxon tradition. That is, instead of serving to reinforce the words' meanings, alliteration can serve to confirm racial identity.[87]

This function of confirming racial identity is the role ultimately played by alliteration in Davenport's novel.[88] While the pairing of English words with Anglo-Saxon alliteration would seem to produce redundant identity criteria, demonstrating English identity *both* through compliance with the language's rules *and* through the presence of these supposedly Anglo-Saxon sounds, these seemingly redundant criteria are, in Davenport's view, quite distinct. Writing at a historical moment when the United States was trying to Americanize large groups of immigrants, which included helping them – among other things – to speak the language, Davenport and those like him who seek a racially "pure" United States fear that such superficial Americanization, while it may produce people who look and sound American, will leave many undesirable racial instincts intact. Shaler, for instance, speaks of the "endurance of ancestral quality . . . among folk who have been thoroughly Americanized" ("European Peasants," 654), and for both Shaler and Davenport the extreme case of such lingering ancestral residue is to be found in people of African descent, people like Davenport's Walter Burton. Although Burton can easily pass as white (his "skin is white" [250] and he can effect "the irreproachable demeanor of a cultured gentleman" [42]), he stands apart from "true" Anglo-Saxons, the alliteration in whose speech confirms – in the way white skin and proper English increasingly cannot – that they are pure Anglo-Saxons.[89]

Davenport, then, is using alliteration to confirm whether visibly white bodies – bodies like those of Walter Burton and Jack Dunlap – are truly Anglo-Saxon, and doing so involves a convergence in thinking about bodies and poems: if cultural practices like alliteration are extensions of race instincts, then the bodies subject to race instincts will display these cultural features. Blood will tell in alliteration. Thus alliteration marks an assertion of Anglo-Saxon antiquity at the locale of the body, and to be a true or "pure" Anglo-Saxon, a person must not only look white but also have the race instincts – the impulse to alliteration – to go with it.[90] This approach to alliteration – treating it as the traditional past asserting itself at the site of the body through these local sound effects – participates in the same supernatural thinking we saw in the doctors discussed above: they argued that since "Black and White are sensibly the same," identifying the source of the racially specific disease patterns requires looking "back beyond the bacillus" and indeed beyond the body itself in order to consider the "diathesis lying behind it," the remote force of racial instincts causing these local effects. Davenport seeks not to diagnose racial instincts through their local disease effects but to confirm racial instincts through their local sound effects, and for him the purity of the Anglo-Saxon tradition is confirmed by the poetic effect by which it is embodied, alliteration. What surviving trachoma indicates to doctors, speaking in alliteration indicates to Davenport, and in each case bodies are treated as sites for the expression of such race instincts.

As we have seen, the racially impure Burton finds alliteration to be inconsistent with his instincts as "a negro," and he is driven away from it toward sounds like "scream" and "murmuring," sounds whose linguistic representations are instances of onomatopoeia. Now if, as I have said, alliteration involves sounds that are supplements to words and onomatopoeia involves words that are reproductions of sounds, then the sounds of alliteration are always an *extension* of linguistic practice and thus have a history that is necessarily bound up with the use of language. The sounds of onomatopoeia, by contrast, need not be introduced into language at all and so always suggest an *intrusion* into language by mere sounds (here the "shrieks" and "murmurs" of panthers and brooks) that can be said to have a history independent of and prior to their *re*production in language. This suggests that while alliteration is redundant, its supposedly Anglo-Saxon sounds confirming the Anglo-Saxonness of the English speech – and speaker – with which it is associated, onomatopoeia is split, its dual status as word and sound perpetually threatening to undo the linguistic standing of the onomatopoetic word. Onomatopoeia, that is, is subject to a form of doubleness (or double consciousness): as words that represent sounds by reproducing those sounds, instances of onomatopoeia have the ever-present potential to return to their prior position outside of language, ceasing to be words that represent a sound and becoming, once again, the mere sound that prompted the onomatopoetic word in the first place. One can ever feel the two-ness of onomatopoeia as a word verges upon a mere "shriek," as the English language borders on mere "murmuring." This potential for onomatopoeia to revert to an earlier, pre-linguistic condition of mere sound reproduces, on the level of language and poetics, the logic that Davenport attributes to Walter Burton's body. While Burton may – like "shriek" or "murmuring" – seem to have a place within Anglo-Saxon institutions, he is only passing as an insider, for he – like these seeming words that are "really" just sounds – has a separate and prior existence, an autonomy apart, his "natural self": "The acquirement of the education, culture and refinement of the white race has made no change in my blood and inherent instincts. I am ever a negro" (250).

The apparent return of these sound-mimicking words to their initial status as mere sound seems, at first, to involve removing them from the domain of culture and relegating them to the domain of nature – the shriek is associated with the "panther" and the murmuring is linked to "brooks." And this would seem to suggest that the corporeal parallel of onomatopoeic words – Walter Burton's sham existence as an Anglo-Saxon – should likewise prompt the same gesture, removing him from culture and relegating him to nature: "I ate and drank more as an untutored tribesman of the jungle than a civilized citizen of our cultured country" (128). But while this pejorative (and alliterative) description reveals Davenport's racism, it should not prevent us from seeing his pluralism, for instead of treating Walter Burton as the antithesis of culture, Davenport ultimately assigns him to a separate culture with its own separate set of racial instincts, and thus racial sounds. Much as Davenport associates the Anglo-Saxons with an instinct for alliteration, so he also associates Africans with an instinct for a different set of sounds, sounds that can only be reproduced in language – if at all – by onomatopoeia. Thus on the island of Haiti, where Burton finally does find the sounds that are natural to him, Mother Sybella speaks in a dialect that "is impossible to describe or reproduce in writing" (74), but if onomatopoeia is not even an option here, Davenport makes limited use of it to describe the sounds that express Sybella's African racial instincts, the sounds of the voodoo drum:

> Mother Sybella . . . was calling her children to worship by the booming of an immense red drum upon which she beat at short intervals. . . . Sybella seemed some tireless fiend incarnate as gradually she animated the multitude and quickened the growing excitement of her emotional listeners by the ceaseless booming of her improv[is]ed tom-tom. (270–71)

These sounds, represented here by the onomatopoetic words "booming" and "tom-tom," are the very sounds that ultimately seem natural to Burton, sounds that lead him to abandon his masquerade of Anglo-Saxon alliteration and become, instead, as the narrator observes, a "flying figure that spun around, transported to the acme of insane emotion, singing in triumphant screeches" (277). The word "screeches," as another instance of onomatopoeia, enacts on the level of poetic effects the very narrative it describes, the narrative of return to the African condition: the word represents a sound existing outside the English language, and that sound is not merely natural sound, for it has been inspired by Sybella, who is infusing Burton with the spirit of Tu Konk. Inducing such a state of possession is, according to voodoo practice, the ritual function of the drum.[91] Thus instead of degenerating from civilized language into mere nature, "screeches" is asserting an alternate culture, embodying a different ancestral past in Burton's body. Just as alliteration embodies Anglo-Saxon ancestry, making those race instincts present in the speech and body of the speaker, so these non-English sounds are likewise embodiments of African ancestors, making those instincts present in the screeches and body of the screecher. This discussion provides us with a better sense of how Davenport uses the doubleness (or double consciousness) of onomatopoeic words like "booming" or "screeches": instead of doubling their status as a word with an additional status as natural sound, they double their status as a word with an additional status as racial sounds, sounds that, according to Davenport, embody the instincts of Africa. Thus unlike alliteration, which supplements English words with compatible Anglo-Saxon sounds (producing a redundancy that confirms Anglo-Saxon racial identity), onomatopoeia undercuts English words with incompatible African sounds (producing a split or doubleness that discloses African-American racial identity).

This account of sounds shows Davenport locating poetics alongside his racialist accounts of bodies and nations: just as onomatopoeia reverts from its artificial existence as an English word to its true status as African sound, so Burton reverts from his fraudulent status as an Anglo-Saxon to the natural self of his "Negro" blood, and likewise Haiti rebels against European rule to revert to tribal African practices. English words (insofar as they are onomatopoeic representations of black sound), white bodies (insofar as they have "black blood"), and European colonies (insofar as they have a black population) are all subject to the same form of possession, a remote racial instinct asserting itself in each context – poetic, corporeal, or colonial – to produce race-specific local effects, effects that ultimately overthrow Anglo-Saxon rule. But even as Davenport stages these multiple instances of black insurgency, he goes on to contain each one by depicting counter-assertions of Anglo-Saxon instincts. For instance, in Haiti Sybella infuses her followers with the resurrected spirits of their ancestors and then leads them in an attack on the whites, but, led by Jack Dunlap, the whites defeat Sybella's charge using "antiquated cutlasses" and appearing as the "supposed resurrection of the ancient buccaneers" (279).[92] A similar battle of racial instincts occurs at Haiti's corporeal correlate, Burton's body. Burton's final gesture of suicide is treated as the ultimate triumph of his Anglo-Saxon instincts over his "Negro" blood: the supposed "predominance of animalism in the negro nature precludes the possibility of suicide in even the extremest cases of conscious debasement" (333), but as an act of self-sacrifice, Burton's suicide is entirely consistent with the supposedly innate nobility of Anglo-Saxon instincts (331), providing the "parting gleam of the nobility begotten by the blood of the superior race within his veins" (333). And perhaps these last two quotes, with their repeated instances of alliteration, suffice to show Davenport's narrative voice favoring a quintessentially Anglo-Saxon sound over the onomatopoeia by which he might represent the now-banished sounds of Africa. The racial purity espoused in the novel's dedication ("To all Americans who deem purity of race an all-important element in the progress of our beloved country" [unpag.]) is accomplished on these several levels, right down to its poetic effects. And given Davenport's commitment to pure Anglo-Saxonism, it should come as no surprise to observe that the subtitle to Davenport's novel reads like an alliterating line of Anglo-Saxon verse: *The Strange Story of a Son of Ham.*

The notion that racial conflict could be acted out through literary effects lies at the heart not only of Davenport's views, but also those of performance poet Vachel Lindsay. In his poem "The Congo: A Study of the Negro Race" (1914)[93] Lindsay treats African-Americans much as Davenport does Walter Burton, enacting in his text what Davenport and the doctors envisioned in black bodies, the voodoo-driven resurgence of an African past acting as an "occult" agency in the present. Like Davenport's character David Chapman, "an amateur Sherlock Holmes" (300) who scrutinizes Walter Burton for any signs of his race, the narrator of Lindsay's poem inspects African-Americans for evidence of their racial past asserting itself through them: "THEN I SAW THE CONGO, CREEPING THROUGH THE BLACK, / CUTTING THROUGH THE JUNGLE WITH A GOLDEN TRACK" (174, 175, 177). These eruptions of the Congo from within these individuals are enacted formally in the poem through the "scream[ing]" sounds of "witch-doctors" that – like the screeches of Davenport's voodoo Queen, Mother Sybella – are conveyed via onomatopoeia:

"Whirl ye the deadly voo-doo rattle,
Harry the uplands,
Steal all the cattle,
Rattle-rattle, rattle-rattle,
Bing.

Boomlay, boomlay, boomlay, BOOM."
. . .
"Be careful what you do,
Or Mumbo-Jumbo, God of the Congo,
. . .
Mumbo-Jumbo will hoo-doo you
Mumbo-Jumbo will hoo-doo you
Mumbo-Jumbo will hoo-doo you."
(174–75)

These instances of onomatopoeia permit the intrusion of supposedly Congo sounds into the poem, thus making the poem itself a repetition on the page of what happens to the body of "THE BLACK" or – in Davenport's *Blood Will Tell* – to the "Negro" body of Walter Burton. Whether these onomatopoetic Congo sounds manifest themselves in poems or bodies, the remote cause imagined in each case is the same, the African "God" that Lindsay names "Mumbo-Jumbo" and that Davenport names "Tu Konk." As a surrogate for the racial body, this poem acts out the features of bodies that doctors were seeking but could not discover, thus using the formal features of poems to assist the medical agenda of diagnosing the presence of racial instincts.

As we saw in Davenport's novel, Burton ultimately contains such intrusions of blackness in his body by killing himself: attributed to the white blood in his veins, suicide pits the occult source of alliteration against the occult source of onomatopoeia, with alliteration emerging triumphant. Like Burton's body, Lindsay's poem also has a distinct white component, a narrator marked as white not only by his safe remove as a mere observer but also by the alliteration of his speech: "Oh, rare was the revel, and well worth while" (176, 177).[94] As in Davenport, this alliterative whiteness seeks to contain onomatopoetic blackness, but where Walter Burton's blackness – and hence the onomatopoetic sounds that were its diagnostic symptoms – could only be silenced by his suicide, here silence seems to come through conversion by "the Apostles" (177):

Pioneer angels cleared the way
For a Congo paradise, for babes at play,
For sacred capitals, for temples clean.
. . .
Oh, a singing wind swept the negro nation
(177–78)

A "singing wind" of supposedly white alliteration is the formal racial correlate of this redemptive Christian theme, and to exemplify this triumph of white alliteration over black onomatopoeia ("boomlay, BOOM"), the poem ends with a distinctively auditory device: in the performance instructions the onomatopoetic representation of black sounds ("Mumbo-Jumbo will hoo-doo you") is described as slowly "*Dying down into a penetrating, terrified whisper*" (178). Yet, given the poem's episodic structure, this persistent whisper of black sounds implies a lingering presence of racial instinct waiting to assert itself. Religious conversion failed to overcome Walter Burton's racial instincts: "I even doubt that my Christianity is genuine and not a hollow mockery! . . . Are my protestations of faith in Christianity . . . merely outward manifestations in imitation of the white race and as deceitful as is the color of my skin?" (250–51; see also 125). Like the drop of black blood in Burton's body, the mere whisper of black sound in poems renders suspect any conversion by "the Apostles." As in Davenport's novel, blood must be made to tell, and making it do so through racial sound effects – whether in bodies or in poems – shows writers like Davenport and Lindsay using their works to advance the wishful thinking of doctors in their medical journals, thinking that imagined a remote racial cause for these bodily and poetic effects.

The central role of poetic effects in making blood tell is confirmed in the writings of Henry Edward Krehbiel, whose *Afro-American Folksongs: a Study in Racial and National Music* was published in 1914, the same year Lindsay published "The Congo." "These idioms," Krehbiel asserts of Afro-American folksongs, "are the crude material which the slaves brought with them from their African homes. This, at least, is the conviction of this writer, and the contention which he hopes to establish by a study of the intervallic and rhythmical peculiarities of the songs and by tracing them to their primitive habitat."[95] Krehbiel seeks the "rhythmical peculiarities" of the race in the songs' formal features, just as earlier doctors like Middleton Michel sought to identify "any determinate pathologic or anatomic peculiarity" of racial bodies.[96] Given this focus on songs rather than bodies, Krehbiel declares anatomy irrelevant to his discussion. Thus when one of his associates suggests a project aimed at showing "a relation between physiology and negro music" (39), proposing an inquiry into "whether or not the negro's vocal cords were differently formed . . . than those of white people" (39), Krehbiel calls this anatomical approach "fantastical": "I did not even try to find a colored subject for the dissecting table or ask for a laryngoscopical examination of the vocal cords" (39). Krehbiel seems to have learned what medical doctors gradually discovered: race need not be localized within the body's anatomy in order for it to be imagined as an occult racial agency exerting its influence upon that body.

Since race can be indexed by the songs these bodies transmit, as well as by the racial anatomy of bodies themselves, Krehbiel's "scientific methods" (39) involve dissecting these songs, relying on formal analysis for "proving the persistence of African idioms in exotic American songs" (35). To do this, Krehbiel focuses on songs associated with "the mysterious voodoo rites practised by the blacks, who clung to a species of snake-worship which had been brought over from Africa" (35). What Krehbiel's formal analysis seeks to reveal, then, is the same sort of information that betrayed the black blood in the veins of Davenport's Walter Burton, and Krehbiel not only attributes it to the same source (Africa), but he also traces it along the same conduit of transmission, the bodies of the immigrants from Africa. Krehbiel describes his own project as "an excursion into the field of primitive African music and also into the philosophy underlying the conservation of savage music. Does it follow," he asks, "that, because the American negroes have forgotten the language of their savage ancestors, they have also forgotten all of their music? May relics of that music not remain in a subconscious memory?" (ix). As we have seen, Nathaniel Southgate Shaler had suggested as much in his 1904 book *The Neighbor*, which credited "Negroes" with a race-based and inherited instinct for music (153–54). Krehbiel agrees, asserting that there is a "persistency of a type of song in spite of a change of environment of sufficient influence to modify the 'civilization' of a people" (7); in other words, the songs remain African even though the singers' environment and "civilization" have become American. Thus Krehbiel is not so much ignoring racial bodies in favor of racial music as he is revising their relation: instead of racially specific anatomy (the "vocal chords") explaining racial music, racially specific music (the "intervallic . . . peculiarities") indexes racial bodies, permitting bodies that participate in American "civilization" to continue to be described nevertheless as African. Far from irrelevant to Krehbiel's analysis, bodies are crucial – and racial – because of their role as repositories and conduits for these African sounds.

One formal parallel Krehbiel observes between African and African-American songs involves musical scales, for both the "prototypes in African music" (69) and their successor slave songs demonstrate the same "intervallic . . . peculiarities" (56).[97] More than this, the slave songs also preserve an African rhythmic feature, the "snap," which he calls "the characteristic rhythmical element of the slave songs" (v). "The rhythmical snap of the American negroes," he asserts, "is in all likelihood an aboriginal relic, an idiom which had taken so powerful a hold on them that they carried it over into their new environment, just as they did the melodic peculiarities which I have investigated. It was so powerful an impulse, indeed," Krehbiel continues,

> that it broke down the barriers interposed by the new language which they were compelled to adopt in their new home. For the sake of the snap the creators of the folksongs of the American negroes did not hesitate to distort the metrical structure of their lines. In scores upon scores of instances trochees like "Moses," "Satan," "mother," "brother," "sister," and so forth, become iambs, while dactyls become amphibrachys, like "No*body*," "No*body* knows," . . . (94–95)

Here Krehbiel imagines poetic effects as a vehicle for demonstrating the impossibility of racial assimilation. An "aboriginal relic" from Africa, the rhythmic "snap" shows that while "negroes" may be "compelled to adopt" the "language" of "their new home," they will nevertheless be overcome by a "powerful impulse" – an impulse resembling the "occult condition" posited by doctors and the "Voo-Doo" force imagined by Davenport and Lindsay – whose influence will be evident in "the metrical structure of their lines." Any "barriers" the "new language" of English might "interpos[e]" will be broken down as trochees become iambs and dactyls amphibrachys, as English metrical structure succumbs to the "innate rhythmical capacity of the Africans . . . In the American songs it finds its expression in the skill with which the negroes constrain their poetry to accept the rhythms of the music" (97). As *no*body becomes no*body*, the "snap" "finds its expression" and racial blood tells. Negro songs might well use English words, but in doing so they are only passing as Anglo-Saxon, for their underlying rhythms are sufficiently distinct to diagnose them as the effects of a particular race. Krehbiel's poetic analysis demonstrates just how far we have come from Lanier's similar commentary on Whitman, discussed in the last chapter: while Lanier invoked the rhythm of poetic lines to argue about the race of a *poem*, claiming that the three-rhythm of Whitman's "Song of Myself" made it not an American but in fact an Anglo-Saxon poem, here Krehbiel invokes the rhythm of poetic lines to argue about the race of *bodies*, claiming that the "metrical structure" of poetic lines reflects a "powerful . . . impulse" embedded within those bodies, a remote racial agency causing discernible bodily effects that reveal that body's race. Distinct from regional dialect, these specifically racial "metrical structures" are the very "forms" that James Weldon Johnson sought in order to give his poems their "racial flavor" – metrical structures that also, Johnson came to see, would have the effect of setting black bodies apart from white ones.

RACIAL FLAVOR

As Krehbiel discusses this "the peculiarly propulsive rhythmical snap, or catch," he adds that it "has several times been described as the basis of 'ragtime'" (48). Vachel Lindsay would make a similar connection, his poem "The Congo" describing the onomatopoetic screams of voodoo witch-doctors as "A roaring, epic, rag-time tune / From the mouth of the Congo" (174). And just as Lindsay describes this rag-time as "the blood-lust song" (174), so too Krehbiel gives a threatening characterization of this rhythmical snap, observing that the "effect of propulsion when frequently repeated becomes very stirring, not to say exciting, and, as has been disclosed by the development of 'ragtime,' leads to a sort of rhythmical intoxication" (92). It is the rhythmical intoxication induced by ragtime that draws Krehbiel into a seeming "digression" from his strictly formal analysis: "in this year of pretended refinement, which is the year of our Lord 1913, the dance which is threatening to force grace, decorum and decency out of the ballrooms of America and England is a survival of African savagery. . . . It was in the dance that the bestiality of the African blacks found its frankest expression" (93). And Krehbiel adds, by now not surprisingly, that in dancing ragtime, "American and English women . . . are imitating the example . . . of the Black Republic" (94), i.e. Haiti. In one sense, then, Krehbiel reverses the plot line of Davenport's *Blood Will Tell*, for instead of Burton imitating Anglo-Saxon culture (the culture of both "American and England"), Anglo-Saxons imitate African culture. In another sense, however, Krehbiel repeats Davenport's plot: barbarism is an infiltrating African "survival" that Anglo-Saxons must seek to contain. Speaking like a J. Dunlap, Krehbiel describes ragtime as a scandal he cannot endure – its "popularity" in the "civilized world" is "deplorable" (v).

Ragtime plays a central role, as well, in the writings of James Weldon Johnson, whose *Autobiography of an Ex-Colored Man* (1912) features "music that demanded physical response, patting of the feet, drumming of the fingers, or nodding of the head in time with the beat. . . . This was ragtime music."[98] While Lindsay and Krehbiel each demonize ragtime, the narrator of Johnson's novel embraces this new music, eventually becoming "the best ragtime-player in New York" (84). Aware of criticism like Krehbiel's, the narrator admits that "American musicians, instead of investigating ragtime, attempt to ignore it, or dismiss it with a contemptuous word. But that has always been the course of scholasticism in every branch of art. . . . In spite of the bans which musicians and music teachers have placed upon it, the people still demand and enjoy ragtime" (73).[99] But if Johnson – through his narrator – disagrees with Krehbiel about ragtime's *valuation*, he agrees about its *derivation*: its "barbaric harmonies" and "intricate rhythms" (72) were "originated . . . by Negro piano players who . . . were guided by natural musical instinct and talent" (72–73) – much like Burton's "inherent instincts" (250) but here valorized as "talent" rather than denigrated. Ragtime, in Johnson's view, stems – as Krehbiel had suggested – from the "natural musical instinct" specific to a particular race.[100]

Although he valorizes it as a talent, this racial instinct for ragtime proves to be a liability for Johnson's narrator, who is trying to become an ex-colored man – that is, to pass as white: "I cursed the drops of African blood in my veins and wished that I were really white" (149). These few drops are not visible ("I noticed the ivory whiteness of my skin" [11]), so he is able, like Burton, to pass as white ("I played my rôle as a white man with a certain degree of nonchalance" [145]). But because of those drops he is, like Burton, not "really white," so the narrator's talent for ragtime is thus an unwelcome symptom threatening to disclose his African blood, just as Walter Burton's "inherent instincts" (250) caused his blood to "tell." As with Burton's attempts to pass, the ex-colored man "began to doubt my ability to play the part. . . . I began even to wonder . . . if there was not, after all, an indefinable something which marked a difference" (146). This invocation of an "indefinable something" recalls the "occult condition" or "something in the blood" that many doctors held responsible for racial differences in disease effects, an agency that Davenport expanded into the voodoo force of Tu Konk. His sense of indefinable difference is what leads Johnson's narrator to view these few drops as his natural self, giving him "my identity as a colored man" (135), and just as Burton had traveled to Haiti to be amidst Sybella and "my people," so Johnson's narrator, "possessed by a strange longing for my mother's people" (153), returns to the US from Europe to visit "the very heart of the South" (104) where he both observes and, like Burton, eventually gets drawn into his people's ceremonies. While Johnson's narrator makes no mention of voodoo possession, he responds to the camp-meeting's preacher in much the same way as Walter Burton responds to Mother Sybella's voodoo drums, with a kind of ecstatic engagement implying possession: "I was a more or less sophisticated and non-religious man of the world, but the torrent of the preacher's words, moving with the rhythm and glowing with the eloquence of primitive poetry, swept me along, and I, too, felt like joining in the shouts of 'Amen! Hallelujah!'" (129).[101]

Johnson's narrator makes this visit to "my people" as part of his larger goal to "take[] ragtime and ma[ke] it classic" (103). Developing the musical materials of his race to the high classic status would provide the Ex-Colored Man with a "way of carrying out the ambition I had formed when a boy" (104), that is, "my ambitions to be a great man, a great colored man, to reflect credit on the race and gain fame for myself" (32). This is why his ultimate failure to compose with ragtime's racial rhythm and his decision, instead, to live his life as a real estate speculator – as "an ordinarily successful white man who has made a little money" (154) – amounts to something more significant than simply making a dissatisfying career choice. The "vague feeling of unsatisfaction, of regret, of almost remorse, from which I am seeking relief" (1–2) stems not from the personal disappointment of failing to develop a rewarding talent but, instead, from failing to place himself among the ranks of Shiny and Booker T. Washington, "colored men who are publicly fighting the cause of their race. . . . Beside them I feel small and selfish. . . . They are men who are making history and a race. I, too, might have taken part in a work so glorious," but instead, "I have chosen the lesser part" (154). The "lesser part" the Ex-Colored Man chooses is the same life Walter Burton chose, and would have continued to live, had he been able to resist Mother Sybella's possessive rhythmic force, return from Haiti to Boston, and resume his place with the J. Dunlap firm. If, in resisting his "longing for my mother's people" (153), Johnson's narrator succeeds where Walter Burton failed, Johnson's novel still makes blood tell – if not in the impulsive public performance of racial rhythm, then in the oppressive psychic awareness of those impulses, an awareness the narrative exists to "tell." Thus the difference between Davenport's Walter Burton and Johnson's Ex-Colored Man (the difference between failed and successful passing) should not obscure their core similarity: in Johnson's novel the Ex-Colored Man understands his own body in precisely the way Burton's body is presented by Davenport (and the way the "Negro" body is presented by medical doctors), as a site where a remote racial agency asserts its effects, causing blood to tell.

In Johnson's *Autobiography of an Ex-Colored Man*, then, racial instincts serve to undermine the goals of the passer, and in doing so they demonstrate their potential – as we saw in Davenport's novel – to advance the goals of racial separation.[102] While *overcoming* this distinction is the apparently futile goal of Johnson's narrator, *preserving* racial distinction would later become a central goal of Johnson himself, a goal made explicit in his contributions to the literary activities of the Harlem Renaissance, particularly the effort to define a "New Negro." Alain Locke's anthology *The New Negro* (1925) included Johnson's poem "The Creation," which contains the following lines:

Then God himself stepped down –
And the sun was on his right hand,
And the moon was on his left;
The stars were clustered about his head,
And the earth was under his feet.
(*God's Trombones*, 18)[103]

In these lines Johnson is careful to use standard speech – for instance, instead of saying "God hisself," Johnson writes "God himself."[104] In doing so, Johnson remains consistent with his earlier "Preface" to *The Book of American Negro Poetry* (1922), where he observes that "newer Negro poets show a tendency to discard dialect."[105] Discarding dialect in favor of standard speech does not, however, involve discarding the racial category "Negro": instead of becoming *former* Negro poets, the writers featured in Johnson's anthology – like Johnson himself, featured in Locke's *The New Negro* – are able to become "newer Negro poets."[106] While older "Negro" poets like Paul Lawrence Dunbar had relied heavily on dialect's regionally specific deviations from standard speech, the "newer Negro poet," according to Johnson, "needs a form that is freer and larger than dialect, but which will still hold the racial flavor" (41). Having called for this new "form" in his own anthology, Johnson goes on to claim to have captured this racial flavor not only in his poem "The Creation" but also in the several related poems collected along with it in *God's Trombones: Seven Negro Sermons in Verse*. As we have seen, Johnson's "Preface" to that volume claims that the voice of the "Negro preacher," reduced to its sound effects, ought to be understood in musical terms, terms rendered using onomatopoetic language: "He often possessed a voice that was a marvelous instrument, a voice he could modulate from a sepulchral whisper to a crashing thunder clap. . . . At such times his language was not prose but poetry" (5). Thus in the poetry quoted above, the reader encounters both the story of the creation and the sound of the trombone. It is within this instrumental sound effect, this "form," that Johnson locates the "racial flavor" of the "New Negro" poem.

What Johnson has in mind in attributing a "racial flavor" to this passage, and particularly to its sound effects, is a notion related to Benjamin Rush Davenport's account of onomatopoetic words like "murmuring" and "screeches." For Davenport, as we have seen, onomatopoetic words seem to assimilate sounds of the natural world into language, but once we view onomatopoeia as sound that merely passes as words (i.e. sound that is simply posing as a representation of a sound while, in fact, exemplifying an authentic instance of that sound), we see onomatopoeia ultimately bringing to the fore a difference between representations of a sound, which are linguistic, and the actual sound, which is not.[107] These exclusive options, we saw, permitted Davenport to advance a corresponding logic of exclusion between "Anglo-Saxon" and "Negro": to represent sounds is to operate in a linguistic mode, a mode where alliteration might occur (and thus Anglo-Saxon blood might tell), whereas to exemplify an actual sound is to operate in a musical mode, a mode where "wild melody" might occur (and thus "Negro" blood might tell). Imagining that a sound can either be represented or exemplified, but not both at once, Davenport uses onomatopoeia to shift from one to the other – from representation to exemplification, from words to authentic sounds, and thus from the rules of language to the phonic symptoms of "Negro" instinct. What Johnson has in mind in *God's Trombones*, however, is slightly different: unlike Davenport's onomatopoeia, which can *either* represent (and hence be language) *or* exemplify (and hence be mere sound), Johnson imagines the lines of poems like "The Creation" to *both* represent *and* exemplify. For Johnson, the representation and exemplification taking place in those lines are oriented not in an *exclusive* manner – toward a sound that, as we saw in Davenport, is either represented or exemplified, but not both – but rather in a *parallel* manner: while the words represent the story of the creation, the poetic effects exemplify the sound of the trombone, and hence contribute the "racial flavor" characteristic of "the Negro." Thus unlike Davenport, who used onomatopoeia to set representation (and the "Anglo-Saxon" alliteration that might accompany it) *against* exemplification (and the "Negro" instinct for "wild melody" that might occasion this exemplification), Johnson's makes English words and racial sounds compatible. For Johnson, the words of his poems can involve standard speech, and thus advance Johnson's goal (as head of the NAACP) of achieving racial uplift and assimilation.[108] At the same time, the sounds of his poem can retain the "racial flavor," making them not just standard speech (which would, by itself, eliminate racial difference[109]), but racial speech, the speech of a "newer Negro poet." By revising Davenport's approach to onomatopoeia, Johnson imagines a more stable form of double consciousness: Johnson's "newer Negro poet" is not required (as Du Bois put it) to throw off the restraint of his English training and surroundings in order for the blood of his fathers to speak through him. The English restraint remains even as blood tells.

But as this statement suggests, for Johnson, blood still tells. If standard speech makes the "Negro poet" "newer," the racial flavor keeps the newer poet "Negro." So despite Johnson's deviations from Davenport, both writers share a fundamental resistance to total assimilation and thus a commitment to racial difference. To assert this racial difference, Johnson characterizes his poems in a manner that more closely resembles Davenport's Walter Burton than his own Ex-Colored Man: whereas the Ex-Colored Man succeeded in passing as white, Johnson's poems must, like Walter Burton, fail to do so. Indeed, Johnson's various prefaces contribute to this failure of poetic passing by cultivating, for "newer Negro poets," a readership among whom poems are viewed in the same way that Davenport viewed Walter Burton's body and the Ex-Colored Man (if not the people he deceived) viewed his own body, as sites that, through their poetic effects, reveal diagnostic signs of racial instinct. In other words, by emphasizing these poems' "racial flavor" in his prefaces, Johnson encourages readers to resist the efforts of these texts to pass as mere standard speech, and thus to become ex-colored texts. Readers are instructed, instead, to view the poems as the Ex-Colored Man viewed his body: just as he was merely passing as white, but was not in fact white, these poems are merely passing as standard speech, but are not simply standard speech – the sound of the trombone is superadded to the words.[110] If readers adopt this perspective, they will see that Johnson's collection of poems – like the Ex-Colored Man's body – derives from its sound effects a "Negro" racial identity. Although dialect has been discarded, the "racial flavor" remains, so the replacement of racial dialect with a combination of standard speech and racial sound effects allows the "Negro" to persist – a "newer Negro," but still a "Negro." Through the "racial flavor" of poetic sound effects, blood will still tell.

What this analysis suggests is that in order to institute a racially distinct poetics for the "New Negro" of the Harlem Renaissance, Johnson sets out to cultivate a readership among whom racially specific poetic effects are not only isolated from standard speech but are also treated as diagnostic symptoms of racial instinct. To detect a "racial flavor," readers must adopt, in their approach to poems, the same analytical stance that late-nineteenth-century physicians brought to bear upon bodies, a stance that sought to diagnose occult racial instincts through their symptomatic effects on the body.[111] Johnson's poetry and criticism not only appropriate this medical logic, they also perpetuate it, helping to extend the views of nineteenth-century physicians well forward into the cultivation of a twentieth-century readership for African-American poetry. Johnson's influence is explicit in the poetic criticism of Stephen Henderson, author of *Understanding the New Black Poetry* (1973). "Johnson's concerns," Henderson writes, "are still the concerns of Black poets, and it is useful to note the terms 'racial spirit' and 'racial flavor' which he employs. . . . In the late 1950's," Henderson continues, "the word 'Soul' . . . came to mean not only a special kind of popular music based on gospel songs and hymns but also the 'racial spirit' and 'racial flavor' which Johnson had spoken of some forty years earlier."[112] Johnson's "new Negro poets" become Henderson's "New Black poets," but "racial flavor" is still what provides racial unity to this group.[113]

The influence of Johnson's criticism is likewise apparent in the more recent work of Jon Michael Spencer, who, like Henderson, sets out to extend the Harlem Renaissance into "the 1940s and 1950s when the maturer phase of the Renaissance evolved" (*New Negroes and their Music*, 136). In order to expand its historical scope, Spencer characterizes the Harlem Renaissance in general terms that are consistent with Johnson's analysis of "newer Negro poets." Thus according to Spencer, "the Negro Renaissance can be generally characterized as an epoch in which art and letters with an inner-African 'mood and spirit,' derived significantly (if not principally) from the remnant of African rhythm, found expression in European 'form and technique" (25–26). This "two-tiered artistic 'mastery'" (27), Spencer asserts, "is exactly what James Weldon Johnson accomplished with his poeticized black sermons in *God's Trombones*" (27). Thus as we have seen, Johnson's "The Creation" balances one tier of "outer European 'form and technique'" (32) (what Johnson conveys by standard speech, rather than dialect) with a second tier of "inner African 'mood and spirit'" (32) (what Johnson calls the "racial spirit" of the poem's trombone sound).[114] As Spencer observes, this second tier of "inner African 'mood and spirit'" was associated, in the minds of many Harlem Renaissance writers, with innate racial instincts. Alain Locke, for instance, who edited *The New Negro* (1925), later observed that although "customs were lost and native cultures cut off in the rude transplantings of slavery . . . , underneath all, rhythm memories and rhythmic skill persisted" (quoted in Spencer, *New Negroes*, 20–21). For Locke, "This racial mastery of rhythm is one characteristic that seems never to have been lost, whatever else was, and it has made and kept the Negro a musician by nature and a music-maker by instinct" (20). It is this same notion of racial instinct that Johnson has in mind when he explains the "Negro preacher's" voices by reference to "the innate grandiloquence of their old African tongues" (*God's Trombones*, 9). And this racial specificity applies not just to the speaker in Johnson's poem but also to Johnson himself who, as one of the "newer Negro poets" he describes, employs this two-tiered system to establish his own standing as someone who can simultaneously assimilate to standard speech practices and also – unlike his Ex-Colored Man – disclose his racial identity.

In addition to demonstrating this account of two-tiered mastery in Johnson's writings, Spencer also adopts this account as a basis for his own critical approach to African-American poetry, thus becoming not just a critic but

Figure 4.2 Jon Michael Spencer, *Sacred Symphony: The Chanted Sermon of the Black Preacher* (New York: Greenwood Press, 1987), 22.

also a student of Johnson. Spencer's application of Johnson's critical views is apparent in Spencer's *Sacred Symphony: The Chanted Sermon of the Black Preacher* (1987). In this work Spencer assembles several chanted sermons, presenting each as both words and accompanying musical notation (see Figure 4.2). By presenting these sermons in this manner, Spenser is able to isolate the same elements that Johnson claimed to be present in his verse sermons, speech and music. Indeed, the first measure of music in Figure 4.2 consists of rhythmic syncopation, the rhythmic effect that Johnson placed at the center of ragtime. The racial specificity of this music is underscored by William C. Turner, whose "Foreword" to Spencer's book asserts that "Black preaching . . . encompasses the atavistic and primal vocabulary of music. . . . [T]here is a surplus (glossa) expressed in music which accompanies the rational content (logos) enunciated in words. . . . For the glossal portion, the preacher becomes an instrument of musical afflatus: a flute through which divine air is blown" (xi–xii).[115] Where Johnson had named the trombone, here Turner invokes the flute, but the larger point is the same: while the words, Turner observes, convey a "message spoken in behalf of God," the music is "rooted in the primal nexus from which manifold expressions of African culture have traditionally effused" (xi). Looking beyond the sermon's "enunciated words" (whether standard speech or dialect) one finds an "atavistic and primal vocabulary" that is imagined, in the manner of voodoo possession, to appropriate the preacher for its own ends.[116]

Turner's observations about Spencer's "chanted sermons," and particularly about the racially atavistic quality of the music, articulate views very much like those Spencer himself would later advance:

> In many traditional African societies. . . . drummers seduced dancers into ready fervor and mobilized the spirits into possessive action. The rhythm that did the seducing is characterizable in the singular as *African rhythm*. . . . But while the drum was deferred in the diaspora, the drumbeats of Africa, I will argue in due course, endured the slave factories and the middle passage and were sold right along with the captive Africans on the auction blocks of the New World. Those drumbeats sat silent in many a gallery of white Protestant and Catholic churches, silent until they could "steal away" and release themselves without reproach in the physical concretizations of those who had carried the rhythm in the bones and blood and souls beneath their flesh.[117]

Spencer's general account closely resembles Benjamin Rush Davenport's account of Walter Burton, whose conversion to Christianity could not prevent his "blood" from telling. For Spencer, however, this expression of "*African rhythm*" now takes place "without reproach." The work of Johnson, we have seen, helped dispel this reproach through its move from the Ex-Colored Man, who hides his instinct for ratgime for fear of reproach, to the "newer Negro poets," who self-consciously display these instincts as a matter of pride. Yet if Davenport's "reproach" is absent from Spencer's account, his original purpose remains intact: just as Davenport imagined a racially specific "Voo-doo" force that would cause "blood" to "tell" in sound effects, so Spencer imagines "spirits" "mobilized . . . into possessive action" in such a way as to "release" a "rhythm" that is "carried . . . in the bones and blood and souls beneath their flesh." The "flesh" that had been the concern of both late nineteenth-century physicians and novelists remains an ongoing concern among literary critics, who continue to employ poetic effects as diagnostic symptoms of the body's occult racial instincts.

Placed alongside Lanier's quite similar musical rendering of the "the half-chanted sermon of the negro" (see Figure 4.1), Spencer's account of the "chanted sermon of the black preacher" illustrates the changing stakes involved in racialized accounts of formal literary effects. Lanier had described the sermon as revealing "a struggle for independence . . . on the part of words as against pure musical tones" (208) and had thus claimed the sermon to be a primitive precursor to the fully independent speech tunes of English poetry. For Lanier, it is not that the sermon's music is itself intrinsically "Negro" but that the presence of music in poetry is, like the "Negro," primitive; hence Lanier prescribes Anglo-Saxon models and oversight in order for the "Negro" to develop toward a more refined or cultivated state. A different approach to the sermon is evident in Spencer's work: following Johnson, Spencer separates the music that is characteristic of an "inner African 'mood and spirit'" from the speech that – once rendered standard rather than dialect – exemplifies "outer European 'form and technique'" (*New Negroes and their Music*, 32). What for Lanier had been the "negro sermon's" primitive failure to separate the arts (music and poetry) becomes, for Spencer (and Johnson), the sermon's pluralist success at separating the races (black music and European speech). As we have seen, in order for this standard European speech to be further characterized as particularly Anglo-Saxon, additional analysis would be necessary: for Lanier, those words would need to employ the characteristically Anglo-Saxon three-rhythm, and for Davenport they would need to use Anglo-Saxon alliteration. But for Davenport, and not for Lanier, the use of those specifically Anglo-Saxon effects would serve as a diagnostic sign of bodily racial instincts. Whereas Lanier's focus was the race of the medium, for later writers like Davenport and Johnson the concern is the instrumentality of the medium in disclosing the race of bodies. Between Lanier and Johnson, then, a substantial change has taken place in the role of formal literary effects: having served Lanier as a way of identifying the racial identity of a text, they serve Johnson as a way of diagnosing the racial identity of a body. As the work of Henderson and Spencer demonstrates, the legacy of this shift from texts to bodies persists in the practice of contemporary literary critics.

Conclusion: the conservation of identities

I have been told by some cautious friends, that the time for such remonstrances as I do most earnestly recommend to our Scottish representatives, would be now . . . unfavourable. . . . Your birthright, proceed these Job's comforters, will be taken from you at all events by superior numbers. Yield it up, therefore, with a good grace, and thank God if they give you a mess of pottage in return – it will be just so much gain.

– Walter Scott, *Letters of Malachi Malagrowther*[1]

I am an ordinarily successful white man who has made a little money . . . . [W]hen I sometimes open a little box in which I still keep my fast yellowing manuscripts, the only tangible remnants of a vanished dream, a dead ambition, a sacrificed talent, I cannot repress the thought that, after all, I have chosen the lesser part, that I have sold my birthright for a mess of pottage.

– James Weldon Johnson, *Autobiography of an Ex-Colored Man*[2]

In the passages quoted above, Walter Scott and James Weldon Johnson each reference the same biblical story of Esau selling his birthright to his brother, Jacob, for a "mess of pottage" (Genesis 25:31). Scott's speaker resists the "cautious friends" who urge him to become an Esau, and Johnson's worries that – passing as a "white man" – he has already done so. Yet even as Scott and Johnson each invoke the loss of a birthright, we have seen that their narratives are ultimately committed – like the biblical narrative they reference – to a people's persistence, not its demise. That is, Scott and Johnson each use their texts to imagine a birthright that cannot be sold, an identity of a people that is in fact beyond loss. Although they may appear to have been absorbed within the British Union, Scots, Scott argues, can always be summoned forth as Scots; and although he may appear to be an ordinary white man, the Ex-Colored Man, Johnson suggests, will always have to conceal his inescapable identity as a "Negro." As we have seen, furthermore, both Scott and Johnson imagine this inalienable identity by reference to poetic effects. In Scott these are apparent in the metrical summons that is, for all Scots, the "language of many recollections," and in Johnson these poetic effects are the "talent" for ragtime rhythm that is an index of the seemingly "white" narrator's invisible "Negro blood." In their respective approaches to national and racial identity, Scott and Johnson demonstrate the central point of the foregoing chapters: despite the apparent differences between a "white" writer concerned with the Scottish nation and a "black" writer concerned with the "Negro" race, they each conceptualize their respective "peoples" by employing the same pattern of thinking about formal effects.

The foregoing chapters have detailed this shared logic in the work of writers ranging from Scott to Johnson, and in doing so those chapters have also revealed an additional commonality among these writers, a commitment to what Walter Scott describes as "Demoniacal possession."[3] As we have seen, when Scott's Elspat MacTavish possesses her son (in much the same way that meter, understood as intrinsically national, is superadded to imperial words) the resulting combination models a subjectivity that can "keep sight of both" nation and empire. For Simms, the possessing demon – the *genius loci* – is not a Highland widow but a Cherokee princess or a Yemassee chief, and once this indigenous history possesses the landscape, Simms is able to characterize that landscape as both poetic and distinctively southern. The Native American *genius loci* possessing Simms's landscape is re-imagined by Sidney Lanier as an Anglo-Saxon genius possessing poetic form: arguing that "our tongue [must] recur to the robust forms – and from these to the underlying and determining genius – of its Anglo-Saxon period,"[4] Lanier imagines that even the "formless" lines of Walt Whitman betray the haunting presence of Anglo-Saxon. While W. E. B. Du Bois adopts a sociological distance when discussing "a pythian madness, a demoniac possession" that "possessed that mass of black folk" attending a "Southern Negro revival,"[5] he later implicates himself in this possession when he describes how he came to write *The Souls of Black Folk*: "The blood of my fathers spoke through me and cast off the English restraint of my training and surroundings."[6] And just as Du Bois imagines an ancestral voice – "the rhythmic cry of the slave" (*SBF*, 205) – speaking through the "Sorrow Songs," so too does Benjamin Rush Davenport imagine ancestral voices speaking through alliteration and onomatopoeia, sounds that, through voodoo possession, allow invisible racial blood to "tell." Finally, in the passage quoted above James Weldon Johnson's Ex-Colored Man hides his "fast yellowing manuscripts" within a "little box," but his talent for ragtime is supposedly hidden within his "Negro blood," so if the "little box" can be sold, his talent can only be concealed. Thus rather than possessing his talent, his talent – his birthright – possesses him. In all of these cases, a more or less explicit form of demoniacal possession is directly associated with poetic effects, and it is this demoniacal possession that allows meter to become Scottish meter, song to become southern or "Negro" song, and rhythm to become Anglo-Saxon or "Negro" rhythm. It is demoniacal possession, in other words, that transforms poetic effects into an index of identity.

If demoniacal possession permits poetic effects to serve as an index of a particular identity, it does so by imbuing those effects with what Walter Scott calls "recollections." For Scott, meter – "the language of many recollections" – bears the memories of Elspat MacTavish, who recalls the independence and autonomy of the Scottish Highlands. For Simms, songs on the shores of Louisiana's Bay of Pascagoula convey the memory of the vanished Biloxi, a legendary Native American tribe. The three-rhythm of Lanier's Battle Songs recalls the history of Anglo-Saxon warriors, and the melodies of Du Bois's Sorrow Songs tell the stories of suffering slaves. Davenport and Johnson, finally, imagine blood to carry the recollections of Anglo-Saxon or African ancestors, recollections that "tell" via poetic effects like alliteration, onomatopoeia, and ragtime rhythm. What differentiates the various writers in this study, then, is not the question of *whether* poetic effects are demoniacally possessed by recollections; rather, it is the question of *whose* recollections are possessing those effects – the recollections of Scots, Southerners, "Negroes," or "Anglo-Saxons" – and *where* those haunted effects are to be found – discovered on the landscape, scanned in poems, or performed by persons (as a symptom of a person's racial "blood").

This list of locations where these effects can be found conveys the shift this book has sought to depict from early nineteenth-century accounts of national poems to later nineteenth-century and early twentieth-century accounts of racial bodies. As we have seen, however, the change is driven by a fundamental continuity linking these earlier accounts of national poems to later accounts of racial bodies. Even as physicians found in the body what they thought were concrete symptoms of racial instinct, these symptoms consistently referred them "back beyond the bacillus" and "outside of the eye" to the "occult condition" responsible for causing these symptoms. The search for this occult racial history led doctors to treat race as an extra-corporeal force capable of inducing effects in bodies, bodies where racial symptoms become evident – where blood will tell. This late nineteenth-century medical account coincides with the occult racial logic in an influential contemporary novel, Thomas Dixon's *The Clansman*

(1905). Celebrating the return to white rule in the post-Reconstruction South, Dixon's novel describes the sheet-clad horsemen of the Ku Klux Klan as "the reincarnated souls of the Clansmen of Old Scotland."[7] This description is consistent not only, as I have noted, with the earlier writings of Walter Scott, who imagined his fellow Scots as demoniacally possessed by recollections of Scottish Highlanders like Elspat MacTavish, but it is also consistent with the understanding of Dixon and his contemporaries about how voodoo possession takes place. In the terminology of voodoo, a person being possessed is called a "horse," and the ancestral spirit doing the possessing is said to "mount" that horse.[8] So just as the ancestral spirits of voodoo "mount" a person's body, so too Dixon's Ku Klux Klansmen – "the reincarnated souls of the Clansmen of Old Scotland" – mount the horses they ride. These horsemen, in turn, figure the "fundamentally spiritual" or occult racial identity of whites in general.[9] While Dixon imagines racial identity by reference to reincarnated souls on horseback, Benjamin Rush Davenport, we have seen, makes a slightly different use of voodoo in *Blood Will Tell*. Davenport's Walter Burton skeptically invokes the idea "that men like horses carried jockeys" (134), only to have his own body become possessed or mounted by ancestral spirits, but Davenport also extends Dixon's voodoo logic even further, imagining racial identity by reference to reincarnated souls in poetic effects. As the previous chapter's discussion of Davenport showed, recollections "mount" alliteration, causing those sounds to be possessed by the souls of Anglo-Saxons of Old England, a presence that lends Anglo-Saxon racial identity to alliterating words (and thus testifies to the race of the body uttering those alliterating words, confirming the racial purity of the white body). A different set of recollections "mounts" onomatopoeia, rendering those sounds haunted by the reincarnated souls of the "Negroes" of Old Africa, ancestral presences who confer "Negro" racial identity to onomatopoetic words (and thus indicate the race of the body uttering those sounds, unmasking the would-be passer). Treating these poetic effects as instances where "blood will tell," Davenport produces an account of racial identity that is fundamentally continuous with the occult logic present both in Dixon's *The Clansman* and in contemporary racial medicine. And this occult logic – demoniacal possession by ancestral recollections – is itself continuous with prior instances outlined in this book's earlier chapters: just as writers like Scott and Simms imagined recollections to possess the meters of poems or the songs of the landscape, Davenport replaces textual and geographic locales with a corporeal site, imagining recollections to possess the sound effects performed by bodies. Whether the ultimate location of these haunted poetic effects is textual, geographic, or corporeal, each exemplifies this general pattern of thinking.

Not only was this pattern of thinking a widespread nineteenth-century phenomenon, it has also persisted into the present. As the Introduction of this book has suggested, contemporary writers like Toni Morrison and Seamus Heaney continue to rely on this pattern of thinking as a way of understanding racial identity. The recent writings of Morrison and Heaney will once again be my focus in the remainder of this conclusion, which will demonstrate in greater detail how the work of these two Nobel laureates exemplifies a commitment to identities embedded in the formal effects of literary texts. As I address these two writers, I will underscore links with the writers examined in the previous chapters, in particular those who treat texts as subject to demoniacal possession by recollections of the past. I will also indicate ways in which Morrison and Heaney have adjusted this flexible pattern of thinking to new circumstances. By tracing these continuities and adjustments, I hope to underscore the relevance of the previous chapters to the identitarian thinking animating current literary discourse. Despite the apparent differences between the nineteenth-century writers examined in earlier chapters and the contemporary works of Morrison and Heaney, these two writers, I will argue, do not challenge but in fact reinforce the basic identitarian premise of those earlier authors, the premise that formal effects can provide an index of a collective identity. By drawing attention to these continuities I will demonstrate that, while accounts of identity may vary in their details, the nineteenth-century commitment to thinking about literary effects in these identitarian terms has remained a consistent feature of the discussion. Once the scope of this pattern of thinking becomes apparent, so too may its potential limitations. These limitations may, in turn, point to genuine alternatives to such long-standing patterns of thinking, alternatives that literary criticism has consistently tended to obscure.

"A SOMEWHERE BEING REMEMBERED"

In his essay "Englands of the Mind" (1976) Seamus Heaney addresses poets who imagine a "relationship between the word as pure vocable, as articulate noise, and the word as etymological occurrence, as symptom of human history, memory and attachments" (150).[10] While Heaney's focus in this early essay is the work of Ted Hughes, his observations likewise apply, as we have seen, to the writings of Sidney Lanier, who imagined that "abrupt vocables" perpetuated the identity of Anglo-Saxon England.[11] Heaney himself goes on to produce his own England of the mind in the "Introduction" to his recent translation of *Beowulf*.[12] After learning that "the word 'whiskey' is the same word as the Irish and Scots Gaelic word *uisce*, meaning water, and that the River Usk in Britain is therefore to some extent the River Uisce (or Whiskey)" (xxiv–xxv), Heaney imagines a way of recasting linguistic heterogeneity (whiskey, *uisce*, and Usk) as linguistic identity ("the same word"):

> The place on the language map where the Usk and the *uisce* and the whiskey coincided was definitely a place where the spirit might find a loophole, an escape route from what John Montague has called "the partitioned intellect," a way into some unpartitioned linguistic country, a region where one's language would not be a simple badge of ethnicity or a matter of cultural preference or official imposition, but an entry into further language. (xxv)

Language becomes "further language" when Heaney stops treating it as merely conventional: while the use of varying signifiers (Usk, *uisce*, and whiskey) to convey a variety of signifieds (the River Usk, water, and whiskey) could be taken as an indication of cultural difference (and hence the source of a partitioned intellect), Heaney seeks to overcome this apparent cultural variety by transforming different local languages into a single "further language." This "further language" is to be located at a "place on the language map" that overcomes the varying local conventions by which speakers communicate their meanings, providing instead a single, mythic locale that the language itself remembers: "in the resulting etymological eddy [arising from the coincidence of Usk, *uisce*, and whiskey] a gleam of recognition flashed through the synapses and I glimpsed an elsewhere of potential which seemed at the time to be a somewhere being remembered" (xxv). The "somewhere being remembered" here is Heaney's England of the mind, "a pristine Celto-British Land" that is "pre-political, prelapsarian, ur-philological" (xxv). The memory of this locale becomes available to be remembered when it is borne by pure vocables like Usk, *uisce*, and whiskey, and once these articulate noises are understood to bear these memories, they become "symptoms of human history, attachments and memory." Thus even though "the English language has changed so much in the last thousand years" (ix), this change can be overcome – different words can be seen as "the same word" – by imaging a single somewhere that those words are remembering.

By referring to these memories in passive terms, as "a somewhere *being* remembered," Heaney suggests that he himself stands apart from them: these memories are not his own. Indeed, these recollections involve a mythic, "pre-political" England of the mind where Heaney has never lived ("a pristine Celto-British Land") and a mythic, "ur-philological" language that Heaney has never spoken ("further language"). The only self for whom memories of such a time and place are possible is the language itself, imagined as a self. We saw the Anglo-Saxon language figured as just such a self in the writings of Sidney Lanier, who called Anglo-Saxon "the Washington of languages," and Heaney likewise figures the language as a self – an Odysseus of languages – when he imagines it embarking from this pristine Celto-British Land in order to undertake a centuries-long "multicultural odyssey": it travels "north into Scotland and then across into Ulster with the planters and then across from the planters to the locals who had originally spoken Irish and then farther across again when the Scots Irish emigrated to the American South in the eighteenth century" (xxvi). Yet even as it participates in this multicultural odyssey, gradually conforming to the many culturally specific conventions that arise from it (i.e. the differences in conventional use between Usk, *uisce*, and whiskey), the language also remains itself, remembering its point or origin – like Odysseus remembering his home in Ithaca. Through this somewhere being remembered, the linguistic Odysseus bridges the gaps between the multiple cultures of Scotland, Ulster, and the American South, supplying in itself the deep unity among them, thus uniting Usk, *uisce*, and whiskey through this remembered "further language."[13] It is this unified linguistic self, with its pre-lapsarian memories, whom Heaney calls upon to provide continuity across an otherwise discontinuous set of linguistic conventions. The linguistic Odysseus thus makes available, in itself, an "escape route" from the "partitioned intellect," permitting Heaney to "collapse[]" the "Irish/English duality, the Celtic/Saxon antithesis" (xxv).[14]

Yet even as Heaney implies that this escape from partition arises outside of himself (since it involves a "somewhere" that is "being remembered" by the linguistic self), he also participates in that escape – "I glimpsed the possibility of release from this kind of cultural determinism" (xxiv). He can do so because he imagines that "further language" is inseparable from his own language and is thus inseparable from himself. Although his language comes to him through people like his aunt, who speaks just one of the language's multi-cultural forms, Heaney comes to realize that "my aunt's language was not just a self-enclosed family possession but an historical heritage" (xxv). Indeed, Heaney finds relics of the linguistic past "surviving in my aunt's English speech generations after her forebears and mine had ceased to speak Irish" (xxiv). Their language thus involves not just the local conventions he has come to possess but the memories of "further language" that have come, through his "historical heritage," to possess him: "I consider *Beowulf* to be part of my voice-right. . . . I was born into its language and . . . its language was born into me" (xxiv). Replacing Odysseus not with Beowulf himself but with the *language* of *Beowulf*, Heaney imagines that the memories of this linguistic self are his own. What results is something he calls "illumination by philology" (xxvi): when the language remembers, so does he.[15] By calling *Beowulf* a "voice-right" that was "born into me," Heaney follows Walter Scott and James Weldon Johnson in imagining a birthright he cannot sell. To do so, Heaney follows a logic quite similar to the one we saw in Benjamin Rush Davenport's novel *Blood Will Tell*: just as the voodoo of Davenport's Mother Sybella mediates Walter Burton's access to the spirit of Tu Konk and the memories of a mythic African past, so too the "further language" of Heaney's aunt mediates his own access to the linguistic Odysseus within *Beowulf* and its memories of a "pristine Celto-British land." Heaney thus understands Anglo-Saxon identity in much the same manner that Davenport understood both "Anglo-Saxon" and "Negro" identity: he imagines his body to be subject to a form of demonaical possession – by the memories embedded within "further language" – such that a specific somewhere is being remembered.

This dynamic of memory operates not only through the pure vocables of *Beowulf's* semantics but also, according to Heaney, through the articulate noise of its metrics. It is the apparent survival of Anglo-Saxon metrics in his own English that reinforces Heaney's commitment to the project of translating *Beowulf*:

> I had an instinct that [the project of translating *Beowulf*] should not be let go. An understanding I had worked out for myself concerning my own linguistic and literary origins made me reluctant to abandon the task. I had noticed, for example, that without any conscious intent on my part certain lines in the first poem in my first book conformed to the requirements of Anglo-Saxon metrics. These lines were made up of two balancing halves, each half containing two stressed syllables – "The spade sinks into gravelly ground: / My father digging. I look down . . ." – and in the case of the second line there was alliteration linking "digging" and "down" across the caesura. Part of me, in other words, had been writing Anglo-Saxon from the start. (xxiii)

Here Anglo-Saxonness is discovered, in retrospect, to have been present all along, dwelling intrinsically within the sounds of "stressed syllables" linked "across the caesura" by "alliteration." Heaney has been doing "from the start" what the translation project would later require, producing lines that "echoed with the sound and sense of the Anglo-Saxon" (xxvii). By making his own poetic effects continuous with Anglo-Saxon ones, Heaney casts his metrics less as a product of his own personal history than as an extension of Anglo-Saxon racial memory. By focusing on "my own linguistic and literary origins," Heaney acquires an Anglo-Saxon racial identity.

If Heaney imagines that "Part of me . . . had been writing Anglo-Saxon from the start," he imagines that a different somewhere is being remembered in the work of black writers. In his account of Caribbean writer Derek Walcott, for instance, Heaney asserts that "Africa and England are in him. The humanist voices of his education and the voices from his home ground keep insisting on their full claims, pulling him in two different directions."[16] If England gets in Walcott through his humanist education in Anglo-Saxon texts like *Piers Plowman* (25), Africa gets in him through the "voices of his home ground," the Caribbean islands. The resulting partition of Walcott's intellect – he "made a theme of the choice and the impossibility of choosing" (24) – is a condition with which Heaney initially identifies, but which he later, as we have seen, uses *Beowulf* to overcome: the "further language" of *Beowulf*, with its memories of a pristine Celto-British land, reconciles the voices of Heaney's English humanist education with those of his Irish home ground. But such a reconciliation does not appear available to black writers like Walcott: "Naturally," Heaney elsewhere observes, "black poets from Trinidad or Lagos . . . will be found arguing that their education in Shakespeare or Keats was little more than an exercise in alienating them from their authentic experience, devalorizing their vernacular and destabilizing their instinctual at-homeness in their own non-textual worlds."[17] If Heaney imagines that *Beowulf* can reconcile the Irish and English partition in himself, he imagines neither a place on the language map nor a linguistic Odysseus whose memories could reconcile the English-African partition within black writers. As a result, the project for black writers will be one not of reconciling the partitioned intellect but instead of isolating the devalorized vernacular voices of their home ground – voices that William Gilmore Simms would call their *genius loci* – from their humanist education and re-investing that devalorized vernacular with value.

It is just such a project that is outlined by Toni Morrison, who valorizes the non-textual sounds of black music as a vernacular source for what she calls "truly black literature":

> I have wanted always to develop a way of writing that was irrevocably black. I don't have the resources of a musician but I thought that if it was truly black literature, it would not be black because I was, it would not even be black because of its subject matter. It would be something intrinsic, indigenous, something in the way it was put together – the sentences, the structure, texture and tone – so that anyone who read it would realize. I use the analogy of the music because you can range all over the world and it's still black. . . . I don't imitate it, but I am informed by it. Sometimes I hear blues, sometimes spirituals or jazz and I've appropriated it. I've tried to reconstruct the texture of it in my writing. . .[18]

When Morrison says that the music her writing seeks to appropriate is "black" "all over the world," she echoes the logic of Heaney's "further language": it is "irrevocably black" in the same way that Usk, *uisce*, and whiskey are residually Anglo-Saxon. That is, like the unity behind Usk, *uisce*, and whiskey, the unity behind the blues, spirituals, and jazz follows from the presumption that in each of these musical forms a single somewhere is being remembered – not a mythic, pre-lapsarian Celto-British land but rather a mythic, pre-diasporic African land.[19] Morrison hopes that her writing, too, can appropriate – or be possessed by – this "irrevocably black" sound, yielding a "truly black literature" such that "anyone who read it would realize" – a literature in which blackness would tell. Indeed, like Davenport's *Blood Will Tell*, which imagines that blackness will be revealed through onomatopoeia, Morrison imagines her own writing as if it, too, were structured like onomatopoeia: just as a word like "BOOM" appropriates and reconstructs the texture of a *loud* sound, 'boom,' so too Morrison's writing deliberately appropriates and reconstructs the texture of a *black* sound, jazz. And just as an onomatopoetic word not only represents a sound but also aspires to embody that sound intrinsically, so too Morrison produces writing that not only represents blackness (in its "subject matter") but also aspires to embody blackness as "something intrinsic, indigenous something in the way it was put together."[20] By valorizing these voices of the home ground, Morrison imagines writing in which Africa is the somewhere being remembered.

While the "somewhere being remembered" in Heaney's criticism (the "pristine Celto-British Land") possesses the language of *persons* ("I was born into [*Beowulf*'s] language and . . . its language was born into me" [xxiv]), we have seen that the somewhere being remembered in Morrison's criticism (a unitary, pre-diasporic Africa) possesses the language of *texts* ("I've tried to reconstruct the texture of it in my writing"). The racial identity of texts is a concern as well in Morrison's influential work *Playing in the Dark*, where she turns her attention to a different textual identity, the identity of American writing. The somewhere being remembered in American writing is not Africa or Anglo-Saxon England but rather a locale on the North American continent – specifically, the plantation of William Dunbar. Quoting from Bernard Bailyn's account of Dunbar's life in colonial Mississippi, Morrison then describes this account as "a succinct portrait of the process by which the American as new, white, and male was constituted."[21] The process Dunbar underwent was, Morrison asserts, crucial "[f]or the settlers and for American writers generally" since "[t]he American nation negotiated both its disdain and its envy in the same way Dunbar did: through a self-reflexive contemplation of fabricated, mythological Africanism" (47). In describing this contemplation as "self-reflexive," Morrison directs her analysis away from the "Africans and their descendants" (16) upon whom these fabrications were projected. This fabrication, Morrison insists, was ultimately not about them: "My project is an effort to avert the critical gaze from the racial object to the racial subject; from the described and imagined to the describers and imaginers; from the serving to the served" (90). With her averted gaze, Morrison associates this fabrication not with Dunbar's slaves but with Dunbar himself: "the subject of the dream is the dreamer. The fabrication of an Africanist persona is reflexive; an extraordinary mediation on the self; a powerful exploration of the fears and desires that reside in the writerly conscious" (17).[22] Dunbar, then, becomes exemplary of a reflexive state of mind available "[f]or the settlers and for American writers generally" (47). Like Dunbar, writers projected their fears and desires outward upon "a resident population, already black, upon which the imagination could play" (37). By occasioning such a projection, "Black slavery enriched the country's creative possibilities. For in that construction of blackness *and* enslavement could be found not only the not-free but also, with the dramatic polarity created by skin color, the projection of the not-me. The result was a playground for the imagination" (38). By projecting this "not-me" away from themselves, American writers were making creative use of the "fears and desires that reside in the writerly conscious" (17). Morrison groups these writers together on the same "playground" of slavery – as her title puts it, they were all "playing in the dark" – and thus suggests widespread agreement among American writers generally who participated together in producing this enabling fabrication. Strong evidence of this agreement comes from the many close readings Morrison presents in *Playing in the Dark*: addressing writers from Poe to Hemingway, she demonstrates a variety of ways in which each author's work either states or implies the proposition of "black surrogacy" (13), the same proposition that permitted Dunbar to rationalize his ownership of slaves.

But even as her author-focused readings suggest that many canonical American writers generally agreed about this "fabricated, mythological Africanism," Morrison ultimately deflects attention away from this focus on the views of authors: "these deliberations," she says of *Playing in the Dark*, "are not about a particular author's attitudes toward race. That is another matter. Studies in American-Africanism, in my view, should be investigations of the ways in which a nonwhite, Africanist presence and personae have been constructed – invented – in the United States, and of the literary uses this fabricated presence has served" (90). Morrison's passive construction elides authors as agents, making her project "Studies in American Africanism," not studies in American authors. Thus instead of examining Dunbar, Poe, Twain, Cather, Hemingway, etc., for evidence of widespread agreement in their respective "attitudes," as I suggested above, Morrison treats Dunbar and the authors she addresses as like instances of a singular national attitude: "[t]he *American nation* negotiated both its disdain and its envy in the same way Dunbar did" (47; my italics). Her concern is thus not particular authorial minds in themselves but a single "national mind" (14), and what Morrison's close readings suggest to be on the minds of particular authors – an "Africanist presence and personae" – is in fact what is "on the 'mind' of the literature of the United States" (39). Dunbar and these writers are alike not so much because they agree with each other about race but because they are each an index of this national "mind," a mind to which is attributable the thinking behind their writings. Standing apart from particular writers, American Africanism turns out to be an independent, autonomous principle: Dunbar's Africanism is not just *like* the Africanism of Hemingway, Cather, Poe, and the rest; it *is* that Africanism. American Africanism turns out to be just like Heaney's Odyssean further language, a self with its own identity.

Indeed, it is this American Africanism, as an entity in its own right, that provides continuity to an otherwise discontinuous American self – it is, one might say, the soul of American folk. For instance, when Morrison invokes the "formative years of the nation's literature" (33) she refers to "Young America" (33), by which she means not only the nationalist politicians and writers of the 1840s but also the nation itself, as a youthful self.[23] During its formative youth, the nation uses its literature to express its conviction of autonomous selfhood: "Young America distinguished itself by, and understood itself to be, pressing toward a future of freedom" (33). This national self-understanding was predicated, however, on an enabling fiction: "the concept of the American self was . . . bound to Africanism" (57–58).[24] It is this "Africanism," Morrison asserts, that "is the vehicle by which the American self knows itself as not enslaved, but free; not repulsive, but desirable" (52). Since this national self is continuously articulated against this "Africanism," "Africanism" remains part of it from its youth through its maturity: "Africanism is inextricable from the definition of Americanness – from its origins on through its integrated or disintegrating twentieth-century self" (65). American literature can express a coherent "self," a persistent national identity, only because Africanism brings together the otherwise disparate stages of an unfolding national life.[25] "It was this Africanism, deployed as rawness and savagery, that provided the staging ground and arena for the elaboration of the quintessential American identity" (44). Thus just as Heaney argued that Usk, *uisce*, and whiskey could be viewed as the "same word" once they were all understood to be remembering a single place, Morrison argues that American literary Romanticism, Realism, and Modernism, despite their differences, each express the same national "self" and "mind" insofar as they all rely upon this same American-Africanism.[26] Like Heaney's linguistic Odysseus, whose "further language" remembers a pristine Celto-British land, Morrison's textual Africanism remembers Dunbar's colonial Mississippi plantation.[27] Just as "further language" is inseparable from Heaney's written English, the "Africanist persona" is inseparable from American literature. Indeed, Morrison asks, "How could one speak of profit, economy, labor, progress, . . . – of almost anything a country concerns itself with – without having as a referent, at the heart of the discourse, at the heart of definition, the presence of Africans and their descendants?" (50). Writing as such, regardless of its author and time period, becomes, in the United States, an index for Africanism. Thus even though Morrison asserts that "My project is an effort to avert the critical gaze from the racial object to the racial subject; from the described and imagined to the describers and imaginers; from the serving to the served" (90), her ultimate goal, we now see, goes even further: she averts the critical gaze not just from black servants to the "white writers" (51) they served but from writers themselves to the "Africanist presence" inhabiting their works. Instead of blacks subject to authorial oppression or white authors engaged in racist suppression, her concern is writing itself subject to demoniacal possession.

While Morrison leaves it to other writers to employ the actual word "possession,"[28] this idea is nevertheless implicit when she calls for a critical approach to American literature in which "world view is taken seriously as agency" (xiii). That is, the "agency" ultimately responsible for producing American literature is less "writers themselves" (15) than a shared "world view" animating their work. A uniquely "American brand of Africanism" (8) thus becomes, for Morrison, an agency behind writing, a "presence – which shaped the body politic, the Constitution, and the entire history of the culture" (5):

> Explicit or implicit, the Africanist presence informs in compelling and inescapable ways the texture of American literature. It is a dark and abiding presence, there for the literary imagination as both a visible and an invisible mediating force. Even, and especially, when American texts are not "about" Africanist presences or characters or narrative or idiom, the shadow hovers in implication, in sign, in line of demarcation. (46–47)

If this "Africanist presence" is "compelling and inescapable" to readers, it was no less so, she suggests, for American writers: "in a wholly racialized society, there is no escape from racially inflected language" (12–13). It is as inescapable to them as an Anglo-Saxon "further language" was to Heaney. Morrison's larger goal, then, is not to show that particular authors espouse racist views but to demonstrate, instead, that the texts themselves are "haunted" (33, 35, 36) by this Africanist presence. "In the scholarship on the formation of an American character and the production of a national literature, a number of items have been catalogued. A major item to be added to the list must be an Africanist presence" (48).[29]

By characterizing American literature in this way, Morrison succeeds in her effort to avoid a mere "exchange of dominations – dominant Eurocentric scholarship *replaced* by dominant Afrocentric scholarship" (8). Instead, what dominates here is an Amerocentrism, and, when it is America – rather than Europe or Africa – that is being remembered, a very different kind of identity results, a "quintessential American identity" (44). Yet, even as Morrison sets this American identity apart, we can also see that she imagines it according to a now familiar logic: just as her own writing, "truly black literature," is (as she asserts above) "informed" by the "texture and tone" of "black music," so too the "Africanist presence *informs* . . . the *texture* of American literature" (my italics). "Truly black" literature and "quintessentially American" literature, it turns out, are each produced in the same manner, by incorporating voices from the home ground, voices in which a particular somewhere – Africa and colonial Mississippi – is being remembered.[30] Within American literature, Dunbar's "founding characteristics extend into the twentieth century" (6), so a twentieth-century writer like Ernest Hemingway "could not help folding into his enterprise of American fiction its Africanist properties" (90–91). Viewed in this light, the work of Hemingway is American in the same way Heaney's writing is "Anglo-Saxon from the start" and Morrison's is "truly black literature" – because each text is imagined to be possessed by the memories of a particular locale, whether a colonial Mississippi plantation, a pristine Celto-British land, or a pre-diaspora Africa. As with her own account of "black" identity and Heaney's account of "Anglo-Saxon" identity, this "quintessential American identity" participates in the same pattern of thinking that nineteenth-century writers brought to bear upon poems and bodies: texts are subject to demoniacal possession by recollections of a local past.

As this analysis suggests, Morrison's versions of this logic emphasize the possession of texts rather than bodies. Yet a closer look at her account demonstrates that, as she imagines textual possession, she figures those texts in terms that are ultimately corporeal. This becomes apparent if we consider the distinction Morrison draws between literature and literary criticism: "I would like it to be clear at the outset," she insists in the first chapter of *Playing in the Dark*, "that I do not bring to these matters solely or even principally the tools of a literary critic" (3). Disappointed by the "paucity of critical material on this large and compelling subject" (9), Morrison nevertheless forges ahead against the critical grain. Africanist "topics surface endlessly when one begins to look carefully, without [literary criticism's] restraining, protective agenda beforehand. They seem to me to render the nation's literature a much more complex and rewarding body of knowledge" (53). By examining this literary "body" directly, without the interference of literary criticism, Morrison can replace literary critical evasions with a more forthright diagnosis: "Africanism" is "a disabling virus within literary discourse" (7). Indeed, by figuring American literature as an infected body whose "Africanist" symptoms belie the whitewashing silence of its critical custodians, Morrison anthropomorphizes American literature in a very specific way – as if it were a sick body trying to pass as healthy and, more particularly, a black body trying to pass for white. According to this analogy, the relation of literary criticism to the Africanist presence in texts parallels the relation of the would-be passer to the "black blood" in his or her body. Just as the would-be passer conceals the presence of the body's one drop of "African blood" and claims instead to be white, so too, according to Morrison, literary criticism conceals the Africanist presence behind assertions of whiteness: the "literary historians and critics . . . . hold[] that traditional, canonical American literature is free of . . . the four-hundred-year-old presence of, first, Africans and then African-Americans in the United States" (4–5). Yet even as criticism proclaims the literature to be "pure" (70) white, "[t]he literature itself suggests otherwise" (46). Just as "blood will tell" in the body of Davenport's Walter Burton, so too in American literature an "Africanist presence . . . . shows" (6). Thus even as she discounts the notion of "telling African blood" (58) in bodies, Morrison recreates, in the American "body of literature" (35), the dynamics of racial bodies we saw at work in the writings of Benjamin Rush Davenport and James Weldon Johnson. If we willingly ignore the Africanism possessing these texts, Morrison warns, we abet the critical effort to present this literature as the passer does his or her body, as if it were white, and in doing so we effectively sell the American literary birthright for a mess of pottage. "All of us, readers and writers," Morrison concludes, "are bereft when criticism remains too polite or too fearful to notice a disrupting darkness before its eyes" (91).

In urging readers to notice this disrupting darkness within American literature, Morrison both revises and retains the ending of Johnson's *Autobiography of an Ex-Colored Man*. She revises that ending, as we have seen, by displacing the question of passing from a human body to the body of American literature. But she also revises the way in which that body is treated, replacing the Ex-Colored Man's fearful decision to conceal blackness with her own critical program for revealing it. And this suggests a further revision: Africanism, for Morrison, is not a scandal but a resource. Thus just as the would-be passer ought to be proud rather than ashamed of his drop of African blood (hence, as Johnson's Ex-Colored Man observes of his decision to conceal his "Negro blood," "I have chosen the lesser part" [154]), so too, according to Morrison, American literature should be celebrated for its textual Africanism: "Linguisic responses to Africanism . . . . give the text a deeper, richer, more complex life than the sanitized one commonly presented to us" (66). Rather than sell this distinctively American birthright for a sanitized mess of pottage, as the Ex-Colored Man does by concealing his black "blood," Morrison's revision discloses the Africanist presence and thereby preserves the birthright of American literature.

If Morrison revises Johnson's ending in these ways, replacing the decision to pass with a refusal to pass, she nevertheless continues to operate within the context of these two options, and thus within the logic of passing. That is, in discouraging passing, she preserves it as a possibility – otherwise it would make no sense to discourage it. Yet even as she retains this general logic, Morrison introduces an additional logical point: if one drop of black blood makes the Ex-Colored Man black, the slightest Africanist presence in literature does not make that literature Africanist – instead, it makes that literature American.[31] Since Africanism is ultimately a New World fabrication motivated by a quintessentially American desire for pure whiteness, Africanism is ultimately an index of that desire, and thus an index of Americanness.[32] Thus while the ending of Johnson's *Autobiography* suggests that someone passing as white is really black, Morrison argues that literary texts passing as white are, by the same logic, really American. By deriving the Americanness of texts in this manner, through a textual one drop rule, Morrison not only places American texts in the position once occupied by "black" bodies, she also transforms a principle of exclusion into a principle of inclusion, employing the logic once used to exclude black bodies from American identity as the logic now used to include literary texts within an American identity. To be American, textually, is what it once was to be black, corporeally. A corporeal logic for asserting black racial identities in bodies is thus transformed or re-tooled as a critical logic for asserting American national identity in texts.

"HARD GRIEVANCE"

As Morrison begins her account of the Africanist presence in American literature, she lists other instances of authors externalizing, through their writing, a disturbing aspect of themselves, mentioning "the way Homer renders a heart-eating cyclops. . . . Faulkner's Benjy, James's Maisie, Flaubert's Emma, Melville's Pip, Mary Shelley's Frankenstein – each of us can extend the list" (3–4). We might well extend her list to include Grendel, the disturbing monster projected by the author of *Beowulf.* The figure of Grendel, it turns out, plays a prominent role in the analysis of *Beowulf* offered by Seamus Heaney. Heaney's analysis appears in a graduation address he delivered at the year 2000 commencement ceremony at Harvard University (where, ten years earlier, Morrison first presented the lectures that would become *Playing in the Dark*). The passage from *Beowulf* that Heaney chooses to analyze turns out to feature, in its own way, an instance of playing in the dark. As Heaney observes, the passage juxtaposes the "light of order, civility and art inside this hall" of Hrothgar, where Beowulf is a welcome guest, to "the monster Grendel [who] is circling in the dark, prowling, listening to the poet inside singing" (67).[33]

> Then a powerful demon, a prowler through the dark,
> nursed a hard grievance. It harrowed him
> to hear the din of the loud banquet
> every day in the hall, the harp being struck
> and the clear song of a skilled poet
> telling with mastery of man's beginnings . . .
>
> (67–68)

As the "skilled poet" sings, he stands apart from the "demon" prowling the external darkness. Attentive to this contrast, Heaney observes that the Hall of Hrothgar presents "an image of both election and exclusion" (68). Borrowing the terms of Morrison's analysis, we might conclude that the poet's song is enabled by this exclusion of the demonic Grendel. That is, just as Africanism is projected by the American mind and imagination, Grendel is projected by an Anglo-Saxon mind and imagination, and by confirming that "savagery is 'out there'" (45), Grendel becomes a "not-me" that permits the poet's "me" to be the opposite, "civilized" (45). The "clear song of the skilled poet" is thus a form of playing in the dark that is crucially enabled by being – as Morrison puts it – "backgrounded by savagery" (44). The fabrication of Grendel would seem to do the same work for *Beowulf* and Anglo-Saxon literature as a fabricated Africanist persona does for American literature. American-Africanism, on this account, has its literary and imaginative counterpart in Anglo-Saxon Grendelism.

Consistent as it may be with Morrison's *Playing in the Dark*, this analysis is not the one Heaney himself offers of the *Beowulf* passage. "Whatever else has happened in our time," Heaney tells the commencement audience, "there has been a recognition of the human affront of relegation and segregation, of the injustice of exclusion on the grounds of race or gender or class or economic status" (68). What "our time" has come to recognize, Heaney suggests, has been anticipated within the *Beowulf* passage, with its willingness to acknowledge the sense of "hard grievance" that Grendel feels when he is excluded from the festivities in the hall of Hrothgar. It is this acknowledgment of Grendel's hard grievance that, for Heaney, makes the passage relevant to "our time" and its "recognition of human affront": "We've learned, in other words, to look at John Winthrop through the eyes of the Native American; to take a Native Irish view of the English expropriations; and indeed, to take a Grendel's eye view of Beowulf" (68). Here, instead of viewing Grendel himself as the enabling fabrication of Anglo-Saxon identity, Heaney views Grendel's "hard grievance" as an allegorical figuration for actual exploitations throughout history. The peoples mistreated in these exploitative acts include not only Native Americans and Native Irish but also, we should add, African-Americans, the people enslaved by that group of Anglo-Saxons whose multicultural odyssey, Heaney observes, led them from a pristine Celto-British land to the "American South" (xxvi) – specifically, to the colonial Mississippi plantation where Dunbar ("a Scot by birth" [*PD* 41]) owned African-Americans. What Heaney registers in Grendel's "hard grievance," then, is not the imaginative play of authors but the harmful exclusion of oppressors. Himself a "scholarship boy" (68), Heaney narrowly escaped becoming just such a Grendel, and the denial of scholarship opportunities to others like him is the kind of social injustice that Heaney imagines *Beowulf* to register. Grendels are thus historical products of exclusionary social practices, and their production constitutes, for Heaney, a "history" that "must be acknowledged" (68).

Left unacknowledged, this history continues – as Morrison's experience shows – to make more Grendels: "My childhood efforts to join America," Morrison observes, "were continually rebuffed. So I finally said, 'you got it'. America has always meant something other to me – them. I was not fully participant in it" ("Living Memory," 179–80).[34] But acknowledging this history – adopting a Morrison's eye view of America, a Grendel's eye view of Beowulf – is not, in itself, sufficient to alleviate the "hard grievance" that Morrison is made to feel. Moreover, if one hopes to alleviate this grievance, one cannot find guidance in the text of *Beowulf* itself since, as Toni Morrison has observed of *Beowulf*, it privileges violence.[35] Appareatly aware of this problem, Heaney shifts his attention from the Hall of Hrothgar to a comparable site, the Halls of Harvard: "great institutions, not only hold promise of fulfillment for those within them, but they can prompt feelings of relegation in those outside them" (68).[36] But what sets Harvard apart, Heaney observes, is its receptiveness toward Grendels, its "determination to open the books and unbar the gates for every student who needs to get in" (68). Transforming Grendels to students, Harvard not only acknowledges the history of hard grievance, it also alters that history – at least for those who have gathered to hear this skilled poet's clear song. "So on the occasion of this millennial Commencement" Heaney tells the graduates, "let us resolve that the open books on the Harvard crest will continue to signify open access to the institution" (68).

Yet if this open access is to continue, it will not do so for these graduates. As in the Hall of Hrothgar, this banquet is finite: it can only accommodate so many, and those few for only so long before the banquet ends and the guests return – as will the graduates Heaney addresses – to the "history" outside its walls, the social context in which hard grievances are formed. If Harvard thus shows how history can be both acknowledged and altered, its alternative of inclusiveness proves to be only partial and temporary. Yet rather than cast graduation as a moment of lapse, a moment when this period of inclusiveness must come to an end, Heaney instead casts that period as a future source of abundant recompense. Having acknowledged and to some extent countered a history of hard grievance, Harvard must return its graduates to that history, but as they once again become Beowulfs and Grendels, they are invited to look beyond this impending future to an alternative, memory. This memory is provided at the close of Heaney's address when he reads a villanelle containing the following recurring lines: "A spirit moves, John Harvard walks the yard. / The books stand open and the gates unbarred" (68). If the "spirit" of John Harvard walks a perpetual sentry duty to enforce open access for future students, this spirit can only preserve the fleeting memory of that access for graduates. These graduates will go on to participate in history's inevitable inequalities, but if hard grievance must return, its temporary suspension will be remembered by the students. A constant presence since the university's founding, the "spirit" of John Harvard becomes the soul of Harvard folk, even though they go on to be Grendels and Beowulfs.

Heaney's repeated lines invoking this ghost of John Harvard align his poem not just with the literary form of the villanelle but also with the literary genre of "inscription," a genre that, as Geoffrey Hartman observes, "was in theory, and often in fact, a dependent form of poetry, in the same sense in which the statues of churches are dependent on their architectural setting or partly conceived in function of it. The inscription was anything conscious of the place on which it was written."[37] The genre of inscription is favored not only by Heaney but also, as we have seen, by William Gilmore Simms who, as Chapter 2 demonstrates, used it as a way of registering the southern *genius loci* and thus a southern national identity. As Simms observed in a lecture prepared for his northern speaking tour, "I will be your medium, to use the language of the Spiritualists, and will put you *en rapport* with the *genius loci* in the wild abodes of the Apalachian."[38] Like Heaney, then, who invokes the spirit of John Harvard, a ghost from the colonial past who serves as the university's *genius loci*, Simms invokes a different set of colonial-era ghosts as the *genius loci* of the South: "In what bold relief," Simms observes, "do we conjure the image of . . . [John Smith]. Following his track, we encounter . . . Powhatan; and behind him, . . . Opechancanough" (7). Through this site-specific memory of his native South, Simms hopes to displace a history of sectional tensions, the hard grievance that would ultimately scuttle his northern lecture tour. For both Heaney and Simms, then, local memory directs attention away from the hard grievances of history, replacing conflict with identity. "This is, after all," argues Roberto Dainotto, "the reactionary trait of the literature of place: it tries to take the question of identity away from the space of politics – away from the space of negotiation. It imposes identity as a rooted absolute," thereby claiming to establish "a place of freedom from the contingent impositions – and crises – of what we have come to know as history."[39]

Heaney replaces history with identity when, as we have seen, he uses the "further language" of *Beowulf* to overcome the political conflict between England and Ireland. That same conflict comes up again in Heaney's Harvard commencement address: "We've learned," Heaney observes, ". . . to take a Native Irish view of the English expropriations; and indeed, to take a Grendel's eye view of Beowulf' (68). Just as Heaney had subsumed English Beowulfs and Irish Grendels within a common Anglo-Saxon identity, so too he will subsume Harvard's graduates within a common Harvard identity: like the pristine Anglo-Saxon language that is dispersed by a linguistic

Odyssey, Harvard's graduates will be dispersed after commencement, and like the words whiskey, *uisce*, and Usk which, while they have become historically distinct, are nevertheless the "same word" (if only for the linguistic Odysseus, who remembers their common point of origin), the Harvard graduates Heaney addresses, while they will henceforth become historically distinct, are nevertheless the same person (if only as a graduating "class," a designation that references their former association with John Harvard's "spirit"). Anglo-Saxon identity thus corresponds to Harvard identity, each identity replacing hard grievance with a mythic, extra-historical somewhere being remembered – whether that somewhere be the pristine Celto-British land remembered by the linguistic Odysseus or the haunted campus remembered by classes of Harvard alumni. Thus even as graduates leave behind this location where Grendels and Beowulfs had once been reconciled and resume their participation in the exclusions that yield "hard grievance," they can nevertheless claim, Heaney suggests, that they are all ultimately "the same." The reconciliation of Beowulfs and Grendels becomes not what these graduates do but – insofar as they have a Harvard identity – who they *are*. One can continue to *be* a reconciler of the conflict between Beowulfs and Grendels even if one does not, thereafter, actively pursue that reconciliation – one is simply a medium through whom prior efforts toward such reconciliation, such a lost cause, are remembered. Thus for Heaney, if history must be acknowledged, there is an even greater imperative, we now see, that such a history must be superceded, the history of conflict replaced by the persistence of identity.

"A RACE-SPECIFIC YET NONRACIST HOME"

The priority given to identity in Heaney's commencement address and his *Beowulf* introduction is apparent as well in Toni Morrison's novel *Jazz*, particularly in that novel's treatment of the character Golden Gray. As was noted in the Introduction, Golden Gray is a character who, like James Weldon Johnson's Ex-Colored Man, easily passes for white – indeed, since he grows up convinced he is white, he is not even aware that he is passing. Morrison's novel, which was published in the year following her *Playing in the Dark*, shares with that work of literary criticism a concern with passing narratives: both her critical account of American literature and her fictional account of Golden Gray feature a body – whether textual or corporeal – aspiring to an unobtainable white purity. The dilemma faced by Golden, then, would seem to be the same dilemma facing American literature in Morrison's *Playing in the Dark*: will he continue to behave in the manner of American literary criticism (and Johnson's Ex-Colored Man) by trying to present himself as if he were white, thus rendering himself "bereft" of a birthright? Or will he, as Morrison's *Playing in the Dark* suggests American literature ought to do instead, embrace the Africanist presence in his body, his one drop of black blood? Put another way, will Morrison use *Jazz* to implement the revisions of the passing narrative called for in her literary criticism? Ultimately, I will suggest, she does not; instead, she makes a different set of revisions. If Morrison's *Jazz* reproduces this dilemma of passing – corporeal as well as textual – in Golden Gray, it does so, I will suggest, to set this formulation of the problem aside in favor of a different account of identity, one that makes Morrison's novel look less like a revision of James Weldon Johnson and more, I will suggest, like a revision of Walter Scott.

This shift unfolds gradually as Morrison presents the character of Golden Gray. Having just learned that his father is black, Golden initially expresses strong hostility toward his black ancestry, setting out on a journey to confront and perhaps kill his father. It is a journey reminiscent of Klan violence, for as the narrator observes, Golden had "Come all that way to insult not his father but his race."[40] During his journey, however, Golden encounters Wild, a pregnant black woman who lives alone, far from others, and seems to haunt the cane fields. "Wild was not a story of a used-to-be-long-ago-crazy girl. . . . She was still out there – and real" (167). Sightings of Wild occasion worried rumors among nearby residents, who view her as a potential source of "harm" (165). Given this account of her – as a haunting, antisocial, and shunned presence – Wild would seem to correspond to the Africanist presence Morrison describes in *Playing in the Dark*.[41] When Wild first sees Golden she is startled and, turning to run, she strikes her head against a tree, falling to the ground unconscious. Given his hostility toward his black father, Golden is not inclined to assist this injured black woman. But he does so anyway, and the narrator, puzzled by this gesture, speculates about his motive for helping her: ". . . perhaps it was because the awful-looking thing lying in wet weeds was everything he was not as well as a proper protection against and anodyne to what he believed his father to be, and therefore (if it could just be contained, identified) – himself" (149). This proposed motive resembles the thinking Morrison attributes to whites like Dunbar in *Playing in the Dark*: in characterizing the black slave as the "not-me" (in Golden's case, characterizing Wild as "everything he is not"), a White American self in fact encounters a self-reflexive projection (in Golden's case, "himself"). Understood in these terms, Golden's motive for helping Wild is consistent with what Morrison calls the quintessential American identity.

By assisting the injured Wild, Golden revises Johnson's Ex-Colored Man, revealing rather than concealing the Africanist presence through which his whiteness is pursued and, thus, upon which his Americanness is founded.[42] But if this account of Golden revises Johnson's Ex-Colored Man by replacing concealment with disclosure, this disclosure takes place within the same pattern of thinking about identity, an identity that is now textual rather than corporeal, now American rather than black. Moreover, this account of Golden helps make explicit the link, implicit in Morrison's *Playing in the Dark*, between corporeal accounts of black bodies and critical accounts of American texts. First, this account of Golden links a corporeal logic of black identity (involving Golden's supposedly "black blood") to the textual logic of American identity (involving a fabricated Africanism): just as a commitment to "black blood" makes Golden's white-seeming body black, so too his commitment to seeing Wild as an Africanist presence makes his white-seeming identity American. Second, this account of Golden extends this logic from the identity of a character like Golden to the identity of the text in which Golden appears: just as Golden's fabrication of Africanism make him American, so too every text's commitment to fabricating such Africanism would make that text American.

Yet if this analysis of Golden's motives casts *Jazz* as an extension and fulfillment of Morrison's earlier critical arguments in *Playing in the Dark*, such an analysis of the novel ultimately seems incomplete. This becomes apparent as the conspicuously uncertain narrator of *Jazz* offers an additional account of Golden's motives for helping Wild. Having suggested a motive that, as I have argued, rehearses Morrison's argument from *Playing in the Dark*, the narrator then considers an alternative motive: "Or," the narrator asks, "was the figure, the vision, as he thought of it" (149) a

> vision that, at the moment when his scare was sharpest, looked also like home comfortable enough to wallow in? That could be it. But who could live in that leafy hair? that unfathomable skin? But he already had lived in and with it: True Belle [Golden's black nurse] had been his first and major love, which may be why two gallops beyond that hair, that skin, their absence was unthinkable. (150)

While the "absence" of Wild is necessary for whiteness – and thus her "presence" is necessary as the element whose exclusion produces that whiteness – her absence is "unthinkable" to Golden. It would ultimately be a mistake, then, to view Golden as a revised Ex-Colored Man, a figure who, like Morrison's preferred form of literary criticism, discloses rather than conceals the denigration of Africanism. Morrison is not, in other words, presenting Wild as just another Africanist persona akin to the earlier ones in American literature. What Wild provides for Golden, ultimately, is not a foil but rather a "home comfortable enough to wallow in." Indeed, Golden and Wild end up living together in Wild's cave dwelling, which is located at a remote site along the banks of "the river whites called Treason" (182). As the river's name suggests, Golden's decision to live with Wild is, from the perspective of whites, not an expression of loyalty to his hidden blackness but an act of treason against his apparent whiteness and consequent Americanness: if repudiating Wild made him pass as white and thereby be American (an Americanism rooted in denigrating a fabricated Africanism), living with Wild undercuts both the pure whiteness to which he had once pretended and the Americanness that such pretensions ultimately conferred.

Within Wild's cave Morrison presents a "domestic" (183) scene, "a stone room where somebody cooked with oil" (183). Thirteen years having passed since they first met (165), Wild and Golden have developed what the narrator describes as "old-time love" (228). The dwelling that Golden and Wild share is a place that Morrison's later essay, "Home," invokes as exemplary of her authorial goal "to inhabit, walk around, a site clear of racist detritus; a place where race both matters and is rendered impotent; a place 'already made for me, both snug and wide open.'"[43] In this final phrase Morrison quotes herself, specifically her own description, in *Jazz*, of the cave shared by Wild and Golden (221). Morrison's aim in invoking this place is to distinguish it from a racist "house," calling it, instead, the "Home" (12) referenced in that essay's title. As such a "Home," Golden and Wild's dwelling represents, Morrison suggests, a response to one of those "questions, which . . . have troubled all of my work. How to be both free and situated; how to convert a racist house into a race-specific yet nonracist home. How to enunciate race while depriving it of its lethal cling?" (5). Having grown up in a United States that is just such a racist house, one reflected in the literature she addresses in *Playing in the Dark*, Morrison has imagined an alternative to that racist house in the home of Golden and Wild (much as Golden himself sees "home" in Wild). Understood as such an alternative, the cave that Golden and Wild make their joint home does more than just revise the Ex-Colored Man's Americanness (a revision, as we have seen, that consisted of revealing rather than concealing the American birthright, i.e. the repudiation of fabricated Africanism). While that earlier revision acknowledged a history of hard grievance, the exclusion of African-Americans from American literature, it did nothing to remedy the exclusion. The cave of Golden and Wild offers such a remedy by entirely displacing that earlier revision and offering in its stead another version of identity – an American national identity in which "race both matters and is rendered impotent." How, then, does Morrison articulate this alternative account of Americanness?

One way to understand her alternative is to consider Wild and Golden's cave alongside a similar dwelling discussed earlier in this book. In Chapter 1 I argued that Scott's story *The Highland Widow* uses the dwelling of Elspat MacTavish to bring together two characters, Elspat and her son Hamish. Like the cave shared by Wild and Golden, Elspat's hut also has treasonous implications: Elspat's son is poised on the threshold of the hut and is thus balanced between his Highlander mother, within, and his British army regiment, without. Induced by his mother to fire his gun at his military comrades, Hamish commits an act of treason for which he is ultimately executed. The antagonistic forces that converge on Scott's Hamish parallel the antagonistic forces converging on Morrison's Golden Gray: just as Hamish wavers between the Highland world of his ancestral past and the imperial context of his personal ambition, Golden likewise appears suspended between two incompatible extremes, the Africanism of his ancestral blood and the pure whiteness to which he aspires.[44] As Golden confronts his black father, his father tells him, "Look. Be what you want – white or black. Choose" (173). Golden is on the verge – like Scott's Hamish – of using his gun to express his choice: "his sober thought was to blow the man's head off" (173). To kill his father, however, would be to prefer whiteness over blackness, and thus to fail, as does Scott's Hamish, to keep sight of both. To do so, moreover, would be to reproduce Morrison's account of Americanness from *Playing in the Dark*: by killing his black father, Golden would be violently expelling the Africanism whose exclusion is central to the American commitment to whiteness. But Golden does not follow through on this impulse to patricide, and as Morrison's narrator says, "It must have been the girl" – Wild – "who changed his mind" (173).

Under Wild's influence, Golden adopts a new outlook. He no longer sees himself according to the racial biology of the one drop rule, as a racial passer driven – in the quintessentially American fashion of Dunbar – to repudiate an internal blackness in favor of an impossibly pure whiteness. Instead, he starts to view himself in terms of the experientially comfortable and familiar blackness he loves – the blackness of his nurse True Belle, the absence of whose blackness is "unthinkable" to him and the presence of which he sees in Wild. Golden exchanges an "intimate relationship to what is being nulled,"[45] his father, for an intimate relationship to what is beloved, Wild.[46] The status of Wild undergoes a corresponding shift: no longer the site where Golden projects a fabricated Africanism that he must exclude, she embodies instead the familiar black features that he cannot live without – home.[47] In shifting his view of Wild, Golden undergoes a shift in identity: while he had been a (quintessentially American) aspirant toward whiteness, which had required the expulsion of Africanism, he now becomes what Morrison elsewhere calls "white" (using the small letter "w" as distinct from the "W" of White).[48] Morrison's *Jazz* thus introduces two substitutions: Golden had aspired to be White (which made him, according to the logic of *Playing in the Dark*, in fact American), but he is now simply white; and Wild had been a surface upon which was projected a fabricated Africanism, but she now becomes a site of genuine blackness.[49]

As a result of these two changes, Golden is no longer, like the quintessential American of *Playing in the Dark*, poised between the extremes of Africanism and Whiteness, but is instead a white who loves blackness. It is this second, revised condition that Morrison presents in her idyllic cave. Thus, unlike Walter Scott, who poises a character (Hamish) between antagonistic or warlike extremes (his Highland mother and his British regiment) and forces that character – with the loaded gun – to choose, Morrison rewrites Scott's political antagonists – nation and empire – as racial lovers – black and white – and recasts the space that separates them from a gap of incompatible choices to the space of erotic desire and intimate embrace. Unlike Scott, then, whose hut scene uses gunfire to separate these political alternatives, assimilating Hamish to just one of them (and thus failing to keep sight of both), Morrison uses sexual intimacy to join these racial alternatives of black and white, this eroticism bringing them together in a way that permits her successfully to keep sight of both. While an older, White racial logic (like that disclosed in Morrison's *Playing in the Dark* and expressed in Davenport's *Blood Will Tell*) might construe this erotic domestic scene as treasonous miscegenation that undermines the stable purity of Whiteness, Morrison's *Jazz* is interested in a new version of American identity in which Wild is neither denigrated as the savage embodiment of "black blood" nor designated as an Africanist persona who, through her exclusion, helps advance an American desire for pure Whiteness. Rather than serve as either of these accessories to Whiteness, Wild is instead embraced by Golden for the "home" that he finds appealing in her.[50] Whereas Americanness had earlier stemmed from keeping blackness out of sight, it now stems from keeping sight of both black and white. Thus if the exclusionary logic of Elspat's hut ultimately undermines Scott's effort to "keep sight of both" nation and empire (by forcing Hamish to choose between them), Morrison's cave succeeds in keeping sight of both black and white – achieving, as she puts it, "race-specificity without race prerogative" (5). This revision of Scott supercedes Morrison's earlier revision of Johnson's Ex-Colored Man (a revision that, as we saw in *Playing in the Dark*, had sought merely to acknowledge the fabrication and denigration of Africanism, not to replace it with something entirely new). As a result of this second revision Morrison is able to find an alternative way to represent American identity, one that involves "imagining race without dominance – without hierarchy" (11).[51] If her earlier criticism had located Americanness at places like Dunbar's colonial Mississippi plantation, a place where Whiteness invented and then repudiated Africanism, *Jazz* locates Americanness at a place like Golden and Wild's dwelling, a place where white and black intimately embrace.

Morrison explores this revised notion of American identity not only, as Scott does, by presenting a domestic "home" scene but also, as Scott likewise does, by focusing on the medium of the text itself. Scott, as we have seen, features the textual medium in his metrical "summons" which, he imagines, affects readers in much the same way that the character Elspat affects her son. Thus just as the hut's threshold brings together uniformed imperial soldiers and Elspat's Highland past, poising Hamish between the two, so too Scott's poetic motto brings together a uniform English language and a traditional Highland meter, poising Scott's readers between the two, a position that leads them – if they are genuine Scots – to be possessed by their recollections of the meter and thus to be summoned forth as the Scots they are. In a similar way, Morrison uses her textual medium as an extension of her domestic scene with Wild and Golden, leading her text to enact that scene's inter-racial eroticism. This textual eroticism is something Morrison herself emphasizes when she discusses this novel's narrative voice: "It sounds like a very erotic, sensual love song of a person who loves you. This is a love song of a book talking to the reader."[52] Morrison then goes on to recite the final lines of *Jazz*, lines in which this loving narrator, speaking enviously of the "old-time love" (228) shared by characters like Wild and Golden, turns to address the reader directly: "I myself have . . . longed . . . to be able to say out loud what they have no need to say at all. . . . If I were able I'd say it. Say make me, remake me. You are free to do it and I am free to let you because look, look. Look where your hands are. Now."[53] This invitation gains its erotic charge, Morrison observes, from the reader's "tactile" relation to the printed page he or she holds: "holding, surrendering to a book, is part of that beautiful intimacy of reading. When it's tactile, your emotions are deeply involved" (42). The reader's tactile relation to the book's medium thus reproduces Golden Gray's situation of holding in his arms Wild's unconscious body. The success of *Jazz* in achieving this tactile intimacy with readers, Morrison observes, stems from its narrative voice, which she says "is the voice of a talking book . . . I deliberately restricted myself using an 'I' that was only connected to the artifact of the book as an active participant in the invention of the story of the book, as though the book were talking, writing itself, in a sense" (42). This active, inventive voice, she continues, "reminded me of a jazz performance" (41).[54]

Applying this invocation of jazz to the novel's closing words, we see the connection between Morrison and Scott's concern with material textual effects: like Scott's metrical summons, which presents readers with a specifically Scottish medium, a Scottish meter superadded to English words, Morrison's closing lines present the reader with a specifically black medium, a jazz texture and tone that she has elsewhere, as we have seen, described as "irrevocably black."[55] In inviting the reader to embrace the novel *Jazz* in its tactile materiality, its irrevocably black texture and tone, these closing lines invite the (white) reader to embrace blackness itself.[56] Such an erotic embrace between black and white, if achieved, would be consistent with Morrison's goal of "imagining race without dominance – without hierarchy" ("Home," 11). Just as Walter Scott assigns Scottish identity to British subjects who are demoniacally possessed by recollections of the Highland past, Morrison assigns American identity to white subjects who are erotically possessed by blackness.[57] Those who surrender to her novel's textual advances contribute to Morrison's goal of producing a new account of American identity, an interracial embrace consistent with her effort "to convert a racist house into a race-specific yet nonracist home" (5).[58]

In confronting readers with this tactile blackness, the closing lines of *Jazz* not only recall the metrical summons of Walter Scott, they also re-stage a scenario that Morrison had addressed in her preface to *Playing in the Dark*, a scenario in which Marie Cardinal is listening to a jazz performance by Louis Armstrong. "My first anxiety attack occurred," Cardinal observes, "during a Louis Armstrong concert. . . . The sounds of the trumpet . . . tore at the nerves. . . . Gripped by a panic . . . I ran into the street like someone possessed" (vi–vii). This response to Armstrong's jazz music, for Morrison, typifies what she will go on to discuss in that volume of literary criticism, the quintessentially American fabrication and repudiation of Africanism. Cardinal's reaction to Armstrong is similar to Golden's initial response to Wild – in Armstrong, Cardinal encounters "the Thing" (vi), and Golden likewise views Wild as "the thing" (149). But Golden, as we have seen, pushes beyond this initial response, eventually viewing Wild as "home" and embracing her as an erotic domestic partner. *Jazz* not only portrays this alternative to Marie Cardinal's response to jazz, it seeks to promote and disseminate that alternative through its own erotic encounter with readers. Morrison's writing, then, replaces Armstrong's playing – as we have seen, her novel's narrative voice "reminded me of a jazz performance" (41) – and the novel's readers, in turn, replace Marie Cardinal, Armstrong's audience, in their bodily proximity to *Jazz*. Instead of fleeing into the street, which would make them White (and thus American in the old sense that we saw in *Playing in the Dark*), they remain curled up with the text's blackness (like Golden in Wild's cave), thus becoming American in this new sense, the sense of loving authentic blackness. Thus unlike Scott's Scottish reader, who is summoned to national identity through demoniacal possession by a national mother, Morrison's American reader is seduced to national identity through erotic possession by an inter-racial lover.[59] In each case, the text's formal medium is imagined to do for readers what it already does for texts – providing an index of collective identity, whether it indexes a Highland history whose familiarity to the British subject makes that subject a Scot or a blackness whose desirability to a white US citizen makes that citizen an American. If Scots are British citizens who have a special relation to a Highland past (a relation of demoniacal possession by Highland recollections), Americans are US citizens who have a special relation to blackness (a relation of sensual desire for genuine blackness), and in each case that relation is mediated by formal textual effects. To underscore the special nature of this relation, Morrison distinguishes European "aficionados" of jazz from their white counterparts in the United States, including musicians like Benny Goodman, the so-called "king of swing," who, "feeding off" the "original musicians," "imitated their music" and thus produced "a sort of bland or played-down reproduction" of jazz ("Interview [with Carabi]," 41). Scott made a similar effort to distinguish those who – like King George IV – merely adopt Scottish garb from those authentic Scots who are genuinely possessed by memories of the Scottish past.[60]

Through these parallels between Morrison and Scott we can observe the larger sweep of what I have been arguing is a specifically literary history of racial identity. Morrison and Scott each present writing as inseparable from formal effects that are, themselves, inseparable from – and thus provide an index of – a particular collective identity. For Scott, the meter superadded to text is itself Scottish, and its superaddition to writing leads to a text demoniacally possessed by a Scottish past and thereby empowered to summon forth Scots. For Morrison the jazz medium erotically embracing her writing is irrevocably black, leading to a text ready to participate in the interracial embrace fundamental to her revised account of American identity. Both Scott and Morrison, moreover, use these accounts of texts to imagine corresponding accounts of persons: Scott's metrical summons provides an index pointing to the Highland past recollected by British subjects, a recollection that makes those subjects Scots, and Morrison's jazz medium provides an index pointing to the blackness desired by US citizens, a desire that makes those citizens Americans. As the previous chapter demonstrated, such an extension of these accounts from texts to persons would invite a slightly different description of formal effects: when associated directly with persons, and thus viewed in corporeal terms, formal effects are not just indices of collective identity but are, more specifically, symptoms of collective identity. Understood as symptoms, formal effects remain indices but now seem to point directly toward the body as their causal source. In this corporeal context, symptoms index a source that, for some late nineteenth-century writers, seemed to be biological, so to these writers, formal effects could provide an index for an instinct, and a particularly racial instinct, located in the blood. Once they were understood as symptoms of racial instincts, and thus as diagnostic signs of racial blood, these formal effects, I have argued, were imagined to make blood tell. Understood in these terms, formal effects underwrote a late nineteenth-century account of bodily racial identity. As a result of this shift to a discourse of bodily symptoms, it became possible to view the texts a writer produced as indexing, through their formal effects, that writer's racial instincts, and thus that writer's racial identity. The following inversion of cause and effect had thus taken place: poetic effects, which had served writers like Scott as a conceptual template for positing a comparable superadded identity demoniacally possessing persons, came to be viewed as a symptomatic consequence of that very identity (now called a biological instinct); and persons, whose identity Scott had presented by analogy to the identity conferred upon literary texts by formal effects, came to be understood as the bodily source of the identity indexed by literary effects. Once the indexical account of formal effects in literary texts had been re-written in this equally indexical vocabulary of bodily symptoms, it came to seem as if this corporeal logic were independent of and separable from literary discourse. As a result, racial identity's literary history became effectively invisible, and what had initially been a literary discourse started to look like an independent medical account of racial identity.

As the previous chapter demonstrates, however, my point has been to emphasize that this seemingly medical account of racial identity has been a literary discourse from the start, and that in appropriating it, the medical sciences have been forced to embrace an occult understanding of causality. Ultimately unable to accommodate that account of causality, the medical sciences have increasingly resisted this notion of bodily racial identity. As Morrison herself has observed, "The idea of scientific racism suggests some serious pathology."[61] But if many medical practitioners now join Morrison in denying any scientific basis to the notion of racial instincts, it is nevertheless the case that the commitment to indices of racial identity – if not bodily symptoms of racial blood – has not disappeared. It has instead taken refuge once again in the literary pattern of thinking from which this corporeal logic was derived, the attribution of racial identity to textual effects. This is why Toni Morrison's insistence on the racial identity of her writing's medium can so closely resemble Walter Scott's account of national identity in his works' formal effects. Skeptical of the emerging discipline of phrenology, Scott shows the same resistance to bodily indices of identity, and the same preference for literary indices of identity, that we see in Morrison. Thus even as she resists one aspect of racial identity's literary history – the aspect that treats textual effects as symptoms of the body's racial instincts – Morrison nevertheless remains true to a larger literary history of which Scott is a vital part, a literary history in which writers treat formal effects as indices of collective identity. Nor is Morrison alone among contemporary adherents to this pattern of thinking, for as we have seen, it is apparent as well in the writings of her fellow Nobel laureat, Seamus Heaney.

As a result of these persistent patterns of thinking, the rejection of corporeal racial instincts and the search for a non-biological vocabulary of racial identity has not led to an alternative logic of racial identity. Instead, that rejection of racial biology has reverted to an earlier fundamentally literary logic of identity, one that played a formative role in establishing those biological accounts in the first place and that extends backward into the nineteenth century's concern with literary indices of another collective identity, nation. It is true, of course, that both Morrison and Heaney introduce a variety of alternatives within this discussion. Morrison, for instance, pursues alternative accounts of American national identity, which in her initial view stems from the repudiation of fabricated Africanism by an aspirant to pure Whiteness and, in her later view, stems from the erotic embrace of genuine blackness by an adoring white aficionado. And Heaney explores alternative contexts for his account of identity, so that the "somewhere" in "a somewhere being remembered" can range from a pristine Celto-British Land to a haunted Harvard yard. But despite these alternative accounts and contexts, the discussion remains committed to treating formal literary effects as indices of collective identity. What might seem like alternative formulations of identity, then, are in fact variations on a theme, with Morrison and Heaney each repeating patterns of thinking that they hold in common with nineteenth-century writers like Walter Scott. Despite these Nobel laureates' various innovations, then, the same basic commitments to and accounts of identity have been conserved.

"FORMIDABLE REVOLUTIONISTS"

Once we observe this fundamental continuity in the literary–critical commitments of these writers, we can gain a better purchase on what might count as a genuine alternative to this long-standing pattern of thinking. We have already seen such an alternative suggested by Seamus Heaney's notion of "hard grievance." As we saw above, Heaney associates hard grievance with the fact that Beowulf is welcome at the Hall of Hrothgar but Grendel is not: only Beowulf is permitted to enjoy the scarce luxuries of that event – to hear "the clear song of the skilled poet / telling with mastery of man's beginnings." Through this fictional scenario Heaney provides an allegory for historically imposed inequalities of access to scarce resources. Beowulf and Grendel, in other words, are figures for social constructs, not identities, and having been constructed by exclusion, they are each subject to being dismantled by the opposite gesture, inclusion. As Heaney sees it, then, one's status as a Grendel is relative to one's circumstances – once Grendels are provided access to resources, they all, in theory, become Beowulfs. This account of hard grievance provides an alternative to identitarian thinking, however, only so long as it is distinguished from the substantially different notion mentioned by Toni Morrison, the "justifiable umbrage" that, she argues, is felt "by Afro-American writers regarding their own exclusion from the 'transcendent "idea of the novel."'"[62] As Heaney imagines it, putting an end to such exclusion would permit writers to exchange their relative status as Grendels for an equally relative status as Beowulfs; Morrison, then, as a celebrated writer of novels, would count as a Beowulf rather than a Grendel, and would be spared "hard grievance." But Morrison's notion of "justifiable umbrage" involves something different: her concern is not just exclusions that lead to "hard grievance" but exclusions that are racially motivated. According to her view, African-American writers are not Grendels because they are excluded, they are excluded because they are Grendels – because they have an identity that Beowulfs (in this case, whites) deride. Here we see the alternative to identity – the alternative represented by the circumstantial notion of "hard grievance" – replaced by a thoroughly identitarian formulation, Morrison's "justifiable umbrage."

One way to underscore the difference is to introduce Morrison's notion into Heaney's allegory of Beowulf and Grendel: in her identitarian formulation, instead of figuring differential degrees of access to scarce resources, Beowulf and Grendel each figure absolute (or essential) identity categories. Thus instead of figuring persons in social contexts of exclusion, Grendel and Beowulf figure identities that – like blackness or Anglo-Saxonness – are independent of one's relative access to resources. Indeed, these identities may be entirely detached from persons and located, as we have seen, in the formal effects of literary texts. So if a lack of material resources for Heaney's Grendels (for instance, non-scholarship boys) is what prompts their hard grievance, a lack of public recognition for Morrison's Grendels (for instance, African-Americans writers) is what prompts their justifiable umbrage. Competition for material resources among persons is thus replaced by competition for recognition among identities. And as we have seen, this competition takes the form of competition for recognition of formal textual effects. Morrison takes this literary competition seriously, working to present her novel, like the jazz music of Louis Armstrong, as the clear song of the skilled poet that provides the entertainment at the American national banquet. Whereas such inclusion would transform Heaney's Grendels (the have-nots outside the Hall) into Beowulfs (the haves within), it leaves Morrison's Grendels (blacks) themselves, Grendels who have gained loving acceptance and appreciation from Morrison's Beowulfs (whites). The socially constructed Grendelism that in Heaney's account had been predicated on exclusion becomes, for Morrison, an identitarian Grendelism that persists regardless of circumstances of exclusion or inclusion. It is by achieving inclusion *as a Grendel* that, for Morrison, justifiable umbrage is assuaged. And as we have seen, this commitment to identity is also where Heaney himself ends up: for Harvard graduates, their shared status as Beowulfs – as institutional insiders – is a temporary condition that must come to an end, but the memory of it – personified as John Harvard – will remain a ghostly presence on the Harvard campus, much like the blackness that remains a ghostly presence in Morrison's written texts.

This account of Morrison and Heaney suggests that they both place greater emphasis on identity than its alternative, the social construction of, and disassembly of, hard grievance. It would be a mistake, however, to deny any relation between the concern with identity in Morrison and Heaney and the project of ameliorating hard grievance. Indeed, one might argue that by gaining recognition for a particular identity, one helps diminish the hard grievance experienced by those who are understood, bodily, to have that identity: the recognition of those effects augurs recognition of the bodies associated with them. This is the logic that Kenneth Warren identifies (and critiques) in critics like Henry Louis Gates., Jr., specifically "his assumption that working in an African-American studies program should be synonymous if not identical with working on behalf of the black community."[63] Alternatively, one might argue – as Marlon Ross does – that identitarian thinking can ameliorate hard grievances not through achieving loving recognition from those with different identities but rather through rallying those who share an identity to work collectively against their circumstance of hard grievance. Thus Ross asserts that "blues, jazz, loud-talk, churchiness, and many other culturally specified manners help to perform and *reproduce* a will to struggle together against the common foe of racism."[64] Responding to such arguments Stephen Greenblatt is willing "to acknowledge the possible tactical efficacy of such artificial memories and fabricated histories" (56), admitting that such a "strategy is by no means necessarily reactionary, that it may serve progressive ends" (56). Greenblatt's concern, however, is that among "Literary critics," "no coherent arguments are made . . . to explain why claims of racial memory or ethnic solidarity that are anything but progressive in . . . real-world politics . . . should somehow be transformed when they are set in verse" (58). Indeed, it is "anything but progressive" – i.e. anything but liberal – ends that, as we have seen, were set in verse by Walter Scott, a fact Scott acknowledges in a letter to John Croker, the British minister whom he had seemed to be opposing in the verse "motto" of his *Letters of Malachi Malagrowther*:

> But Scotland, completely liberalized, as she is in a fair way of being, will be the most dangerous neighbour to England that she has been since 1639. There is yet time to make a stand, for there is yet a great deal of good and genuine feeling left in the country. But if you *unscotch* us you will find us damned mischievous Englishmen. The restless and yet laborious and constantly watchful character of the people, their desire for speculation in politics or any thing else, only restrained by some proud feelings about their own country, now become antiquated and which late measures will tend much to destroy, will make them, under a wrong direction, the most formidable revolutionists who ever took the field of innovation.[65]

The goal here is to "make a stand" against Scotland becoming "completely liberalized," and the means to that end is not to "*unscotch*" the Scots but, instead, to inspire in Scots "proud feelings about their own country," about their Scottish identity. Scott, as we have seen, prompted these feelings by means of formal literary effects, assuaging his justifiable umbrage at the slighting of Scottish identity while making no fundamental changes in the Union's political structure – indeed, countering any efforts to make such changes. Scott's letter confirms not only the concern of Greenblatt but also the related observation of Adolph Reed who, critiquing southern identities similar to those envisioned by William Gilmore Simms and Sidney Lanier, observes that "the preservationist impulse is by no means automatically politically progressive. It can come just as easily from a reactionary nostalgia about 'tradition' as from models of harmonious, democratic social life."[66] Indeed, this "ambivalence of the preservationist impulse" (182) is precisely what leads a critic like Reed – who is interested in blacks becoming unblacked, or completely liberalized – to castigate literary criticism as an obstacle to projects like his own, projects that seek to galvanize a liberalized populace into the very "formidable revolutionists" whom Scott and Croker each fear.[67]

What this suggests is that literary criticism of formal effects, with its concern for assuaging the justifiable umbrage of particular identities, is at best an ambivalent vehicle for alleviating hard grievance and at worst a genuine obstacle to such ends. While a focus on the identity of formal textual effects might help produce coalitions of those who might then go on to alleviate hard grievance, this focus might just as easily distract them from that goal, becoming an end in itself rather than a means to that end. This distraction is exploited by anti-progressive writers like Scott and it is inadequately registered, I would argue, by writers like Morrison and Heaney, writers who tie their work to a more progressive political agenda. When such distractions are in place, political leadership is replaced by literary criticism, a discipline whose practitioners, whatever their political intentions, are trained to address matters of aesthetic judgment rather than matters of social justice.[68] In such hands, with such a focus on textual identity, politics does not of course disappear, but it courts distraction – of the kind Scott welcomes – from progressive political goals. The question, then, is not whether the attribution of collective identity to formal textual effects is a political gesture, but rather which political ends – assuaging justifiable umbrage or alleviating hard grievance – it serves.

The question of how one ought to proceed in such cases has not been a central focus of this study, but one conclusion to which this study does point is that, in the various cases in which it has been in effect, whether it involved the national identities of texts or the racial identities of bodies, this literary logic has generally hampered progressive politics by undermining the liberal subject and thereby marginalizing the account of the subject upon which such a progressive politics relies.[69] This outcome need not, of course, be viewed as a problem; indeed, for some writers a progressive politics is precisely to be avoided, and literary criticism of the kind I have been describing provides them with a welcome alternative to progressive or liberal goals.[70] But if one's primary goal is progressive political engagement on behalf of alleviating the hard grievance of underserved citizens, one would be well advised, this project suggests, to avoid the distractions from that end that can arise from embracing the pattern of thinking whose literary history this book has presented. While analyzing literary texts that participate in this pattern of thinking might make one a more informed critic of the rhetorical techniques used to challenge the notion of the liberal subject and, thereby, to undermine progressive political reforms on behalf of such subjects, that analysis – and indeed (to borrow a phrase from Morrison) this book "where your hands are. Now" (*Jazz*, 229) – is not sufficient in itself to achieve those progressive ends. If one seeks to advance progressive reforms on behalf of those excluded from scarce resources, one must begin, I am arguing, not with a loving embrace that conserves identities but with a critical resistance to that seductive call. And for those who truly aspire to become "formidable revolutionists," the most direct avenue to that end is not more extensive formal analysis of literary texts but, instead, a more equitable distribution of resources to the population at large.

Notes

INTRODUCTION: THE POETICS OF IDENTITY

1. Toni Morrison, "Living Memory: A Meeting with Toni Morrison," with Paul Gilroy. Paul Gilroy, *Small Acts: Thoughts on the Politics of Black Cultures* (London: Serpent's Tail, 1993), 181–82. Subsequent citations will appear parenthetically in the text.
2. Seamus Heaney, "Introduction," *Beowulf: A New Verse Translation*, trans. Seamus Heaney (New York: Farrar, Straus and Giroux, 2000), xxiii. Subsequent citations will appear parenthetically in the text.
3. In her discussion with Paul Gilroy, Morrison distinguishes herself from black Americans who have chosen to distance themselves from a black underclass: "I feel very estranged from black Americans. . . . When I say that phrase, what pops before me is a kind of bourgeois 'I have made it' person who is more foreign to me than a sympathetic white American" (180). In an earlier (1987) interview Morrison similarly makes blackness a function of chosen affiliation: "Now people choose their identities. Now people choose to be Black. They used to be *born* Black. That's not true anymore. You can be Black genetically and choose not to be" (*Conversations with Toni Morrison*, ed. Danille Taylor-Guthrie [Jackson: University Press of Mississippi, 1994], 236).
4. In *The Redress of Poetry* (New York: Farrar, Straus and Giroux, 1995) Heaney, speaking of his residence in the north of Ireland, seeks "to be understood as having full freedom to the enjoyment of an Irish name and identity within that northern jurisdiction. Those who [like Heaney himself] want to share that name and identity in Britain's Ireland should not be penalized or resented or suspected of a sinister motive because they draw cultural and psychic sustenance from an elsewhere supplementary to the one across the water. . . . [T]hey, in turn, must not penalize or resist the at-homeness of their neighbours who cherish the primacy of the British link" (201–02).
5. Henry Louis Gates, Jr., *Figures in Black: Words, Signs, and the "Racial" Self* (New York: Oxford University Press, 1987), 275, 179, 187. Although Gates here describes music as the "referent," he earlier says of dialect that there is "a musicality inherent in the form itself" (179), collapsing the distinction between dialect writing and music and thus reinforcing Morrison's notion that blackness is "intrinsic" to the writing itself.

6. Houston Baker, *Modernism and the Harlem Renaissance* (University of Chicago Press, 1987), 68, 60.
7. See Ted Hughes, "Myths, Metres, Rhythms," *Winter Pollen: Occasional Prose*, ed. William Scammell (Boston: Faber and Faber, 1994), 360, 366. For a useful discussion of Hughes's influence on Heaney, see Raphaël Ingelbien, "Mapping the Misreadings: Ted Hughes, Seamus Heaney, and Nationhood," *Contemporary Literature* 40:4 (Winter 1999): 627–58.
8. Northrop Frye, *Anatomy of Criticism: Four Essays* (Princeton University Press, 1957), 251. To demonstrate this point Frye proposes the following experiment: "If we read many iambic pentameters 'naturally,' giving the important words the heavy accent that they do have in spoken English, the old four-stress line stands out in clear relief against its metrical background" (251).
9. See Sculley Bradley, "The Fundamental Metrical Principle in Whitman's Poetry" [1939], *On Whitman: The Best from* American Literature, ed. Edwin H. Cady and Louis J. Budd (Durham, NC: Duke University Press, 1987), 50, 53, 50, 54 note 19. For a symptomatic discussion of these claims of an Anglo-Saxon essence within literary effects, see Joseph Malof, "The Native Rhythm of English Meters," *Texas Studies in Literature and Language* 5:4 (Winter 1964): 580–94.
10. Benedict Anderson, for instance, has written that "nationality, . . . nation-ness, as well as nationalism, are cultural artefacts of a particular kind," and he argues that "the creation of these artefacts towards the end of the eighteenth century was the spontaneous distillation of a complex 'crossing' of discrete historical forces," specifically, "the convergence of capitalism and print technology"; Benedict Anderson, *Imagined Communities: Reflections on the Origin and Spread of Nationalism*, revised edn. (New York: Verso, 1991), 4, 4, 46. Just as Anderson focuses specifically on nation, Kwame Anthony Appiah ("Race, Culture, Identity: Misunderstood Connections," in K. Anthony Appiah and Amy Gutmann, *Color Conscious: The Political Morality of Race* [Princeton University Press, 1996]) focuses on race when he addresses "the history of the race concept" (71): "current ways of talking about race," Appiah argues, "are the residue, the detritus, so to speak, of earlier ways of thinking about race; so that it turns out to be easiest to understand contemporary talk about 'race' as the pale reflection of a more full-blooded race discourse that flourished in the last century" (38). Comparing the account of race in Shakespeare's *Othello* to the writings of Thomas Jefferson, Appiah argues that "Jefferson's discussion is representative of a transition in the way the word 'race' is used" (50). A further transition comes in the work of Matthew Arnold: "Arnold . . . invokes race – which in Jefferson is invoked to account for division – in a context where he is arguing toward universality" (58–59). Arnold's account of race is itself modified by the scientific thinking of Darwin: "Darwin . . . thought of the species as essentially a classificatory convenience. . . . To believe this was already to move away from the sort of racial essences that we find in Arnold" (67). In the course of his analysis of race, Appiah does suggest a link between racial and national identity, an observation to which I am

indebted: "Between Carlyle's essay and Arnold's lectures, talk of 'nations' was displaced by talk of 'race'" (62). I will argue that this displacement was possible because, in the writers I address, it also involved a fundamental logical continuity, an ongoing commitment to formal literary effects as a vehicle for conferring collective identity, whether national or racial.

11. Anthony W. Marx, for instance, has argued that "[t]he process of defining the nation with rules of citizenship is of obvious relevance for how racial categories are established and reinforced. Coercive powers have been used to define citizenship according to race. . . . Official exclusion, as by race, legitimates these categories as a form of social identity"; Anthony W. Marx, *Making Race and Nation: A Comparison of South Africa, The United States, and Brazil* (New York: Cambridge University Press, 1998), 5–6. For a related analysis see Etienne Balibar, "Racism and Nationalism," *Race, Nation, Class: Ambiguous Identities* (New York: Verso, 1991), 49–54.
12. Benedict Anderson, "Exodus," *Critical Inquiry* 20 (Winter 1994): 314–27; hereafter cited parenthetically in the text.
13. Anderson's discussion of nationalist projects addresses a notion of "home" that "was less experienced than imagined" (319) and places "the locomotive along with the printed newspaper as the material points of juncture between the classical nation-state project and capitalism at the stage of primary industrialization" (320). By invoking imagined communities and print capitalism, Anderson effectively links this discussion of nineteenth-century classical nationalism to his well-known analysis of national identity in *Imagined Communities: Reflections on the Origins and Spread of Nationalism*, rev. edn. (New York: Verso, 1991), 61–62.
14. Referring to them as a "transposable theme," Anderson treats racial identity and ethnicity as interchangeable concepts: "The purpose of the program [Alex Haley's "Roots"] was to counter melting pot ideology by underlining the continuous 'Africanness' that Haley's ancestors maintained as it were *despite* their Americanization. There can be little doubt that the popularity of 'Roots' owed much to this transposable theme, given the rush, especially during the 1980s, of thoroughly American youngsters to lobby for various *ethnic* [my italics] studies programs at universities and their eagerness to study languages that their immediate parents had so often been determined to abandon. Out of these and other impulses has emerged the ideological program of multiculturalism, which implies that a simple nineteenth-century version of Americanism is no longer adequate or acceptable" (325).
15. In his *Imagined Communities* Anderson acknowledges that "a certain inventive legerdemain was required to permit the empire to appear attractive in national drag" (87), but he participates in this sleight of hand by treating the British and American nations from the perspective of the empire rather than the perspective Scott and Simms take themselves to hold, that of the colonized. Accordingly, Anderson argues that Scotland never satisfied the criteria for being described as an independent nation (90), and he makes only brief mention of the Southern Confederacy (201). This exclusive focus on the imagined communities of

print-capitalism (whether nations or races) overlooks the competing accounts of nation underwritten by the literary history I am providing here.

16. Walter Benn Michaels, *Our America: Nativism, Modernism, and Pluralism* (Durham, NC: Duke University Press, 1995), 13. This is so, Michaels argues, because "it is only when we know which race we are that we can tell which culture is ours" (15). As he observes, "the fact that some people before you did some things that you do does not in itself make what they did part of your past. To make what *they* did part of *your* past, there must be some prior assumption of identity between you and them, and this assumption is . . . racial" (127). Given this prior assumption of race, Michaels concludes, "The modern concept of culture is not, in other words, a critique of racism; it is a form of racism" (129). Thus even the notion of an American culture, Michaels argues, is implicated in this logic of racial identity; see Michaels, *Our America*, 8–9, 127–28.
17. Michaels writes, "U.S. social relations have been and continue to be organized in part by race. My point has been to assert that insofar as this organization cannot be scientifically defended, it is the consequence of a mistake, and that anti-essentialist defenses of race amount to nothing more than new ways of making the mistake" (*Our America*, 134). Naomi Zack offers a similar critique of "attachment to identities based on outdated science"; see her *Philosophy of Science and Race* (New York: Routledge, 2002), 116.
18. Allen Grossman, *Summa Lyrica*, in *The Sighted Singer: Two Works on Poetry for Readers and Writers* (Baltimore: Johns Hopkins University Press, 1992), 235.
19. By broadening my discussion from Michaels's focus on racial biology to my own focus on literary effects, I introduce corresponding limits on the kind of critique that my analysis can advance. After all, central to Michaels's critique of both cultural and racial identity is their mutual reliance on racial biology, with racial identity relying on it empirically and cultural identity relying on it logically. Thus Michaels critiques identities that are racial on the empirical grounds that their commitment to racial biology lacks empirical scientific support: "My point has been to assert that insofar as this organization [of U.S. social relations by race] cannot be scientifically defended, it is the consequence of a mistake" (*Our America*, 123). And Michaels critiques identities that are cultural on the logical grounds that since their proponents claim to stand apart from the acknowledged mistake of racial biology but in fact perpetuate that same mistake, their discussions are internally contradictory and thus logically incoherent: "what's wrong with cultural identity is that, without recourse to the racial identity that (in its current manifestations) it repudiates, it makes no sense" (*Our America*, 142). Since the empirical and logical avenues of these critiques are each made available by the commitment to racial biology, my argument that these commitments are ultimately textual rather than biological removes the ground – racial biology – for both of these critiques. One could, of course, shift the empirical critique from biology to formal textual effects and argue that these effects cannot – any more than the human body – provide empirical support for such claims. But as I will show, these claims about textual

effects, for all of their emphasis on acoustics, end up being not empirical but supernatural, ultimately relying on the notion that formal effects are haunted by the ghostly *genius loci* of a given culture or race. Such claims are of course subject to empirical critique, but my point is that the writers I am addressing, who are already committed to such non-empirical notions of a ghostly *genius loci* in texts, have already rejected empiricism, so they differ from the writers Michaels addresses (whom he presents as having been committed to racial biology as an empirical science). So unlike the writers Michaels addresses, who can be critiqued for failing to muster empirical support for their overtly empirical claims of racial biology, the writers I address can be critiqued only for failing to advance their claims about textual identity in empirical (rather than supernatural) terms, a critique they reject (out of apparent contempt for mere empiricism). And since claims of cultural identity, like those of Morrison and Heaney, are returning to this notion of haunted textuality rather than repudiating it, it is not possible to challenge their account of cultural identity in texts (as Michaels does accounts of cultural identity in bodies) on the logical grounds that they require what they repudiate (and thus of internal contradiction); indeed, I am arguing that, while these writers may not be aware of their coincidence with nineteenth-century predecessors, they are not logically committed to repudiating that coincidence, so when there is such a coincidence they are not in danger of logical incoherence. Indeed, Morrison and Heaney each reveal themselves to be aware, to some extent, of their work's alignment with, rather than repudiation of, earlier claims about textuality and cultural identity. As Heaney has observed, in direct reference to his comments about translating *Beowulf*, the embarrassment of his account of Anglo-Saxon identity isn't its absence of empiricism but its potential for conservatism: "The movement between a deep past and what is going on around us is necessary, I think, if we are to hold on to ourselves as creatures of culture. The literary deep past, I mean, and the historical present. . . . I know all that sounds very Eliotesque, very un-post-modern, but it's based on my own experience as a reader and as a writer" (Seamus Heaney, *Seamus Heaney in Conversation with Karl Miller* [London: Between The Lines, 2000], 42). Thus rather than repudiating (while in fact relying on) earlier empirical commitments (as Michaels argues of those whose accounts of cultural identity repudiate racial biology while in fact relying on it), Heaney acknowledges (however apologetically) his consistency with earlier commitments (those of T. S. Eliot) to textuality and "culture," so his commitment to cultural identity inhering in text – to Anglo-Saxon identity inhering in his metered lines – is not logically incoherent, just culturally conservative. A similar observation can be made of Toni Morrison, who provides her own Eliotesque account of writing, which she says must "keep in touch with the ancestor. . . . When you kill the ancestor you kill yourself. I want to point out the dangers, to show that nice things don't always happen to the totally self-reliant if there is no conscious historical connection" ("From 'Rootedness: The Ancestor as Foundation' (1984)," *African American Literary Criticism, 1773–2000*, ed. Hazel Arnett Ervin [New York: Twayne, 1999], 202).

While Heaney is more reticent than Morrison about this commitment to a "literary deep past," neither makes the move Michaels critiques (of repudiating while at the same time relying on a prior stance), so neither Morrison's nor Heaney's account of cultural identity in texts is (as Michaels observes of accounts of cultural identities in bodies) committed to a principle it repudiates, and thus neither suffers from the logical incoherence of internal contradiction. In my analysis, then, I can rely on neither the empirical nor the logical grounds for critique advanced in Michaels's *Our America*. I do not wish to suggest, however, that in shifting the discussion of identity from Michaels's focus on empirical biology to my own focus on supernatural textuality I rule out any avenue for a critique of identity. As I will argue in the conclusion, the formulations of identity that I am addressing here are susceptible to a different kind of critique, one that proceeds on historical and pragmatic rather than empirical and logical grounds.

20. Thomas C. Holt, *The Problem of Race in the 21st Century* (Cambridge: Harvard University Press, 2000), 21; hereafter cited in the text.

21. Michael Banton, *Racial Theories* (New York: Cambridge University Press, 1987), xiv. The second of three phases in Banton's analysis, this is the one in which "Physical features of the kind called racial were taken as indicators that the individuals in question were usefully assigned to particular populations" (xii). As recent criticism has shown, this emphasis on physical characteristics displaced a much earlier notion of races as primitive tribes like Teutons and Saxons, tribes identified not by physical characteristics but by social practices – especially religion, language, and political institutions; see Hugh B. MacDougall, *Racial Myth in English History: Trojans, Teutons, and Anglo-Saxons* (Montreal: Harvest House, 1982), 48–50. MacDougall elaborates, "Out of the Renaissance and the Reformation a myth developed of an original Germanic people with roots reaching back to Adam, possessing a language and culture richer than and independent from any other. In this myth the Germanic achievement was everything and the contributions of other peoples, whether classical or medieval, irrelevant. As the persecuted Germanic people wrested European hegemony from the Romans by virtue of their might, so the Reformation represented a sweeping away by Germans of the false pretensions of Latin Christianity" (44). This Renaissance approach to race was, as Winthrop Jordan observes in *White Over Black*, evident in early colonial encounters in the New World: "for Englishmen settling in America, the specific religious difference was initially of greater importance than color"; see Winthrop Jordan, *White Over Black: American Attitudes Toward the Negro, 1550–1812* (New York: W. W. Norton & Co., 1968), 97–98. Jordan adds, however, that "[a]s time went on . . . the colonists turned increasingly to the striking physiognomic difference" (95–96), and Jordan traces this emergent commitment to physiognomic classification through the colonial period and into the early United States. For a recent study that makes similar observations about the shift from customs to color as a basis for racial difference, see Roxanna Wheeler, *The Complexion of Race: Categories of Difference in Eighteenth-Century British*

Culture (Philadelphia: University of Pennsylvania Press, 2000). For a discussion in which the centrality of color to race is presented as a development of early twentieth-century racial discourse, see Matthew Pratt Guterl, *The Color of Race in America, 1900–1940* (Cambridge, MA: Harvard University Press, 2001).

22. As Maurice L. Wade has recently observed, "Most eighteenth-century taxonomies of human kinds were evaluative hierarchies as well as descriptive categorizations," so they "did not simply sort human beings into categories on the basis of physical differences. They also looked to the 'inner' features of the person as correlated with such differences." Maurice L. Wade, "From Eighteenth- to Nineteenth-Century Racial Science: Continuity and Change," *Race and Racism in Theory and Practice*, ed. Berel Lang (New York: Rowman & Littlefield, 2000), 32. For more extended critiques of such hierarchical racial structures, see Charles W. Mills, *The Racial Contract* (Ithaca: Cornell University Press, 1997) and *Blackness Visible: Essays on Philosophy and Race* (Ithaca: Cornell University Press, 1998).
23. William Gilmore Simms, "Introduction" to "The Morals of Slavery," *The Pro-Slavery Argument; As Maintained by the Most Distinguished Writers of the Southern States* (1852; reprint New York: Negro Universities Press, 1968), 179. For a discussion of Simms's place in the larger southern effort to defend slavery, see Drew Gilpin Faust, *A Sacred Circle: The Dilemma of the Intellectual in the Old South, 1840–1860* (Baltimore: Johns Hopkins University Press, 1977), 112–31.
24. See William Stanton, *The Leopard's Spots: Scientific Attitudes Toward Race in America, 1815–59* (University of Chicago Press, 1960); John S. Haller, *Outcasts from Evolution: Scientific Attitudes of Racial Inferiority, 1859–1900* (Urbana: University of Illinois Press, 1971); Nancy Stepan, *The Idea of Race in Science: Great Britain, 1800–1960* (Hamden, CT: Archon Books, 1982); and Elazar Barkan, *The Retreat of Scientific Racism: Changing Concepts of Race in Britain and the United States Between the World Wars* (New York: Cambridge University Press, 1992).
25. For Stowe, this plan of "colonization" was compatible with the agenda of antislavery, and Stern is careful to critique the former as she praises the latter: "we must remember that America's most imaginative abolitionist was also a romantic racialist who believed that free blacks could make no place for themselves in an America without slavery"; see "Spanish Masquerade and the Drama of Racial Identity in *Uncle Tom's Cabin*," *Passing and the Fictions of Identity*, ed. Elaine K. Ginsberg (Durham, NC: Duke University Press, 1996), 122.
26. Kenneth Warren asserts, "the realistic authors who published their works in such magazines as the *Century* revealed the multifaceted role that realism played in this process" of the "rapid and often violent erosion of black civil rights"; see his *Black and White Strangers: Race and American Literary Realism* (University of Chicago Press, 1993), 47.
27. Eric Sundquist, *To Wake the Nations: Race in the Making of American Literature* (Cambridge, MA: Harvard University Press, 1993), 111. Sundquist adds, "What

[Douglass] added to the attack on proslavery appeals to domestic sentiment and paternal protection was a meditation upon the patriarchy in its most profoundly American form: the revolutionary principles of equal rights" (94). For a discussion that probes the limits of Douglass's appeal to equal rights, see Mills, *Blackness Visible*, 167–200.

28. Gates, "Editor's Introduction: Writing 'Race' and the Difference It Makes," *"Race," Writing, and Difference*, ed. Henry Louis Gates, Jr. (University of Chicago Press, 1986), 12. See also Gates, *Figures in Black*, 25–27.
29. For a useful overview of the literature of racial passing see Werner Sollors, *Neither Black Nor White Yet Both: Thematic Explorations of Interracial Literature* (New York: Oxford University Press, 1997), 246–84.
30. Elaine K. Ginsberg, "Introduction: The Politics of Passing," *Passing and the Fictions of Identity*, ed. Elaine K. Ginsberg (Durham, NC: Duke University Press, 1996), 13; hereafter cited parenthetically in the text.
31. This textual approach to passing – which analogizes the race of bodies to the meaning of words – is made explicit in Martha Cutter's analysis of Nella Larson's novel *Passing*: "In the galaxy of signs that is the novel *Passing*, Clare functions as a signifier whose meaning cannot be stabilized, fixed, confined, limited; and 'passing' becomes the ultimate mechanism for creating a text that refuses to be contained, consumed, or reduced to a unitary meaning"; see Martha J. Cutter, "Sliding Significations: Passing as a Narrative and Textual Strategy in Nella Larsen's Fiction," *Passing and the Fictions of Identity*, ed. Elaine K. Ginsberg (Durham, NC: Duke University Press, 1996), 76. A comparable statement comes from Amy Robinson: "Considered as a hostile encounter between two *ways of reading*, the pass offers competing rules of recognition in the place of discrete essences or 'natural' identities. . . . To imagine identity politics as a skill of reading is to replace the inadequate dichotomy of visibility and invisibility with an acknowledgement of multiple codes of *intelligibility*"; see Amy Robinson, "It Takes One to Know One: Passing and Communities of Common Interest," *Critical Inquiry* 20 (Summer 1994): 716. Steven Knapp has linked such accounts of textuality, and the political resistance associated with them, to the theoretical writings of Paul de Man, at the same time challenging the claim that such accounts of textual instability can contribute meaningfully to political resistance; see Steven Knapp, *Literary Interest: The Limits of Anti-Formalism* (Cambridge, MA: Harvard University Press, 1993), 93–97.
32. In her discussion of passing in Stowe, Julia Stern concludes that "identity is not a stable fact but a fluid and reversible category"; see Stern, "Spanish Masquerade," 123. In her book *Crossing the Line: Racial Passing in Twentieth-Century US Literature and Culture* (Durham, NC: Duke University Press, 2000), Gayle Wald argues that "racial passing can 'work' . . . only because race is more liquid and dynamic, more variable and random, than it is conventionally represented to be within hegemonic discourse," and Wald's aim is "to investigate how this instability and fluidity of race is negotiated in various exemplary culture representations of racial passing" (6, 6–7).

33. Toni Morrison, *Jazz* (New York: Penguin, 1992), 139; hereafter cited parenthetically in the text.
34. Indeed, Golden's decision to confront his father amounts to more than a meeting with a specific individual: "Come all that way to insult not his father but his race" (143) – not the person of his father but the blackness that, by the logic of the one drop rule, his father's blood has imparted to Golden as "his race."
35. For useful discussions of this development see F. James Davis, *Who is Black?: One Nation's Definition* (University Park: Pennsylvania State University Press, 1991), 8–11 and 54–66; and Sundquist, *To Wake the Nations*, 233–51.
36. Defending his mother's decision to conceal his black ancestry, Golden asserts, "She protected me! If she'd announced I was a nigger, I could have been a slave!" (172).
37. Werner Sollors, *Neither White Nor Black Yet Both*, 250.
38. As Walter Benn Michaels has observed, "The very idea of passing – whether it takes the form of looking like you belong to a different race or of acting like you belong to a different race – requires an understanding of race as something separate from the way you look and the way you act"; these forms of passing, Michaels adds, "are tributes to, not critiques of, racial essentialism"; see *Our America* 133.
39. As this formulation suggests, my project differs in important respects from Cathy Boeckmann's recent book *A Question of Character: Scientific Racism and the Genres of American Fiction, 1892–1912* (Tuscaloosa: University of Alabama Press, 2000). While Boeckmann's study likewise draws links between race and literary texts, her study attends to racial character rather than racial identity, focusing on the "descriptive language" (15) employed by various literary genres rather than formal textual effects: "an emphasis on inherited race character brought racial theory into a close relationship with literary notions about characterization. And as different genres have different conventions for characterization, it also follows that different genres can be used to present race differently. . . . By implication, the aesthetic debates over realism, romance, and sentimental fiction were in some cases implicated in racial debates" (15). In her useful epilogue, Boeckmann distinguishes the symbolic mode of representation characteristic of the texts she addresses from the very different mode of indexical representation that is the focus of my own analysis (209, 211).
40. John Hollander, *Vision and Resonance: Two Senses of Poetic Form* (New York: Oxford University Press, 1975), 162.
41. Unlike Heaney, however, Hollander views the role of poetic effects to be a matter of shifting "convention" rather than persistent racial identity, observing that "metrical forms take on new modal significances with each new use, and with different sorts of awareness of past ones"; see *Vision and Resonance*, 196.
42. The account of the symbol I have in mind here is quite different from the more familiar account made famous by Samuel Taylor Coleridge, who observes of the literary symbol that "[i]t always partakes of the reality which it renders intelligible" (quoted in James C. McKusick, "Symbol," *The Cambridge*

Companion to Coleridge, ed. Lucy Newlyn [Cambridge University Press, 2002], 223). McKusick observes that for Coleridge, "The concept of symbol . . . was in large part an effort to overcome the arbitrariness of the linguistic sign" (217), but the symbolic code I have in mind here is closer to the ideas of Charles S. Peirce, whose notion of the symbol involves just such an arbitrary and conventional stipulation of symbolic elements; see Chares Sanders Peirce, *Elements of Logic*, vol. ii of *Collected Papers of Charles Sanders Peirce*, ed. Charles Hartshorne and Paul Weiss (Cambridge, MA: Harvard University Press, 1965), paragraph 297, page 167.

43. Paul Gilroy, *The Black Atlantic: Modernity and Double Consciousness* (Cambridge: Harvard University Press, 1993), 76; hereafter cited parenthetically in the text. Gilroy quotes Morrison on p. 78.

44. In his more recent writings Gilroy has shown a greater affinity for the analytic orthodoxy that *The Black Atlantic* resists; see his *Against Race: Imagining Political Culture Beyond the Color Line* (Cambridge, MA: Harvard University Press, 2000).

45. Keith Negus and Patria Román Velázquez, "Belonging and Detachment: Musical Experience and the Limits of Identity," *Poetics* 30 (2002): 135; hereafter cited parenthetically in the text.

46. Ronald Radano and Philip V. Bohlman, "Introduction: Music and Race, Their Past, Their Presence," *Music and the Racial Imagination*, eds. Ronald Radano and Philip V. Bohlman (University of Chicago Press, 2000); hereafter cited parenthetically in the text.

47. Radano and Bohlman are thus careful to differentiate themselves, and the contributors to their collection, from "the 'end of racism' that both the Right and the Left are calling for. The essays in this book militate against the rhetoric that foresees an end to race and racism. When the authors turn to music in the racial imagination, the evidence just isn't there. World music and postmodern hybridities have yet to eliminate racial barriers and they show no signs of masking the conditions that give rise to racial differences" (37).

48. Gilroy's *The Black Atlantic* describes his effort to bridge a gap "between those who see the music as the primary means to explore critically and reproduce politically the necessary ethnic essence of blackness and those who would dispute the existence of any such unifying, organic phenomenon" (100), an effort that leads him to describe his own position as "anti-anti-essentialism" (102). For critics like Radano and Bohlman, however, this position collapses back into essentialism: after addressing recent criticism emphasizing migration, of which Radano and Bohlman argue that "a racial metaphysics lives on in the very efforts to demystify the interpretation of culture" (31), they then refer specifically to Gilroy's *The Black Atlantic*, with its central concept of "diaspora," arguing that, "in the end he adheres to a purely sonic projection of black music that enables proposals of transhistorical consistencies . . . of meaning" (45 note 12). Such a critique of a black musical diaspora would apply as well, of course, to Gilroy's chief example, Toni Morrison, and her commitment to a written medium that, like black music, is black "all over the world."

49. Understood in terms of "imagination," these notions constitute, for Radano and Bohlman, a form of "ideology": "As an ideology, . . . the racial imagination remains forever on the loose, subject to reformation within the memories and imaginations of the social. . . . The imagination of race not only informs perceptions of musical practice but is at once constituted within and projected into the social through sound" (5).
50. For related discussions by these same authors, see Philip V. Bohlman, "Musicology as a Political Act," *Journal of Musicology* 11:4 (Fall 1993): 411–36; and Ronald Radano, "Black Noise/White Mastery," *Decomposition: Post-Disciplinary Performance*, ed. Sue-Ellen Case, Philip Brett, and Susan Leigh Foster (Bloomington: Indiana University Press, 2000), 39–49.
51. When other critics have employed Peirce's symbolic categories to describe poetic effects they have tended to use his notions of icon or symbol rather than an index; see Annie Finch, *The Ghost of Meter: Culture and Prosody in American Free Verse* (Ann Arbor: University of Michigan Press, 1993), 141 n. 2.
52. Chares Sanders Peirce, *Elements of Logic*, paragraph 248, page 143.
53. For discussion of these examples, see Thomas A. Sebeok, "Indexicality," *Peirce and Contemporary Thought*, ed. Kenneth Laine Ketner (New York: Fordham University Press, 1995), 233; James Jakób Liszka, *A General Introduction to the Semeiotic of Charles Sanders Peirce* (Bloomington: Indiana University Press, 1996), 38, 49–50; and, C. J. Misak, *Truth and the End of Inquiry: A Peircean Account of Truth* (New York: Oxford University Press, 1991), 17.
54. Floyd Merrell, *Peirce, Signs, and Meaning* (University of Toronto Press, 1997), 54. Sebeok observes, "Temporal succession, relations of a cause to its effect or, vice versa, of an effect to its cause, or else some space/time vinculum between an index and its dynamic object . . . lurks at the heart of indexicality"; see Sebeok, "Indexicality," 228.
55. Charles Sanders Peirce, *Pragmatism and Pragmaticism*, vol. v of *Collected Papers of Charles Sanders Peirce*, eds. Charles Hartshorne and Paul Weiss (Cambridge, MA: Harvard University Press, 1965), paragraph 75, page 52.
56. Charles Sanders Peirce, *Reviews, Correspondence, and Bibliography*, in vol. viii of *Collected Papers of Charles Sanders Peirce*, ed. Arthur W. Burks (Cambridge, MA: Harvard University Press, 1966), 241 note 23.
57. Charles Sanders Peirce, *Reviews, Correspondence, and Bibliography*, 242 note 23.
58. Charles Sanders Peirce, *Science and Philosophy*, vol. vii of *Collected Papers of Charles Sanders Peirce*, ed. Arthur W. Burks (Cambridge, MA: Harvard University Press, 1966), paragraph 628, page 373.
59. Charles Sanders Peirce, *Reviews, Correspondence, and Bibliography*, paragraph 335, page 228.
60. That is, whether the formal effect in question is located on the landscape, in a poem, or in a bodily performance, the notion that it is an index of a discrete "people" implies that this "people" be viewed as a powerful agency – whether supernatural or biological – capable of producing that effect at that site, thereby permitting a formal effect to serve as an index of that agency; and when that agential source is described in identitarian terms – as the agency of a national or

racial people, as the agency of that people's memory, history, or "blood" – then the formal effects that this identity-agency supposedly produces can be imagined as an indexical sign of that particular identity.

61. On immigration from Scotland to the southern United States, see Bernard Bailyn, *Voyagers to the West: A Passage in the Peopling of America on the Eve of the Revolution* (New York: Alfred A. Knopf, 1987), 205–06, 502–07. On Scotland's intellectual influence on the United States generally, see Robert Crawford, *Devolving English Literature*, 2nd edn. (Edinburgh University Press, 2000), 176–215. On Walter Scott's influence on the writing of Simms specifically, see C. Hugh Holman, "The Influence of Scott and Cooper on Simms," *The Roots of Southern Writing: Essays on the Literature of the American South* (Athens: University of Georgia Press, 1972), 50–60; and George Dekker, *The American Historical Romance* (New York: Cambridge University Press, 1987), 61–63.
62. Kwame Anthony Appiah, *In My Father's House: Africa in the Philosophy of Culture* (New York: Oxford University Press, 1992), 30. Speaking in particular of W. E. B. Du Bois, Appiah observes, "what Du Bois attempts, despite his own claims to the contrary, is not the transcendence of the nineteenth-century scientific conception of race – as we shall see, he relies on it – but rather, as the dialectic requires, a revaluation of the Negro race in the face of the sciences of racial inferiority" (30). I will argue, by contrast, that the nineteenth-century conception upon which Du Bois ultimately relies is not the scientific and empirical conception of biological racial identities but the literary and supernatural conception of textual national identities.
63. Benedict Anderson, *Imagined Communities*, 6; hereafter cited parenthetically in the text.
64. Hazel V. Carby, *Race Men* (Cambridge, MA: Harvard University Press, 1998), 13.
65. For a concise recent statement of this view, see Alan H. Goodman, "Bred in the Bone?," *The Sciences* 37:2 (March/April 1997): 20–25.
66. For a useful critique of racial authenticity see Appiah, "Race, Culture, Identity: Misunderstood Connections," 93–96.
67. For a clear general discussion of this point, see Walter Been Michaels, "Autobiography of an Ex-White Man: Why Race is Not a Social Construction," *Transition* 73 (1998): 122–43; and Walter Benn Michaels, "Posthistoricism," *Transition* 70 (1995): 4–19, especially his observation that "false beliefs can be as consequential as true ones without thereby becoming true" (9). See also Naomi Zack's observation that "[r]ace is like the liar who says he speaks the truth, the social construction that is constructed around denial that it is a social construction" (*Philosophy of Science and Race*, 117).
68. Consider, for instance, Toni Morrison's response when confronted with assertions of racial identity's falsity, the assertion that it might be "imagined" in the sense of being a "fabrication": "Suddenly . . . 'race' does not exist. . . . When blacks discovered they had shaped or become a culturally formed race, and that it had specific and revered difference, suddenly they were told there is no such thing as 'race,' biological or cultural, that matters and that genuinely

intellectual exchange cannot accommodate it. In trying to come to some terms about 'race' and writing, I am tempted to throw my hands up"; see Morrison's "Unspeakable Things Unspoken: The Afro-American Presence in American Literature," *Within the Circle: An Anthology of African American Literary Criticism from the Harlem Renaissance to the Present*, ed. Angelyn Mitchell (Durham, NC: Duke University Press, 1994), 370. By throwing up her hands Morrison registers more than indecision about whether she will participate in a particular style of imagining; her gesture shows her confronting the question whether there is a fundamental falsity or genuineness to racial identities, the very question that Anderson's analysis would set aside.

1. METER AND NATIONAL IDENTITY IN SIR WALTER SCOTT

1. Walter Scott, *The Journal of Sir Walter Scott*, ed. W. E. K. Anderson (Oxford: The Clarendon Press, 1972), 98–99. Hereafter cited as *J* parenthetically in the text.
2. Lord Melville, *The Arniston Memoirs: Three Centuries of a Scottish House, 1571–1838*, ed. George W. T. Omond (Edinburgh: David Douglas, 1887), 318, 319; John Wilson Croker, *Two Letters on Scottish Affairs*, in *Thoughts on the Proposed Change of Currency & Two Letters on Scottish Affairs*, ed. David Simpson and Alastair Wood (New York: Barnes & Noble, 1972), 18; Great Britain, Parliament, *The Parliamentary Debates*, new series, vol. XIV (London: HM Stationery Office, 1826), 1,386.
3. Both David Johnson and William Donaldson suggest that Jacobite songs were written well after the Scottish rebellions of 1715 and 1745 and were merely passed off as products of those moments; see Johnson, *Music and Society in Lowland Scotland in the Eighteenth Century* (London: Oxford University Press, 1972), 4, 130, 146; and Donaldson, *The Jacobite Song: Political Myth and National Identity* (Aberdeen University Press, 1988), 3–4, 72, 89, 90, 98. This practice of projecting recent cultural works backward into a remote mythic past and then treating them as if they were a shared national heritage is consistent with what Eric Hobsbawm critiques as the "invention of tradition"; see Hobsbawm, "Introduction: Inventing Traditions," *The Invention of Tradition*, ed. Eric Hobsbawm and Terence Ranger (Cambridge University Press, 1983), 1–14.
4. J. G. Checkland, *Scottish Banking: A History, 1695–1973* (Glasgow: Collins, 1975), 436. For a record of Parliament's discussion of these issues, see, *The Parliamentary Debates*, new series, vol. XIV. This reform measure should be seen within the larger history of attempts to return the English banking system to specie payments after their suspension in 1793 (in response to threats of war with France). For useful discussions of these currency manipulations, see Elie Halevy, *The Liberal Awakening, 1815–1830*, trans. E. I. Watkin (New York: Peter Smith, 1949), 46–53, 113–17, 230–37; and Frank Whitson Fetter, *Development of*

British Monetary Orthodoxy, 1797–1875 (Cambridge, MA: Harvard University Press, 1965), 1–164.

5. Walter Scott, *Letters from Malachi Malagrowther, Esq. on the Proposed Change of Currency, The Miscellaneous Prose Works of Sir Walter Scott*, vol. 1 (Edinburgh: R. Cadell, 1847), 742. This is one of many titles given to the set of three letters that appeared in the *Edinburgh Weekly Journal* on February 21, February 28, and March 7 of 1826. I will refer to them collectively as *Letters of Malachi Malagrowther*; subsequent references will be to this edition and will be cited parenthetically in the text.
6. As one historian notes, "these famous letters created an enormous sensation . . . . and were often quoted during the discussions which afterwards took place in Parliament. The proposed measure was, so far as Scotland was concerned, abandoned; and the fact that the Scottish banks retained the privilege of issuing £1 notes was universally said to be the work of Sir Walter Scott"; *The Arniston Memoirs*, 315. For similar observations, see also Andrew William Kerr, *History of Banking in Scotland*, 3rd edn. (London: A. & C. Black, 1918), 177; and Graham McMaster, *Scott and Society* (Cambridge University Press, 1981), 88–90.
7. Malagrowther himself asserts this retreat from economic theory (744, 728, 751), and many subsequent critics have likewise de-emphasized the contribution of these letters to currency theory; see, for instance, William Graham, *The One Pound Note in the History of Banking in Great Britain* (Edinburgh: James Thin, 1911), 181; Paul Henderson Scott, "The Malachi Episode," *Blackwood's Magazine* 320 (1976): 247, 250; and Fetter, *Development of British Monetary Orthodoxy*, 122.
8. For a discussion of how a currency of precious metals can participate either in a money economy or in a barter economy, see Joyce Oldham Appleby, "Locke, Liberalism and the Natural Law of Money," *Past and Present* 71 (May 1976): 45.
9. Andrea Henderson, *Romantic Identities: Varieties of Subjectivity, 1774–1830* (Cambridge University Press, 1996), 44, quoting Henry Mackenzie. In her useful discussion of the figure of the smooth shilling, Henderson asserts that coins are interchangeable not, as Malagrowther suggests, because they contain equal quantities of precious metal bullion but, on the contrary, because they are "money," and what makes them money (and not just a commodity for barter) is that they are not at all smooth, that their surface bears an inscription or "impress" that permits them to participate in "the sense of identity as mere sign" (52). When identity involves a "mere sign," Henderson asserts, "Characters whose only interest is in matters of form and appearance are immediately suspicious" (50), for they raise the possibility of an empty form, of a form that is "indeterminate" (51, 53, 54, 57). Thus Henderson presents Mackenzie and David Hume as precursors to the cultural context in which "characters resemble the reified form of the exchange value of the commodity: money" (52); in this "prototype of the gothic world" (45) "people tend to become as interchangeable as coins" (52). Malagrowther, by contrast, is unconcerned about the emptiness of these forms and in fact embraces them as the basis for national identity. Thus where Henderson's version of the Gothic sees a troubling uniformity in the

presence of a coin's impress, Malagrowther sees a troubling uniformity in the absence of that impress; where Henderson's account of the Gothic finds such signs "suspect" (50), Malagrowther is suspicious of ministers who would eliminate them; where Henderson's Gothic takes the presence of this impress as threatening the loss of personal identity (51), Malagrowther views it as ensuring the persistence of national identity. As we will see, Malagrowther will go on to substitute poetic meter for this impress as the guarantee of national identity, but in either case, his concern is not to explore the indeterminacy of Gothic identity but rather to ensure the stability of national identity by insisting that a specifically national representation can coexist with the imperial resource of the commodity.

10. Malagrowther's simultaneous commitment to national identity and paper money contradicts many recent critical accounts that view a commitment to essential identity categories – categories ranging from personal identity to national identity, from gender to race – as consistent with a repudiation of paper money and a commitment, instead, to hard money. For such an account that addresses Scott's contemporaries, see Andrea Henderson, *Romantic Identities*, 46–47; for a similar argument about "the dual essentialism of race and money" (389) in America, see Michael O'Malley, "Specie and Species: Race and the Money Question in Nineteenth-Century America," *The American Historical Review* 99:2 (April 1994): 377, 379. One might argue that Malagrowther's commitment both to Scottish national identity and to paper money demonstrates a failure to register these critics' insight that essential or intrinsic accounts of identity are logically consistent only with essential or intrinsic accounts of money. In my view, however, Malagrowther is not missing this point but presenting an alternative to it, an alternative that does not conflate methods of accounting for value with methods of accounting for identity.
11. Indeed, contemporary opponents to the *Letters of Malachi Malagrowther* assert the fundamentally international nature of these institutional practices; see Melville's response to these letters in *The Arniston Memoirs*, 319.
12. See, for instance, Malagrowther's extensive discussion of a boundary stone, which secures national integrity only if it is both detected and obeyed (740).
13. For a recent account that shows conversion to be central to English accounts of national identity, see Michael Ragussis's *Figures of Conversion: "The Jewish Question" & English National Identity* (Durham, NC: Duke University Press, 1995).
14. "Scotland's motto is *Nemo me impune lacesset*, or 'Wha daur meddle wi' me'." This Scots dialect translation comes from Anderson's footnote in *J*, 97 n. 2.
15. This song verse can be traced to two prominent collections published in Scott's lifetime. The first is James Johnson's *The Scots Musical Museum: 1787–1803*, vol. 1 (Amadeus Press, 1991), 178; the second is James Hogg's *The Jacobite Relics of Scotland* [1819] (New York: AMS Press, 1974), 110–11. Thanks to Tony Inglis and Caroline M. Jackson-Houlston for help in identifying these sources.
16. The entry for "tutti-tait(e)" in the *Scottish National Dictionary* (vol. 9, p. 451) describes it as "an exclamation to represent the sound of a trumpet." Although Scott replaces trumpets with pipes, he preserves the onomatopoeia.

17. On the necessity of thematic context (or "semantic field") to identify the sound embodied by onomatopoeia, see the entry for "Onomatopoeia" in *The New Princeton Encyclopedia of Poetry and Poetics*, ed. Alex Preminger and T. V. F. Brogan (Princeton University Press, 1993), 861a.
18. Walter Scott, "Introductory Remarks on Popular Poetry, and on the Various Collections of Ballads of Britain, Particularly Those of Scotland" [1830], *The Poetical Works of Sir Walter Scott* (Boston: Phillips, Sampson, and Company, 1856); see also 538.
19. For related observations about the effects of poetic meter see Adela Pinch, "Female Chatter: Meter, Masochism, and the *Lyrical Ballads*," *ELH* 55 (1988): 846.
20. Note that Malagrowther's view maps fully onto neither of the two "alternatives" that J. C. D. Clark (*English Society, 1688–1832* [Cambridge University Press, 1985]) associates with accounts of "aristocratic status": "The royalist case was that 'Nobility is defined as a quality which the sovereign power imprints upon private persons in order to place them and their descendants above other citizens': that is, that the monarch could so honour anyone he chose. Its antithesis was the nobility's conviction, as one of them put it in 1839, that 'La noblesse . . . tient au sang': that is, that their status was independent and indefeasible" (96). Malagrowther is treating these two positions not as alternatives but as mutually reinforcing notions, where one's noble blood provides the conduit along which is transmitted ongoing credit for ancestral distinctions; the blood is not sufficient, but it is necessary for laying out the trajectory along which is transmitted credit for ancestral acts. For further discussion of these alternative accounts of aristocracy, see Jerome Christensen, *Lord Byron's Strength* (Baltimore: Johns Hopkins University Press, 1993), 11–15, 33, 47.
21. My formulation of this logic draws upon the helpful discussion in Walter Benn Michaels's *Our America*, esp. 84, 87, 90, and 122.
22. The passage is indeed somewhat mangled. It comes from William Mason's *Caractacus* (1759) (*The Works of William Mason*, vol. II [London: T. Cadell and W. Davies, 1811], 99–100), a poem that dramatizes how inhabitants of northern Britain, aided by the local Druids, unsuccessfully resist the encroachments of the Roman Empire. The lines Scott has in mind are an invocation to the musical spirits whose aid is required to induct Caractacus – an embattled indigenous leader and opponent of the Romans – into the Druidical tribe. Joining the Druids as an alternative to continued resistance is (like the retreat of nation into meter) not quite the same as surrender. The poem's overall aim is to show that the southern part of the island relies on the northern part as a way of resisting integration within the expansive Roman Empire (see esp. 168–69). Such a plot is consistent with Malagrowther's own wish to see the northern part of the island as a site of resistance to imperial uniformity, but I wish to emphasize that Malagrowther's interest is as much the passage's supposedly Scottish meter as its anti-imperial themes.
23. Johnson introduces his *Dictionary of the English Language* (New York: AMS Press, 1967) not only with the "Preface," which sought to replace the "boundless variety" (4) of the language's semantics with "steadiness and uniformity" (7),

but also with "A Grammar of the English Tongue," which asserts that "the laws of metre are included in the idea of a grammar" and that "Versification is the arrangement of a certain number of syllables according to certain laws" (unpag.). After describing the precise syllable counts available for English prosody, Johnson concludes that "To these measures, and their laws, may be reduced every species of English verse" (unpag.), and "every line considered by itself is more harmonious, as this rule is more strictly observed" (unpag.). This insistence on metrical uniformity had a profound influence on subsequent prosodic practice; for further discussion see A. Dwight Culler, "Edward Bysshe and the Poet's Handbook," *PMLA* 63:3 (September 1948): 881; and Paul Fussell, *Theory of Prosody in Eighteenth-Century England* (Archon Books, 1966), 25.

24. Johnson's emphasis on syllable counts faced increasing challenges from advocates of accentual prosody, an approach to verse that drew upon the ballad revival as well as German writings (both of which Scott knew well) to culminate in Coleridge's *Christabel* (1797, 1800; 1816) and Scott's own *Lay of the Last Minstrel* (1805). For accounts of this shift from syllabic metrics to accentual verse, see Culler, "Edward Bysshe and the Poet's Handbook," 878–85; Fussell, *Theory of Prosody in Eighteenth-Century England*, 101 ff.; T. S. Omond, *English Metrists* (New York: Phaeton Press, 1968), 108–09, 114–16; and Brennan O'Donnell, *The Passion of Meter: A Study of Wordsworth's Metrical Art* (Kent State University Press, 1995), 28–32, 253 n. 8. For Scott's own comments on his deviations from Johnson's metrical standard, see his "Introduction to Edition 1830 [of *The Lay of the Last Minstrel*]," *The Poetical Works of Sir Walter Scott*, 14; and "Essay on Imitations of the Ancient Ballad," *The Poetical Works of Sir Walter Scott*, 560–63. Even as he embraced metrical variety, Scott advocated standard English words, a view apparent in the "Dedicatory Epistle" of *Ivanhoe*, where he insists that remote historical topics "should be, as it were, translated into the manners, as well as the language, of the age we live in" (*Ivanhoe*, ed. A. N. Wilson [New York: Penguin Books, 1984], 526).

25. For Scott's statements regarding national metrical forms, see his "Introductory Remarks on Popular Poetry," *Poetical Works of Sir Walter Scott*, 538, 542–43; and his "Essay on Imitations of the Ancient Ballad," 567–68. The account of "tension" that I am advancing here differs somewhat from most prosodic criticism: most locate it entirely *within* the domain of prosody, between variable and uniform patterns of sound (i.e. a varying rhythm or diction within a uniform metrical structure). On this version of tension, see Fussell, *Theory of Prosody*, esp. 152–53; Derek Attridge, *The Rhythms of English Poetry* (New York: Longman, 1982), 9, 17–18, 306–14; O'Donnell, *The Passion of Meter*, 31, 67; and Allen Grossman, *The Sighted Singer*, 290–98; 373–74. Scott's *Letters of Malachi Malagrowther*, I am suggesting, relocates this tension from *within* prosody (i.e. between each line's uniform and varying sound patterns) to *between* meter and words, thus permitting these to be assigned, respectively, to nation and empire.

26. For Wordsworth's use of the word "superadded" to describe the relation of meter to words, see his "Preface" (1802) to the *Lyrical Ballads* in *The Oxford*

Authors: William Wordsworth (Oxford University Press, 1990), 602, 609. For an account of Wordsworth's general tendency to exploit tensions between words and superadded meter, see O'Donnell, *The Passion of Meter*, 27–28. For a recent effort to describe poems in general in these terms, as simultaneous and irreducible domains of word and meter, see Amittai F. Aviram, *Telling Rhythm: Body and Meaning in Poetry* (Ann Arbor: University of Michigan Press, 1994), 7–8, 19–21, 24–25, 223.

27. See *The Oxford Authors: William Wordsworth*, 83. All subsequent references to Wordsworth will come from this collection and will be cited parenthetically in the text. The missing words are "dear brother Jem," which were suggested to Wordsworth by Coleridge but were later removed; see *The Oxford Authors: William Wordsworth*, 690 n. 84.
28. For an alternate account of this exchange, one that sees it less in terms of political conflict than of conceptual agreement, see Frances Ferguson, *Solitude and the Sublime: Romanticism and the Aesthetics of Individuation* (New York: Routledge, 1992), 164–69.
29. Scott was joined by his contemporary, Thomas De Quincey, in this gesture of appropriating the stance of the little maid in "We Are Seven." For an extended discussion of De Quincey's investment in this role, see Margaret Russett, *De Quincey's Romanticism: Canonical Minority and the Forms of Transmission* (Cambridge University Press, 1997), 10, 15–27, 46–49.
30. Consider also the later moment in the "Preface" when Wordsworth asserts that "all men feel an habitual gratitude, and something of an honourable bigotry for the objects which have long continued to please them; we not only wish to be pleased, but to be pleased in that particular way in which we have been accustomed to be pleased" (614).
31. See James K. Chandler, *Wordsworth's Second Nature: A Study of the Poetry and Politics* (University of Chicago Press, 1984), esp. 172–73.
32. For a similar view see O'Donnell, *The Passion of Meter*, 43–48. Compare to Adela Pinch's account, which aligns the meter in Wordsworth's "Goody Blake and Harry Gill" with a woman's voice of suffering; for Pinch, both meter and the female voice exercise a power that does *not* stem from acquired habits, for, as Pinch puts it, they induce a novel circumstance, "the masculine subject's masochistic introjection of a woman's suffering" ("Female Chatter," 845–46).
33. See Coleridge's notebooks for the years of his stay in Germany: *The Notebooks of Samuel Taylor Coleridge*, ed. Kathleen Coburn, vol. 1. (New York: Pantheon Books, 1957), entries 372–73.
34. *The Oxford Authors: Samuel Taylor Coleridge*, ed. H. J. Jackson (Oxford University Press, 1985), 66. All subsequent references to Coleridge will come from this collection and will be cited parenthetically in the text.
35. Scott singles out "the striking fragment called Christabel, by Mr. Coleridge, which, from the singularly irregular structure of the stanzas, and the liberty which it allowed the author, to adapt the sound to the sense, seemed to be exactly suited to such an extravaganza as I meditated . . . . it is to Mr. Coleridge that I am bound to make the acknowledgment due from the pupil to his master"; see

Scott's "Introduction to Edition 1830 [of *The Lay of the Last Minstrel*]," *Poetical Works of Sir Walter Scott*, 13.

36. Sir Walter Scott, *The Highland Widow*, in *Chronicles of the Canongate*, vol. 1 (Philadelphia, PA: Henry T. Coates & Co., 1900), 91. Subsequent references will appear parenthetically in the text. The collection did not appear until 1827 because Scott's financial problems led to legal wrangling over who owned it, Scott or his creditors. The composition of the work occurred much earlier, and *The Highland Widow* itself was composed in late May and early June of 1826, less than four months after Scott's first involvement with the currency crisis; see *J*, 150.
37. That is, whether or not Coleridge intended Geraldine as a figure for meter's power, Scott, I am suggesting, read her in this way. Coleridge's own views on meter have occasioned extensive critical discussion. While his mature metrical theory (as set out in *Biographia Literaria* [1817]) tends to subordinate metrical effects to a poem's overall unity (see O'Donnell, *The Passion of Meter*, 49), his early poetry has led many recent critics to observe in his metrical practice what I am suggesting Scott saw there – an autonomous and powerful force responsible for very specific effects. See Karen Swann, "'Christabel': The Wandering Mother and the Enigma of Form," *Studies in Romanticism* 23 (Winter 1984): 552; Jerome Christensen, "Ecce Homo: Biographical Acknowledgment, the End of the French Revolution, and the Romantic Reinvention of English Verse," *Contesting the Subject: Essays in the Postmodern Theory and Practice of Biography and Biographical Criticism*, ed. William H. Epstein (West Lafayette, IN: Purdue University Press, 1991), 71–79; and Rachel Crawford, "Thieves of Language: Coleridge, Wordsworth, Scott, and the Contexts of 'Alice du Clos,'" *European Romantic Review* 7:1 (Summer 1996): 2, 8.
38. Scott made this point in an 1827 letter to the Reverend Charles McCombie; the letter is reprinted as "Sir Walter Scott on the Scottish Metrical Psalms," *Life and Work* (Feb. 1884), 17–19.
39. It first occurs when Geraldine embraces Christabel (l. 263) and again – a circumstance more apt to inspire the misquotation of "wound" – when Bracy relates a dream in which "I saw a bright green snake/ Coiled around" the "wings and neck" of a dove (ll. 549–50), the snake figuring Geraldine and the dove, Christabel.
40. For Coleridge's use of the term "superadded" to describe meter's relation to poetic lines, see his *Biographia Literaria*, Chapter XVII, in *The Oxford Authors: Samuel Taylor Coleridge*, ed. H. J. Jackson (Oxford: Oxford University Press, 1985), 353–54.
41. John Barrell, *The Infection of Thomas De Quincey* (New Haven: Yale University Press, 1991), 33. The substitution of an oak for a palm redirects the reference from Judaea to the Jacobite cause; on the role of oak trees in Jacobite iconography, see Paul Kléber Monod, *Jacobitism and the English People, 1688–1788* (New York: Cambridge University Press, 1989), 71–72.
42. "She associated so little with others, went so seldom and so unwillingly from the wildest recesses of the mountains, where she usually dwelt with her goats,

that she was quite unconscious of the great change which had taken place in the country around her, the substitution of civil order for military violence . . ." (105). "To be brief, Elspat was one who viewed the present state of society with the same feelings with which she regarded the times that had passed away" (112).

43. The story mentions the Highland regiments sponsored by the Earl of Chatham; they wore tartan plaid but fought "for the defence of the colonies" (132). For more on this see Hugh Trevor-Roper's "The Invention of Tradition: The Highland Tradition of Scotland," *The Invention of Tradition*, ed. Eric Hobsbawm and Terence Ranger (Cambridge University Press, 1983), 25.
44. As Scott's narrator observes, "By nature and habit, every Highlander was accustomed to the use of arms, but at the same time totally unaccustomed to, and impatient of, the restraints imposed by discipline upon regular troops" (132). Scott makes this same point much earlier in his review of the "Culloden Papers," *Quarterly Review* 14:28 (January 1816), 283–333.
45. Elspat's successful resistance to the imperial structure sets her apart from what Jan Gordon ("'Liquidating the Sublime': Gossip in Scott's Novels," *At the Limits of Romanticism: Essays in Cultural, Feminist, and Materialist Criticism*, ed. Mary A. Farret and Nicola J. Watson [Bloomington: Indiana University Press, 1994]) calls the "gossip-figure" (257). While Gordon's analysis suggests that Scott's narratives ultimately assimilate these outlaw figures, the standoff at Elspat's threshold suggests that Elspat overcomes such attempts at assimilation. It is through this ongoing resistance that she, and the meter she embodies, offer an alternative to imperial structures and, in turn, preserve the national impress from the encroachments of imperial uniformity.
46. Thomas Reid, *Essays on the Active Powers of Man* (1788), in *Thomas Reid: Philosophical Works* (New York: Georg Olms Verlag, 1983). Even more forceful statements of this point are rehearsed in Dugald Stewart's *Elements of the Philosophy of the Human Mind* (Philadelphia, PA: William Young, 1793), which cites these passages and then explicitly disagrees, reclaiming habit's seemingly mechanical force on behalf of voluntary action; see esp. 103–05. Stewart was Scott's teacher in 1792, when this response was first published, so it seems likely that Scott would have been aware of the debate; see John Sutherland, *The Life of Walter Scott* (Cambridge, MA: Blackwell, 1995), 41.
47. On the importance of this concept to Scottish writers of the period, see Susan Manning, "'This Philosophical Melancholy': Style and Self in Boswell and Hume," *New Light on Boswell*, ed. Greg Clingham (Cambridge University Press, 1991), 126–40.
48. Hume, *A Treatise of Human Nature* [1739] ed. L. A. Selby-Bigge, 2nd edn. (Oxford: Clarendon Press, 1978), 133; a fuller description of habit reads as follows: "the supposition, *that the future resembles the past*, is not founded on arguments of any kind, but is deriv'd entirely from habit, by which we are determin'd to expect for the future the same train of objects, to which we have been accustom'd"; see Hume's *A Treatise of Human Nature*, 134. See also Hume's *Enquiries Concerning Human Understanding* [1777], ed. L. A. Selby-Bigge, 3rd

edn. (Oxford: Clarendon Press, 1975) for the following account of "Custom or Habit. For wherever the repetition of any particular act or operation produces a propensity to renew the same act or operation, without being impelled by any reasoning or process of the understanding, we always say, that this propensity is the effect of *Custom*" (43); "Custom, then, is the great guide of human life. It is that principle alone which renders our experience useful to us, and makes us expect, for the future, a similar train of events with those which have appeared in the past" (44). Such custom "is nothing but a species of instinct or mechanical power, that acts in us unknown to ourselves; and in its chief operations, is not directed by any such relations or comparisons of ideas, as are the proper objects of our intellectual faculties" (108).

49. Such an account of psychology is Scott's own invention, for it is finally inconsistent with Hume's own analysis: Hume speaks explicitly of "a contradiction, *viz.* a habit acquir'd by what was never present to the mind"; see *A Treatise of Human Nature*, 197.

50. Scott, *Letters on Demonology and Witchcraft* (London: John Murray, 1831); hereafter cited parenthetically in the text. Scott had been contemplating such a work as early as 1809 and had begun writing it as early as 1823, well before the currency crisis; see Edgar Johnson, *Sir Walter Scott: The Great Unknown*, vol. 2 (New York: The Macmillan Company, 1970), 1,126.

51. Katie Trumpener, *Bardic Nationalism: The Romantic Novel and the British Empire* (Princeton University Press, 1997). Subsequent references will appear parenthetically in the text.

52. Homi K. Bhabha, "DissemiNation," *Nation and Narration*, ed. Homi K. Bhabha (New York: Routledge, 1990), 291–322. References to specific pages are given parenthetically in the text.

53. "The signs of cultural difference cannot then be unitary or individual forms of identity because their continual implication in other symbolic systems always leaves them 'incomplete' or open to cultural translation" (313).

54. For a recent effort to defend the notion of Scottish meter, see Douglas Dunn, "'A Very Scottish Kind of Dash': Burns's Native Metric," *Robert Burns and Cultural Authority*, ed. Robert Crawford (Iowa City: University of Iowa Press, 1997), 58–85.

55. Benedict Anderson, *Imagined Communities*. References to specific pages are given parenthetically in the text.

56. Indeed, such expansiveness is characteristic of Anderson's account of nation, for even though in practice national "solidarities had an outermost stretch limited by vernacular legibilities" (77), nothing in principle prevents an ever-expanding range of literacy and the corresponding production of those solidarities (133–34). Thus even though a "community imagined through language" might at first seem to be "simultaneously open and closed" (146), the "untranslatable" features of language that seem to underwrite closure are "always open to new speakers, listeners, and readers" (146), so the apparent closure of knowing a language – whether its syntax, its semantics, or its songs – is always undercut by potential openness to new speakers, readers, and singers. Anderson invokes

this essential openness to explain the absence of nationalism in a Scotland effectively absorbed within the uniformity of Britain's English language (88–90).

57. See *The Letters of Sir Walter Scott*, vol. IX, ed. H. J. C. Grierson (London: Constable & Co. Ltd., 1935), 471–72.
58. On the remoteness of Elspat, see Susan Manning: "Scott's stories . . . tend to be 'twice told' and reach the reader framed by prefatory paraphernalia which remove them from the actuality of experience without preventing him from participating in the process of meaning. 'The Highland Widow' (1827), for example, is introduced as 'a story' of 'the state of the highlands'. . . . The ineluctable otherness of the widow is conveyed by her refusal to be touched by sympathy; the observer cannot possess her experience, and it seems impertinent to try" (*The Puritan-Provincial Vision* [Cambridge University Press, 1990], 96).
59. In his discussion of the Ossian controversy Peter Murphy registers MacPherson's "use of a style that connotes translation": "By calling this prose poetry, MacPherson conjures up the shadowy original, marching dim Gaelic feet through unknown Gaelic meters, and at the same time his humble refusal to recreate this meter is always before our eyes" ("Fool's Gold: The Highland Treasures of MacPherson's Ossian," *ELH* 53:3 [Fall 1986]: 576). On Scott's involvement with the Ossian controversy, see Susan Manning, "Ossian, Scott, and Nineteenth-Century Scottish Literary Nationalism," *Studies in Scottish Literature* 17 (1982): 39–54.
60. Murphy, "Fool's Gold," 588. Murphy criticizes MacPherson's tendency, evident in the Ossian poems, to achieve the imperial "absorption" of distinct national cultures through the elimination of their peculiar poetic features: "The ease of mixture, of absorption, is utterly dependent on this erasure of distinguishing form" (588), including "foreign meter" (576). Scott's writings of this period draw similar links between national identity and unassimilable – i.e. untranslatable – literary features; see, for instance, Scott's discussion of Henry Fielding in *Lives of the Novelists* (1825), quoted in William Warner, *Licensing Entertainment: The Elevation of Novel Reading in Britain, 1684–1750* (Berkeley: University of California Press, 1998), 22–23; see also Scott's 1827 letter to the Reverend Charles McCombie, "Sir Walter Scott on the Scottish Metrical Psalms," 17–19.
61. Just as a translation of a poem can be said to have lost metrical effects that it, the translation, never had, so Scots in Britain can claim to have lost a nationality that they, themselves, never had. Indeed, one is only a Scot insofar as one claims this loss as one's own, as a national *dis*possession (which implies, of course, the prior possession) consequent upon one's translation from a national subject into an imperial subject. If imperial subjects understand themselves to have been, like Croftangry, alienated from meter (and the nationality it embodies), what they now possess is meter's absence, and even if this meter is just as absent from them as it is from other imperial subjects, its absence from them is seen as peculiarly their own because their orientation toward the prior state in which it was present is not one of successor to predecessor but of translation to original. Paradoxically, but quite powerfully, asserting one's status as a translation elevates

the loss involved into a possession in its own right, but a possession crucially different from the "demonaical possession" Scott associates with Elspat and Hamish.

62. As K. Anthony Appiah has observed, early post colonial novels "are in the tradition of Scott" in precisely this sense – insofar as "they authorize a 'return to traditions' while at the same time recognizing the demands of a Weberian rationalized modernity"; see Appaiah's *In My Father's House,* 150.
63. James Chandler, "The Historical Novel Goes to Hollywood: Scott, Griffith, and Film Epic Today," *The Romantics and Us: Essays on Literature and Culture*, ed. Gene W. Ruoff (New Brunswick, NJ: Rutgers University Press), 249.
64. For a discussion of "redemption" and its relation to Dixon's novel see Joel Williamson, *A Rage For Order: Black/White Relations in the American South Since Emancipation* (New York: Oxford University Press, 1986), 39, 98–99.
65. Thomas Dixon, *The Clansman*: *An Historical Romance of the Ku Klux Klan* (Lexington: University Press of Kentucky, 1970), 326; hereafter cited parenthetically in the text.
66. On the centrality of the body in Dixon's *The Clansman*, see Walter Benn Michaels, "The Souls of White Folk," *Literature and the Body: Essays on Populations and Persons*, ed. Elaine Scarry (Baltimore: Johns Hopkins University Press, 1988), 200–01.
67. On Edinburgh as a center for medical and anatomical study, see T. V. N. Persaud, *A History of Anatomy: The Post-Vesalian Era* (Springfield, IL: Charles C. Thomas, 1997), 155–71. It was not until 1850 that the prominent Edinburgh anatomist Robert Knox published *Races of Men*, a text that brought anatomy forth as a tool for distinguishing among peoples.
68. "Doctor Hartley . . . settle[d] in Madras in a medical capacity. . . . His practice was not confined to his countrymen, but much sought after among the natives, who, whatever may be their prejudices against the Europeans in other respects, universally esteemed their superior powers in the medical profession" (136). Dr. Hartley's Scottish mentor, Dr. Gray, likewise asserts the universality of medical knowledge, which is "that noble profession, by means of which, wherever your lot casts you, you may always gain your bread, and alleviate, at the same time, the distresses of your fellow-creatures" (86). See Walter Scott, *The Surgeon's Daughter* in *Chronicles of the Canongate*, vol. 1 (Philadelphia, PA: Henry T. Coates & Co., 1900).
69. Quoted in James Reed, *Sir Walter Scott: Landscape and Locality* (London: The Athlone Press, 1980), 15.
70. "I, the Chronicler of the Canongate," Scott confided in his journal, "will have to take up my residence in the Sanctuary for a week or so, unless I prefer the more airy residence of Calton Jail" (*J*, 371). See also Eric Quayle, *The Ruin of Sir Walter Scott* (New York: C. N. Potter, 1968). On the function of the Canongate as a debtor's sanctuary, see John MacKay, *History of the Burgh of Canongate with Notices of the Abbey and Palace of Holyrood* (Edinburgh: Oliphant Anderson & Ferrier, 1900), 216–19.

2. NATION AND *GENIUS LOCI* IN HAWTHORNE AND SIMMS

1. Peter Ginna, "Taking Place," *American Places: Encounters with History*, ed. William E. Leuchtenburg (New York: Oxford University Press, 2000), xvii.
2. Originally appearing in the Charleston *City Gazette* (July 4, 1831), this poem is reprinted as "Union and Liberty" in Simms's *Southward Ho!* (New York: Redfield, 1856), 256–57. See James E. Kibler, Jr., *The Poetry of William Gilmore Simms: An Introduction and Bibliography* (Spartanburg, SC: Reprint Company, 1979), 306.
3. Calhoun's nullification doctrine was published anonymously on December 19, 1828 as the "South Carolina Exposition and Protest." Calhoun's authorship of that document had become public knowledge by the time Simms wrote his response in his July 4 newspaper poem. Just three weeks later, on July 26, 1831, Calhoun presented his "Fort Hill Address: On the Relations of the States and the Federal Government," a document that further details his nullification stance. For an historical overview of the events in which Simms and his poem were participating, see Merrill G. Christophersen, "The Anti-Nullifiers," *Oratory in the Old South, 1828–1860*, ed. Waldo W. Braden (Baton Rouge: Louisiana State University Press, 1970), 73–103.
4. William Gilmore Simms, "To James Lawson, Summerville, Nov. 25. [1832]," *The Letters of William Gilmore Simms*, ed. Mary C. Simms Oliphant, *et. al.*, vol. 1 (Columbia, SC: University of South Carolina Press, 1952), 47. Hereafter cited parenthetically in the text.
5. For general discussions of Simms's changing relation to the Union and southern sectionalism, see John W. Higham, "The Changing Loyalties of William Gilmore Simms," *The Journal of Southern History* 9:2 (May 1943): 210–23; Jon L. Wakelyn, *The Politics of a Literary Man: William Gilmore Simms* (Westport, CT: Greenwood Press, 1973).
6. Simms's language makes clear his sense of himself as tour guide: "As you enter from the sea, . . . the city opens before you in the foreground" (2); "As you advance . . ." (3); "In front of you . . . is Fort Sumter"; "On the right you see . . ."; "On the left are . . ."; "Here, at the very portals of the city, you encounter Castle Pinckney . . . ; and here we propose to give you a bird's-eye view of the city itself. We are now in the ancient city itself – the Palmetto City!" (3). See Simms, "Charleston: The Palmetto City," *Harper's New Monthly Magazine* 15:85 (June 1857): 1–22.
7. In the period between Simms's July 4 poem and his "Calhoun – Ode," Calhoun's strategies for resisting federal legislation would undergo a change: where his writings of 1829 advocated nullification by states in the Union, his writings of the 1840s advocated a veto by minority interests (for instance, the South) within a "concurrent majority." In either case, Calhoun's concern was constitutional procedure for the management of legal sovereignty. For an overview of Calhoun's changing views see the "Introduction" by C. Gordon Post to John C. Calhoun's

A Disquisition on Government and Selections from the Discourse, ed. C. Gordon Post (New York: Macmillan, 1953), xii–xviii, xxi–xxv.

8. For recent criticism relevant to the issues I am addressing in Simms, see Leonard Lutwack, *The Role of Place in Literature* (Syracuse University Press, 1984); Frederick Turner, *Spirit of Place: The Making of an American Literary Landscape* (San Francisco, CA: Sierra Club Books, 1989); Lawrence Buell, *The Environmental Imagination: Thoreau, Nature Writing, and the Formation of American Culture* (Cambridge, MA: Harvard University Press, 1995), especially his chapter on "Place" (252–79); Roberto M. Dainotto, *Place in Literature: Regions, Cultures, Communities* (Ithaca, NY: Cornell University Press, 2000), 1–33 and 171–73; and Robert Eric Livingston, "Glocal Knowledges: Agency and Place in Literary Studies," *PMLA* 116:1 (January 2001): 145–57.
9. For a recent discussion that speaks more generally of Simms's commitment to locales and his emphasis on guided tours of those locales, see James E. Kibler, "Stewardship and Patria in Simms's Frontier Poetry," *William Gilmore Simms and the American Frontier*, ed., John Caldwell Guilds and Caroline Collins (Athens: University of Georgia Press, 1997), 209–20, esp. 211–12, 215–17.
10. Debates about the shape of Hawthorne's career have taken a variety of forms. For a summary and analysis of that debate, see Lawrence Buell, *New England Literary Culture: From Revolution through Renaissance* (New York: Cambridge University Press, 1986), 239–40. For a subsequent treatment of that debate, see Lauren Berlant, *The Anatomy of National Fantasy: Hawthorne, Utopia, and Everyday Life* (University of Chicago Press, 1991).
11. William Gilmore Simms, *Geography of South Carolina: Being a Companion to the History of that State* (Charleston, SC: Babcock & Co., 1843), and *History of South Carolina*, new and revised edn. (New York: Redfield, 1860).
12. William Gilmore Simms, "Jocassée, A Cherokee Legend," *The Wigwam and the Cabin* (New York: Redfield, 1856), 209. This story first appeared in *The Gift of 1837* (1836) bearing the one-word title "Jocassée," but it is more accessible as a reprint in the later collection. Subsequent citations from *The Wigwam and the Cabin* will be abbreviated *W&C* and will appear parenthetically in the text.
13. The lingering presence of Aborigines is something Simms underscores by urging that Native American place names be restored to the region. See "Summer Travel in the South," *The Southern Quarterly Review*, ns 2 (September, 1850), 64.
14. Geoffrey H. Hartman, "Romantic Poetry and the Genius Loci," *Beyond Formalism: Literary Essays 1958–1970* (New Haven: Yale University Press, 1971), 311. Subsequent citations will appear parenthetically in the text. For Hartman's discussion of personification see 315, 331–35: "What modern literary theory tends to call an epiphany involves a confrontation with a second self in the form of genius loci or Persona. There is a djinee in every well-wrought urn" (333). It is my contention that Simms is presenting, as such Personae, the historical figures Calhoun and Jocassée, associating them not just with urns, or poems, but also with places.

15. Geoffrey H. Hartman, "Wordsworth, Inscriptions, and Romantic Nature Poetry," *Beyond Formalism: Literary Essays 1958–1970* (New Haven: Yale University Press, 1971), 207. Subsequent citations will appear parenthetically in the text. Hartman traces the inscription to classical precedents, including the influential comments of Lessing: "The true inscription is not to be thought of apart from that whereon it stands, or might stand. Both together make the whole from which arises the impression which, speaking generally, we ascribe to the inscription alone. First, some object of sense which arouses our curiosity; and then the account of this same object, which satisfies that curiosity" (209).
16. "What Wordsworth did," Hartman observes, "is clear: he transformed the inscription into an independent nature poem, and in so doing created a principal form of the Romantic and modern lyric" (221). Note the significance Hartman accords the *genius loci* in Wordsworth's early development: "How did Wordsworth raise himself from his obsession with specific place to the key notion of spots of time? I suspect the intermediate concept to have been that of *genius loci*, or 'spirit of place.' The renovating energy flowing from the spots of time is really spirit of place reaching through time with a guardian's care" (*Wordsworth's Poetry* [New Haven: Yale University Press, 1964], 212). For Hartman's more recent discussion of these same issues, see his *The Fateful Question of Culture* (New York: Columbia University Press, 1997) 3–4, 66, 151. My ultimate concern here is Hartman's discussion of the *genius loci* rather than his account of Wordsworth, which is critiqued by Jerome J. McGann in *The Romantic Ideology* (University of Chicago Press, 1983), 41, and defended by Jonathan Bate in *Romantic Ecology: Wordsworth and the Environmental Tradition* (New York: Routledge, 1991), 90–91.
17. This account of identity stands apart, in Hartman's view, from an account focused on trauma. Thus in a recent interview with Cathy Caruth, Hartman observes, "Implicit in much I have done is a meditation on place and its relation to memory and identity (individual rather than collective). It wasn't the study of Wordsworth that led me to study the Holocaust. There is a clear separation between these two subjects. . . . I sensed a loss of memory place, of the Wordsworthian memory place, after the Holocaust"; see Cathy Caruth, "An Interview with Geoffrey Hartman," *Studies in Romanticism* 35 (Winter 1996): 645.
18. This concern with a place's "moral presence" sets these works apart from contemporary texts that are concerned with the landscape's picturesque beauty, for as Beth L. Lueck has observed, writings "commenting on local inhabitants, customs, politics, legends, and history" amounted to "digressions" from the central aims of the picturesque tour; see Lueck's *American Writers and the Picturesque Tour: The Search for National Identity, 1790–1860* (New York: Garland Publishing, 1997), 13. Instead, Simms's concern with a place's "moral presence" aligns his work more closely with what Lawrence Buell calls the "Spirit of Place"; see Buell's *New England Literary Culture*, 286–94. While Buell attributes this concern primarily to New England writers, Kristie Hamilton has argued that Buell's observations can be extended to include writers in the South;

see Hamilton's *America's Sketchbook: The Cultural Life of a Nineteenth-Century Literary Genre* (Athens: Ohio University Press, 1998), 68–69.

19. On the Cherokee Removal see *Cherokee Removal: Before and After*, ed. William L. Anderson (Athens: University of Georgia Press, 1991); and *The Cherokee Removal: A Brief History with Documents*, ed. Theda Perdue and Michael D. Green (New York: Bedford Books, 1995).

20. Simms's earliest writings treat the *genius loci* strictly as a convention of "imaginative" writing following German models. Thus in 1838, when Simms first collects the Jocassée legend in a volume of short stories, he places it among other tales that, although set in geographically unrelated locations, nevertheless employ this same "imaginative" topos of the *genius loci*. The tale "Logoochie," for instance, features a haunted site in Georgia while "Carl Werner" portrays a haunted site in Germany. (See William Gilmore Simms, *Carl Werner, An Imaginative Story; With Other Tales of Imagination* [New York: George Adlard, 1838].) Eight years later, in 1845, Simms places the Jocassée legend in yet another collection, this one casting its *genius loci* as an index of "border history." In this collection, superstitions like the Jocassée legend persist beyond the "border" of advancing European "civilization," so the *genius loci* marks not so much the exterior boundaries of a nation but the advancing frontier of "progress." Neither case, then, draws a constitutive link between *genius loci* and national identity. Later writings, however, will feature such a link.

21. William Gilmore Simms, "Summer Travel in the South," 31, 33. Hereafter cited parenthetically in the text.

22. William Gilmore Simms, "The Apalachian, a Southern Idyll: In Two Lectures," ed. Miriam J. Shillingsburg, *Appalachian Journal* 1 (Autumn 1972): 2–11; (Spring, 1972): 147–60. Hereafter cited parenthetically in the text. For further discussion of this lecture, see Miriam J. Shillingsburg, "William Gilmore Simms and the Myth of Appalachia," *Appalachian Journal* 6 (Winter 1979): 110–19. For further discussion of the tour itself, see Merrill Christophersen, "Simms' Northern Speaking Tour in 1856: A Tragedy," *Southern Speech Journal* 36 (Winter 1970): 139–51; John Hope Franklin, *A Southern Odyssey: Travelers in the Antebellum North* (Baton Rouge, LA: Louisiana State University Press, 1976), 237–43; and James Perrin Warren, *Culture of Eloquence: Oratory and Reform in Antebellum America* (University Park, PA: Pennsylvania State University Press, 1999), 155–67.

23. Charles S. Watson notes both Simms's use of the *genius loci* in his poetry and his shift from American nationalism to southern secessionism, but he does not suggest what I am claiming, that Simms sees these two issues as fundamentally related, the first being an avenue to the second. I want to demonstrate that Simms treats this literary device as a basis for national identity: it is only because he had a *genius loci* that he could have an independent South capable of seceding. See Charles S. Watson, *From Nationalism to Secessionism: The Changing Fiction of William Gilmore Simms* (Westport, CT: Greenwood Press, 1993), 11–12.

24. For further discussion of this distinction see Eric H. Walther, "Fire-Eaters and the Riddle of Southern Nationalism," *Southern Studies* 3:1 (Spring 1992): 67–77.
25. By focusing his attention on the *genius loci*, Simms conveniently ignores both the social history of southern slavery and the political history of southern efforts to extend slavery into the territories. For a discussion of slavery's social history, see Eugene D. Genovese, *Roll Jordan Roll: The World the Slaves Made* (New York: Vintage Books, 1976); for a discussion of efforts to extend slavery into the territories, see Eric Foner, *Free Soil, Free Labor, Free Men: The Ideology of the Republican Party before the Civil War* (New York: Oxford University Press, 1970).
26. Nathaniel Hawthorne, "An Old Woman's Tale," *Hawthorne: Tales and Sketches* (New York: Library of America, 1982), 25. Subsequent citations of Hawthorne's tales and sketches will refer to this edition and appear parenthetically in the text.
27. John L. O'Sullivan's "Introduction" to the first issue of the *United States Magazine and Democratic Review* begins with the following statement:

> The character and design of the work of which the first number is here offered to the public, are intended to be shadowed forth in its name, the "United States Magazine and *Democratic Review*." It has had its origin in a deep conviction of the necessity of such a work, at the present critical stage of our national progress, for the advocacy of that high and holy DEMOCRATIC PRINCIPLE which was designed to be the fundamental element of the new social and political system created by the "American experiment."(*United States Magazine and Democratic Review* 1:1 [October 1837]: 1)

Michael Rogin writes of the *Democratic Review*, "For almost two decades, from 1837 well into the 1850s, it was the leading spokesman for American literary and political nationalism." See *Subversive Genealogy: The Politics and Art of Herman Melville* (Berkeley: University of California Press, 1983), 72.
28. The clearest instance of this claim comes from Robert Fossum ("Time and the Artist in 'Legends of the Province House,'" *Nineteenth-Century Fiction* 21:4 [March 1967]):

> [N]owhere in Hawthorne's canon . . . is the purpose of the fiction clearer than in the "Legends." For these tales imaginatively reforge nineteenth-century America's link to the past. Through such historical fictions, Hawthorne hoped to create the conscience and consciousness of his race, to make all Americans aware of the historical matrix which gave them birth and from which they can detach themselves only by relinquishing their national identity. Since we can know what we are only by knowing what we have been, our identity is contingent on recognizing the nature of our heritage. (337–38)

To recognize "our heritage" is to acknowledge shared "birth" from a specific "historical matrix" – i.e. it is for Americans to acknowledge themselves as children of an American past.
29. Those who see Hawthorne opposing Hancock include Fossum, Neal Frank Doubleday (*Hawthorne's Early Tales, a Critical Study* [Durham, NC: Duke University Press, 1972], 133), and Michael Colacurcio (*The Province of Piety*

[Cambridge, MA: Harvard University Press, 1984], 451 ff.]; those who see Hawthorne supporting Hancock include Geoffrey D. Smith ("The Reluctant Democrat and the Amiable Whig: Nathaniel Hawthorne, Edmund Quincy and the Politics of History," *Nathaniel Hawthorne Review* 18:2 [1992]: 9–14) and Nina Baym (*The Shape of Hawthorne's Career* [Ithaca, NY: Cornell University Press, 1976], 78). Other critics see *Legends of the Province House* as ultimately about Hawthorne's ongoing ambivalence about this choice: see Julian Smith, "Hawthorne's *Legends of the Province House,*" *Nineteenth-Century Fiction* 24:1 (June 1969): 44; Evan Carton, "Hawthorne and the Province of Romance," *ELH* 47 (1980): 331–54; and George Dekker, *The American Historical Romance* (New York: Cambridge University Press, 1987), 180–85.

30. The following sentence gives an even better view of Esther Dudley as storytelling guide: "Thus, without affrighting her little guests, she led them by the hand into the chambers of her own desolate heart, and made childhood's fancy discern the ghosts that haunted there" (673). The "ghosts" in her heart are the ones in her magic mirror, which contains the Province-House's past (671). Other early tales in which Hawthorne's narrators take on this role include "Alice Doane's Appeal" (1835) and "A Rill from the Town-Pump" (1835). While I take the force of Berlant's choice (in *The Anatomy of National Fantasy*) to label this recurrent figure as a "sibyl" (169) and attribute it to Hawthorne's knowledge of "epic" (250–51 n. 5), the term I prefer is guide to the *genius loci*, and to me the more compelling source is the one Hartman offers, the conventions of eighteenth-century British poetry and the genre of the "inscription."
31. As he describes Esther Dudley's expulsion, the storytelling guide suddenly finds himself bereft of a subject: "As the old loyalist concluded his narrative, the enthusiasm which had been fitfully flashing within his sunken eyes and quivering across his wrinkled visage, faded away, as if all the lingering fire of his soul were extinguished" (677).
32. Hawthorne's frame narrator repeatedly complains of this commercial involvement. Tavern customers and stagecoach schedules show the Province-House's historic associations besieged by contemporary commerce, and Hancock, who is described not as a revolutionary patriot but as "this New England merchant" (676), finally secures commercial supremacy when he expels Esther Dudley. By expelling Esther Dudley, then, Hancock terminates the Province-House's aristocratic distinctiveness, effectively immersing it within this new nation's "tiresome identity" (640) of commerce.
33. William Gilmore Simms, "Sectional Literature," *The Magnolia* (April 1842): 251. Hereafter cited parenthetically in the text.
34. William Gilmore Simms, *Views and Reviews in American Literature, History and Fiction, First Series*, ed. C. Hugh Holman (Cambridge: Harvard University Press, 1962) 55–56. Subsequent citations will be abbreviated *V&R* and will appear parenthetically in the text.
35. For discussion of Simms's locally oriented approach to historiography of the Revolution, see William L. Welch, "Lorenzo Sabine and the Assault on Sumner," *New England Quarterly* 65 (1992): 298–302.

36. "Review of Simms's *Views and Reviews* and Hood's *Poems*," The Scarlet Letter *& Related Writings by Nathaniel Hawthorne*, ed. H. Bruce Franklin (Philadelphia, PA: J. B. Lippincott, 1967), 286. Hereafter cited parenthetically in the text. Hawthorne offered even sharper criticism of Simms's *Views and Reviews* in the letter that accompanied his manuscript: "naturally I am no critic. I know well enough what I like, but am always at a loss to render a reason. Mr. Simms I do not like at all." See Randall Stewart, "Hawthorne's Contributions to *The Salem Advertiser*," *American Literature* 5 (1934): 330 n. 12.
37. Simms makes this explicit in his discussion of the Pocahontas theme: "the life of the Virginia princess [i.e. Pocahontas] furnishes other materials . . . which are fully equal, in intrinsic capabilities, to any of those which have been employed by Scott. The tone of the story may be pitched with that of the Lady of the Lake" (*V&R*, 121). Similarly, Simms observes of Native American traditions: "We should not need a Milton, or a Homer, for the performance. The material would have suited Scott's poetical genius better, perhaps, than that of better bards" (*V&R*, 146). For Scott's own views on what he calls "this local sympathy," see James Reed, *Sir Walter Scott: Landscape and Locality*, 15.
38. Geoffrey Hartman, *The Fateful Question of Culture*, 4. On this transformation from *genius loci* to *genius* in Hawthorne's writing career, see Kenneth Dauber, *The Idea of Authorship in America: Democratic Poetics from Franklin to Melville* (Madison: University of Wisconsin Press, 1990), 177–78.
39. Nathaniel Hawthorne, "Review of Whittier's *The Supernaturalism of New England*," The Scarlet Letter *& Related Writings by Nathaniel Hawthorne*, ed. Franklin, 291. Note that Hawthorne sees these gathered legends working to particularize a region, not – as Simms had suggested – to constitute a given region's contribution to America as a whole.
40. For a related discussion, see Dekker, *The American Historical Romance*, 185.
41. Nathaniel Hawthorne, "The Custom-House," *The Norton Anthology of American Literature*, 4th edn., vol. 1 (New York: W. W. Norton & Company, 1994), 1,253. Subsequent citations will appear parenthetically in the text.
42. Hawthorne's "Preface" to the 1851 edition of *Twice-Told Tales* looks back upon his place from the other side of this divide: "The circulation of the two volumes was chiefly confined to New England; nor was it until long after this period, if it even yet be the case, that the Author could regard himself as addressing the American public, or, indeed, any public at all. He was merely writing to his known or unknown friends" (*Hawthorne: Tales and Sketches* 1,151).
43. This turn against local history exemplifies at once the "American liberalism" that Sacvan Bercovitch critiques Hawthorne for praising and the "National Symbolic" that Lauren Berlant praises Hawthorne for critiquing. That each critic's account could have such force is, I want to argue, evidence of this novel's emergence out of Hawthorne's ongoing struggle with the Simms program. See Sacvan Bercovitch, *The Office of* The Scarlet Letter (Baltimore: Johns Hopkins University Press, 1991), 29–31; and Lauren Berlant, *The Anatomy of National Fantasy*, 7.

44. Nathaniel Hawthorne, *Life of Franklin Pierce* (Boston: Ticknor, Reed, and Fields, 1852), 111. Subsequent citations will refer to this edition and will appear parenthetically in the text.
45. William Gilmore Simms, *Father Abbot, or, The Home Tourist* (Charleston, SC: Miller & Browne, 1849), 20. Subsequent citations will refer to this edition and will appear parenthetically in the text.
46. For a similar discussion of the sectionalist tendencies within Simms's Americanism, a discussion that focuses on Simms's July 4 oration "The Sources of American Independence" (1844), see Warren, *Culture of Eloquence*, 146–48.
47. Simms, "Summer Travel in the South," 33. Hereafter cited parenthetically in the text.
48. William Gilmore Simms, "The Apalachian, a Southern Idyll," 5; hereafter cited parenthetically in the text. Describing himself as "nursed in those mysterious regions" and "gifted with the faculty of the clairvoyant," Simms claims to have attained, "in dream and vision, the wild aspects of [the region's] legendary lore" (5): "In what bold relief do we conjure the image of . . . [John Smith]. Following his track, we encounter . . . Powhatan; and behind him, . . . Opechancanough. . . . Hovering in the shadow, on the edge of the thicket, you behold . . . the damsel Pocahontas" (7).
49. Simms, *The Letters of William Gilmore Simms*, 1:47.
50. Nathaniel Hawthorne, *The House of the Seven Gables* (New York: Penguin Books, 1981), 3. Hereafter cited parenthetically in the text.
51. "The question briefly is – What are the standards of the modern Romance? . . . The domestic novel of [Richardson and Fielding], confined to the felicitous narration of common and daily occurring events, and the grouping and delineation of characters in ordinary conditions of society, is altogether a different sort of composition. . . . It [Romance] invests individuals with an absorbing interest . . . and it seeks for its adventures among the wild and wonderful. It does not confine itself to what is known, or even what is probable. It grasps at the possible" (23–24). See Simms's preface to the 1856 edition of *The Yemassee: A Romance of Carolina* [1835] rev. edn. (New York: W. J. Widdleton, 1856).
52. In *The American Historical Romance* George Dekker observes that Simms "crowded the plots of his romances with the notable figures and incidents that also appeared in his *History of South Carolina*" (63).
53. Nathaniel Hawthorne, *A Wonder Book for Boys and Girls, Hawthorne: Tales and Sketches* (New York: Library of America, 1974), 1,163; hereafter cited parenthetically in the text.
54. The formal layout of the book underscores this point, for the myths themselves are set off from introductory and concluding sections that point to the local landscape. Never do myth and landscape occupy the same page.
55. See Simms's poem "Sketches in Hellas," Part 3, "Thessaly" in *Selected Poems of William Gilmore Simms*, ed. James Everett Kibler, Jr. (Athens, GA: University of Georgia Press, 1990), 282–85.

56. William Gilmore Simms, *Poems Descriptive, Dramatic, Legendary and Contemplative*, vol. 1 (New York: Redfield, 1853), 209–327. Specific poems will be cited parenthetically in the text.
57. Edgar Allan Poe, "The Raven," *The Norton Anthology of American Literature*, 4th edn, vol. 1 (New York: W. W. Norton & Company, 1994), 1,447.
58. In his writings of the 1840s Simms did, like Poe, focus on the sounds of poems themselves; see *Views and Reviews*, 34, 49, 54, 56, 76, 99, 110–12, 127. As I have suggested, however, the 1850s show Simms moving away from the commitment to text while retaining the commitment to literary effects, and he accomplishes this by displacing those effects onto the landscape itself, treating landscape itself as poem. For a clearer statement of this see "The Legend of the Happy Valley, and the Beautiful Fawn," *Southern Literary Messenger* 20 (July, 1854), where Simms writes, "We lack rather the student than the matter; rather the novelist than the tradition; rather the bard than the hero; rather the art than the raw material, upon which it exercises itself. That we shall yet have the Poet, and that he will explore the wilderness, and embody for us in glorious forms the mysterious legends which it hides, is a fond persuasion in our hearts" (397).
59. This poem first appeared in 1841 under a different title, "The Last Song of the Biloxi. A Tradition of the South." The 1853 version, then, replaces "Song" with "Fields," displacing the emphasis from the song itself to its location on the map. On this shift in the poem's title see James Everett Kibler, Jr., *The Poetry of William Gilmore Simms: An Introduction and Bibliography* (Spartanburg, SC: Reprint Company Publishers, 1979), 186.
60. Simms would make an explicit call for such guidebooks in his *Southward Ho!* (1856): "What a pity," one of the characters laments, "that handbooks for the South are not provided by some patriotic author!" (381):

    In the old countries of Europe, the . . . . handbook which you carry distinguishes the spot with some strange or startling history. In our world of woods, we lack these adjuncts. If we had the handbook, we should doubtlessly discover much to interest us in the very scenes by which we hurry with contempt. Dull and uninteresting as the railroad rout appears through North and South Carolina, were you familiar with the facts in each locality – could you couple each with its local history or tradition – the fancy would instantly quicken. . . . (380–81)

    Note that the passage also references Scott: "It is a great pity that for these we have no guide-books – no monuments along the wayside – no 'Old Mortality' to show us where the stone lies half buried, and, with the chisel, to deepen all its features to our eyes" (380; see also 388).
61. William Gilmore Simms, "Poetical Works of Wordsworth," *Southern Quarterly Review* 18 (September 1850): 6. This essay on Wordsworth seeks to specify the nature of poetry, ruling out meter and even imagination before settling on this notion of immediacy. Unlike our experience of "the landscape itself," where "our sensations have their origin in that tangible reality," "in poetry, what we feel is produced causelessly, as it were, within ourselves" (4). This,

moreover, is how Simms later (in *Southward Ho!*) describes the experience of South Carolina's "gloomy wastes of pine and swamp forest": these scenes, once linked to "events and traditions," "commend themselves to sympathies which lie much deeper than any which we can reach through the medium of the external senses" (381). "With a considerable knowledge of the history of the country in all these states, I am able to identify scenes of interest as I pass; and I find, at every step, in my course along these regions which seem so barren to the stranger, fruitful interests and moving influences, which exercise equally the memory and the imagination – the imagination through the memory"; see *Southward Ho!*, 381. To someone without such memory, who did not have a grandmother to tell him/her as a child, an ordinary guidebook will do, and this allows traditional locales to function just like poems – as they do for the maid in "The Cassique of Accabee."

62. Simms makes this same point in "The Legend of the Happy Valley" (1854): "To one who rambles in the lovely valleys of the Catawba, the memory of the gallant savages, who occupied them, at the first coming of the white race, and who distinguished themselves in arms for a long while after, will vividly recur" (396).
63. William Gilmore Simms, *Paddy McGann; Or, The Demon of the Stump*, *The Writings of William Gilmore Simms, Centennial Edition*, vol. III (Columbia, SC: University of South Carolina Press, 1972), 220. Subsequent citations will be to this edition and will appear parenthetically in the text.
64. A similar approach to the Appalachians appears in 1842 when Simms, the new editor of *The Magnolia*, renamed it *The Magnolia; or Southern Apalachian*. At the time he presumably did not consider this a tautology, but by 1863 he had come to view it as one.
65. For a useful discussion of the supernatural element in *Paddy McGann*, see Linda E. McDaniel, "American Gods and Devils in Simms's *Paddy McGann*," *Long Years of Neglect: The Work and Reputation of William Gilmore Simms*, ed. John Caldwell Guilds (Fayetteville, AR: University of Arkansas Press, 1988), 60–75.
66. For an account of the novel that focuses on these class relations, see Renée Dye, "A Sociology of the Civil War: Simms's *Paddy McGann*," *Southern Literary Journal* 28:2 (Spring 1996): 3–23. While Dye sees the novel forecasting the decay of social hierarchies in the South, I view it as announcing the advent of national identity, an Appalachian identity to which class differences can be subordinated.
67. Nathaniel Hawthorne, "Chiefly About War-Matters," *The Atlantic Monthly* 10 (July 1862): 54, 57, 55. Hereafter cited parenthetically in the text.
68. Those who have "sided with the South" (61), he concedes, have "plausible arguments" (48): "They have a conscientious, though mistaken belief, that the South was driven out of the Union by intolerable wrong on our part, and that we are responsible for having compelled true patriots to love only half their country instead of the whole" (61). For discussions that place greater emphasis on this ambivalence see Berlant, *The Anatomy of National Fantasy*,

205–06; Larzer Ziff, *Literary Democracy* (New York: Viking Press, 1981), 124–27; and James Bense, "Nathaniel Hawthorne's Intention in 'Chiefly About War Matters,'" *American Literature* 61:2 (May 1989): 214.

69. Simms's poem is printed in William Drayton, *An Oration Delivered in the First Presbyterian Church, July 4,* 1831 (Charleston, SC: W. S. Blain and J. S. Burges, 1831), 74–79. The quoted passage appears on p. 74; this poem is hereafter cited parenthetically in the text. The quotation from Walter Scott is the first three lines of the sixth canto of *The Lay of the Last Minstrel* (1805). The same lines figure prominently in Edward Everett Hale's popular Unionist short story "The Man Without a Country," which was first published in the *Atlantic Monthly* in December, 1863; see Hale's *The Man Without a Country*, ed. Carl Van Doren (New York: The Heritage Press, 1936), 16. I am indebted to Caroline Levander for bringing this connection to my attention.

70. William Gilmore Simms, "Preface," *War Poetry of the South*, ed. William Gilmore Simms (New York: Richardson & Company, 1867), vi; hereafter cited parenthetically in the text.

71. Nathaniel Hawthorne, "Chiefly About War-Matters," 49.

72. Henry James, "Preface," *The American Scene* [1907], ed. Leon Edel (Bloomington, IN: Indiana University Press, 1968), unpag. Hereafter cited parenthetically in the text.

73. Nathaniel Hawthorne, *Tanglewood Tales For Girls and Boys; Being a Second Wonder Book* [1853], *Hawthorne: Tales and Sketches* (New York: Library of America, 1974), 1,309.

74. Hawthorne's influence on James as a model of authorship is underscored by Richard Broadhead's effort to locate James within a "School of Hawthorne." Addressing the revised account of Hawthorne that James elucidated in his late career, the period in which James wrote *The American Scene*, Brodhead observes that "a new *invention* of Hawthorne as a source of tradition – is what James performs in his late return to Hawthorne . . . . This new-found or new-made Hawthorne then helps him find how to meet the requirements of his own new position: how to write a close to his career, and how to adapt his work to the modern situation of literary expression"; see Richard Brodhead, *The School of Hawthorne* (New York: Oxford University Press, 1986), 176.

75. As Brodhead observes, "What James recovers in *The Golden Bowl*, I am trying to suggest, is not just Hawthornesque romance's stylistic mannerisms, but its stylistic insistence on itself as something radically constructed – something wholly artificial, in the sense of being wholly artificed; a perfect fabrication, in the sense that a maker's act has fashioned it all" (*The School of Hawthorne*, 188).

76. William Gilmore Simms, "Charleston: The Palmetto City," 1–22. Hereafter cited parenthetically in the text.

77. Kenneth W. Warren, *Black and White Strangers*: 121. For additional discussion of James's *The American Scene* and its relation to Du Bois, see Beverly Haviland, *Henry James's Last Romance: Making Sense of the Past and The American Scene* (New York: Cambridge University Press, 1997), 108–134.

78. William Gilmore Simms, "The Apalachian, a Southern Idyll," 5.
79. Robert Stepto, *From Behind the Veil: A Study of Afro-American Narrative*, 2nd edn. (Chicago: University of Illinois Press, 1991), 76. Hereafter cited parenthetically in the text.
80. "One lingers thoughtfully among the ruins of Jamestown," Simms writes in *Southward Ho!* (1856); but since "There is little or nothing to be seen" there, "It is, of course, the mere *site* which will now interest you . . . . the association only, the *genius loci*. . . . What stores of tradition . . . are yet to be turned up with the soil of this neighborhood" (131).
81. W. E. B. Du Bois, *The Souls of Black Folk* (New York: Penguin Books), 93. Hereafter cited parenthetically in the text.
82. Stepto discusses the travel dimension of *The Souls of Black Folk* on 66–82; for specific discussion of "the geography of the *genius loci*" (77), see 70–74 and 76–78. Houston Baker makes the similar observation that "Du Bois's South sings" (*Modernism and the Harlem Renaissance*, 67). According to Baker, "A FOLK is always . . . possessed of a guiding or tutelary spirit" (63), and Baker associates that tutelary spirit with the "melodies of ancient spiritual song" that are "resident on the southern landscapes presented in *Souls*" (66).
83. William Gilmore Simms, "The Last Fields of the Biloxi; A Tradition of Louisiana," *Poems Descriptive, Dramatic, Legendary, and Contemplative*, I: 273.
84. See I.ii.374 and I.ii.388 in William Shakespeare, *The Tempest*, ed. Stephen Orgel (New York: Oxford University Press, 1987), 121–22.
85. Simms, "The Apalachian, a Southern Idyll," 5; hereafter cited parenthetically in the text.
86. For Baker's alignment of Du Bois and Caliban, see *Modernism and the Harlem Renaissance*, 53–61; hereafter abbreviated *MHR*. Although Baker mentions "Caliban's singing" (*MHR*, 60), his remarks elsewhere associate Caliban with "sounds and sweet airs" and "a thousand twangling instruments" ("Caliban's Triple Play," *"Race," Writing, and Difference*, ed. Henry Louis Gates, Jr. [University of Chicago Press, 1986], 392), both of which are phrases used by Caliban to refer to the tabor and pipe playing of Ariel; see *The Tempest*, 162 (III.ii.134–35). These are the sounds that for Baker are "truly foundational" ("Caliban's Triple Play," 392), so the overall effect of comparing Du Bois and Caliban is to cast Du Bois not as a lyric singer but as someone who – like Caliban guiding visitors to Ariel, and like Simms guiding visitors to the Biloxi – mediates an audience's relation to these ambient sounds of the locale. "Du Bois's South sings" (*MHR*, 67), Baker asserts, but Du Bois himself does not, and "The whole of *Souls*," Baker argues, "moves in fact toward the moment . . . when a phaneric narrator reveals that he *knows the score*" (*MHR*, 57), a musical score that he did not compose but for which he – like Caliban and Simms – can serve as mediating guide.
87. In his discussion of Du Bois's trip to the South, Eric Sundquist likewise links Du Bois with the concern we have seen in Simms, a concern with haunted locales. "The South is a land inhabited by white ghosts of the Confederacy but also the living ghosts of African American slavery" (*To Wake the Nations*,

508). For Simms, as we have seen, a concern for Confederate ghosts succeeds an earlier concern with Native American ghosts, each serving Simms as a basis for southern identity.

88. Roberto M. Dainotto, *Place in Literature*, 17; hereafter cited parenthetically in the text.
89. Houston A. Baker, Jr., *Turning South Again: Re-Thinking Modernism/Re-Reading Booker T.* (Durham, NC: Duke University Press, 2001), 69, 24; hereafter cited parenthetically in the text.
90. On the capacity of the *genius loci* to support claims of both nation and race, see Hartman, *The Fateful Question of Culture*, 87, 184.
91. See Walter Benn Michaels, "Jim Crow Henry James?," *The Henry James Review* 16:3 (1995): 286–91. For a subsequent discussion that supports these claims see Gert Buelens, *Enacting History in Henry James: Narrative, Power, and Ethics* (Cambridge University Press, 1997), 173.
92. Of course it is precisely the US Constitution – or rather the Supreme Court's interpretation of it in the 1896 *Plessy v. Ferguson* case – that imposes the color line Du Bois seeks to transcend, so the point is not that the Constitution itself provides a cosmopolitan escape from locale, but that the cosmopolitanism (through Union citizenship) that Hawthorne imagines via the Constitution's ability to apply anywhere, regardless of *genius loci*, anticipates the cosmopolitanism (through intellectualism) that Du Bois imagines via his own intellectual ability to engage with any great thinker, regardless of race. On Du Bois as a cosmopolitan intellectual, see Houston Baker, "The Black Man of Culture: W. E. B. Du Bois and *The Souls of Black Folk*," *Long Black Song: Essays in Black American Literature and Culture* (Charlottesville: University Press of Virginia, 1972), 96–108; and Ross Posnock, *Color and Culture: Black Writers and the Making of the Modern Intellectual* (Cambridge, MA: Harvard University Press, 1998).
93. Nathaniel Hawthorne, "Chiefly About War-Matters," 48.
94. Support for this account of double consciousness comes from the shifting readings of Du Bois presented in the work of Houston Baker. In a 1972 essay Baker asserts that Du Bois "felt that a new stage in the growth of the black man in America had been reached. . . . The realization of the 'pastness of the past' and the sense of a new age that inform *The Souls of Black Folk* are not surprising when we consider that Du Bois was a man of the twentieth-century" ("The Black Man of Culture," 96). Bakers's characterization of Du Bois resembles Hawthorne's characterization of John Hancock, who, as we saw, expelled Esther Dudley, the New England *genius loci*: "you are a symbol of the past," Hancock tells her, "And I, and these around me – we represent a new race of men, living no longer in the past, scarcely in the present – but projecting our lives forward into the future. Ceasing to model ourselves on ancestral superstitions, it is our faith and principle to press onward, onward!" (676). In Baker's later account, as we have seen, he casts Du Bois in precisely the opposite way, as a guardian of this *genius loci*. Baker acknowledges that his later account amounts to a reversal (*MHR*, 64) – that he in effect shifts Du

Bois from the position of John Hancock to that of Esther Dudley. My point is that both of Baker's analyses, early and late, equally apply to Du Bois, and it is this ambivalence between them – between Hancock and Esther Dudley (and later, between Hawthorne and Simms) – that produces a civil war mindset, the mischievous anomaly of two allegiances characteristic of double consciousness.

95. On hyphenated identity in Du Bois, see David Levering Lewis, *W. E. B. Du Bois: Biography of a Race, 1868–1919* (New York: Henry Holt, 1993), 281. On the possible sources for Du Bois's term "double consciousness," see Lewis, *W. E. B. Du Bois*, 96; Arnold Rampersad, *The Art and Imagination of W. E. B. Du Bois* (Cambridge, MA: Harvard University Press, 1976), 74; and Dickerson D. Bruce, Jr. "W. E. B. Du Bois and the Idea of Double Consciousness," *American Literature* 64:2 (June 1992): 299–309. My concern is less the textual source of Du Bois's term than the cultural logic he uses that term to convey, a logic consistent, I am arguing, with Hawthorne's notion of an exceedingly mischievous anomaly of two allegiances. Others critics see Du Bois's double consciousness in psychoanalytic and indeed Lacanian terms; see for instance Sandra Adell, *Double-Consciousness/Double Bind: Theoretical Issues in Twentieth-Century Black Literature* (Chicago: University of Illinois Press, 1994), 72; and Gwen Bergner, "Myths of Masculinity: The Oedipus Complex and Douglass's 1845 *Narrative*," *The Psychoanalysis of Race*, ed. Christopher Lane (New York: Columbia University Press, 1998), 241–42. My concern, however, is not the future psychoanalytic theory Du Bois may be anticipating but rather the Civil War history he had thoroughly studied.
96. W. E. B. Du Bois, "The Conservation of Races," *W. E. B. Du Bois: A Reader*, ed. David Levering Lewis (New York: Henry Holt and Company, 1995), 23. For a discussion that puts this essay in the context of Du Bois's larger career, a career that moves away from such racial exclusivism, see Lewis, *W. E. B. Du Bois*, 173–74.
97. See Cecil Carus-Wilson's "The Production of Musical Notes from Non-Musical Sands," *Nature* 44:1136 (August 6, 1891): 322; hereafter cited parenthetically in the text.
98. See W. C., "On the Production of Musical Notes from Non-Musical Sands," *Chemical News* 64:1650 (July 10, 1891): 25.
99. This impulse continues into the present – see "Natural and Artificial 'Singing' Sands," *Nature* 386:6620 (March 6, 1997): 29.

3. THE MUSIC OF RACIAL IDENTITY

1. For an audio recording of this work see Dudley Buck and Sidney Lanier, "The Centennial Meditation of Columbia," *The Union Restored: 1861–76*, record 6 of *The Sounds of History; A Supplement to The Life History of the United States* (Time Inc., 1963), side 2, track 12.
2. In his discussion of the "Centennial Meditation of Columbia," Charles Hamm observes that "the idea was to have a 'Yankee' and a 'Rebel' combine talents, as a symbol of reconciliation between North and South" (*Music in the New World* [London: W. W. Norton and Company, 1983], 325).

3. Sidney Lanier, "The Centennial Meditation of Columbia," in *Poems and Poem Outlines*, ed. Charles R. Anderson, vol. I of *The Centennial Edition of the Works of Sidney Lanier*, ed. Charles R. Anderson (Baltimore: Johns Hopkins University Press, 1945), 61. Further references to this poem will be to this edition and will be cited parenthetically in the text as "CMC"; subsequent references to *Poems and Poem Outlines* will be cited parenthetically in the text as *PPO*.
4. Walt Whitman, "Preface 1876 – *Leaves of Grass* and *Two Rivulets*," *Leaves of Grass*, ed. Sculley Bradley and Harold W. Boldgett (New York: W. W. Norton and Company, 1973), 751, 746–47; further references to "Preface 1876" and to Whitman's poems will be to this edition and will be cited parenthetically in the text as *LG*.
5. See Exodus 3:14, where God reveals himself to Moses with a name that can be translated as either "I am what I am" or "I will be what I will be"; see also Revelation 1:8: "'I am the Alpha and the Omega,' says the Lord God, who is and who was and who is to come, the Almighty" (*The New Oxford Annotated Bible*, new rev. standard version [New York: Oxford University Press, 1991]).
6. Lanier, "The Centennial Cantata," "*The Science of English Verse" and Essays on Music*, ed. Paull Franklin Baum, vol. II of *The Centennial Edition of the Works of Sidney Lanier*, ed. Charles R. Anderson (Baltimore: Johns Hopkins University Press, 1945), 272–73. Further references to this essay will be to this volume and will be cited parenthetically in the text as "CC." Subsequent references to "*The Science of English Verse" and Essays on Music* will be cited parenthetically in the text as "*SEV*."
7. See Houston A. Baker Jr., *Modernism and the Harlem Renaissance*, 57, 62; and Eric Sundquist, *To Wake the Nations*, 529–30.
8. Thomas Jefferson, quoted in Stanley R. Hauer, "Thomas Jefferson and the Anglo-Saxon Language," *PMLA* 98 (October 1983): 880. For further discussion of Jefferson's Anglo-Saxonism, see Reginald Horsman, *Race and Manifest Destiny* (Cambridge, MA: Harvard University Press, 1981), 18–23; and Allen J. Frantzen, *Desire for Origins* (New Brunswick, NJ: Rutgers University Press, 1990), 203–07.
9. For discussions of the role played by Anglo-Saxon in accounts of Manifest Destiny, see Horsman, *Race and Manifest Destiny*, 1–6; and J. R. Hall, "Mid-Nineteenth-Century American Anglo-Saxonism: The Question of Language," *Anglo-Saxonism and the Construction of Social Identity*, ed. Allen J. Frantzen and John D. Niles (Gainesville: University Press of Florida, 1997), 134.
10. Arthur Mann, *The One and the Many: Reflections on the American Identity* (University of Chicago Press, 1979), 128.
11. Gregory A. VanHoosier-Carey, "Byrhtnoth in Dixie: The Emergence of Anglo-Saxon Studies in the Postbellum South," *Anglo-Saxonism and the Construction of Social Identity*, ed. Allen J. Frantzen and John D. Niles (Gainesville: University Press of Florida, 1997), 165.
12. See VanHoosier-Carey, "Byrhtnoth in Dixie," 161–63; and J. R. Hall, "Nineteenth-Century America and the Study of the Anglo-Saxon Language: An Introduction," *Preservation and Transmission of Anglo-Saxon Culture*, ed.

Paul E. Szarmach and Joel T. Rosenthal (Kalamazoo: Western Michigan University, 1997), 47–49.

13. Lanier, Letter to Daniel C. Gilman, 22 October 1876, *Letters 1874–1877*, ed. Charles R. Anderson and Aubrey H. Starke, vol. IX of *The Centennial Edition of the Works of Sidney Lanier*, ed. Charles R. Anderson (Baltimore: Johns Hopkins University Press, 1945), 406.
14. Lanier, Letter to Daniel C. Gilman, 13 July 1879, *Letters 1878–1881*, ed. Charles R. Anderson and Aubrey H. Starke, vol. X of *The Centennial Edition of the Works of Sidney Lanier*, ed. Charles R. Anderson (Baltimore: Johns Hopkins University Press, 1945), 130.
15. On the activities of Gilman, Lanier, and Whitney at Johns Hopkins, see Hugh Hawkins, *Pioneer: A History of the Johns Hopkins University, 1874–1889* (Ithaca, NY: Cornell University Press, 1960).
16. William Dwight Whitney, *The Life and Growth of Language* (New York: Dover, 1979), 145, 24; hereafter this source will be cited parenthetically in the text as *LGL*. Whitney's position was later invoked by Ferdinand de Saussure: "To emphasize the fact that language is a genuine institution, Whitney quite justly insisted upon the arbitrary nature of signs; and by so doing, he placed linguistics on its true axis" (*Course in General Linguistics*, trans. Wade Baskin [New York: Philosophical Library, 1959], 76).
17. Kenneth Cmiel, *Democratic Eloquence: The Fight over Popular Speech in Nineteenth-Century America* (New York: William Morrow, 1990), 156. For a useful discussion of the contemporary debate between scientific philologists like Whitney and verbal critics like Richard Grant White, see chapters 4–6, esp. 153–56.
18. Lanier, "From Bacon to Beethoven," in "*SEV*," 276. Further references to this essay will be to this volume and will be cited parenthetically in the text as "BB."
19. While Lanier's early public defense of his "The Centennial Meditation of Columbia" pairs "conventionally significant words" with "unconventionally significant tones," taking the "general idea" of the words to be "reproducible . . . by orchestral effects" ("CC," 267, 271), he later explicitly distances himself from this central commitment of "programme-music" (see "The Physics of Music," in "*SEV*," 252; and "BB," 278–81).
20. Lanier, quoted in introduction to "*SEV*," xiii.
21. See Lanier, "CC," 268; and "Appendix," "*SEV*," 338.
22. Richard Wagner, *Beethoven; With a Supplement from the Philosophical Works of Arthur Schopenhauer*, trans. Ed Dannreuther (London: New Temple Press, 1870), 88; further references to this source will be cited parenthetically in the text as *B*.
23. A slightly longer passage helps clarify Wagner's views: "Music loses nothing of its character when very different words are set to it; and this fact proves that the relation of music to the *art of poetry* is an entirely illusory one; for it holds true that when music is heard with singing added thereto, it is not the poetical thought . . . that is grasped by the auditor; but, at best, only that element of

it which, to the musician, seemed suitable for the music, and which his mind transmuted into music" (*B*, 74).

24. For useful discussions of Wagner's changing views on opera, with particular reference to the influence of Schopenhauer, see Carl Dahlhaus, *Between Romanticism and Modernism: Four Studies in the Music of the Later Nineteenth Century*, trans. Mary Whittall (Berkeley and Los Angeles: University of California Press, 1980), 33–39; and Bryan Magee, *The Philosophy of Schopenhauer* (New York: Oxford University Press, 1997), 350–402.
25. Lanier, *The Science of English Verse*, in "*SEV*," 42. Further references to this source will be to this volume and will be cited parenthetically in the text as *SEV*.
26. Whitney goes on to assert, "The very earliest dialects are as exclusively conventional as the latest; the savage has no keener sense of etymological connection than the man of higher civilization" (*LGL*, 297; see also 19).
27. Lanier, "Lecture XI: The Sonnet-Makers from Surrey to Shakspere," *Shakspere and His Forerunners: The Peabody Lectures*, in *Shakspere and His Forerunners*, ed. Kemp Malone, vol. III of *The Centennial Edition of the Works of Sidney Lanier*, ed. Charles R. Anderson (Baltimore: Johns Hopkins University Press, 1945), 87.
28. Here I emphasize Lanier's notion of Anglo-Saxon self-identity (that is, the language's relation to itself over time) rather than his notion of Anglo-Saxon superiority (the language's relation to other languages at a given moment), but the latter notion is also present in Lanier's thinking. For a discussion that emphasizes this aspect of Lanier's work, see VanHoosier-Carey, "Byrhtnoth in Dixie," 169–70.
29. Lanier, "Lecture I," *Shakspere and His Forerunners*, 7.
30. On the remote grammar of Anglo-Saxon, see Lanier, "Lecture VII: *Beowulf* and *Midsummer Night's Dream*," *Shakspere and His Forerunners*, 24; on its remote pronunciation, see "Lecture XVI: Pronunciation of Shakspere's Time," *Shakspere and His Forerunners*, 173; and on its remote semantics, see "Lecture X: The Wife in Middle English Poetry," *Shakspere and His Forerunners*, 83. For Whitney's similar statements about the dramatic changes in English, see *LGL*, 32–44.
31. Lanier, "Lecture VII," *Shakspere and His Forerunners*, 23.
32. See Hauer, "Thomas Jefferson and the Anglo-Saxon Language," 882, 880.
33. See Lanier's focus on sound in "Introduction to the Boy's Froissart," *"The English Novel" and Essays on Literature*, ed. Clarence Gohdes and Kemp Malone, vol. IV of *The Centennial Edition of the Works of Sidney Lanier*, ed. Charles R. Anderson (Baltimore: Johns Hopkins University Press, 1945), 353; and "Introduction to the Boy's King Arthur" (*"The English Novel" and Essays on Literature*, 361–64).
34. While the word "sound" here refers specifically to rhythm, rhythm is just one aspect of Lanier's complex account of sound, an account that addresses questions of duration, intensity, pitch, and tone color (see *SEV*, 23–29). I focus on rhythm because Lanier singles it out to do the work of racial continuity.

35. Lanier offers the following account of why the word "English" appears at all in the title of his *The Science of English Verse*: "The science of verse, then, observes and classifies all the phenomena of rhythm, of tune, and of tone-color, so far as they can be exhibited to the ear directly by spoken words, – or to the ear, through the eye, by written or printed signs of spoken words, – or to the mind by the conception of spoken words; and, The science of *English* verse observes and classifies these phenomena so far as they can be indicated through the medium of spoken English words" (*SEV*, 48; Lanier's emphasis). Here *English* is transformed from an institution of arbitrary signs into a "medium" for sound notation. But if, as we have seen, English is sufficient but not necessary to record the sounds of poems, then calling this the science of *English* verse seems mistaken: the sounds in question may coincide with the sounds in English, but without meanings attached they have ceased to be English and belong instead to the (in his view) extralinguistic domain of music. To continue to describe these sounds as Anglo-Saxon is to imagine this Anglo-Saxonness residing within them at a level deeper than conventional meaning: for Lanier, these sounds are an index of Anglo-Saxon.
36. For a thorough summary of the critical reception of Lanier's theories up to 1945, see the introduction to "*SEV*," xxx–xliv. For more recent treatments, see W. K. Wimsatt and Monroe C. Beardsley, "The Concept of Meter: An Exercise in Abstraction," *PMLA* 74:5 (December 1959): 588; W. K. Wimsatt and Monroe C. Beardsley, "A Word for Rhythm and a Word for Meter," *PMLA* 76:3 (June 1961): 308; Paul C. Boomsliter, Warren Creel, and George S. Hastings, Jr., "Perception and English Poetic Meter," *PMLA* 88:2 (March 1973): 200, 205; Jane S. Gabin, *A Living Minstrelsy: The Poetry and Music of Sidney Lanier* (Macon, GA: Mercer University Press, 1985), 153–56; and Harvey Gross and Robert McDowell, *Sound and Form in Modern Poetry*, 2nd edn (Ann Arbor: University of Michigan Press, 1996), 5.
37. The concern with musical sound among nineteenth-century writers involved not only poems but also, as Caroline Levander observes, "the tone of the female voice" (*Voices of the Nation: Women and Public Speech in Nineteenth-Century Literature and Culture* [New York: Cambridge University Press, 1998], 14). The writers Levander addresses "increasingly identified the nation's integrity with the voices of American women" (9) and thus, in "attempt[ing] to ensure the exclusive tonality of women's speech" (21), sought to perpetuate not racial but national identity. Consolidating this national identity involved preserving the "purity" of women's voices rather than perpetuating the rhythm of poems, and the vehicle of the former was "women's relegation to the private sphere" (16, 22) while the vehicle of the latter was the attribution of racial form to poetic texts.
38. See David S. Reynolds, *Walt Whitman's America: A Cultural Biography* (New York: Knopf, 1995), 514–15.
39. Whitman, quoted in Robert D. Faner, preface to *Walt Whitman & Opera* (Philadelphia: University of Pennsylvania Press, 1951), v.

40. This essay was later retitled "Poetry To-day in America – Shakspere – The Future" (see Whitman, *Prose Works 1892*, 2 vols., ed. Floyd Stovall [New York: New York University Press, 1964], II:474). Subsequent references to this essay and to others in *Prose Works* will be cited parenthetically in the text as *PW*.
41. Whitman elaborates on this point in his "Slang in America" (1885) (in *PW*, II:572–77). Jonathan Arac usefully observes a problem that, contrary to Whitman's own aims, often arises as critics discuss Whitman's celebration of nonstandard usage: "[H]aving been used to define one set of bounds (America versus the Old World), vernacular becomes a means for drawing further bounds within the United States, as to what will count as authentically 'American'" ("Whitman and Problems of the Vernacular," *Breaking Bounds: Whitman and American Cultural Studies*, ed. Betsy Erkkila and Jay Grossman [New York: Oxford University Press, 1996], 48).
42. Lanier, "Lecture III," *"English Novel" and Essays on Literature*, 50.
43. Lanier, "Lecture II," *"English Novel" and Essays on Literature* 27, 50; further references to this lecture will be to this volume and will be cited parenthetically in the text as "LII."
44. For his part, Whitman accused Lanier of all too strong an immersion in melody and sound: "Study Lanier's choice of words . . . . [which] are too often fit rather for sound than for sense. . . . [H]is over-tuning of the ear, this extreme deference paid to oral nicety, reduced the majesty, the solid worth, of his rhythms" (quoted in Aubrey Starke, "Lanier's Appreciation of Whitman," *The American Scholar* 2 [October 1933]: 408).
45. Many subsequent critics follow Lanier in locating Whitman's poetics in an ongoing Anglo-Saxon tradition. For early versions of this view, see Sculley Bradley, "The Fundamental Metrical Principle in Whitman's Poetry," 437–59; and John E. Bernbrock, "Walt Whitman and 'Anglo-Saxonism'" (Ph.D. diss., University of North Carolina, 1961), 159–88. In a more recent version of this approach, Dana Phillips laments that Whitman "merely *refers*" to "the sounds of different cultures from all around the world" instead of providing a "degree of onomatopoeia, or actual physical likeness to the sounds." Having been filtered through Whitman as "medium," the sounds of other cultures are thereby subordinated to the sounds of Whitman's speaker who – as Lanier would say – speaks in racial sounds, the sounds of a "White Father" ("Nineteenth-Century Racial Thought and Whitman's 'Democratic Ethnology of the Future,'" *Nineteenth-Century Literature* 49:3 [December 1994]: 292, 293 n. 4). The difference between Phillips and Lanier, then, is that while Lanier considers the racial identity intrinsic to Whitman's sounds a good thing (since Anglo-Saxon rhythm thereby perpetuates itself, even in a speaker explicitly resistant to the Old World), Phillips finds it objectionable, since Whitman's essentially "White" sound excludes other sounds and the racial identities embodied in them. Martha C. Nussbaum defends Whitman's ambition to speak for "excluded people," but in her account Whitman succeeds not because of his poems' formal features but because his "commitment both to narrative

and to the concrete depiction of different ways of life brings him into close contact with the novel" (*Poetic Justice: The Literary Imagination and Public Life* [Boston: Beacon Press, 1995], 119, 7).

46. Lanier, "Lecture XII: The Sonnet-Makers," *Shakspere and His Forerunners*, 114.
47. Lanier, "Lecture VII," *Shakspere and His Forerunners*, 33. This emphasis on Scottish sounds is apparent in the concluding words of Lanier's *The Science of English Verse*: "King James has summed up the whole matter in his homely Scotch words: 'Zour eare maun be the onely iudge, as of all the other parts of *Flowing*,' (that is, of *rhythmic movement*) 'the verie twichestane quhairof is musique'" (*SEV*, 244).
48. Lanier fought for the Confederacy as "a full-blooded secessionist" (introduction to *"Tiger-Lilies" and Southern Prose*, ed. Garland Greever, vol. v of *The Centennial Edition of the Works of Sidney Lanier*, ed. Charles R. Anderson [Baltimore: Johns Hopkins University Press, 1945], liv). Although Lanier ultimately accepted the North's victory, his poems of the period immediately following the war frequently criticize the policies of Reconstruction; see "To Our Hills" (1867; *PPO*, 167); "Laughter in the Senate" (1868; *PPO*, 14); and "Steel in Soft Hands" (1868; *PPO*, 169). See also Lanier, "Furlow College Address" (1869; *"Tiger-Lilies" and Southern Prose*, 258); "Confederate Memorial Address" (1870; *"Tiger-Lilies" and Southern Prose*, 269); "Retrospects and Prospects" (1871; *"Tiger-Lilies" and Southern Prose*, 303); and Aubrey Harrison Starke, *Sidney Lanier: A Biographical and Critical Study* (Chapel Hill: University of North Carolina Press, 1933), 112–13.
49. According to Eric Foner, "This measure . . . made it illegal for places of public accommodation and entertainment to make any distinction between black and white patrons, and outlawed racial discrimination in public schools, jury selection, churches, cemeteries, and transportation" (*Reconstruction: America's Unfinished Revolution, 1863–1877* [New York: Harper & Row, 1988], 532–33). Subsequent references to this source will be cited parenthetically in the text as *R*.
50. Joel Williamson describes this change as "a beginning of 'white soul.' In the end," Williamson continues, "the essence of the old order, the sense of Southernness and whiteness as qualities uniquely valuable, was saved. . . . The term that they applied to regaining control of their states was as fully laden with meaning as the Christian view of the rebirth of the spirit. They called it 'Redemption'" (*A Rage for Order*, 39).
51. Ohio governor Rutherford B. Hayes, who would ascend to the presidency through the compromise that ended Reconstruction, wrote to a southern friend, "'The let alone policy' seems now to be the true course; at any rate nothing but good will now exists towards you" (quoted in *R*, 558; see also 567).
52. *Nation*, 5 April 1877; quoted in *R*, 582.
53. Starke, *Sidney Lanier*, 186.
54. W. E .B. Du Bois, *The Souls of Black Folk*, 205. Subsequent references to this source will be to this edition and will be cited parenthetically in the text as *SBF*.

55. J. B. T. Marsh, *The Story of the Jubilee Singers: With Their Songs. With Supplement Containing an Account of Their Six Years' Tour around the World, and Many New Songs, by F. J. Loudin*, new edn. (Cleveland Printing & Publishing, 1892), 17, 18; hereafter, this source will be cited parenthetically in the text as *SJS*. On the array of contemporary editions of this text, see Dena J. Epstein, "The Story of the Jubilee Singers: An Introduction to its Bibliographic History," *New Perspectives on Music: Essays in Honor of Eileen Southern*, ed. Josephine Wright (Warren, MI: Harmonie Park Press, 1992), 151–62.
56. John Lovell Jr., *Black Song: The Forge and the Flame; The Story of How the Afro-American Spiritual Was Hammered Out* (New York: Macmillan, 1972), 406.
57. Their successes included gaining an audience with the queen, earning an invitation to Gladstone's residence, and prompting the following comment from Lord Shaftsbury: "I don't want them to become white, but I have a strong disposition myself to become black. If I thought color . . . brought with it their truth, piety, and talent, I would willingly exchange my complexion to-morrow" (*SJS*, 50, 84, 80).
58. For discussion of the religious orientation of the Jubilee Singers, see G. D. Pike, *The Jubilee Singers, and Their Campaign for Twenty Thousand Dollars* (Boston: Lee and Shepard, 1873), 9–24; Louis D. Silveri, "The Singing Tours of the Fisk Jubilee Singers: 1871–1874," in *Feel the Spirit: Studies in Nineteenth-Century Afro-American Music*, ed. George R. Keck and Sherrill V. Martin (New York: Greenwood, 1988), 106–9; and Andrew Ward, *Dark Midnight When I Rise: The Story of the Jubilee Singers Who Introduced the World to the Music of Black America* (New York: Farrar, Straus and Giroux, 2000), 100–105.
59. Lovell, *Black Song*, 415. For a related discussion, see Paul Gilroy, *The Black Atlantic: Modernity and Double Consciousness* (Cambridge, MA: Harvard University Press, 1993), 87–90.
60. Whitman states, "Lately, I have wonder'd whether the last meaning of this cluster of thirty-eight States is not only practical fraternity among themselves . . . but for fraternity over the whole globe" (*PW*, II:484).
61. Antonín Dvořák, "Letter to the Editor," *New York Herald*, May 28, 1893; reprinted in *Dvořák in America: 1882–1895*, ed. John C. Tibbetts (Portland, OR: Amadeus Press, 1993), 359; subsequent references to *Dvořák in America* will appear parenthetically in the text as *DA*.
62. Dvořák, "The Real Value of Negro Melodies," *New York Herald*, May 21, 1893; reprinted in *DA*, 356–57.
63. As John Higham notes, this shift in immigration patterns altered the reception new immigrants received: "No longer scorned simply for 'mere habits of life,' each of the major groups from southern and eastern Europe stood forth as a challenge to the nation, either endangering American institutions by unruly behavior or threatening through avarice to possess them" (*Strangers in the Land: Patterns of American Nativism 1860–1925* [New York: Atheneum, 1963], 94). This perceived challenge led some to respond with plans for legal restriction and others with programs of aggressive assimilation (97–105, 74–75).

64. Dvořák, "Music in America," *Harper's*, February 1895; reprinted in *DA*, 376.
65. See Dvořák's claim in "Real Value of Negro Melodies" that "Many of the negro melodies – most of them, I believe – are the creations of negroes born and reared in America. That is the peculiar aspect of the problem. The negro does not produce music of that kind elsewhere. I have heard black singers in Hayti for hours and, as a rule, their songs are not unlike the monotonous and crude chantings of the Sioux tribes. It is so also in Africa. But the negro in America utters a new note, full of sweetness and as characteristic as any music of any country" (*DA*, 357–58).
66. Dvořák, "Real Value of Negro Melodies," in *DA*, 355–56.
67. Dvořák, "Music in America," in *DA*, 377.
68. Dvořák, "Hear the 'Old Folks at Home,'" *New York Herald*, 23 January 1894; quoted in *DA*, 366.
69. Dvořák, "For National Music," *Chicago Tribune*, August 13, 1893; reprinted in *DA*, 362.
70. Henry Burleigh, quoted in Thomas L. Riis, "Dvořák and his Black Students," *Rethinking Dvořák: Views from Five Countries*, ed. David R. Beveridge (New York: Oxford University Press, 1996), 266. For a skeptical reading of Dvořák's nationalism, see Michael Beckerman, "The Master's Little Joke: Antonín Dvořák and the Mask of Nation," *Dvořák and His World*, ed. Michael Beckerman (Princeton University Press, 1993), 134–54.
71. Theodore F. Seward, "Preface to the Music," *SJS*, 156.
72. Quoted in "Dvořák on His New Work," *New York Herald*, December 15, 1893; reprinted in *DA*, 363.
73. "Dvořák seems to be describing familiar pentatonic and Dorian scales" (Riis, "Dvořák and His Black Students," 267).
74. Michael Beckerman responds to this question by arguing, "Composers who wish to employ exotic material are often in search of what I call 'multicultural puns,' that is, musical figures or devices that are common to at least two cultures"; Dvořák, then, is choosing sounds that belong both to his own culture and to US culture ("Henry Krehbiel, Antonín Dvořák, and the Symphony 'From the New World,'" *Notes* 49:2 [December 1992]: 462). But if the example of the pun demonstrates how multiple meanings (signifieds) can be associated with the same sound (signifier), this *linguistic* analogy relegates cultural difference to signifieds and thus begs the question of how multiple cultures can be embodied in the same nonlinguistic, or *musical*, sound.
75. James Huneker, "Dvořák's New Symphony: The Second Philharmonic Concert," *Musical Courier*, December 20, 1893; reprinted in *Dvořák and His World*, ed. Beckerman, 163; see also 160.
76. Booker T. Washington, "The Atlanta Exposition Address," *Up from Slavery*, in *Three Negro Classics* (New York: Avon Books, 1965), 148.
77. For a similar account, which likewise reads Wagner's music as "white," see Sundquist, *To Wake the Nations*, 523. For an alternative reading, which interprets Wagner's music in this scene as symbolizing Du Bois's "desire for a race-blind love," see Russell A. Berman, "Du Bois and Wagner: Race, Nation,

and Culture between the United States and Germany," *German Quarterly* 70:2 (Spring 1997): 130.

78. In other words, just as Lanier had opposed the Civil Rights Bill and sought instead to consolidate one people – Anglo-Saxons – out of northern and southern whites, so Du Bois opposes both the Redeemers' oppressions and Booker T. Washington's concessions, seeking instead to consolidate one people – Negroes – out of northern and southern blacks (*SBF*, 47). Just as Lanier tried to consolidate Anglo-Saxon people by asserting the race inherent in poetic rhythm, so Du Bois consolidates a Negro people by asserting the race inherent in the Sorrow Songs. For a useful critical discussion of Du Bois's effort to achieve racial unity and that effort's problematic legacy, see Kenneth Warren, "Delimiting America: The Legacy of Du Bois," *American Literary History* 1 (Spring 1989): 172–89.
79. Sundquist notes that Du Bois's analysis of the Sorrow Songs "reduces language to *sound*" (*To Wake the Nations*, 529), and Sundquist follows Du Bois's lead in racializing that sound when he argues that since the Sorrow Songs enter "the domain of sheer sound," they inhabit "the extremity of African American cultural expression, the domain where the cry fades into an articulacy reaching beyond European American apprehension" (531). My analysis suggests, however, that in the writers of this period, the domain of sheer sound is providing a new opportunity to assert the existence of race, whether Anglo-Saxon or Negro. Although Sundquist denies that his own account of Du Bois is "a brief for Afrocentrism" (15), he is generally more appreciative than critical as he repeatedly highlights Du Bois's assertions of sound as intrinsically African (472, 511, 525–39). Houston Baker shares Sundquist's commitment to identifying a specifically African-American sound in *The Souls of Black Folk* (*Modernism and the Harlem Renaissance*, 56–68). Shamoon Zamir likewise takes race to be "embodied" in the spirituals (*Dark Voices: W. E. B. Du Bois and American Thought, 1888–1903* [University of Chicago Press, 1995], 170–72, 175), but he sees the spirituals less as a vehicle for consolidating racial identity ("an essentialized idea of *communitas*" [181]) than as a vehicle for Du Bois's own autobiographical narrative of "self-transformation" (184). Paul Gilroy recognizes that Du Bois installs "slave music . . . in its special position of privileged signifier of black authenticity," but he goes on to cite "powerful reasons for resisting the idea that an untouched, pristine Africanity resides inside these forms" (*The Black Atlantic*, 91, 101). For a related statement of resistance, see Ronald M. Radano, "Soul Texts and the Blackness of Folk," *Modernism/Modernity* 2:1 (January 1995): 84.
80. This melody undoubtedly came to the United States from Africa (see Sundquist, *To Wake the Nations*, 519–20), but the question of its provenance is not the same as the question of its essence, and it is this latter question – the question of what people, if any, the song embodies – that I am addressing here.
81. Lanier, "Lecture XVI: Pronunciation of Shakspere's Time," *Shakspere and His Forerunners*, 169.

82. Du Bois, "The Conservation of Races," *W. E. B. Du Bois: A Reader*, 25; further references to this source will be to this edition and will be cited parenthetically in the text as "CR."
83. Anthony Appiah and Ross Posnock have shown that in his later career Du Bois sought to achieve something Lanier never imagined: abandoning race as a central category of social organization. While Appiah argues that this effort failed and Posnock counters that it succeeded, they agree that Du Bois's early writings set out the commitment to race from which he would later seek to retreat. It is these early writings and their commitment to "the unifying ideal of Race" that I am addressing here (*SBF*, 11); see Anthony Appiah, *In My Father's House*, 28–46; and Ross Posnock, *Color & Culture*, 88–89, 18–19.
84. Israel Zangwill, *The Melting-Pot* [1909] (New York: The Macmillan Company, 1932). Hereafter cited parenthetically in the body of the text.
85. See Mann, *The One and the Many*, 98–101; and Philip Gleason, *Speaking of Diversity: Language and Ethnicity in Twentieth-Century America* (Baltimore: Johns Hopkins University Press, 1992), 5–10.
86. See Joel Williamson, *A Rage For Order*, 122.
87. In his *Our America*, Walter Benn Michaels observes that "in the Americanizing discourse of Progressive racism . . . the 'Negro' defines the limits of Americanization" (145 n. 22), and he locates this exclusion of African-Americans within Zangwill's *The Melting-Pot* (60).
88. Zangwill responds to a similar charge five years later, but his response (Zangwill, "Afterword," *Race and Ethnicity in Modern America*, ed. Richard J. Meister [Lexington, MA: D. C. Heath and Company, 1974]) in effect underscores the way in which African-Americans are pushed aside in the play. Noting the "present barbarous pitch" of "Negrophobia," Zangwill asserts that "it is as much social prejudice as racial antipathy that today divides black and white in the New World" (24). If the potential of overcoming this "prejudice" holds open the prospect that "even upon the Negro the melting pot of America will not fail to act" (24), this eventuality remains unachieved in the play itself, a play whose assimilationist plot, as Werner Sollors argues, is "very much interested in 'gamic interaction' of the exceptional, 'heroic souls' who (like Zangwill himself) 'dare the adventure of intermarriage'" (*Beyond Ethnicity: Consent and Descent in American Culture* [New York: Oxford University Press, 1986], 71).
89. See H. Wiley Hitchcock, *Music in the United States: A Historical Introduction*, 2nd edn. (Englewood Cliffs, NJ: Prentice-Hall, Inc., 1974), 25, 90.
90. On the British roots of Zangwill's assimilationism, see Joseph H. Udelson, *Dreamer of the Ghetto: The Life and Works of Israel Zangwill* (Tuscaloosa: University of Alabama Press, 1990), 25–29, 190–99.
91. For a discussion of Dixon's stage adaptation of *The Clansman*, which toured the United States for five years, see Raymond Allen Cook, *Fire from the Flint: The Amazing Careers of Thomas Dixon* (Winston-Salem, NC: John F. Blair, 1968), 136–49. On the contemporary touring productions of *The Melting-Pot*, see Arthur Mann, "The Melting Pot," *Uprooted Americans: Essays to Honor Oscar Handlin* (Boston: Little, Brown and Company, 1979), 294–95; and Joe Kraus, "How *The Melting Pot* Stirred America: The Reception of Zangwill's

Play and Theater's Role in the American Assimilation Experience," *MELUS* 24:3 (Fall 1999): 3–19.

92. For discussion of Redemption, see Williamson, *A Rage for Order*, 39.
93. The phrase "photo-drama" appears in the program for the film's first public performance, under the title *The Clansman*, in 1915. This program is reproduced in Martin Miller Marks, *Music and the Silent Film: Contexts and Case Studies, 1895–1924* (New York: Oxford University Press, 1997), 134. On the links between Dixon's work and *The Birth of a Nation*, see Russell Merritt, "Dixon, Griffith, and the Southern Legend: A Cultural Analysis of *The Birth of a Nation*," *Cinema Examined: Selections from* Cinema Journal, ed. Richard Dyer MacCann and Jack C. Ellis (New York: E. P. Duton, Inc., 1982), 165–84; Michael Rogin, "'The Sword Became a Flashing Vision': D. W. Griffith's *The Birth of a Nation*," *The Birth of a Nation: D. W. Griffith, Director*, ed. Robert Lang (New Brunswick, NJ: Rutgers University Press, 1994), 250–93; and Jeffrey B. Martin, "Film out of Theatre: D. W. Griffith, *Birth of a Nation* and the Melodrama *The Clansman*," *Literature/Film Quarterly* 18:2 (1990): 87–95. For more general discussions of the racial politics of *The Birth of a Nation*, see Richard Dyer, "Into the Light: The Whiteness of the South in *The Birth of a Nation*," *Dixie Debates: Perspectives on Southern Cultures*, ed. Richard H. King and Helen Taylor (London: Pluto Press, 1996), 165–76; and Cedric J. Robinson, "In the Year 1915: D. W. Griffith and the Whitening of America," *Social Identities* 3:2 (1997): 161–92.
94. In his *Music and the Silent Film* Marks discusses both the early practice of musical accompaniment (see 9–12 and 67–68) and the later development of the "special score" (62), of which the score to *The Birth of a Nation* is a conspicuous but not a unique example (64).
95. On Wagner's role in the Philadelphia centennial, see William Pierce Randel, *Centennial: American Life in 1876* (New York: Chilton Book Company, 1969), 291; and Joseph Horowitz, *Wagner Nights: An American History* (Berkeley: University of California Press, 1994), 59–60.
96. See Henry T. Finck, *Wagner and His Works: The Story of His Life with Critical Documents*, vol. II (1893; New York: Haskell House Publishers, 1968), 509.
97. Wagner did, of course, see his musical compositions as racially charged; see Paul Lawrence Rose, *Wagner: Race and Revolution* (New Haven: Yale University Press, 1992).
98. Lanier's poem "Them Ku Klux," *PPO*, is (like the poem "Civil Rights" discussed above) spoken in dialect, the sound effects that Lanier considers to be essentially Anglo-Saxon, by a speaker who implies hidden knowledge of the Klan's activities.
99. Breil's unpublished and incomplete essay "On Motion Picture Music" is quoted in Marks, *Music and the Silent Film*, 138. Elsewhere Breil mentions Wagner by name as an influence on his compositional approach; see Marks, *Music and the Silent Film*, 283 n. 50.
100. See Marks, *Music and the Silent Film*, 283 n. 50.
101. Recalling the efforts that went into composing the film score, Lillian Gish asserts that "The greatest dispute was over the Klan call, which was taken

from *The Ride of the Valkyries* by Richard Wagner" (quoted in Marks, *Music and the Silent Film*, 140).

102. On the role played by Griffith in composing this theme, and the similarities and differences between it and Wagner's *Ride*, see Marks, *Music and the Silent Film*, 139–40.

103. The text of Griffith's film is quoted from John Cuniberti, *The Birth of a Nation: A Formal Shot-by-Shot Analysis Together with Microfiche* (Woodbridge, CT: Research Publications, Inc., 1979), 115.

104. For a list of the three moments in the film where "The Call to the Ku Klux Klansmen" appears, see Marks, *Music and the Silent Film*, 216; for a description of where these instances occur within the film's narrative structure, see Marks, *Music and the Silent Film*, 204–06.

105. See Cuniberti, *Birth of a Nation: A Formal Shot-by-Shot Analysis*, 134.

106. Cuniberti, *Birth of a Nation: A Formal Shot-by-Shot Analysis*, 142. Zangwill was not, of course, a member of the Ku Klux Klan; indeed, in his essay "Mr Zangwill Criticizes the Klan" published in the *Chicago Daily News* in 1924 Zangwill opposes the comments of Dr. H. W. Evans, one of the Klan's "Imperial Wizards," by invoking a scene from his play: after quoting David Quixano's pledge of allegiance to the American flag, Zangwill asks, "Has the 'Nordic' pledge or oath of the Ku Klux klan anything better than this pledge of the Jew?" (quoted in Edward Price Bell, "Creed of the Klansmen and Those Who Debate It," *Chicago Daily News Reprints* 8 [1924]: 12–13). Zangwill's point is that Jews are, contrary to Evans's contentions, fully willing to "intermarry with gentiles" (12). By advocating the assimilation of Jewish immigrants with other European immigrants in the United States, Zangwill sets out a view that is consistent, as Walter Benn Michaels has observed, with the assimilation program advocated by Thomas Dixon's *Trilogy of Reconstruction*, which included *The Clansman*, the novel upon which *The Birth of a Nation* was based; see Michaels, *Our America*, 10, 22, 24, 60–61.

107. Breil, "On Motion Picture Music," quoted in Marks, *Music and the Silent Film*, 286 n. 76.

108. On the use of this phrase to catalogue sections of Breil's score, see Marks, *Music and the Silent Film*, 130.

109. Breil, "On Motion Picture Music," quoted in Marks, *Music and the Silent Film*, 286 n. 76.

110. Breil, "On Motion Picture Music," quoted in Marks, *Music and the Silent Film*, 286 n. 76.

111. Marks, *Music and the Silent Film*, 156.

112. Cuniberti, *The Birth of a Nation: A Formal Shot-by-Shot Analysis*, 36–37.

113. Breil, "On Motion Picture Music," quoted in Marks, *Music and the Silent Film*, 286 n. 76. For a list of the theme's several recurrences, see Marks, *Music and the Silent Film*, 210. For discussions of the manner in which Breil's "Negro theme" comes to be associated with a variety of African-American characters, see Marks, *Music and the Silent Film*, 153; and Gaines and Lerner, "The Orchestration of Affect: The Motif of Barbarism in Breil's *The Birth of a Nation* Score," *The Sounds of Early Cinema*, ed. Richard Abel

and Rick Altman (Bloomington: Indiana University Press, 2001), 257, 258, 262; hereafter cited parenthetically in the text.

114. See Marks, *Music and the Silent Film*, 128–29.

115. James Chandler, "The Historical Novel Goes to Hollywood," 247.

116. Gaines and Lerner argue that since Thomas Dixon associated Breil's opening theme not with the "Negro" in Africa but rather with "a low cry of the anguished South being put to torture" ("The Ochestration of Affect," 256), and since Francis Hackett of the NAACP associated it with "'hoochy-coochy' music" (264), the "Negro theme" is therefore subject to "selective reception, or, better, political receptivity, that aspect of reading we hesitate to call simply subjective" (256). This interpretive variety among listeners suggests that the "Negro theme" is semantically rather than intrinsically "Negro." But if this observation implies a theoretical critique of the claim that such formal effects can have an indexical force, such a critique should not obscure the historical commitment of these writers to indexical representations, a commitment that helped them to underwrite their belief in race as an essential identity inseparable from particular sound effects.

117. Indeed, Gaines and Lerner suggest this very point when they ask about the concerns that motivated various municipalities to ban the film: "Is it that the music 'makes' some people do things they can't help doing, or does the music suggest to others that it will make certain people (notably blacks and women) do things?" ("The Ochestration of Affect," 264). These are the very concerns present in the writings of Scott, who also thought in terms of involuntary action, both hoping and worrying that "certain people" – Scots – would do things they could not help, i.e. be summoned forth as Scots.

118. Richard Aldrich, "Henry Edward Krehbiel," *Musical Discourse from* The New York Times (1928; Freeport, NY: Books For Libraries Press, Inc., 1967), 282. More recently, Mark N. Grant has described Krehbiel as "the most esteemed and influential newspaper music critic America had yet seen"; see Mark N. Grant, *Maestros of the Pen: A History of Classical Music Criticism in America* (Boston: Northeastern University Press, 1998), 81.

119. Henry Krehbiel, *The Afro-American Folksongs: A Study in Racial and National Music* (New York: G. Schirmer, 1914); hereafter cited parenthetically in the text.

120. For a useful summary of the debate regarding the origins of African-American music, see Eric Sundquist, *To Wake the Nations*, 318.

121. A tension between the views of Krehbiel and Dvořák dates back to the premier of Dvořák's symphony *From the New World*, which Krehbiel discussed in the pages of the New York *Tribune* (see Beckerman, "Henry Krehbiel, Antonín Dvořák, and the Symphony," 447–73). There Krehbiel argues that Dvořák's supposedly American rhythm is "a pervasive element in African music" (462) and that his American melody "has the same right to be called an aboriginal African element as the rhythmical figure already discussed" (463). While Krehbiel is willing to set these differences aside in his discussion of Dvořák's symphony ("Enough that [the melody] is popular here, and, therefore, justified in a symphony designed to give expression to American feeling"

[463]), Krehbiel's later work advances a pluralism more overtly at variance with Dvořák's views: "there is no American music and can be none: Every element of our population must have its own characteristic musical expression, and no one element can set up to be more American than another" (154). For Krehbiel, "independence of European influence" (83) makes sounds African, whereas for Dvořák it had made them American. The racially pluralist view advanced in Krehbiel's *Afro-American Folksongs* led him not only to quote favorably from Du Bois's account of the "Sorrow Songs" (27–28) but also to be invoked, in turn, as a musical authority on African-American music, an authority quoted by both Du Bois and by James Weldon Johnson; see Du Bois's "The Black Man Brings his Gifts," *Survey Graphic* 6:6 (March 1925): 655; and James Weldon Johnson's "Preface," *The Book of American Negro Spirituals*, ed. James Weldon Johnson (New York: Viking Press, 1925), 14, 18, 47–48.

122. Krehbiel writes, "the creator of the folksong is an unindividualized representative of his people. . . . [H]is identity as [the song's] creator is swallowed up in that of the people. . . . His potentiality is racial or national, not personal, and for that reason it is enduring, not ephemeral" (4). In Krehbiel's account of the "Afro-American folksongs," the traditions shared by a race are more significant than the meanings communicated by an individual talent.

123. As Thomas Cripps observes, "More than any other director Griffith gave future moviemakers a model, a cinematic language, and a rich romantic tradition that would define an Afro-American stereotype. He was the bridge between nineteenth-century southern melodramatic and literary tradition and the new art of the cinema" (*Slow Fade to Black: The Negro in American Film, 1900–1942* [New York: Oxford University Press, 1977], 29). See also Donald Bogle, *Toms, Coons, Mulattoes, Mammies, & Bucks: An Interpretive History of Blacks in American Films*, 4th edn. (New York: Continuum, 2001), 3–18.

124. James Weldon Johnson, "Uncle Tom's Cabin and the Clansman," *New York Age*, March 4, 1915; reprinted in *The Selected Writings of James Weldon Johnson, Vol. I: The* New York Age *Editorials (1914–1923)*, ed. Sondra Kathryn Wilson (New York: Oxford University Press, 1955), 13; hereafter cited parenthetically in the text.

125. For Johnson's additional editorial comments against *The Birth of a Nation*, see *The Selected Writings of James Weldon Johnson, Vol. I: The* New York Age *Editorials (1914–1923)*, 16, 156–58, and 265.

4. LITERARY EFFECTS AND THE DIAGNOSIS OF RACIAL INSTINCT

1. Josh White, "Free and Equal Blues," *Black Folk Singers: Leadbelly & Josh White (1937–46)*, DOCD-1018, (Vienna, Austria: Document Records, 1999), track 30.

2. Joel Chandler Harris, *Uncle Remus: His Songs and His Sayings* [1880], ed. Robert Hemenway (New York: Penguin Books, 1982), 40. Hereafter cited parenthetically in the text.
3. Sidney Lanier, *SEV*, 214, 196. Hereafter cited parenthetically in the text.
4. James Weldon Johnson, "Preface to the First Edition," *The Book of American Negro Poetry* [1922, 1931], revised edn., ed. James Weldon Johnson (New York: Harcourt Brace & Co., 1969), 41. Hereafter abbreviated *BANP* and cited parenthetically in the text.
5. James Weldon Johnson, *God's Trombones: Seven Negro Sermons in Verse* [1927] (New York: Penguin Books, 1990), 8. Hereafter cited parenthetically in the text.
6. Johnson's writings have continued to be influential in subsequent studies of the African-American sermon; see, for instance, Albert J. Raboteau, *A Fire in the Bones: Reflections on African-American Religious History* (Boston: Beacon Press, 1995), 146; William H. Pipes, *Say Amen, Brother!: Old-Time Negro Preaching: A Study in American Frustration* (1951; reprint Westport, CT: Negro Universities Press, 1992), 149–55; and Dolan Hubbard, *The Sermon and the African American Literary Imagination* (Columbia: University of Missouri Press, 1994), 12–14, 24.
7. Lanier's distinction is important to a thorough understanding of his relation to Johnson, which requires that it be quoted at length. Lanier speaks of

   > that differentiating process we are now to trace, which has resulted in the complete independence of music on the one hand and of poetry on the other, the former having found its fullest expression in the purely instrumental symphony, while the latter finds its fullest expression in the purely vocal tunes of the speaking-voice. [205] . . . At this time [the 16th century] music is striving as hard on its side for separate existence as poetry on its side: until Palestrina and Haydn and Bach and Beethoven finally bring-out the perfect glory of harmony and of instrumentation, on the one hand, while Shakspere and Milton and Keats and Tennyson bring-out the perfect glory of poetic words on the other hand. Now, we find music almost exclusively expressed through the instrumental tune – a term including the song, which belongs to the singing-voice as a reed-instrument [or, for Johnson, the *preaching*-voice as a *brass*-instrument, the trombone] – while poetry is expressed through the speaking-voice tune. Now, the musician uses the voice simply as a reed-instrument, and the word simply as a tone-color; while the word-artist, the poet, uses music only in that range of it comprehended between the limits of the speaking-voice. In fine we have on the one hand the Symphony: on the other the Tunes of Verse. The advantage to each art in thus setting-up for itself and growing alone is seen in the wonderful development of both.[210]

   Poetry, as Lanier defines it, involves the *sui generis* sounds of spoken words, the sounds of the speaking voice no longer "subordinated to the music" (209) of instruments like Johnson's trombones.
8. When he describes dialect as the "mere mutilation of English spelling and pronunciation," Johnson understands dialect in the same terms set out by both Michael North, who understands it as language practice deviating from the standard usage set out in the *Oxford English Dictionary* (see North's *The Dialect of Modernism: Race, Language, and Twentieth-Century Literature* [New York: Oxford University Press, 1994], 11–12) and Richard Brodhead, who asks, "what else is dialect?" but "Ethnically deformed speech" (see Brodhead's "Regionalism

and the Upper Class," *Rethinking Class: Literary Studies and Social Formations*, ed. Wai Chee Dimock and Michael T. Gilmore [New York: Columbia University Press, 1994], 166). Elsewhere Johnson will describe dialect in different terms, treating it as converging with music; hence the dialect poet Paul Lawrence Dunbar, Johnson asserts, "took the humble speech of his people and in it wrought music" (*BANP*, 37). This view is more consistent with the music-centered discussions of dialect set out in such works as Henry Louis Gates, Jr.'s *Figures in Black*, 177–87, Houston Baker's *Modernism and the Harlem Renaissance*, 42–47, and Eric Sundquist's *To Wake the Nations*, 309–23. While Johnson uses the term dialect in these two ways, the point I wish to emphasize is not the common term but the divergence in its definitions. The point, that is, is not the ambiguity of the term dialect itself but the distinction between the two meaning Johnson uses it to convey, the distinction between nonstandard speech and musical sound effects. Johnson wishes to abandon the former in favor of the latter, an outcome he takes to be achieved in the voice of the "Negro preacher."

9. Not only does Lanier characterize the music of "Southern negroes" as "primitive" (*SEV*, 214; see also 146 and 192), he also associates it with his own primitive state of childhood, the earliest phase in his personal development toward musical sophistication; see "Appendix," *SEV*, 339–40.
10. In her essay "James Weldon Johnson and the Autobiography of an Ex-Colored Musician" (*American Literature* 72:2 [June 2000]) Christina L. Ruotolo asserts Johnson's "refusal to give up the possibility of an authentic black musicality" (258) and acknowledges the consequence that the "color line is . . . maintained" (260); see also 250, 262, 268.
11. For Johnson's extensive discussions of black music, see his "Preface" to *The Book of American Negro Spirituals*, 11–50; and his "Preface" to *The Second Book of Negro Spirituals*, ed. James Weldon Johnson (New York: Viking Press, 1926), 11–24. Johnson's racialization of musical sounds participates in a larger cultural dynamic that is well captured by Paul Anderson's *Deep River: Music and Memory in Harlem Renaissance Thought* (Durham, NC: Duke University Press, 2001).
12. In his autobiography *Along This Way* (New York: Viking Press, 1933) Johnson describes *The Souls of Black Folk* as "a work which, I think, has had a greater effect upon and within the Negro race in America than any other single book published in this country since *Uncle Tom's Cabin*" (203).
13. Rudolph Matas, "The Surgical Peculiarities of the Negro: A Statistical Inquiry Based Upon the Records of the Charity Hospital of New Orleans (Decennium 1884–94)," *Transactions of the American Surgical Association* 4 (1896): 507.
14. Carlo Ginzburg usefully describes this late nineteenth-century pattern of thinking to involve a "double skill," a "combination of the doctor's and the connoisseur's perceptions"; Carlo Ginzburg, "Clues: Morelli, Freud, and Sherlock Holmes," in *The Sign of Three: Dupin, Holmes, Peirce*, ed. Umberto Eco and Thomas A. Sebeok (Bloomington: Indiana University Press, 1983), 95. Concerning the perceptions of doctors, Ginzburg focuses on "Hippocratic

medicine, which clarified its methods by analyzing the central concept of symptom (*sēmeîon*). Followers of Hippocrates argued that just by carefully observing and registering every symptom it was possible to establish precise 'histories' of each disease, even though the disease as an entity would remain unattainable" (91). Ginzburg notes the centrality of such thinking to art historians, or connoisseurs, like Giovanni Morelli, who sought methods for detecting forged paintings: "Morelli's idea was to trace out within a culturally determined sign-system the conventions of painting signs which, like symptoms (and like most clues), were produced involuntarily. Not just that: in these involuntary signs. . . . Morelli located the most certain clue to artistic identity" (104). My concern will be the detection not of forged paintings but of forged or inauthentic racial bodies, so my concern will be with efforts to confirm collective rather than individual identities; further, the diagnostic skills used to detect those forgeries will, in my analysis, be those not of the art critic but of the literary critic. Nevertheless, Ginzberg's general concern – the confirmation of authentic identity using the diagnostic skills common to both an artistic connoisseur and a physician – remains consistent with my own focus on formal literary effects and racial identities.

15. On the early history of challenges to racial medicine, see Nancy Leys Stepan and Sander L. Gilman, "Appropriating the Idioms of Science: The Rejection of Scientific Racism," *The "Racial" Economy of Science: Toward a Democratic Future*, ed. Sandra Harding (Bloomington: Indiana University Press, 1993), esp. 183–88; and Elazar Barkan, *The Retreat of Scientific Racism*, 262–66. These issues continue to be a matter of debate among physicians. For critical surveys of past efforts to study race and disease, see Richard Cooper, "A Note on the Biologic Concept of Race and its Application in Epidemiologic Research," *American Heart Journal* 108 (1984): 717–19, 721, 722; and Phyllis Jones, Thomas A. LaVeist, and Marsha Lillie-Blanton, "'Race' in the Epidemiologic Literature: An Examination of the *American Journal of Epidemiology*, 1921–1990," *American Journal of Epidemiology* 134:10 (1991): 1079–84. For cautionary remarks about the role of racial categories in future studies, see Newton G. Osborne and Marvin D. Feit, "The Use of Race in Medical Research," *Journal of the American Medical Association* 267 (1992): 275–79; Stephen H. Caldwell and Rebecca Popenoe, "Perceptions and Misperceptions of Skin Color," *Annals of Internal Medicine* 122:8 (15 April 1995): 614–17; Edward J. Huth, "Identifying Ethnicity in Medical Papers," *Annals of Internal Medicine* 122:8 (15 April 1995): 619–21; Ritchie Witzig, "The Medicalization of Race: Scientific Legitimization of a Flawed Social Construct," *Annals of Internal Medicine* 125 (1996): 65–79; and Paul D. Stolley, "Race in Epidemiology," *International Journal of Health Services* 29:4 (1999): 908.
16. W. E. B. Du Bois, "On *The Souls of Black Folk*," *The Oxford W. E. B. Du Bois Reader*, ed. Eric J. Sundquist (New York: Oxford University Press, 1996), 305.
17. Benjamin Rush Davenport, *Blood Will Tell; The Strange Story of a Son of Ham* (Cleveland, OH: Caxton Book Co., 1902); hereafter cited parenthetically in the text.

18. While Du Bois asks, "Would America have been America without her Negro people?" (W. E. B. Du Bois, *The Souls of Black Folk*, 215), Davenport equates Americanness with whiteness, dedicating his novel "To all Americans who deem purity of race an all-important element in the progress of our beloved country" (unpag.).
19. Sidney Lanier, "The Death of Byrhtnoth: A Study in Anglo-Saxon Poetry," *The English Novel and Essays on Literature*, vol. IV of *The Centennial Edition of The Works of Sidney Lanier*, ed. Clarence Gohdes and Kemp Malone (Baltimore: Johns Hopkins University Press, 1945), 290, my italics; see this same phrase repeated on p. 296. This essay is hereafter cited parenthetically in the text. The essay was assembled from Lanier's manuscripts and published posthumously in the *Atlantic Monthly* 82 (August 1898): 165–74. The *Atlantic Monthly* version, reprinted in Lanier's *Music and Poetry* [1898] (New York: Haskell House Publishers, 1969), speculates of the Anglo-Saxons praised in these poems, "it may be that their blood flows in our own veins" (149), but the editors of the *Centennial Edition* were unable to trace these words to Lanier's manuscripts and thus excluded them from their edition (The English Novel *and Essays on Literature*, 298 n.). The excluded statement reflects a concern with racial blood that is consistent with 1898 but separable from Lanier's earlier concern with racial poetic effects.
20. These editions are *The Boy's Froissart* (1879), *The Boy's King Arthur* (1880), *The Boy's Mabinogion* (1881), and *The Boy's Percy* (1882). In "The Death of Byrhtnoth" Lanier observes, "English poetry written between the time of Aldhelm and Caedmon in the seventh century and that of Chaucer in the fourteenth century has never yet taken its place by the hearths and in the hearts of the people whose strongest prayers are couched in its idioms. . . . [T]here are no illuminated boy's editions of it. . . . [E]very boy . . . can give some account of the death of Hector; but how many boys . . . in America could do more than stare if asked to relate the death of Byrhtnoth?" (290, 291–92).
21. On Shaler as a popularizer of science, see David N. Livingstone, *Nathaniel Southgate Shaler and the Culture of American Science* (Tuscaloosa: University of Alabama Press, 1987), 41.
22. Nathaniel S. Shaler, *The Neighbor; a Natural History of Human Contacts* (Boston: Houghton Mifflin Company, 1904), hereafter cited parenthetically in the text. For a detailed discussion of Shaler's racial theories, see John S. Haller, *Outcasts from Evolution*, 166–87; for a discussion that places him in the context of nineteenth-century southern radicalism, see Joel Williamson, *A Rage for Order*, 86–88.
23. On Shaler's Lamarckism, see Livingstone, *Nathaniel Southgate Shaler and the Culture of American Science*, 55–85. Lamarckism provided Shaler with a way of thinking of racial instincts as an inescapable impediment to assimilating new immigrants to the United States. In the hands of assimilationists, by contrast, Lamarckism could be made to support the notion that new arrivals on US shores would acquire new habits that, once transmitted to their children, would effectively Americanize those subsequent generations. Thus Lamarckism could

be used to defend both sides of the assimilation question: the transmission of long-standing ancestral traits acquired by remote ancestors would supposedly impede the Americanization of children who inherited those traits (as Shaler argues), but the transmission of traits acquired recently by immigrant parents would aid Americanization of those immigrants' children. George W. Stocking describes those holding these views as, respectively, "hard and soft Lamarckians"; see his "The Turn-of-the-Century Concept of Race," *Modernism/Modernity* 1:1 (1994): 16.

24. The court's majority opinion endorses state segregation laws on the grounds, in part, that "Legislation is powerless to eradicate racial instincts or to abolish distinctions based upon physical differences, and the attempt to do so can only result in accentuating the difficulties of the present situation"; see *Plessy v. Ferguson; A Brief History with Documents*, ed. Brook Thomas (Boston: Bedford Books, 1997), 51.
25. Williamson, *A Rage for Order*, 87. Nathaniel Southgate Shaler, "The Negro Problem," *The Atlantic Monthly* 54 (November 1884): 696–709; hereafter cited parenthetically in the text.
26. Nathaniel Southgate Shaler, "Science and the African Problem," *The Atlantic Monthly* 66 (July 1890): 36, 44, 45. Hereafter cited parenthetically in the text.
27. See Shaler, "The Negro Problem," *The Atlantic Monthly* 54 (November 1884): 699; Shaler, "Science and the African Problem," 37; and Shaler, "European Peasants as Immigrants," *The Atlantic Monthly* 71 (May 1893): 654.
28. Richard S. Cooper, "Celebrate Diversity – Or Should We?," *Ethnicity & Disease* 1:1 (Winter 1991): 6, 7. For a related critique of what is called "black box epidemiology," see Raj Bhopal, "Is Research Into Ethnicity and Health Racist, Unsound, or Important Science?," *BMJ* 314 (June 14, 1997): 1,752.
29. Nancy Kreiger, "Shades of Difference: Theoretical Underpinnings of the Medical Controversy on Black/White Differences in the United States, 1830–70," *International Journal of Health Services* 17:2 (1987): 275. William H. Tucker has similarly observed, "The question of genetic differences between races has arisen not out of purely scientific curiosity or the desire to find important scientific truth or to solve some significant scientific problem but only because of the belief, explicit or unstated, that the answer has political consequences"; see *The Science and Politics of Racial Research* (Chicago: University of Illinois Press, 1994), 5.
30. Thomas A. LaVeist, "Why We Should Continue to Study Race . . . But Do a Better Job: An Essay on Race, Racism and Health," *Ethnicity & Disease* 6 (1996): 23. This same question is built into the title of another journal's editorial; see Nancy Moss, "What are the Underlying Sources of Racial Differences in Health?," *Annals of Epidemiology* 7 (1997): 320–21.
31. For the nineteenth-century history of medical approaches to race, see Kreiger, "Shades of Difference"; John S. Haller, Jr., "The Negro and the Southern Physician: A Study of Medical and Racial Attitudes, 1800–1860," *Medical History* 16 (1972): 238–53; John S. Haller, "The Physician Versus the Negro: Medical and Anthropological Concepts of Race in the Late Nineteenth Century," *Bulletin*

of the History of Medicine 44 (1970): 154–67; Haller, *Outcasts from Evolution*, 3–68; Kenneth F. Kiple and Virginia Himmelsteib King, *Another Dimension to the Black Diaspora: Diet, Disease, and Racism* (New York: Cambridge University Press, 1981), 161–90; and W. Michael Byrd and Linda A. Clayton, "An American Health Dilemma: A History of Blacks in the Health System," *Journal of the National Medical Association* 84:2 (1992): 194–95.

32. "Racial differences in mortality are in all likelihood not due to fundamental biological differences, but are in large part due to racism and discrimination. Racisms are conditions based on the fabrication of race" (Allen A. Herman, "Toward a Conceptualization of Race in Epidemiologic Research," *Ethnicity & Disease* 6 [1996]: 13). For similar statements see Richard Cooper and Richard David, "The Biological Concept of Race and its Application to Public Health and Epidemiology," *Journal of Health Politics, Policy, and Law* 11:1 (Spring 1986): 98, 106–07, 113; Fatimah Linda Collier Jackson, "Race and Ethnicity as Biological Constructs," *Ethnicity & Disease* 2 (1992): 121; James O. Mason, "Understanding the Disparities in Morbidity and Mortality Among Racial and Ethnic Groups in the United States," *Annals of Epidemiology* 3:2 (March 1993): 121; Rueben C. Warren, "The Morbidity/Mortality Gap: What is the Problem?," *Annals of Epidemiology* 3:2 (March 1993): 127; and Marsha Lillie-Blanton and Thomas LaVeist, "Race/Ethnicity, the Social Environment, and Health," *Social Sciences and Medicine* 43:1 (1996): 83–91.

33. L. S. Joynes, "Remarks on the Comparative Mortality of the White and Colored Populations of Richmond," *Virginia Medical Monthly* 2 (1875): 159. Although he ultimately favors environmental explanations, Joynes does not rule out race itself as a source of these effects: "White people placed in the same conditions would no doubt succumb to their influence in equal proportions," so "we are therefore, under no necessity of appealing to diversity of race for an explanation of the facts in the present instance [i.e. Richmond mortality tables]" (159, 161).

34. J. Wellington Byers, "Diseases of the Southern Negro," *Medical and Surgical Journal* 63 (1888): 736.

35. See, for instance, the debate in the pages of the journal *Medical News* over the issue of the relative importance of race and environment in producing the racial disparities seen in mortality statistics. In 1893 Dr. Robert Reyburn, former chief medical officer of the Freedmen's Bureau, sought to "disprove the statements so commonly made concerning the extreme liability of the colored race to scrofula and pulmonary tuberculosis. So far from these two diseases being almost universally prevalent among the colored people in the Southern States, these people seem to be no more subject to them than the whites who live under like conditions in our larger cities. Scrofula and pulmonary tuberculosis are, in great part, caused by a neglect of the laws of hygiene and sanitary science. These diseases do not seem to be any more destructive to the colored race than to the white"; see Robert Reyburn, "Type of Disease Among the Freed People (Mixed Negro Races) of the United States," *Medical News* 63 (December 2, 1893): 625. In 1894, just two months after Reyburn's article, Dr. R. M. Cunningham compared death rates of white and black convicts and

concluded that, given the disparity even under the identical circumstances of incarceration, there must be a "physical inferiority" that predisposes blacks to diseases; see R. M. Cunningham, "The Morbidity and Mortality of Negro Convicts," *Medical News* 64 (February 3, 1894): 115. Doctor M. V. Ball referred to this article two months later when making the counter-claim that no disease predisposition exists: "I would refer the differences commonly found in the death-rates of the colored race, as compared with the white, to differences in the environment . . . and not to any physical distinctions"; see M. V. Ball, "The Mortality of the Negro," *Medical News* 64 (April 7, 1894): 390.

36. On the relation between racial classification and life insurance, see John S. Haller, "Race, Mortality, and Life Insurance: Negro Vital Statistics in the Late Nineteenth Century," *Journal of the History of Medicine and Allied Sciences* 25:3 (July 1970): 247–61.
37. Frederick L. Hoffman, *Race Traits and Tendencies of the American Negro* (New York: American Economic Association, 1896), 146. For background on the influence of Hoffman's *Race Traits and Tendencies* see Haller, *Outcasts from Evolution*, 60–68; and George M. Fredrickson, *The Black Image in the White Mind* (New York: Harper & Row, 1971), 249.
38. See Eugene R. Corson, "The Vital Equation of the Colored Race and its Future in the United States," *The Wilder Quarter-Century Book* (Ithaca, NY: Comstock Publishing Co., 1893), 115, 124.
39. On Corson's place amidst this general context of pessimism, see Haller, *Outcasts from Evolution*, 41, 47–48.
40. Swan M. Burnett, "Racial Influence in the Etiology of Trachoma," *Medical News* (November 22, 1890): 543.
41. In 1891, for instance, one article summarized statistical data, saying, "The conclusion is reached that the negro race does not withstand the attacks of acute inflammation, such as pneumonia, nor do they recover from long-continued illnesses, such as typhoid fever, so well as the white race; but, on the other hand, the negro's power of repair after injuries and following surgical operations is believed to be superior to that of the white race"; see "Predisposition to Disease in the Negro," *Medical News* (July 11, 1891): 52. Another article, of 1896, refers to "Billings [who], in a statistical study of the influence of race on disease, states that the colored race . . . is especially liable to tuberculosis and pneumonia, and less liable to malaria, yellow fever, scarlet fever, and cancer"; see J. Morrison Ray, "Observations Upon Eye Diseases and Blindness in the Colored Race," *New York Medical Journal* 64 (July 18, 1896): 86.
42. Ray, "Observations Upon Eye Diseases," 88, 87.
43. This problem occurred to Dr. E. H. Gregory, one of the respondents to a presentation by Dr. Tiffany: "I believe that it is only the weakest possible body that entertains the tubercle bacillus, regarding it as the weakest of all infective organisms, and the body that entertains that bacillus represents the lowest possible degree of organization, that it is at the bottom of the scale. . . . It strikes me that such an assumption is irreconcilable with the observation, I

believe, of both Dr. Tiffany and Dr. Johnson, that negroes do better after injury than do white men. It seems to me that the reparative processes are always proportional to the energy and perfection of the body, and that when we are low in the scale of organization our reparative processes are relatively feeble. If the negro has better plastic [i.e. reparative] processes than the white man, I can scarcely reconcile it with the statement that he has more tubercle"; see Tiffany, "Comparison Between the Surgical Diseases of the White and Colored Races," *Transactions of the American Surgical Association* 5 (1887): 268.

44. Louis McLane Tiffany, "Comparison Between the Surgical Diseases of the White and Colored Races," 273.
45. See Matas, "The Surgical Peculiarities of the Negro," 527, 528.
46. See Warwick M. Cowgill, "Why the Negro Does Not Suffer from Trachoma," *Journal of the American Medical Association* 34 (1900): 399; hereafter cited parenthetically in the text.
47. Edward A. Balloch, "The Relative Frequency of Fibroid Processes in the Dark-Skinned Races," *Medical News* 64 (January 13, 1894): 34, 35.
48. William Benjamin Smith, *The Color Line: A Brief in Behalf of the Unborn* (1905), reprinted in *Racial Determinism and the Fear of Miscegenation, Post-1900*. Series *Anti-Black Thought, 1863–1925*, vol. VIII, ed. John David Smith (New York: Garland Publishing, Inc., 1993), 270–71.
49. Burnett, "Racial Influence in the Etiology of Trachoma," 542–43.
50. W. A. Dixon, "The Morbid Proclivities and Retrogressive Tenedencies in the Offspring of Mulattoes," *Medical News* 61 (August 13, 1892): 180–82. Also reprinted in *Journal of the American Medical Association* 20 (January 7, 1893): 1–2.
51. E. H. Sholl, "The Negro and his Death Rate," *Alabama Medical and Surgical Age* 3 (1890–91): 340–41.
52. Cunningham, "The Morbidity and Mortality of Negro Convicts," 113; hereafter cited parenthetically in the text.
53. F. Tipton, "The Negro Problem from a Medical Standpoint," *New York Medical Journal* 63 (May 22, 1886): 570–71.
54. As Laënnec Hubron observes, Americans have frequently cast voodoo as "essentially a heap of superstitions, and of magical practices and sorcery, stripped of coherence" ("American Fantasy and Haitian Vodou," *Sacred Arts of Haitian Vodou*, ed. Donald J. Cosentino [Los Angeles: Fowler Museum of Cultural History, 1995], 183).
55. In his essay "Occult Truths: Race, Conjecture, and Theosophy in Victorian Anthropology" (in *Excluded Ancestors, Inventible Traditions: Essays Toward a More Inclusive History of Anthropology*, ed. Richard Handler [Madison: University of Wisconsin Press, 2000]), Peter Pels observes that supernatural or occult reasoning played a prominent role in medical diagnostics as that discipline took shape in the course of the nineteenth century. "In the theory and practice of phreno-mesmerism," Pels observes, "the empirically tangible signs of race were made subordinate to its occult qualities in terms of innate character and natural disposition. . . . Both paradigms [i.e. phrenology and mesmerism]

were part of a political battle over scientific expertise – medical expertise in particular. The battleground for both parties was, to a large extent, the field of the conjectural method or medical semiotics, which, by hypothesizing invisible causes from perceived minute effects, was very much engaged with occult qualities" (18–19). Pels continues that "the conjectural method defines certain occult qualities as causes, which, *because* they are occult and imponderable, are impossible to refute by subsequent testings" (35). Through such methods, Pels observes, "what was later classified as 'occult science' . . . promised to conjecture spiritual essences from minute visible effects by means that did not lend themselves to elite appropriation through method, scientific institutionalization, or technical complication" (37). On the related "model of medical semiotics or symptomatology – the discipline which permits diagnosis, though the disease cannot be directly observed, on the basis of superficial symptoms or signs, often irrelevant to the eye of the layman," see Carlo Ginzburg, "Clues: Morelli, Freud, and Sherlock Holmes," 87.

56. Middleton Michel, "Carcinoma Uteri in the Negro," *Medical News* (October 8, 1892): 400.
57. Michel, "Carcinoma Uteri in the Negro," 400.
58. Balloch, "The Relative Frequency of Fibroid Processes," 29.
59. Michel, "Carcinoma Uteri in the Negro," 400. Michel objects, for example, that "hare-lip" and "carcinoma of the uterus" have been presented as rare in blacks when they are quite common (400) and that "fibroid tumors" of the uterus have been presented as common to blacks when "we have not found fibroids of the uterus so frequent – much less a constant condition of the negress's womb" (401). In expressing the concern that these features be not just "frequent" but in fact "constant," Michel reflects an important aspect of this anatomical study for many doctors.
60. One way in which color showed itself to be unnecessary to racial classification was through the phenomenon of albinoism; see David DeBeck, "Albinoism in the Negro," *Ohio Medical Journal* 7 (1896): 277. Such an absence of color was also of concern in the case of newborn babies. Although some doctors claimed that an African-American baby "comes into the world black" (see T. L. Robertson, "The Color of Negro Children When Born," *Alabama Medical and Surgical Age* 10 [1897–98]: 414), most asserted that, for a few days at least, black babies were "just like white babies" (see Benjamin H. Brodnax, "Correspondence," *New York Medical Times* 23 [1895)]: 322). "Often it would be a difficult matter to decide," confessed one doctor, "whether the child was of white or negro origin unless the parents were known"; see "The Color of Negro Babies," *Medical News* (December 24, 1898): 845. Related ambivalences concerned adults. An 1896 study in *The Journal of Experimental Medicine* concluded that "the pigment of the negro's hair is not different from the dark pigment found in the hair of the white races, and we may infer that the pigment of the black skin differs only in amount and not in kind from that deposited in the skin of the white man"; see John J. Abel and Walter S. Davis, "On the Pigment of the Negro's Skin and Hair," *Journal of Experimental Medicine* 1 (1896): 400.

Such a finding struck the authors as important because it "might throw great light on many anomalous cases of pigmentation" occurring "in the skin of the white races," as in the high amounts of pigmentation associated with Addison's disease (362). This finding and the others showed that neither the presence of pigment nor the amount could constitute a "determinant . . . peculiarity" of the "Negro."

61. In 1892 a doctor presented "a description of an anatomic feature observed in the eyes of our negro population particularly." This feature was "seen in negroes alone" and was "very frequent, at least, in the negro"; see Middleton Michel, "Plica Circularis Conguncticæ in the Negro," *Medical News* (October 22, 1892): 463.

62. In 1868 Dr. E. B. Turnipseed proposed that "the hymen of the negro woman is not at the entrance of the vagina, as in the white woman" and suggested "that this may be one of the anatomical marks of non-unity of the races"; see E. B. Turnipseed, "Letter from South Carolina," *Richmond and Louisville Medical Journal* 6 (1868): 195. Eleven years later Turnipseed published a follow-up in *The American Journal of Obstetrics* in which he noted that "there has been no refutation; therefore I conclude the profession has accepted the truths" that the racially specific positioning of the hymen is "one of the anatomical indications Providence has given us of the non-unity of the races"; see Edward B. Turnipseed, "Some Facts in Regard to the Anatomical Differences Between the Negro and White Races," *American Journal of Obstetrics* 10 (1877): 33. This journal's next issue contained several responses to this claim, one of which concurred in this assessment: "I am satisfied from actual observation that every hymen I have ever seen or examined in the negro or mulatto is placed farther within the vagina than any I ever saw or examined in the white race, and as soon as I saw Dr. Turnipseed's article above referred to I was convinced that it is an anatomical peculiarity of the negro race; so much so, indeed, that I sincerely believe that this peculiarity . . . would enable any practiced physician to distinguish the negro from the white race, even in the dark, by the aid of touch alone"; see C. H. Fort, "Some Corroborative Facts in Regard to the Anatomical Difference Between the Negro and White Races," *American Journal of Obstetrics* 10 (1877): 259. The two other respondents, however, offered dissenting opinions, one saying he had "never seen any marked difference" in his examinations of white and black women (H. Otis Hyatt, "Note on the Normal Anatomy of the Vulvo-Vaginal Orifice," *American Journal of Obstetrics* 10 [1877]: 254) and the other that "I have found but little uniformity in the location of the hymen in either race" (A. G. Smythe, "The Position of the Hymen in the Negro Race," *American Journal of Obstetrics* 10 [1877]: 639).

63. Matas, writing in 1896, observes, "it has been proven that the negro is subject to many anomalies of the muscular system. In this country Baker, Michel, the writer, and others confirm the existence of these variations in the myology of the negro. . . . Among the more important variations that have been claimed as peculiar to the negro, we may mention the greater frequency of the psoas

parvus, the greater persistence and development of the plantaris . . . [etc.]"; see Matas, "The Surgical Peculiarities of the Negro," 499.

64. For a discussion of flat feet, see Albert H. Freiberg and J. Henry Schroeder, "A Note on the Foot of the American Negro," *American Journal of the Medical Sciences* 76 (1903): 1,033–36. For a discussion of chorea see R. W. I'Anson, "Chorea in the Negro," *Virginia Medical Monthly* 2 (1875): 284; and Philip S. Roy, "A Case of Chorea in a Negro," *Medical Record* (August 20, 1892): 215. For a discussion of keloid see Balloch, "The Relative Frequency of Fibroid Processes," 33–35.

65. D. K. Shute, "Racial Anatomical Peculiarities," *American Anthropologist* 9 (1896): 125. Shute was careful to distinguish those deviations that occurred in a forward and backward direction along the path of evolutionary "progress" from the seemingly random variations produced by the arbitrary process of evolutionary change: "But in the study of these variations a sharp distinction must be made between those that are atavistic . . . and those that are prophetic . . . ; also, in the study of all variations, whether muscular or otherwise, due care must be exercised in eliminating fortuitous cases – that is to say, sports or monstrosities – such as supernumerary digits or incisors" (125). Shute's premise is that races evolve from a prior form or type, so there can be reversions to that type. For discussions of racial types, see Nancy Stepan, *The Idea of Race in Science*, 93–103; and Michael Banton, *Racial Theories* (New York: Cambridge University Press, 1987), 28–64.

66. A doctor writing in 1894 in *Medical News* quotes a source who "has noted, in two among thirty-three negro brains examined by him, the existence of an internal *pli du passage*, as well marked as in any of the Simiadæ. . . . its absence had been regarded as a distinguishing characteristic of human as compared with anthropoid brains." Its presence in these two "Negroes," in other words, shows them, through their tendency to atavistic variation, to be closer to this anthropoid. The suggestion is that perhaps they and, by association, the others in their "Negro" type do not have far to go before they revert fully to the ape type; see Balloch, "The Relative Frequency of Fibroid Processes," 29. Matas, writing in 1896, notes several muscular anomalies, "all of which have been pointed out as marked atavistic traits which make the negro a nearer kin to the quadrumana, or lower species, than the white man." He refers to this phenomenon as "atavism or reversion of type to ancestral animal forms"; see Matas, "The Surgical Peculiarities of the Negro," 499, 498. Another article, appearing in 1897 in the *Journal of Anatomy and Physiology*, admitted that "the question is still open whether or not negro myology reveals a greater relative frequency of variations which may be regarded as atavistic." The article goes on, however, to report on the dissection of "a pure-bred negro" and to make the following observation: ". . . it is very interesting to note the concurrence in one individual of so many variations, which remind one of the descriptions of anthropoid myology"; see Thomas H. Bryce, "Notes on the Myology of a Negro," *Journal of Anatomy and Physiology* 31 (1897): 607, 614. A 1904 article held much the same view, stating, "Many rudimentary or vestigial

organs and structures that are constant in the case of the animals below man, appear far more frequently in the negro than in the white man," for example "the supracondyloid foramen of the humerus (feline carnivora – gorilla) is frequently present in the negro, and I have found that the psoas parvus muscle undoubtedly is"; see R. W. Shufeldt, "Comparative Anatomical Characters of the Negro," *Medical Brief* 32 (1904): 27–28.

67. William Lee Howard, "The Negro as a Distinct Ethnic Factor," *Medical News* 84 (May 7, 1904): 905.

68. Paul B. Barringer, "The American Negro, His Past and Future" (1900), reprinted in *Racial Determinism and the Fear of Miscegenation, Pre-1900*, series *Anti-Black Thought, 1863–1925*, vol. VII, ed. John David Smith (New York: Garland Publishing, Inc., 1993), 437–57. Subsequent references will appear parenthetically in the text.

69. William Lee Howard asserts, "In the increase of rape on white women we see the explosion of a long train of antecedent preparation. The attacks on defenseless white women are evidences of racial instincts that are about as amenable to ethical culture as is the barrier which keeps the philanthropist and moralist from realizing that the phylogenies of the Caucasian and African races are divergent, almost antithetical"; see "The Negro as a Distinct Ethnic Factor," 905–06. Similar claims are advanced in *Virginia Medical Monthly*: "When we take into consideration the ancestry of the American negro, and reflect upon the peculiar sexual relations sustained by that ancestry, it is by no means surprising that ancestral traits crop out occasionally. Marriage among certain negro tribes is as close a simulation of what is designated as rape in civilized communities as could well be imagined. When the Ashantee warrior knocks down his prospective bride with a club and drags her off into the woods, he presents an excellent prototype illustration of the criminal sexual acts of the negro in the United States." The authors go on to call rape an "atavistic manifestation of savagery"; see Frank G. Lydston and Hunter McGuire, "Sexual Crimes Among the Southern Negroes – Scientifically Considered," *Virginia Medical Monthly* 20 (1893): 110. For a general discussion of the racist positions advanced using the concept of phylogeny, see Stephen Jay Gould, *Ontogeny and Phylogeny* (Cambridge, MA: Harvard University Press, 1977), 126–35.

70. Frederick Douglass, "Lecture on Haiti, World's Fair, Chicago, January 2, 1893," *The Life and Writings of Frederick Douglass*, vol. IV, ed. Philip S. Foner (New York: International Publishers, 1955), 483; hereafter cited parenthetically in the text.

71. For a useful discussion that places Douglass within a larger nineteenth-century context of celebratory views of Haitian history, see David Nicholls, *From Dessalines to Duvalier: Race, Colour and National Independence in Haiti* (New York: Cambridge University Press, 1979), 5–7.

72. Douglass singles out the writings of James Anthony Froud (480), whose *The English in the West Indies; or The Bow of Ulysses* (1888) calls Haiti "the most ridiculous caricature of civilization in the world"; quoted in Joan Dayan,

"Vodoun, or the Voice of the Gods," *Sacred Possessions: Vodou, Santería, Obeah, and the Caribbean*, ed. Margarite Fernández Olmos and Lizabeth Paravisini-Gebert (New Brunswick, NJ: Rutgers University Press, 1997), 13. For a similar contemporary account see Sir Spenser St. John, *Hayti; or the Black Republic*, 2nd edn. [1889] (London: Frank Cass and Company Limited, 1971), vii–ix.

73. Shaler, "The Negro Problem," 698; and "European Peasants as Immigrants," 647.
74. On the role of possession in voodoo, see Alfred Métraux, *Voodoo in Haiti*, trans. Hugo Charteris (New York: Schocken Books, 1972), 120–40.
75. See Shaler, "European Peasants as Immigrants," 654–55.
76. To be possessed by a spirit is often described among practitioners of voodoo as being mounted by a horse; see Métraux, *Voodoo in Haiti*, 120.
77. Chapman even looks like High Priestess Sybella, with his bald head and cadaver-like appearance (25) paralleling the bald head and skeleton-like body of Sybella (83). Chapman has not married because he has "given, in the intense way that is part of my nature, all the love of my heart and consecrated all my devotion to the business . . . submerg[ing] my every emotion in the glory and honor of the house of 'J. Dunlap'" (148). This priest-like devotion has a doctrinal side as well, for "All established rules of the house of 'J. Dunlap' were . . . to David Chapman, inviolable" (288).
78. Métraux, *Voodoo in Haiti*, 146. See also Marilyn Houlberg, "Magique Marasa: The Ritual Cosmos of Twins and Other Sacred Children," *Sacred Arts of Haitian Vodou*, ed. Donald J. Consentino (Los Angeles: Fowler Museum of Cultural History, 1995), 267–85.
79. See Métraux, *Voodoo in Haiti*, 88. Joan Dayan similarly observes that although the "loa come to visit their 'children,'" the people the loa visit are not actually descendants: although "they share their home with the ancestors," the loa are "clearly distinguished from *les morts*, the spirits of the dead"; see Joan Dayan, "Vodoun, or the Voice of the Gods," 17.
80. For a useful general discussion of the voodoo pantheon and the dynamics of possession, see Métraux, *Voodoo in Haiti*, 82–141. As Métraux acknowledges, generalizations about voodoo religious practice (typically referred to with the alternate orthography of vodou or vodun) are notoriously difficult to make due to the immense variety within this syncretic religious practice; for a useful discussion of this issue see Donald J. Cosentino, "Imagine Heaven," *Sacred Arts of Haitian Vodou*, ed. Donald J. Consentino (Los Angeles: Fowler Museum of Cultural History, 1995), 44–55.
81. The presumption of a coincidence between black bodies and the practice of voodoo was a frequent reaction to the 1802 Haitian revolution, but this presumption became particularly widespread following the United States' occupation of Haiti in 1915; for useful discussions of this coincidence between blackness and possession, as well as its varying uses (whether to denigrate blacks as "savage" or to celebrate them as "primitive") see David Nicholls, *From Dessalines to Duvaalier*, 6, 11–12; J. Michael Dash, *Haiti and the United States: National Stereotypes and the Literary Imagination* (London: Macmillan

Press Ltd., 1988), 1–3 and 30–36; and Laënnec Hurbon, "American Fantasy and Haitian Vodou," 181–83. As I am trying to suggest, however, the work of Davenport makes explicit an effort to imagine something different, not only that certain forms of ancestral possession coincide with black bodies (and particularly with "Negro" "blood") but also that other forms of ancestral possession coincide with "Anglo-Saxon" bodies (and particularly with "Anglo-Saxon" "blood").

82. As Walter Benn Michaels has observed, *Plessy v. Ferguson* appeals to "physical differences" between races but then concedes that these "physical differences" are not a required basis for racial segregation, thus implying that race is ultimately not physical but "spiritual"; see Walter Benn Michaels, "The Souls of White Folk," 190.

83. For contemporary views on the centrality of alliteration to Anglo-Saxon poetry and, in turn, to the subsequent poetic tradition in English, see Sidney Lanier, *SEV*, 239–40; and Francis B. Gummere, "The Translation of Beowulf, and the Relations of Ancient and Modern English Verse," *American Journal of Philology* 7 (1886): 57, 64, 70–73.

84. Unlike onomatopoeia, then, which involves sounds that are linguistic outsiders and can only be mimicked within language, alliteration involves sounds that are linguistic insiders, that arise only in the context of language. John Hollander, in his *Vision and Resonance*, follows I. A. Richards in describing this distinction in slightly different terms, as two sorts of onomatopoeia, primary or "natural" and secondary or "conventional" (156): "Certain primary onomatopoetic representations of non-linguistic sounds, such as the characteristic noises of animals, become morphemes of a language quite early in its development; the result is that they seem 'natural' to it. . . . Secondary, or conventional onomoatopoeia" operates differently; "In it, words are made to sound not like the noises of nature or of physical processes, but like other words" (156). Secondary onomatopoeia, then, serves "to associate words already given us with others having common sounds. Assonance, alliteration, and even rhyme" (157), Hollander observes, are examples of secondary onomatopoeia. By distinguishing alliteration, as secondary onomatopoeia, from primary onomatopoeia, Hollander captures, in different terms, the distinction I am drawing here between alliteration and onomatopoeia. Hollander is appropriately skeptical about the "illusory" (156) claim that primary onomatopoeia can escape convention, and indeed Seymour Chatman asserts that "onomatopoetic words turn out to be doubly conventional. For the reference of ordinary words already operates by convention. . . . To that convention, onomatopoeia adds another, namely the convention that certain words not only signal certain things but also sound like them" (Seymour Chatman, *A Theory of Meter* [London: Mouton & Co., 1965], 194); for a similar statement emphasizing the ultimate conventionality of onomatopoeia, see Ferdinand de Saussure, *Course in General Linguistics*, trans. Wade Basian (New York: Philosophical Library, 1959), 69. Rather than distinguishing between those formal effects that seem natural and those that are conventional, it is perhaps more

useful to distinguish, as do the texts I am addressing, between those (ultimately conventional) formal effects (effects which I am calling onomatopoeia) that seek to imitate the extra-linguistic sounds of nature and those formal effects (effects which I am calling alliteration) that seek to imitate the sounds of culture, specifically the sounds of words. Thus in Tennyson's famous lines, "The moan of doves in immemorial elms / And murmuring of innumerable bees" (Hollander, *Vision and Resonance*, 157), the word "murmuring" would be onomatopoeia, in my sense, if one takes it to be imitating the sounds of bees, but it would be alliteration, in my sense, if one takes it (as Hollander does) to be imitating the sounds of "immemorial elms," the words that immediately precede it (157).

85. The phrase appears in a 1913 letter in which Frost asserts, "I alone of English writers have consciously set myself to make music out of what I may call the sound of sense"; see Robert Frost, "To John T. Bartlett," *Robert Frost on Writing*, ed. Elaine Barry (New Brunswick, NJ: Rutgers University Press, 1973), 58–59.

86. For discussions of this use of alliteration, see Hollander, *Vision and Resonance*, 154–56; and *The New Princeton Encyclopedia of Poetry and Poetics*, 1,175–76, 1,180–82.

87. In an account of the Ku Klux Klan first published in 1884, J. C. Lester and D. L. Wilson observe the importance of alliteration in the selection of the organization's name: "The committee appointed to select a name . . . . mentioned several which they had been considering. In this number was . . . the Greek word *Kuklos* (Kuklos), meaning a band or circle. At mention of this someone cried out: 'Call it Ku Klux.' 'Klan' at once suggested itself, and was added to complete the alliteration. So instead of adopting a name, as was the first intention, which had a definite meaning, they chose one which to the proposer of it, and to every one else, was absolutely meaningless. . . . [I]t is difficult to resist the conclusion that the order would never have grown to the proportions which it afterward assumed, or wielded the power it did, had it not borne this name or some other equally as meaningless and mysterious – mysterious because meaningless"; see J. C. Lester and D. L. Wilson, *Ku Klux Klan: Its Origin, Growth and Disbandment*, ed. Walter L. Fleming (1905; New York: AMS Press, 1971), 55–56. As meaningless alliteration, the organization name becomes a mere sound effect that is separable from, and thus a potential supplement to, linguistic communication. Like the sheets that abstract race from bodies of Klan members (see Michaels, "The Souls of White Folk," 190), alliteration abstracts whiteness from language; so like the sheets draped over the bodies of the Klan members, alliteration drapes language in the cloak of race.

88. See Sidney Lanier's complaint, in "The Death of Byrhtnoth," that "with regard to the first seven hundred years of our poetry we English-speaking people appear never to have confirmed ourselves unto ourselves" (290). Such self-confirmation comes, Lanier goes on to say, from reading Anglo-Saxon poetry and enjoying "the beauty of its rhythm" (296). For Davenport, I am arguing, Anglo-Saxon rhythm is in the blood, not in texts, so Anglo-Saxons confirm

themselves unto themselves by attending not to poems but to themselves and by noting, in their bodies, an innate propensity to alliteration.

89. This account is consistent with Davenport's other published work, which evolves toward a concern with asserting racial unity (see his *Anglo-Saxons Onward!; a Romance of the Future* [1898]) following his early concern with fighting class difference (see *The Crime of Caste in our Country; Americans Enforce Equality. No Sham Aristocracy of Wealth Permitted by the People* [1892] and *"Uncle Sam's" Cabins; A Story of American Life, Looking Forward a Century* [1895]).

90. My discussion here is indebted to an account of the whiteness of the Ku Klux Klan set out in Walter Benn Michaels, "The Souls of White Folk," 190.

91. See Robert Farris Thompson, "From the Isle Beneath the Sea: Haiti's Africanizing Vodou Art," *The Sacred Arts of Haitian Vodou*, ed. Donald J. Cosentino (Los Angeles: Fowler Museum of Cultural History, 1995), 93, 98; and Métraux, *Voodoo in Haiti*, 178.

92. This image of whites possessed by the spirits of their ancestors anticipates by three years the description offered by Thomas Dixon in his 1905 novel *The Clansman*. There the Clansmen bear not cutlasses but the fiery cross of the Scottish Highlanders, and they are not resurrected buccaneers but "the reincarnated souls of the Clansmen of Old Scotland" (2). As reincarnated ghosts, the horsemen of Dixon's Clan coincide with the voodoo image of ancestral spirits who "mount" the person to be possessed, called a "horse"; on the role of this terminology in voodoo, see Métraux, *Voodoo in Haiti*, 120. The relation of a Clansman to his horse in Dixon's novel thus reproduces the voodoo image of the possessed individual as a "horse" ridden by a reincarnated ancestral spirit. Thus Dixon's Clansmen rely on the same logic of voodoo possession as Davenport's Anglo-Saxons and "Negroes." Davenport's occult Anglo-Saxons and Dixon's occult Clansmen each set out a notion of a supernatural whiteness that problematizes the typology of tropes offered by Cynthia Schrager (in "Both Sides of the Veil: Race, Science, and Mysticism in W. E. B. Du Bois," *American Quarterly* 48:4[1996]:551–86), tropes that "figure blackness in terms of the spiritual and whiteness in terms of the material" and rational (554). Davenport demonstrates that you do not have to be a rationalist to be a racialist or indeed a racist, and thus if, as Schrager suggests, "the discourse of visionary prophecy permits the articulation of alternative political arrangements" to those of Jim Crow ("Both Sides of the Veil," 573), occult spiritualism can likewise be a vehicle for enforcing Jim Crow as the racial status quo.

93. Vachel Lindsay, "The Congo: A Study of the Negro Race," *The Poetry of Vachel Lindsay*, vol. 1, ed. Dennis Camp (Peoria, IL: Spoon River Poetry Press, 1984), 174–78. Hereafter cited parenthetically in the text.

94. Although she does not address the whiteness embodied in the alliteration of Lindsay's "The Congo," Rachel Blau DuPlessis provides an effective discussion of another way in which whiteness is constructed in this poem, via the narrative containment of blackness. My own analysis has benefited from her thorough

critique of this and other poems of the period that use their formal features to construct whiteness; see her "'HOO, HOO, HOO': Some Episodes in the Construction of Modern Whiteness," *American Literature* 67:4 (December 1995): 667–700.

95. Henry Edward Krehbiel, *Afro-American Folksongs*, 56. Subsequent citations will appear parenthetically in the text.
96. Middleton Michel, "Carcinoma Uteri in the Negro," 400.
97. Krehbiel offers a Lamarckian "hypothesis" (77) for these peculiarities by suggesting that "centuries of habit might atrophy the musical faculty of a people so as to make the production of a tone as part of an intervallic system difficult and lead to its modification when occasion called for its introduction" (76).
98. James Weldon Johnson, *Autobiography of an Ex-Colored Man* (New York: Penguin Books, 1990), 72. Hereafter cited parenthetically in the text.
99. The views of Johnson's narrator here coincide with those of Johnson himself, who elsewhere praises ragtime as an important musical accomplishment; see his "Preface" to *The Book of American Negro Poetry*, 11–17.
100. It is not clear when Johnson first read Krehbiel's book, but he cites certain parts of it approvingly in his "Preface" to *The Book of American Negro Spirituals* (New York: Viking Press, 1925), 18, 23, 48.
101. See Johnson's "Preface" to *The Book of American Negro Spirituals* for his discussion of the "ecstatic state" induced by the "ring shout" (33), which he associates with similar practices he witnessed in Haiti (34). For related observations about the Ex-Colored Man, see Ruotolo, "The Autobiography of an Ex-Colored Musician," 266; and J. Martin Favor, *Authentic Blackness: The Folk in the New Negro Renaissance* (Durham, NC: Duke University Press, 1999), 42–52.
102. For related discussion see Jon Michael Spencer, who argues, "This wish not to sacrifice the magnificence of black cultural particularity for a nonracial universality was also the sentiment behind some of Johnson's passages in *The Autobiography of an Ex-Colored Man*" (*The New Negroes and Their Music: The Success of the Harlem Renaissance* [Knoxville: University of Tennessee Press, 1997], 35); Walter Benn Michaels, who argues that "If race, to be what it is, *must* be essential, then Johnson's ex-colored man, because he once was black, can never stop being black" ("Autobiography of an Ex-White Man, 125); Favor, who asserts that "the narrator's lament for his birthright reflects a belief in – or a desire for – a genetic boundary" (51) between races; and Ruotolo, who identifies a "'color line' that this novel, with all its subversions of 'race,' refuses to cross. An essential, if mutable, difference inheres for Johnson between 'black' and 'white' models of music production: for the rag player, as for the narrator's mother, music remains inseparable from the moment of its performance and from the body of its performer" (262).
103. Johnson's poem was first published in *The New Negro: An Interpretation*, ed. Alain Locke (New York: Albert and Charles Boni, 1925), 138–41.

104. In a 1938 letter to Flora M. Todd, Johnson asserts that the words of "The Creation" have largely excluded the "traditional plantation atmosphere" and the "artificial atmosphere of the jungle"; Johnson is quoted in Spencer, *The New Negroes and Their Music,* 4. Critics of Johnson debate the effectiveness of his poetry in capturing a racially specific sound. For a criticism of Johnson's results, see Eric J. Sundquist, *The Hammers of Creation: Folk Culture in Modern African-American Fiction* (Athens: University of Georgia Press, 1992), 62–64; for praise of Johnson's results see George Hutchinson, *The Harlem Renaissance in Black and White* (Cambridge, MA: Harvard University Press, 1995), 417; and Fahamisha Patricia Brown, *Performing the Word: African American Poetry as Vernacular Culture* (New Brunswick, NJ: Rutgers University Press, 1999), 20–25. My ultimate concern is not to assess whether Johnson achieved an authentic black sound but to demonstrate that he aspired to do so through the formal effects of his verse, and it is this aspiration that I am viewing as an important feature of the literary history of racial identity I am presenting.

105. James Weldon Johnson, "Preface," *The Book of American Negro Poetry*, 40. Hereafter cited parenthetically in the text.

106. For a discussion of Johnson's retention of the category "Negro" see Spencer, *The New Negroes and their Music*, 30, 33–35.

107. Roger Scruton asks, "what is poetry if not sound? But," he continues, "the representational nature of poetry is a consequence of the medium of language; poetry achieves representation by describing things, according to the pre-established semantic rules. If the sounds of music were likewise to be put to a linguistic use – if there were literally a musical language – then of course music would be capable of representation. But then it would cease to be music"; see Roger Scruton, *The Aesthetics of Music* (New York: Oxford University Press, 1997), 138.

108. For a discussion of Johnson's place within the larger goals of racial uplift and access to equal rights, see Kevin Gaines, *Uplifting the Race: Black Leadership, Politics, and Culture in the Twentieth Century* (Chapel Hill: University of North Carolina Press, 1996), 207, 224, 248.

109. The commitment to good English grammar above all, is, as Michael North has argued, consistent with the escape from racial difference; see his *Dialect of Modernism*, 143–44.

110. As J. Martin Favor observes, "The narrator of *Ex-Colored Man* is caught in a great paradox of race; he is both part of and apart from 'race'" (*Authentic Blackness*, 50).

111. For a dissenting view see Favor's *Authentic Blackness*, which seeks to separate Johnson from the "pernicious racial stereotype" set out by his Ex-Colored Man, the view that "musical talent is really ethnic" (44). Favor argues that "Johnson seems to understand the necessity of denaturalizing historical categories" (51–52) and of thinking, instead, in terms of "an identity that forms from an amalgam of positions . . . that are always in negotiation and contestation" (52). Tempting as it may be to rescue Johnson from the logical implications of his narrative, it is nevertheless the case that Johnson willingly characterizes musical talent as an "instinct" (17, 20) and as "innate"

(31) in his "Preface" to *The Book of American Negro Spirituals*. Doing so does not make Johnson a bad person so much as a subscriber to and proponent of a cultural logic that is, as Favor suggests and as Walter Benn Michaels asserts, "a mistake" (Michaels, "Autobiography of an Ex-White Man," 131, 143).

112. Stephen E. Henderson, *Understanding the New Black Poetry: Black Speech and Black Music as Poetic References* (New York: William Morrow & Co., 1973), 74.

113. More recently Henderson has made similar observations about Johnson's lasting influence; speaking specifically in reference to Johnson's *God's Trombones*, Henderson asserts the "confluence of the oral tradition, the verse of James Weldon Johnson, and the New Black Poetry"; see Stephen E. Henderson, "Worrying the Line: Notes on Black American Poetry," *The Line in Postmodern Poetry*, ed. Robert Frank and Henry Sayre (Chicago: University of Illinois Press, 1988), 63. If Johnson's terms permit Henderson to make "racial flavor" central to his understanding of the new black *poetry*, Henderson in turn inspires the more recent work of Houston Baker, who makes this "racial flavor" central to his understanding of the new black *criticism*, vernacular criticism:

> [S]cholars like . . . Henderson . . . had *faith* in the ultimate significance of the vernacular. Which is to say, they had an explicit and unshakable trust in the value of their *own* explicitly racial instincts and experiences. They entertained no doubts about the absolute necessity to allow the spirit of a culture's expressive genius to dictate the form and guide the presentation and purpose of their own work. (Houston Baker, *Afro-American Poetics: Revisions of Harlem and the Black Aesthetic* [Madison: University of Wisconsin Press, 1988], 89)

Subject to the "dictates" of the "culture's expressive genius," the vernacular critic is deferring not only to "experiences" but also "racial instincts." Here we see the language of racial medicine ("racial instincts") paired with the language of voodoo possession (where a "spirit . . . dictate[s] the form" of the critic's "work"). This passage takes the late nineteenth-century physicians' approach to bodies and extends it to include not just poems but also literary criticism. According to Baker, vernacular critics should be able to say of their own scholarship what, as we have seen, Du Bois said about the "style" of his *The Souls of Black Folk*: "The blood of my fathers spoke through me and cast off the English restraint of my training and surroundings." For vernacular critics like Baker, the interpretive goals of African-American poetics have continued to be "explicitly racial," and those goals thus perpetuate a long-standing search for textual symptoms through which blood will tell. Other recent critics who have affiliated themselves with the criticism of Henderson, and thus with its foundations in the criticism of Johnson, include Joyce A. Joyce, "*Bantu, Nkodi, Ndungu,* and *Nganga*: Language, Politics, Music, and Religion in African American Poetry," *The Furious Flowering of African American Poetry*, ed. Joanne V. Gabbin (Charlottesville: University Press of Virginia, 1999), 103–04; and Brown, *Performing the Word*, 4.

114. At a later point in his analysis (109–10 and 135–37) Spencer asserts the compatibility of these two "tiers" of "mastery" with the two accounts of mastery central to Houston Baker's account of the Harlem Renaissance, "mastery of form" and "deformation of mastery." In the case of James Weldon Johnson, however, Baker's terms seem not to apply. As Spencer himself observes, "Johnson evidently would have considered it self-denigrating to succumb to the demands of white patrons, publishers, and critics for the traditional sounds of the plantation or the minstrel stage" (13), so Johnson's "mastery of form" (i.e. discarding dialect and using standard speech) does not involve placating whites through appropriations of minstrelsy, which is how Baker describes the "mastery of form" (*Modernism and the Harlem Renaissance*, 25–36). And while Baker sees his two forms of mastery as deeply incompatible (*Modernism and the Harlem Renaissance*, 49–51, 56), Johnson can combine his two forms of mastery in what Spencer describes as a "balance": "Johnson did an excellent job of mastering the balance of the two-tiered 'mastery' in *God's Trombones*" (24). It is a similar balance that Favor attributes to Johnson's Ex-Colored Man, whose character, according to Favor, "suggests the viability of a discourse of black identity somewhere between the 'inauthenticity' of European high culture and the 'authenticity' of African American vernacular culture" (*Authentic Blackness*, 44).
115. William C. Turner, "Foreword," in Jon Michael Spencer, *Sacred Symphony: The Chanted Sermon of the Black Preacher* (New York: Greenwood Press, 1987), xi–xii; hereafter cited parenthetically in the text.
116. For similar accounts of the preacher's activity, see Raboteau, *Fire in the Bones*, 150, and Hubbard, *The Sermon and the African American Literary Imagination*, 7.
117. Jon Michael Spencer, *Re-Searching Black Music* (Knoxville: University of Tennessee Press, 1996), 11–12.

CONCLUSION: THE CONSERVATION OF IDENTITIES

1. Walter Scott, *Letters of Malachi Malagrowther*, 735.
2. James Weldon Johnson, *Autobiography of an Ex-Colored Man*, 154.
3. Walter Scott, *Letters on Demonology and Witchcraft*, 68.
4. Sidney Lanier, "The Death of Byrhtnoth," 296.
5. Du Bois, *The Souls of Black Folk*, 155, 155, 154.
6. W. E. B. Du Bois, "On *The Souls of Black Folk*," *The Oxford W. E. B. Du Bois Reader*, 305.
7. Dixon, *The Clansman*, 2.
8. See Alfred Métraux, *Voodoo in Haiti*, 120.
9. As Walter Benn Michaels argues, "Identity in *The Clansman* is always fundamentally spiritual. . . . [It is] an identity that can't be seen in people's skins . . . but can be seen in the Klan's sheets"; see "The Souls of White Folk," 190.
10. Heaney, "Englands of the Mind" (*Preoccupations; Selected Prose, 1968–78* [New York: Farrar, Straus, Giroux, 1980]), 150. Heaney goes on to associate such

ghostly "reincarnations of the Norsemen" "resurrected in all their arctic mail" (155) with the metrics of Ted Hughes (151–56), the writer to whose memory Heaney's 1999 verse translation of *Beowulf* is dedicated.

11. Lanier, "CC," 273.
12. Seamus Heaney, "Introduction," *Beowulf.* Subsequent citations will appear parenthetically in the text.
13. In an interview with Mike Murphy (entitled "Seamus Heaney" and appearing in *Reading the Future: Irish Writers in Conversation with Mike Murphy*, ed. Cliodhana Ni Anluain [Dublin: The Lilliput Press, 2000]) Heaney observes of his *Beowulf* project, "There was mischievous element in it, all right. It confounded the identity politics of things" (94). Critically targeting this "identity politics," Heaney states, "one function of writing or of a writer, in fact, may be to disrupt all that. One of your functions is to say that your language and your consciousness are as wide as the world" (94). But the scope he then attributes to *Beowulf* is in fact much narrower: "it's actually European. Its subject is somebody from the south west of Sweden coming down into Denmark and helping the Danes" (94–95). Heaney, then, doesn't confound identity politics so much as he adjusts its categories, subsuming a discussion of English and Irish identities within a larger – but equally identitarian – discussion of European identity. Thus although Stephen Greenblatt, in his essay "Racial Memory and Literary History," *PMLA* 116:1 (January 2001), presents Heaney's *Beowulf* as an example of global cosmopolitanism, and hence as an alternative to racial memory (59), I see it as yet another example of racial memory. Greenblatt critiques "recent attempts from a wide range of positions within current identity politics . . . to forge a usable past" (55–56), arguing that "there is no authentic home, no *nostos* to conjure up" (56). For Greenblatt, Heaney expresses this lack of an authentic home in his "'nostalgia for world culture.' That culture is in fact our home, our *nostos* from which we have long wandered, and it is time to return to it" (59). But as I have argued, Heaney does indeed imagine a *nostos* for that culture, a return to a mythic Celto-British land that, despite the dispersion of Anglo-Saxon language as a diasporic world culture, remains available as a somewhere being remembered. Thus Greenblatt's critical claim about racial memory would seem to apply, as well, to Heaney: "If the assumptions of an originary or primordial culture or of a stable linguistic identity progressively unfolding through time . . . are misguided, then they must not be embraced" (57).
14. This escape from partition signals a move beyond his earlier claims (in *The Redress of Poetry*) that advocated "two-mindedness" (202).
15. For additional discussions of haunting in Heaney's work, see Lucy McDiarmid, "Joyce, Heaney, and 'That Subject People Stuff,'" *James Joyce and his Contemporaries*, ed. Diana A. Ben-Merre and Maureen Murphy (New York: Greenwood Press, 1989), 131–39; Michael R. Molino, *Questioning Tradition, Language, and Myth: The Poetry of Seamus Heaney* (Washington, DC: Catholic University of America Press, 1994), 51; Sammye Crawford Greer, "'Station Island' and The Poet's Progress," *Seamus Heaney: The Shaping Spirit*, ed. Catharine Malloy and Phyllis Carey (Newark: University of Delaware

Press, 1996), 106–19; and Raphaël Ingelbien, "Mapping the Misreadings," 634–35.

16. Heaney, "The Murmur of Malvern," *The Government of the Tongue* (New York: Farrar, Straus and Giroux, 1989), 24. Hereafter cited parenthetically in the text.
17. *The Redress of Poetry*, 7.
18. Toni Morrison, "Living Memory," 181–82. Subsequent citations will appear parenthetically in the text.
19. For a critique of such mythic claims of African homogeneity, see Kwame Anthony Appiah, *In My Father's House*: "the very invention of Africa (as something more than a geographical entity) must be understood, ultimately, as an outgrowth of European racialism; the notion of Pan-Africanism was founded on the notion of the African, which was, in turn, founded not on any genuine cultural commonality but, as we have seen, on the very European concept of the Negro. . . . But the reality is that the very category of the Negro is at root a European product: for the 'whites' invented the Negroes in order to dominate them. Simply put, the course of cultural nationalism in Africa has been to make real the imaginary identities to which Europe has subjected us" (62).
20. Morrison does not specify the particular effects within her own writing that embody this blackness, but some critics have sought to do this for her. Taking their cues from Morrison's invocation of jazz, as well as from the title of her novel *Jazz*, many critics argue that her writing contains jazz riffs and improvisation. See Eusebio L. Rodrigues, "Experiencing *Jazz*," *Modern Fiction Studies* 39:3–4 (Fall-Winter 1993): 733–54; Alan J. Rice, "Jazzing it up a Storm: The Execution and Meaning of Toni Morrison's Jazzy Prose Style," *Journal of American Studies* 28 (1994): 423–32; and Robin Small-McCarthy, "The Jazz Aesthetic in the Novels of Toni Morrison," *Cultural Studies* 9:2 (1995): 293–300. For a critique of this line of analysis see Alan Munton, "Misreading Morrison, Mishearing Jazz: A Response to Toni Morrison's Jazz Critics," *Journal of American Studies* 31:2 (August 1997): 235–51.
21. Toni Morrison, *Playing in the Dark: Whiteness and the Literary Imagination* (New York: Vintage Books, 1992), 43; hereafter cited parenthetically in the text.
22. Thus in her discussion of Willa Cather, Morrison is led to "the inescapable conclusion that Cather was dreaming and redreaming her problematic relationship with her own mother" (27). Although Charles Mills's *The Racial Contract* cites Morrison with approval, he in fact deviates from her analysis at this point. While Morrison turns away from black victims of this Africanism to celebrate the literary imagination that produced it, Mills is concerned with ongoing victims of racist practices that, in his view, stem less from America's literary imagination than from whites' "consensual hallucination," a "racial fantasyland" in which "There will be white mythologies, invented Orients, invented Africas, invented Americas, with a correspondingly fabricated population, countries that never were, inhabited by people who never were – Calibans and Tontos, Man Fridays and Sambos – but who attain a virtual reality through their existence in travelers' tales, folk myth, popular and highbrow

fiction, colonial reports, scholarly theory, Hollywood cinema, living in the white imagination and determinedly imposed on their alarmed real-life counterparts" (*The Racial Contract*, 18–19).

23. For a useful discussion of the nineteenth-century writers associated with the nationalist Young America movement, as well as their rivalry with the more Anglophile writers associated with the New York *Knickerbocker* magazine, see Perry Miller, *The Raven and the Whale: The War of Words and Wits in the Era of Poe and Melville* (New York: Harcourt, Brace and Company, 1956), 88–103; on the tensions between the political and literary branches of Young America, see Michael Paul Rogin, *Subversive Genealogy*, 71–76, 148–50.
24. Adding that this American self was "covert about its dependency" (58) on a denigrated Africanism, Morrison asserts "the parasitical nature of white freedom" (57), suggesting that "this Africanist presence may be something the United States cannot do without" (47).
25. Morrison sets out to "observe and trace the transformation of American Africanism" (63) through a variety of stages, but even as it is transformed it goes by the same name, thus providing continuity across otherwise changing times and circumstances. Elsewhere Morrison underscores this continuous national selfhood: observing that "Older America is not always distinguishable from its infancy," Morrison goes on to align the 1848 writings of Poe with the 1986 writings of Kenneth Lynn as comparable manifestations of this American-Africanism; see Morrison's "Unspeakable Things Unspoken: The Afro-American Presence in American Literature" (1989), *Within the Circle: An Anthology of African American Literary Criticism from the Harlem Renaissance to the Present*, ed. Angelyn Mitchell (Durham, NC: Duke University Press, 1994), 380 n.
26. For a critique of Morrison that is directed at precisely this assumption of a deep continuity in accounts of race across texts from different US writers in different periods, see Walter Benn Michaels, "Jim Crow Henry James?," 286–91.
27. The link to Heaney is even more clear in Morrison's novel *Jazz*, where she construes this word "remembering" in corporeal terms, as the restoration of bodily wholeness to the severed limbs, or members, of a body: "I will locate it so the severed part can remember the snatch, the slice of its disfigurement. Perhaps then the arm will no longer be a phantom, but will take its own shape, grow its own muscle and bone, and its blood will pump from the loud singing that has found the purpose of its serenade. Amen" (159).
28. In her "Preface" to *Playing in the Dark*, for instance, Morrison discusses a writer who, upon hearing the music of Louis Armstrong, "ran into the street like someone possessed" (vii). This episode of possession exemplifies for Morrison how all American writers experience the Africanist presence. Later quoting from an A. S. Byatt novel – entitled, aptly, *Possession* – Morrison asserts that even as writers seek to create what is "wholly new, never before seen," they in fact produce what was "*always there*" and has been "*always known*" (xi). Implicit here is the idea that writers do not create new ideas so much as they are possessed by the ideas that predate them. Listing

the "key elements" of "Morrison's language," Linden Peach has emphasized "above all, the way in which community memory is not accessed through but stored in the language" (*Toni Morrison* [New York: St. Martin's Press, 1995], 134).

29. For a recent example of such scholarship, see Houston Baker's critical memoir, *Turning South Again*, 10, 97–98.

30. According to Morrison, her own writing process requires her "to call [the "unburied"] by their names and ask them to reappear" (*Conversations with Toni Morrison*, 209), and her focus on slavery in *Beloved*, she observes, is motivated by her conviction that "We have to re-inhabit those people. . . . The struggle to forget, which was important in order to survive is fruitless and I wanted to make it fruitless" (Morrison, "Living Memory," 179). As other critics have demonstrated, Morrison not only writes about ghosts, but she also imagines her texts themselves to be haunted by memories of the past. See Walter Benn Michaels, "'You Who Never Was There': Slavery and the New Historicism, Deconstruction and the Holocaust," *Narrative* 4:1 (January 1996): 5–8; Avery F. Gordon, *Ghostly Matters: Haunting and the Sociological Imagination* (Minneapolis: University of Minnesota Press, 1997), 165–69, 194–201; Kathleen Brogan, *Cultural Haunting: Ghosts and Ethnicity in Recent American Literature* (Charlottesville: University Press of Virginia, 1998), 5–8 and Chapter 3; and many of the selections in *Critical Essays on Toni Morrison's* Beloved, ed. Barbara H. Solomon (New York: G. K. Hall & Co., 1998).

31. As Morrison observes, "I am using the term 'Africanism' not to suggest the larger body of knowledge on Africa that the philosopher Valentine Mudimbe means by the term 'Africanism,' nor to suggest the varieties and complexities of African people and their descendants who have inhabited this country" (6).

32. This reasoning, linking Americanness with a desire for purity from blackness, is apparent in the words that Benjamin Rush Davenport offers in the dedication to his novel *Blood Will Tell*: "To all Americans who deem purity of race an all-important element in the progress of our beloved country" (*Blood Will Tell* [unpaginated]).

33. Seamus Heaney, "Book Learning," *Harvard Magazine* 103:1 (September–October 2000): 66–68; hereafter cited parenthetically in the text.

34. As she says in *Playing in the Dark*, "I do not have quite the same access to these traditionally useful constructs of blackness. . . . because I am a black writer" (x).

35. The violence of *Beowulf* figures centrally in Toni Morrison's unpublished addresses entitled "The Humanities After 9/11," which was presented in June of 2001 as the inaugural address in a lecture series sponsored by and presented before the United Nations.

36. In an interview with Karl Miller (*Seamus Heaney in Conversation with Karl Miller* [London: Between the Lines, 2000]) Heaney acknowledges his predilection for drawing parallels between *Beowulf*'s Hall of Hrothgar and other encircled citadels: "I did a lecture on *Beowulf* at Harvard, where I enjoyed sporting with the analogies that could be made between Boston surrounded by native

Americans, Edmund Spenser in his castle surrounded by Gaels, Ulster planters surrounded by Gaels, and Hrothgar with his minstrel in his Hall surrounded by Grendel" (41).

37. Geoffrey H. Hartman, "Wordsworth, Inscriptions, and Romantic Nature Poetry," *Beyond Formalism: Literary Essays 1958–1970* (New Haven: Yale University Press, 1971), 207.
38. William Gilmore Simms, "The Apalachian, a Southern Idyll," 5; hereafter cited parenthetically in the text.
39. Roberto Dainotto, *Place in Literature*, 33. "If history is moved by this clash of classes," Dainotto observes, "identity entails, in turn, the very suspension of historical process and the return to a Golden Age of unity" (30). Dainotto, via Geoffrey Hartman, associates this account of place with the writings of Heaney; see Dainotto, *Place in Literature*, 12.
40. Toni Morrison, *Jazz*, 143; hereafter cited parenthetically in the text.
41. For useful discussions that advance this point, see Michael Nowlin, "Toni Morrison's *Jazz* and the Racial Dreams of the American Writer," *American Literature* 71:1 (March 1999): 157–60; and J. Brooks Bouson, *Quite as it's Kept: Shame, Trauma, and Race in the Novels of Toni Morrison* (Albany: State University of New York Press, 2000), 175–78.
42. As Bouson observes, "By professing Golden Gray's desire to take ownership of his projected shame and to embrace his own 'blackness,' *Jazz* acts out a reparative fantasy" (*Quite as it's Kept*, 178).
43. Toni Morrison, "Home," *The House that Race Built: Black Americans, U. S. Terrain*, ed. Wahneema Lubiano (New York: Pantheon Books, 1997), 9. Hereafter cited parenthetically in the text.
44. On the general tendency toward wavering in the heroes of Scott's Waverley novels, see Alexander Welsh, *The Hero of the Waverley Novels; With New Essays on Scott* rev. edn. (Princeton University Press, 1992), 27. This wavering is reproduced not only in Golden Gray of Morrison's *Jazz* but also in Walter Burton of Benjamin Rush Davenport's *Blood Will Tell*, where Burton wavers between his training among New England Anglo-Saxons and the instinctive impulses of his Haitian great-grandmother, Sybella.
45. Morrison, "Unspeakable Things Unspoken," 384.
46. Indeed, in an interview with Angels Carabi, Morrison links Wild with the title character of her previous novel *Beloved*, asserting "The woman they call Wild . . . . could be Sethe's daughter, Beloved"; see Toni Morrison, "Interview [With Angels Carabi]," *Belles Lettres* 10.2 (Spring 1995): 43.
47. Noting this transformation of Wild, Bouson describes her as "an embodiment of the Africanist presence in literature, a white projective and shame-ridden image that Morrison redeems by associating it with the deeper unconscious sources of African-American art. Reconfigured as the African-American muse, Wild is the maternal inspiration for the *Jazz* narrator's art" (*Quite as it's Kept*, 187). Nowlin notes "the collision [Morrison] stages between" a "blackness alien to outside (predominantly white) readers . . . and the blackness familiar to the white literary imagination" ("Toni Morrison's *Jazz*," 156; see also 159–60). Morrison herself distinguishes two accounts of blackness in her "Preface" to *Playing*

in the Dark: "I do not have quite the same access to these traditionally useful constructs of blackness. Neither blackness nor 'people of color' stimulates in me notions of excessive, limitless love, anarchy, or routine dread. . . . My vulnerability would lie in romanticizing blackness rather than demonizing it" (x, xi).

48. In her interview with Paul Gilroy, Morrison references "a sympathetic white American who has never been a White Person to me," and Gilroy notes that she is making "use of James Baldwin's important distinction between people who make a political choice to be White with a capital W and those who merely have 'white' skin"; see "Living Memory," 180.
49. While Morrison's *Playing in the Dark* is concerned primarily with an Africanism fabricated by whites, her contemporaneous essay, "Unspeakable Things Unspoken," concerns itself primarily with this alternate account of blackness, a genuine blackness distinct from and heretofore obscured by white fabrications of Africanism: "Now that the Afro-American artistic presence has been 'discovered' actually to exist, now that serious scholarship has moved from silencing the witnesses and erasing their meaningful place in the contribution to American culture, it is no longer acceptable merely to imagine us and imagine for us. We have always been imagining ourselves. We are not Isak Dinesen's 'aspects of nature,' nor Conrad's unspeaking. We are the subjects of our own narrative, witnesses to and participants in our own experience" (375). Morrison's goal to represent this actually existing blackness is something she associates with her novel *Sula*: "I always thought of Sula as quintessentially black, metaphysically black, if you will" ("Unspeakable Things Unspoken," 390).
50. In her analysis of this passage, Bouson argues that the attraction between Wild and Golden "subverts and also rewrites the classic script of nineteenth-century American literature" (177), leading to a "reparative fantasy" (178) in which Golden Gray seeks "to take ownership of his projected shame and to embrace his own 'blackness'" (178). I concur in this account of subversion, but I am offering a different account of reparation: while the ownership of shame by the passer is the solution Morrison proposes in *Playing in the Dark*, I am arguing that she offers a different solution here, one in which, for whites (as opposed to Whites), blackness is not a psychologically internal source of shame but a racially external object of desire.
51. Noting the implicit commitment here to black and white races, Nowlin observes that Morrison's goal of "negation and transcendence of the 'mandate to conquest' must proceed through an affirmation of the effects of conquest, the most inescapable being the racialization of the American" ("Toni Morrison's *Jazz*," 158; see also 152–53).
52. Morrison, "Interview [With Angels Carabi]," 42.
53. Morrison, "Interview [With Angels Carabi]," 42; hereafter cited in the text.
54. Further evidence that Morrison associates this talking book with blackness and jazz is apparent from her essay "Unspeakable Things Unspoken," where she describes her "quintessentially black" (390) character Sula as "Improvisational" (390). Commenting about her novel *Jazz*, Morrison distinguishes "the original musicians" of jazz from "the white people who imitated their music,"

including "Benny Goodman," asserting that this white jazz involved "a sort of bland or played-down reproduction of it," an imitation that was less appealing to the more appreciative "aficionados" in Europe ("Interview [With Angels Carabi]," 41).

55. As with Scott, Morrison uses the word "summon" to describe the language practice that achieves this irrevocably black result: "I hope you understand that in this explication of how I practice language is a search for and deliberate posture of vulnerability to those aspects of Afro-American culture that can inform and position my work. I sometimes know when the work works, when *nommo* has effectively summoned, by reading and listening to those who have entered the text. I learn nothing from those who resist it" ("Unspeakable Things Unspoken," 397). She can know if her works have served as a summons by the responses of those whom it has summoned. Here the agency of summoning is not Morrison herself but the text, an agency she calls "*nommo*," a West African term which William R. Handley defines as "the magic power of the word to call things into being"; see Handley, "The House a Ghost Built: *Nommo*, Allegory, and the Ethics of Reading in Toni Morrison's *Beloved*," *Contemporary Literature* 36:4 (Winter 1995): 677.

56. On the implicit whiteness of Morrison's reader, see Nowlin, "Toni Morrison's *Jazz*," 156. It is not just white readers, however, who are implicated in the analogy that aligns Golden's relation to Wild with the reader's relation to the book, for Golden is also – according to the "one drop rule" – black, so in addition to providing a model for how whites might love Wild's authentic blackness, his relationship with Wild provides a model for how African-Americans might love their own authentic blackness.

57. Morrison thus replaces an identitarian fear of being possessed demoniacally (as in Scott's Hamish being possessed by his Highland mother Elspat, Davenport's Walter Burton being possessed by his Haitian great-grandmother Sybella, or Morrison's literary critics who fear an American literature possessed by an Africanist presence) with an equally identitarian desire for being possessed erotically (what Morrison calls "surrendering" to a "tactile" text). As a result, these prior accounts of possession, which involved one body with two distinct identities (a formulation central to passing narratives), are replaced by an erotic scenario of two different bodies each belonging to different races. Given its reliance on two bodies, Morrison's revised account of American identity precludes passing.

58. In a different interpretation of these closing lines of *Jazz*, Roberta Bernstein emphasizes not the reader's intimacy with the text's medium but rather the reader's contribution to the text's meaning: "Morrison explicitly places in the reader's hands the responsibility for constructing the meaning of her text" ("History and Story, Sign and Design: Faulknerian and Postmodern Voices in *Jazz*," *Unflinching Gaze: Morrison and Faulkner Re-Envisioned*, ed. Carol A. Kolmerten, Stephen M. Ross, and Judith Bryant Wittenberg [Jackson: University Press of Mississippi, 1997], 162). Similarly emphasizing meaning, Gurleen Grewal argues of these closing lines that "The narrator's plea/permission is an acknowledgment of the reader's agency in producing the text's meaning" (*Circles of*

Sorrow, Lines of Struggle: The Novels of Toni Morrison [Baton Rouge: Louisiana State University Press, 1998], 137). Nowlin's "Toni Morrison's *Jazz*" describes these closing lines as "an invitation to participate in a kind of marriage of reading and writing" (168), where the reading is performed by "a new American reader open to the possibilities this literature affords when one confronts its investment in the category of race" (156). I am arguing, more precisely, that this openness to possibilities involves receiving this literature not through more informed capacity for semantic decoding but through a willingness to attribute blackness to the novel's formal features, its tactile texture and tone.

59. In her discussion of Morrison's *Jazz* Drucilla Cornell writes, "I know Wild too and I address her when I write. I will go one step further. I love her. How could I not?" See Drucilla Cornell, "The Wild Woman and All That Jazz," *Feminism Beside Itself*, ed. Diane Elam and Robyn Wiegman (New York: Routledge, 1995), 320.

60. Thus in Scott's *The Highland Widow* Hamish fires upon British soldiers of a Highland regiment who, despite "the plaids and bonnets which they wore" (146), are not, like Hamish, possessed by the memories of Elspat and thus are not genuine or authentic Scots. This emphasis on authenticity stands in contrast to King George IV's state visit to Edinburgh just five years earlier, in 1822, a visit organized and orchestrated by Walter Scott, where the King played a role similar to the one Morrison attributes to the "king of swing," Benny Goodman: appearing publicly in the tartan costume, George IV (as Hugh Trevor-Roper observes) "played his part in the Celtic pageant, and at the climax of the visit solemnly invited the assembled dignitaries to drink a toast not to the actual or historic elite but to 'the chieftans and clans of Scotland'"; see Hugh Trevor-Roper, "The Invention of Tradition," 31. In contrast to invented traditions fabricated by imitators, Scott and Morrison each seek authentic traditions, an authenticity they believe to be indexed by formal textual effects possessed by Scottishness or blackness.

61. Toni Morrison, "Living Memory," 178.

62. Toni Morrison, "Unspeakable Things Unspoken," 372.

63. Kenneth W. Warren, "The End(s) of African-American Studies," *American Literary History* 12:3 (Fall 2000): 641. Warren adds, "A considerable body of writing has taken up the task of telling white readers just 'what the Negro wants' and 'who the Negro is.' Rather, it is precisely this understanding of the enterprise of black studies that I want to call into question, chiefly because the belief that black studies can provide us with some access to the inner thought of some collective black subject or black community is a belief fraught with problems" (643).

64. "For racially oppressed groups like American Blacks," Ross adds, ". . . cultural practices constitute a *means* for survival as well as pleasurable *ends* whereby the pleasure taken in identificatory cultural practices cements the bonds enabling survival" (837); see Marlon B. Ross, "Commentary: Pleasuring Identity, or the Delicious Politics of Belonging," *New Literary History* 31 (2000): 837.

65. See *The Letters of Sir Walter Scott*, vol. IX, 471–72.

66. Adolph Reed, *Class Notes: Posing as Politics and Other Thoughts on the American Scene* (New York: The New Press, 2000), 182; hereafter cited in the text.
67. As Reed observes, there is "an ideological current within the post-segregation-era black petite bourgeoisie that is troubling because of its fundamentally conservative and depoliticizing effects on black American intellectual life. This orientation to the history of Afro-American thought is linked most immediately to the prominence of literary studies in contemporary Afro-Americanist scholarship"; *W. E. B. Du Bois and American Political Thought: Fabianism and the Color Line* (New York: Oxford University Press, 1997), 130. For similar criticisms directed at literary studies of regional identity, rather than racial identity, see Dainotto, *Place in Literature*, 1–33. For a related critique of "post-Marxist" criticism see Daniel T. McGee, "Post-Marxism: The Opiate of the Intellectuals," *MLQ* 58:2 (June 1997): 201–25.
68. As Kenneth Warren observes, "I for one cannot say whether or not the hip-hop trained scholar has indeed accurately discerned in the slick choreography of young men dancing on the street corner the truth of their political aspirations. But I do know that the future of those young men should not hang on that contingency. . . . The task of figuring out what people really want should not rely on ingenious textual interpretation. And the academic hubris that leads us to think that we know something about the minds of the people whose lives and expressions we study is best tempered by a society in which other voices have the power to counter our own" ("The End(s) of African-American Studies," 651, 653).
69. For recent efforts to resist racial identity and thereby to defend the liberal subject, see K. Anthony Appiah, "Liberalism, Individuality, and Identity," 331–32; and Naomi Zack, *Race and Mixed Race* (Philadelphia, PA, Temple University Press, 1993), 165.
70. Lucius Outlaw, for instance, searches for alternatives to "modern liberal individualism" in his book *On Race and Philosophy* (New York: Routledge, 1996), 8; see also 140–41, 149. For Outlaw, "knowledge must be protected, if not revised, and maintained. So, too, must 'the order of things' be protected. Hence, the necessary creation of a canopy (often sacred) of cognitive and normative interpretation. . . . The production of protective, legitimating canopies requires, of course, particular folk, namely, those who 'figure out' such matters. But their functions are socially vital, which is why their positions and roles must be valorized in ways to give them 'authority' and, thereby, power: the power to *define the real, the true, and the good*, including the characterizing and identifying definitions of members of the group and of 'others' . . . . This, in general, is what I take to be the social location of those who have come to be called 'philosophers'" (18–19; italics in original). Himself a philosopher, Outlaw illustrates here not only the temptations to self-authorization (faced by literary critics and Nobel Laureates as well as philosophers) but also the social consequences that arise for a group when such self-authorizing gestures go unchallenged. For Outlaw's defense of his project in the explicit terms of Du Bois's nineteenth-century essay "The Conservation of Races" (1897) see *On Race and Philosophy*, 151–57.

Bibliography

Abel, John J. and Walter S. Davis. "On the Pigment of the Negro's Skin and Hair." *Journal of Experimental Medicine* 1 (1896): 361–400.

Adell, Sandra. *Double-Consciousness/Double Bind: Theoretical Issues in Twentieth-Century Black Literature*. Chicago: University of Illinois Press, 1994.

Aldrich, Richard. "Henry Edward Krehbiel." *Musical Discourse from* The New York Times. 1928; Freeport, NY: Books For Libraries Press, Inc., 1967, 282–92.

Anderson, Benedict. *Imagined Communities: Reflections on the Origin and Spread of Nationalism*. Rev. edn. New York: Verso, 1991.

"Exodus." *Critical Inquiry* 20 (Winter 1994): 314–27.

Anderson, Paul. *Deep River: Music and Memory in Harlem Renaissance Thought*. Durham, NC: Duke University Press, 2001.

Appiah, K. Anthony. *In My Father's House: Africa in the Philosophy of Culture*. New York: Oxford University Press, 1992.

"Liberalism, Individuality, and Identity." *Critical Inquiry* 27:2 (Winter 2001): 305–32.

"Race, Culture, Identity: Misunderstood Connections." In K. Anthony Appiah and Amy Gutmann, *Color Conscious: The Political Morality of Race*. Princeton University Press, 1996, 30–105.

Appleby, Joyce Oldham. "Locke, Liberalism and the Natural Law of Money." *Past and Present* 71 (May 1976): 43–69.

Arac, Jonathan. "Whitman and Problems of the Vernacular." *Breaking Bounds: Whitman and American Cultural Studies*. Ed. Betsy Erkkila and Jay Grossman. New York: Oxford University Press, 1996, 44–61.

The Arniston Memoirs: Three Centuries of a Scottish House, 1571–1838. Ed. George W. T. Omond. Edinburgh: David Douglas, 1887.

Attridge, Derek. *The Rhythms of English Poetry*. New York: Longman, 1982.

Aviram, Amittai F. *Telling Rhythm: Body and Meaning in Poetry*. Ann Arbor: University of Michigan Press, 1994.

Bagley, Christopher. "A Plea for Ignoring Race and Including Insured Status in American Research Reports on Social Science and Medicine." *Social Science and Medicine* 40:8 (1995): 1,017–19.

Bailyn, Bernard. *Voyagers to the West: A Passage in the Peopling of America on the Eve of the Revolution*. New York: Alfred A. Knopf, 1987.

Baker, Houston A. *Afro-American Poetics: Revisions of Harlem and the Black Aesthetic.* Madison: University of Wisconsin Press, 1988.

Modernism and the Harlem Renaissance. University of Chicago Press, 1987.

Turning South Again: Re-Thinking Modernism/Re-Reading Booker T. Durham, NC: Duke University Press, 2001.

"The Black Man of Culture: W. E. B. Du Bois and *The Souls of Black Folk.*" *Long Black Song: Essays in Black American Literature and Culture.* Charlottesville: University Press of Virginia, 1972, 96–108.

"Caliban's Triple Play." *"Race," Writing, and Difference.* Ed. Henry Louis Gates, Jr. University of Chicago Press, 1986, 381–95.

Balibar, Etienne. "Racism and Nationalism." *Race, Nation, Class: Ambiguous Identities.* New York: Verso, 1991, 37–67.

Ball, M. V. "The Mortality of the Negro." *Medical News* 64 (April 7, 1894): 389–90.

Balloch, Edward A. "The Relative Frequency of Fibroid Processes in the Dark-Skinned Races." *Medical News* 64 (January 13, 1894): 29–35.

Banton, Michael. *Racial Theories.* New York: Cambridge University Press, 1987.

Barkan, Elazar. *The Retreat of Scientific Racism: Changing Concepts of Race in Britain and the United States Between the World Wars.* New York: Cambridge University Press, 1992.

Barrell, John. *The Infection of Thomas De Quincey.* New Haven: Yale University Press, 1991.

Barringer, Paul B. "The American Negro, His Past and Future." Reprinted in *Racial Determinism and the Fear of Miscegenation, Pre-1900.* Anti-Black Thought, 1863–1925, vol. VII. Ed. John David Smith. New York: Garland Publishing, Inc., 1993, 435–58.

Bate, Jonathan. *Romantic Ecology: Wordsworth and the Environmental Tradition.* New York: Routledge, 1991.

Baym, Nina. *The Shape of Hawthorne's Career.* Ithaca, NY: Cornell University Press, 1976.

Beckerman, Michael. "Henry Krehbiel, Antonín Dvořák, and the Symphony 'From The New World.'" *Notes* 49:2 (December 1992): 447–73.

"The Master's Little Joke: Antonín Dvořák and the Mask of Nation." *Dvořák and His World.* Ed. Michael Beckerman. Princeton University Press, 1993, 134–54.

Bense, James. "Nathaniel Hawthorne's Intention in 'Chiefly About War Matters.'" *American Literature* 61:2 (May 1989): 200–14.

Bercovitch, Sacvan. *The Office of* The Scarlet Letter. Baltimore: Johns Hopkins University Press, 1991.

Bergner, Gwen. "Myths of Masculinity: The Oedipus Complex and Douglass's 1845 *Narrative.*" *The Psychoanalysis of Race.* Ed. Christopher Lane. New York: Columbia University Press, 1998, 241–60.

Berlant, Lauren. *The Anatomy of National Fantasy: Hawthorne, Utopia, and Everyday Life.* University of Chicago Press, 1991.

Berman, Russell A. "Du Bois and Wagner: Race, Nation, and Culture between the United States and Germany." *German Quarterly* 70:2 (Spring 1997): 123–35.

Bernbrock, John E. "Walt Whitman and 'Anglo-Saxonism.'" Ph.D. Dissertation. University of North Carolina, 1961.

Bernstein, Roberta. "History and Story, Sign and Design: Faulknerian and Postmodern Voices in *Jazz*." *Unflinching Gaze: Morrison and Faulkner Re-Envisioned*. Ed. Carol A. Kolmerten, Stephen M. Ross, and Judith Bryant Wittenberg. Jackson: University Press of Mississippi, 1997, 152–64.

Bhabha, Homi K. "DissemiNation." *Nation and Narration*. Ed. Homi K. Bhabha. New York: Routledge, 1990, 291–322.

Bhopal, Raj. "Is Research Into Ethnicity and Health Racist, Unsound, or Important Science?" *BMJ* 314 (June 14, 1997): 1752.

Boeckmann, Cathy. *A Question of Character: Scientific Racism and the Genres of American Fiction, 1892–1912*. Tuscaloosa: University of Alabama Press, 2000.

Bogle, Donald. *Toms, Coons, Mulattoes, Mammies, & Bucks: An Interpretive History of Blacks in American Films*. 4th edn. New York: Continuum, 2001.

Bohlman, Philip V. "Musicology as a Political Act." *Journal of Musicology* 11:4 (Fall 1993): 411–36.

Boomsliter, Paul C., Warren Creel, and George S. Hastings, Jr. "Perception and English Poetic Meter." *PMLA* 88:2 (March 1973): 200–08.

Bouson, J. Brooks. *Quite as it's Kept: Shame, Trauma, and Race in the Novels of Toni Morrison*. Albany: State University of New York Press, 2000.

Bradley, Sculley. "The Fundamental Metrical Principle in Whitman's Poetry." *American Literature* 10 (January 1939): 437–59. Reprinted in *On Whitman: The Best from* American Literature. Ed. Edwin H. Cady and Louis J. Budd. Durham, NC: Duke University Press, 1987, 49–71.

Brodhead, Richard. *The School of Hawthorne*. New York: Oxford University Press, 1986.

"Regionalism and the Upper Class." *Rethinking Class: Literary Studies and Social Formations*. Ed. Wai Chee Dimock and Michael T. Gilmore. New York: Columbia University Press, 1994, 150–74.

Brodnax, Benjamin H. "Correspondence." *New York Medical Times* 23 (1895): 322.

Brogan, Kathleen. *Cultural Haunting: Ghosts and Ethnicity in Recent American Literature*. Charlottesville: University Press of Virginia, 1998.

Brown, Fahamisha Patricia. *Performing the Word: African American Poetry as Vernacular Culture*. New Brunswick, NJ: Rutgers University Press, 1999.

Bruce, Jr., Dickerson D. "W. E. B. Du Bois and the Idea of Double Consciousness." *American Literature* 64:2 (June 1992): 299–309.

Bryce, Thomas H. "Notes on the Myology of a Negro." *Journal of Anatomy and Physiology* 31 (1897): 607–18.

Buck, Dudley and Sidney Lanier. "The Centennial Meditation of Columbia." *The Union Restored: 1861–76*. Record 6 of *The Sounds of History; A Supplement to The Life History of the United States*. Time Inc., 1963. Side 2, track 12.

Buelens, Gert. *Enacting History in Henry James: Narrative, Power, and Ethics*. Cambridge University Press, 1997.

Buell, Lawrence. *The Environmental Imagination: Thoreau, Nature Writing, and the Formation of American Culture*. Cambridge, MA: Harvard University Press, 1995.

New England Literary Culture: From Revolution through Renaissance. New York: Cambridge University Press, 1986.

Burke, Edmund. *Reflections on the Revolution in France.* New York: Macmillan, 1988.

Burnett, Swan M. "Racial Influence in the Etiology of Trachoma." *Medical News* (November 22, 1890): 542–43.

Byers, J. Wellington. "Diseases of the Southern Negro." *Medical and Surgical Journal* 63 (1888): 734–37.

Byrd, W. Michael and Linda A. Clayton. "An American Health Dilemma: A History of Blacks in the Health System." *Journal of the National Medical Association* 84:2 (1992): 194–95.

Cable, George Washington. *The Grandissimes.* New York: Penguin Books, 1988.

Caldwell, Stephen H. and Rebecca Popenoe. "Perceptions and Misperceptions of Skin Color." *Annals of Internal Medicine* 122:8 (April 15, 1995): 614–17.

Carton, Evan. "Hawthorne and the Province of Romance." *ELH* 47 (1980): 331–54.

Carus-Wilson, Cecil. "The Production of Musical Notes from Non-Musical Sands." *Nature* 44:1136 (August 6, 1891): 322–23.

Caruth, Cathy. "An Interview with Geoffrey Hartman." *Studies in Romanticism* 35 (Winter 1996): 631–52.

Chandler, James K. *Wordsworth's Second Nature: A Study of the Poetry and Politics.* University of Chicago Press, 1984.

"The Historical Novel Goes to Hollywood: Scott, Griffith, and Film Epic Today." *The Romantics and Us: Essays on Literature and Culture.* Ed. Gene W. Ruoff. New Brunswick, NJ: Rutgers University Press, 1990, 237–73.

Chatman, Seymour. *A Theory of Meter.* London: Mouton & Co., 1965.

Checkland, J. G. *Scottish Banking: A History, 1695–1973.* Glasgow: Collins, 1975.

Cherokee Removal: Before and After. Ed. William L. Anderson. Athens: University of Georgia Press, 1991.

The Cherokee Removal: A Brief History with Documents. Ed. Theda Perdue and Michael D. Green. New York: Bedford Books, 1995.

Christensen, Jerome. *Lord Byron's Strength.* Baltimore: Johns Hopkins University Press, 1993.

"Ecce Homo: Biographical Acknowledgment, the End of the French Revolution, and the Romantic Reinvention of English Verse." *Contesting the Subject: Essays in the Postmodern Theory and Practice of Biography and Biographical Criticism.* Ed. William H. Epstein. West Lafayette, IN: Purdue University Press, 1991, 53–83.

Christophersen, Merrill G. "The Anti-Nullifiers." *Oratory in the Old South, 1828–1860.* Ed. Waldo W. Braden. Baton Rouge, LA: Louisiana State University Press, 1970, 73–103.

"Simms' Northern Speaking Tour in 1856: A Tragedy." *Southern Speech Journal* 36 (Winter 1970): 139–51.

Clark, J. C. D. *English Society, 1688–1832.* Cambridge University Press, 1985.

Cmiel, Kenneth. *Democratic Eloquence: The Fight over Popular Speech in Nineteenth-Century America.* New York: William Morrow, 1990.

Colacurcio, Michael. *The Province of Piety.* Cambridge, MA: Harvard University Press, 1984.

Coleridge, Samuel Taylor. *Christabel.* In *The Oxford Authors: Samuel Taylor Coleridge.* Ed. H. J. Jackson, Oxford University Press, 1985, 66–84.

The Notebooks of Samuel Taylor Coleridge. 3 Vols. Ed. Kathleen Coburn. New York: Pantheon Books, 1957.

The Oxford Authors: Samuel Taylor Coleridge. Ed. H. J. Jackson. Oxford University Press, 1985.

"The Color of Negro Babies." *Medical News* (December 24, 1898): 844–45.

Cook, Raymond Allen. *Fire from the Flint: The Amazing Careers of Thomas Dixon.* Winston-Salem, NC: John F. Blair, 1968.

Cooper, Richard. "A Note on the Biologic Concept of Race and its Application in Epidemiologic Research." *American Heart Journal* 108 (1984): 715–22.

Cooper, Richard S. "Celebrate Diversity – Or Should We?" *Ethnicity & Disease* 1:1 (Winter 1991): 3–7.

Cooper, Richard and Richard David. "The Biological Concept of Race and its Application to Public Health and Epidemiology." *Journal of Health Politics, Policy, and Law* 11:1 (Spring 1986): 97–116.

Cornell, Drucilla. "The Wild Woman and All That Jazz." *Feminism Beside Itself.* Ed. Diane Elam and Robyn Wiegman. New York: Routledge, 1995, 313–21.

Corson, Eugene R. "The Vital Equation of the Colored Race and its Future in the United States." *The Wilder Quarter-Century Book.* Ithaca, NY: Comstock Publishing Co., 1893, 115–75.

Cosentino, Donald J. "Imagine Heaven." *Sacred Arts of Haitian Vodou.* Ed. Donald J. Consentino. Los Angeles: Fowler Museum of Cultural History, 1995, 44–55.

Cowgill, Warwick M. "Why the Negro Does Not Suffer from Trachoma." *Journal of the American Medical Association* 34 (1900): 399–400.

Crawford, Rachel. "Thieves of Language: Coleridge, Wordsworth, Scott, and the Contexts of 'Alice du Clos.'" *European Romantic Review* 7:1 (Summer 1996): 1–25.

Crawford, Robert. *Devolving English Literature.* 2nd Edn. Edinburgh University Press, 2000.

Cripps Thomas. *Slow Fade to Black: The Negro in American Film, 1900–1942.* New York: Oxford University Press, 1977.

Critical Essays on Toni Morrison's Beloved. Ed. Barbara H. Solomon. New York: G. K. Hall & Co., 1998.

Croker, John Wilson. *Two Letters on Scottish Affairs.* In *Thoughts on the Proposed Change of Currency & Two Letters on Scottish Affairs.* Ed. David Simpson and Alastair Wood. New York: Barnes & Noble, 1972.

Culler, A. Dwight. "Edward Bysshe and the Poet's Handbook." *PMLA* 63:3 (September 1948): 858–85.

Cuniberti, John. *The Birth of a Nation: A Formal Shot-By-Shot Analysis Together with Microfiche.* Woodbridge, CT: Research Publications, Inc., 1979.

Cunningham, R. M. "The Morbidity and Mortality of Negro Convicts." *Medical News* 64 (February 3, 1894): 113–17.

Cutter, Martha J. "Sliding Significations: Passing as a Narrative and Textual Strategy in Nella Larsen's Fiction." *Passing and the Fictions of Identity.* Ed. Elaine K. Ginsberg. Durham, NC: Duke University Press, 1996, 75–100.

Dahlhaus, Carl. *Between Romanticism and Modernism: Four Studies in the Music of the Later Nineteenth Century.* Trans. Mary Whittall. Berkeley and Los Angeles: University of California Press, 1980.

Dainotto, Roberto M. *Place in Literature: Regions, Cultures, Communities.* Ithaca, NY: Cornell University Press, 2000.

Dash, J. Michael. *Haiti and the United States: National Stereotypes and the Literary Imagination.* London: Macmillan Press Ltd., 1988.

Dauber, Kenneth. *The Idea of Authorship in America: Democratic Poetics from Franklin to Melville.* Madison: University of Wisconsin Press, 1990.

Davenport, Benjamin Rush. *Blood Will Tell.* Cleveland: Caxton Book Co., 1902.

Davis, F. James. *Who is Black?; One Nation's Definition.* University Park: Pennsylvania State University Press, 1991.

Dayan, Joan. "Vodoun, or the Voice of the Gods." *Sacred Possessions: Vodou, Santería, Obeah, and the Caribbean.* Ed. Margarite Fernández Olmos and Lizabeth Paravisini-Gebert. New Brunswick, NJ: Rutgers University Press, 1997, 13–36.

DeBeck, David. "Albinoism in the Negro." *Ohio Medical Journal* 7 (1896): 276–77.

Dekker, George. *The American Historical Romance.* New York: Cambridge University Press, 1987.

Dixon, Thomas. *The Clansman: An Historical Romance of the Ku Klux Klan.* Lexington, KY: University Press of Kentucky, 1970.

Dixon, W. A. "The Morbid Proclivities and Retrogressive Tendencies in the Offspring of Mulattoes." *Medical News* 6 (August 13, 1892): 180–82. Reprinted in *Journal of the American Medical Association* 20 (January 7, 1893): 1–2.

Donaldson, William. *The Jacobite Song: Political Myth and National Identity.* Aberdeen University Press, 1988.

Doubleday, Neal Frank. *Hawthorne's Early Tales, a Critical Study.* Durham, NC: Duke University Press, 1972.

Douglass, Frederick. "Lecture on Haiti, World's Fair, Chicago, January 2, 1893." *The Life and Writings of Frederick Douglass.* Vol. IV. Ed. Philip S. Foner. New York: International Publishers, 1955, 483.

Drayton, William. *An Oration Delivered in the First Presbyterian Church, July 4, 1831.* Charleston, SC: W. S. Blain and J. S. Burges, 1831.

Du Bois, W. E. B. *The Souls of Black Folk.* New York: Penguin Books, 1989.

"The Black Man Brings his Gifts." *Survey Graphic* 6:6 (March 1925): 655–58.

"The Conservation of Races." *W. E. B. Du Bois: A Reader.* Ed. David Levering Lewis. New York: Henry Holt and Company, 1995, 17–27.

"On *The Souls of Black Folk.*" *The Oxford W. E. B. Du Bois Reader.* Ed. Eric J. Sundquist. New York: Oxford University Press, 1996, 304–05.

Dunn, Douglas. "'A Very Scottish Kind of Dash': Burns's Native Metric." *Robert Burns and Cultural Authority.* Ed. Robert Crawford. Iowa City: University of Iowa Press, 1997, 58–85.

DuPlessis, Rachel Blau. "'HOO, HOO, HOO': Some Episodes in the Construction of Modern Whiteness." *American Literature* 67:4 (December 1995): 667–700.

Dvořák, Antonín. "[Dvořák's] Letter to the Editor." *Dvořák in America: 1882–1895*. Ed. John C. Tibbetts. Portland, OR: Amadeus Press, 1993, 359–61.

"Dvořák on His New Work." *Dvořák in America: 1882–1895*. Ed. John C. Tibbetts. Portland, OR: Amadeus Press, 1993, 362–64.

"For National Music." *Dvořák in America: 1882–1895*. Ed. John C. Tibbetts. Portland, OR: Amadeus Press, 1993, 361–62.

"Hear the 'Old Folks at Home.'" *Dvořák in America: 1882–1895*. Ed. John C. Tibbetts. Portland, OR: Amadeus Press, 1993, 365–66.

"Music in America." *Dvořák in America: 1882–1895*. Ed. John C. Tibbetts. Portland, OR: Amadeus Press, 1993, 370–80.

"The Real Value of Negro Melodies." *Dvořák in America: 1882–1895*. Ed. John C. Tibbetts. Portland, OR: Amadeus Press, 1993, 355–59.

Dye, Renée. "A Sociology of the Civil War: Simms's *Paddy McGann*." *Southern Literary Journal* 28:2 (Spring 1996): 3–23.

Dyer, Richard. "Into the Light: The Whiteness of the South in *The Birth of a Nation*." *Dixie Debates: Perspectives on Southern Cultures*. Ed. Richard H. King and Helen Taylor. London: Pluto Press, 1996, 165–76.

Epstein, Dena J. "The Story of the Jubilee Singers: An Introduction to its Bibliographic History." *New Perspectives on Music: Essays in Honor of Eileen Southern*. Ed. Josephine Wright. Warren, MI: Harmonie Park Press, 1992, 151–62.

Faner, Robert D. *Walt Whitman & Opera*. Philadelphia: University of Pennsylvania Press, 1951.

Faust, Drew Gilpin. *A Sacred Circle: The Dilemma of the Intellectual in the Old South, 1840–1860*. Baltimore: Johns Hopkins University Press, 1977.

Favor, J. Martin. *Authentic Blackness: The Folk in the New Negro Renaissance*. Durham, NC: Duke University Press, 1999.

Ferguson, Frances. *Solitude and the Sublime: Romanticism and the Aesthetics of Individuation*. New York: Routledge, 1992.

Fetter, Frank Whitson. *Development of British Monetary Orthodoxy, 1797–1875*. Cambridge, MA: Harvard University Press, 1965.

Finch, Annie. *The Ghost of Meter: Culture and Prosody in American Free Verse*. Ann Arbor: University of Michigan Press, 1993.

Finck, Henry T. *Wagner and His Works: The Story of His Life with Critical Documents*. Vol. II. New York: Haskell House Publishers, 1968.

Fleishman, Avrom. *The English Historical Novel*. Baltimore: Johns Hopkins Press, 1971.

Foner, Eric. *Free Soil, Free Labor, Free Men: The Ideology of the Republican Party Before the Civil War*. New York: Oxford University Press, 1970.

Reconstruction: America's Unfinished Revolution, 1863–1877. New York: Harper & Row, 1988.

Forbes, Duncan. "The Rationalism of Sir Walter Scott." *Cambridge Journal* 7 (1953): 20–35.

Fort, C. H. "Some Corroborative Facts in Regard to the Anatomical Difference Between the Negro and White Races." *American Journal of Obstetrics* 10 (1877): 258–59.

Fossum, Robert. "Time and the Artist in 'Legends of the Province House.'" *Nineteenth-Century Fiction* 21:4 (March 1967): 337–48.

Franklin, John Hope. *A Southern Odyssey: Travelers in the Antebellum North.* Baton Rouge: Louisiana State University Press, 1976.

Frantzen, Allen J. *Desire for Origins.* New Brunswick, NJ: Rutgers University Press, 1990.

Fredrickson, George M. *The Black Image in the White Mind.* New York: Harper & Row, 1971.

White Supremacy: A Comparative Study in American and South African History. New York: Oxford University Press, 1981.

Freiberg, Albert H. and J. Henry Schroeder. "A Note on the Foot of the American Negro." *American Journal of the Medical Sciences* 76 (1903): 1,033–36.

Frost, Robert. "To John T. Bartlett." *Robert Frost on Writing.* Ed. Elaine Barry. New Brunswick, NJ: Rutgers University Press, 1973, 58–60.

Frye, Northrop. *Anatomy of Criticism: Four Essays.* Princeton University Press, 1957.

Fussell, Paul. *Theory of Prosody in Eighteenth-Century England.* Archon Books, 1966.

Gabin, Jane S. *A Living Minstrelsy: The Poetry and Music of Sidney Lanier.* Macon, GA: Mercer University Press, 1985.

Gaines, Jane and Neil Lerner. "The Orchestration of Affect: The Motif of Barbarism in Breil's *The Birth of a Nation* Score." *The Sounds of Early Cinema.* Ed. Richard Abel and Rick Altman. Bloomington: Indiana University Press, 2001, 251–68.

Gaines, Kevin. *Uplifting the Race: Black Leadership, Politics, and Culture in the Twentieth Century.* Chapel Hill: University of North Carolina Press, 1996.

Garside, P. D. "Scott and the 'Philosophical' Historians." *Review of English Studies* 23 (1972): 147–61.

Gates, Jr., Henry Louis. *Figures in Black: Words, Signs, and the "Racial" Self.* New York: Oxford University Press, 1987.

"Editor's Introduction: Writing 'Race' and the Difference it Makes." *"Race," Writing, and Difference.* Ed. Henry Louis Gates, Jr. University of Chicago Press, 1986, 1–20.

Genovese, Eugene D. *Roll Jordan Roll: The World the Slaves Made.* New York: Vintage Books, 1976.

Gilroy, Paul. *Against Race: Imagining Political Culture Beyond the Color Line.* Cambridge, MA: Harvard University Press, 2000.

The Black Atlantic: Modernity and Double Consciousness. Cambridge, MA: Harvard University Press, 1993.

Ginna, Peter. "Taking Place." *American Places: Encounters with History.* Ed. William E. Leuchtenburg. New York: Oxford University Press, 2000, xvii–xviii.

Ginsberg, Elaine K. "Introduction: The Politics of Passing." *Passing and the Fictions of Identity.* Ed. Elaine K. Ginsberg. Durham, NC: Duke University Press, 1996, 1–18.

Ginzburg, Carlo. "Clues: Morelli, Freud, and Sherlock Holmes." *The Sign of Three: Dupin, Holmes, Peirce.* Ed. Umberto Eco and Thomas A. Sebeok. Bloomington: Indiana University Press, 1983, 81–118.

Gleason, Philip. *Speaking of Diversity: Language and Ethnicity in Twentieth-Century America.* Baltimore: Johns Hopkins University Press, 1992.

Goehr, Lydia. *The Quest for Voice: Music, Politics, and the Limits of Philosophy.* New York: Oxford University Press, 1998.

Goodman, Alan H. "Bred in the Bone?" *The Sciences* 37:2 (March/April 1997): 20–25.

Goodson, A. C. *Verbal Imagination: Coleridge and the Language of Modern Criticism.* New York: Oxford University Press, 1988.

Gordon, Avery F. *Ghostly Matters: Haunting and the Sociological Imagination.* Minneapolis: University of Minnesota Press, 1997.

Gordon, Jan. "'Liquidating the Sublime': Gossip in Scott's Novels." *At the Limits of Romanticism: Essays in Cultural, Feminist, and Materialist Criticism.* Ed. Mary A. Favret and Nicola J. Watson. Bloomington: Indiana University Press, 1994, 247–67.

Gossett, Thomas F. *Race: The History of an Idea in America.* Dallas, TX: Southern Methodist University Press, 1963.

Gould, Stephen Jay. *The Mismeasure of Man.* Rev. edn. New York: W. W. Norton & Company, 1996.

Ontogeny and Phylogeny. Cambridge, MA: Harvard University Press, 1977.

Graham, William. *The One Pound Note in the History of Banking in Great Britain.* Edinburgh: James Thin, 1911.

Grant, Mark N. *Maestros of the Pen: A History of Classical Music Criticism in America.* Boston: Northeastern University Press, 1998.

Great Britain, Parliament. *The Parliamentary Debates.* New series, vol. 14. London: H. M. Stationery Office, 1826.

Greenblatt, Stephen. "Racial Memory and Literary History." *PMLA* 116:1 (January 2001): 48–63.

Greer, Sammye Crawford. "'Station Island' and The Poet's Progress." *Seamus Heaney: The Shaping Spirit.* Ed. Catharine Malloy and Phyllis Carey. Newark: University of Delaware Press, 1996, 106–19.

Grewal, Gurleen. *Circles of Sorrow, Lines of Struggle: The Novels of Toni Morrison.* Baton Rouge: Louisiana State University Press, 1998.

Griffith, D. W. "The Continuity Script." *The Birth of a Nation, D. W. Griffith, Director.* Ed. Robert Lang. New Brunswick, NJ: Rutgers University Press, 1994, 43–156.

Gross, Harvey and Robert McDowell. *Sound and Form in Modern Poetry.* 2nd edn. Ann Arbor: University of Michigan Press, 1996.

Grossman, Allen. *Summa Lyrica: A Primer of the Commonplaces in Speculative Poetics.* In Allen Grossman, with Mark Halliday. *The Sighted Singer: Two Works on Poetry for Readers and Writers.* Baltimore: Johns Hopkins University Press, 1992, 205–374.

Gummere, Francis B. "The Translation of Beowulf, and the Relations of Ancient and Modern English Verse." *American Journal of Philology* 7 (1886): 46–78.

Guterl, Matthew Pratt. *The Color of Race in America, 1900–1940.* Cambridge, MA: Harvard University Press, 2001.

Hale, Edward Everett. *The Man Without a Country.* Ed. Carl Van Doren. New York: The Heritage Press, 1936.

Halevy, Elie. *The Liberal Awakening, 1815–1830.* Trans. E. I. Watkin. New York: Peter Smith, 1949.

Hall, J. R. "Mid-Nineteenth-Century American Anglo-Saxonism: The Question of Language." *Anglo-Saxonism and the Construction of Social Identity.* Ed. Allen J. Frantzen and John D. Niles. Gainesville: University Press of Florida, 1997, 133–56.

"Nineteenth-Century America and the Study of the Anglo-Saxon Language: An Introduction." *Preservation and Transmission of Anglo-Saxon Culture.* Ed. Paul E. Szarmach and Joel T. Rosenthal. Kalamazoo: Western Michigan University, 1997, 37–71.

Haller, John S. *Outcasts from Evolution: Scientific Attitudes of Racial Inferiority, 1859–1900.* Urbana: University of Illinois Press, 1971.

"The Negro and the Southern Physician: A Study of Medical and Racial Attitudes, 1800–1860." *Medical History* 16 (1972): 238–53.

"The Physician Versus the Negro: Medical and Anthropological Concepts of Race in the Late Nineteenth Century." *Bulletin of the History of Medicine* 44 (1970): 154–67.

"Race, Mortality, and Life Insurance: Negro Vital Statistics in the Late Nineteenth Century." *Journal of the History of Medicine and Allied Sciences* 25:3 (July 1970): 247–61.

Hamilton, Kristie. *America's Sketchbook: The Cultural Life of a Nineteenth-Century Literary Genre.* Athens: Ohio University Press, 1998.

Hamilton, Paul. *Coleridge's Poetics.* Stanford University Press, 1983.

Hamm, Charles. *Music in the New World.* London: W. W. Norton and Company, 1983.

"Dvořák, Stephen Foster, and American National Song." *Dvořák In America: 1892–1895.* Ed. John C. Tibbetts. Portland, OR: Amadeus Press, 1993, 149–56.

Handley, William R. "The House a Ghost Built: *Nommo*, Allegory, and the Ethics of Reading in Toni Morrison's *Beloved.*" *Contemporary Literature* 36:4 (Winter 1995): 676–701.

Harris, Joel Chandler. *Uncle Remus: His Songs and His Sayings.* Ed. Robert Hemenway. New York: Penguin Books, 1982.

Hartman, Geoffrey H. *Beyond Formalism: Literary Essays 1958–1970.* New Haven: Yale University Press, 1971.

The Fateful Question of Culture. New York: Columbia University Press, 1997.

Wordsworth's Poetry. New Haven: Yale University Press, 1964.

"Romantic Poetry and the Genius Loci." *Beyond Formalism: Literary Essays 1958–1970.* New Haven: Yale University Press, 1971, 311–36.

"Wordsworth, Inscriptions, and Romantic Nature Poetry." *Beyond Formalism: Literary Essays 1958–1970.* New Haven: Yale University Press, 1971, 206–30.

Hauer, Stanley R. "Thomas Jefferson and the Anglo-Saxon Language." *PMLA* 98 (October 1983): 879–98.

Haviland, Beverly. *Henry James's Last Romance: Making Sense of the Past and The American Scene.* New York: Cambridge University Press, 1997.

Hawkins, Hugh. *Pioneer: A History of the Johns Hopkins University, 1874–1889.* Ithaca, NY: Cornell University Press, 1960.

Hawthorne, Nathaniel. *Hawthorne: Tales and Sketches.* New York: Library of America, 1982.

The House of the Seven Gables. New York: Penguin Books, 1981.

Life of Franklin Pierce. Boston: Ticknor, Reed, and Fields, 1852.

The Scarlet Letter. In *The Norton Anthology of American Literature.* 4th edn. Vol. 1. New York: W. W. Norton & Company, 1994. 1273–1386.

Tanglewood Tales For Girls and Boys; Being a Second Wonder Book. Hawthorne: Tales and Sketches. New York: Library of America, 1974, 1,303–469.

A Wonder Book for Boys and Girls. Hawthorne: Tales and Sketches. New York: Library of America, 1974, 1,159–302.

"Chiefly About War-Matters." *The Atlantic Monthly* 10 (July 1862): 43–61.

"The Custom-House." In *The Norton Anthology of American Literature.* 4th edn. Vol. 1. New York: W. W. Norton & Company, 1994, 1,249–73.

"Review of Simms's *Views and Reviews* and Hood's *Poems.*" The Scarlet Letter *& Related Writings by Nathaniel Hawthorne.* Ed. H. Bruce Franklin. Philadelphia, PA: J. B. Lippincott, 1967, 285–87.

"Review of Whittier's *The Supernaturalism of New England.*" The Scarlet Letter *& Related Writings by Nathaniel Hawthorne.* Ed. H. Bruce Franklin. Philadelphia, PA: J. B. Lippincott, 1967, 289–91.

Heaney, Seamus. *The Redress of Poetry.* New York: Farrar, Straus and Giroux, 1995.

Seamus Heaney in Conversation with Karl Miller. London: Between the Lines, 2000.

"Book Learning." *Harvard Magazine* 103:1 (September – October 2000): 66–68.

"Englands of the Mind." *Preoccupations; Selected Prose, 1968–78.* New York: Farrar, Straus, Giroux, 1980, 150–69.

"Introduction." *Beowulf: A New Verse Translation.* Trans. Seamus Heaney. New York: Farrar, Straus and Giroux, 2000, ix–xxx.

"The Murmur of Malvern." *The Government of the Tongue.* New York: Farrar, Straus and Giroux, 1989, 23–29.

"Seamus Heaney." *Reading the Future: Irish Writers in Conversation with Mike Murphy.* Ed. Cliodhna Ni Anluain. Dublin: The Lilliput Press, 2000, 80–97.

Henderson, Andrea. *Romantic Identities: Varieties of Subjectivity, 1774–1830.* Cambridge University Press, 1996.

Henderson, Stephen E. *Understanding the New Black Poetry: Black Speech and Black Music as Poetic References.* New York: William Morrow & Co., 1973.

"Worrying the Line: Notes on Black American Poetry." *The Line in Postmodern Poetry.* Ed. Robert Frank and Henry Sayre. Chicago: University of Illinois Press, 1988, 60–82.

Herman, Allen A. "Toward a Conceptualization of Race in Epidemiologic Research." *Ethnicity & Disease* 6 (1996): 7–20.

Higham, John. *Strangers in the Land: Patterns of American Nativism, 1860–1925.* New York: Atheneum, 1963.

Higham, John W. "The Changing Loyalties of William Gilmore Simms." *The Journal of Southern History* 9:2 (May 1943): 210–23.

Hitchcock, H. Wiley. *Music in the United States: A Historical Introduction.* 2nd edn. Englewood Cliffs, NJ: Prentice-Hall, Inc., 1974.

Hobsbawm, Eric. "Introduction: Inventing Traditions." *The Invention of Tradition.* Ed. Eric Hobsbawm and Terence Ranger. Cambridge University Press, 1983, 1–14.

Hoffman, Frederick L. *Race Traits and Tendencies of the American Negro.* New York: American Economic Association, 1896.

Hogg, James. *The Jacobite Relics of Scotland.* New York: AMS Press, 1974.

Hollander, John. *Vision and Resonance: Two Senses of Poetic Form.* New York: Oxford University Press, 1975.

Holman, C. Hugh. "The Influence of Scott and Cooper on Simms." *The Roots of Southern Writing: Essays on the Literature of the American South.* Athens: University of Georgia Press, 1972, 50–60.

Holt, Thomas C. *The Problem of Race in the 21st Century.* Cambridge, MA: Harvard University Press, 2000.

Horowitz, Joseph. *Wagner Nights: An American History.* Berkeley: University of California Press, 1994.

Horsman, Reginald. *Race and Manifest Destiny.* Cambridge, MA: Harvard University Press, 1981.

Howard, William Lee. "The Negro as a Distinct Ethnic Factor." *Medical News* 84 (May 7, 1904): 905–06.

Houlberg, Marilyn. "Magique Marasa: The Ritual Cosmos of Twins and Other Sacred Children." *Sacred Arts of Haitian Vodou.* Ed. Donald J. Consentino. Los Angeles: Fowler Museum of Cultural History, 1995, 267–85.

Hubbard, Dolan. *The Sermon and the African American Literary Imagination.* Columbia: University of Missouri Press, 1994.

Hubron, Laënnec. "American Fantasy and Haitian Vodou." *Sacred Arts of Haitian Vodou.* Ed. Donald J. Cosentino. Los Angeles: Fowler Museum of Cultural History, 1995, 181–97.

Hughes, Ted. "Myths, Metres, Rhythms." *Winter Pollen: Occasional Prose.* Ed. William Scammell. Boston: Faber and Faber, 1994, 310–72.

Hume, David. *Enquiries Concerning Human Understanding.* Ed. L. A. Selby-Bigge. 3rd edn. Oxford: Clarendon Press, 1975.

Treatise of Human Nature. Ed. L. A. Selby-Bigge. 2nd edn. Oxford: Clarendon Press, 1978.

Huneker, James. "Dvořák's New Symphony: The Second Philharmonic Concert." *Dvořák and His World.* Ed. Michael Beckerman. Princeton University Press, 1993, 159–65.

Hutchinson, George. *The Harlem Renaissance in Black and White.* Cambridge, MA: Harvard University Press, 1995.

Huth, Edward J. "Identifying Ethnicity in Medical Papers." *Annals of Internal Medicine* 122:8 (April 15, 1995): 619–21.

Hyatt, H. Otis. "Note on the Normal Anatomy of the Vulvo-Vaginal Orifice." *American Journal of Obstetrics* 10 (1877): 253–58.

I'Anson, R. W. "Chorea in the Negro." *Virginia Medical Monthly* 2 (1875): 284.

Ingelbien, Raphaël. "Mapping the Misreadings: Ted Hughes, Seamus Heaney, and Nationhood." *Contemporary Literature* 40:4 (Winter 1999): 627–58.

Jackson, Fatimah Linda Collier. "Race and Ethnicity as Biological Constructs." *Ethnicity & Disease* 2 (1992): 120–25.

James, Henry. *The American Scene.* Ed. Leon Edel. Bloomington: Indiana University Press, 1968.

Johnson, David. *Music and Society in Lowland Scotland in the Eighteenth Century.* London: Oxford University Press, 1972.

Johnson, Edgar. *Sir Walter Scott: The Great Unknown.* Vol. II. New York: The Macmillan Company, 1970.

Johnson, James. *The Scots Musical Museum: 1787–1803.* Vol. I. Amadeus Press, 1991.

Johnson, James Weldon. *Along This Way.* New York: Viking Press, 1933.

Autobiography of an Ex-Colored Man. New York: Penguin Books, 1990.

God's Trombones: Seven Negro Sermons in Verse. New York: Penguin Books, 1990.

"Preface." *The Book of American Negro Spirituals.* Ed. James Weldon Johnson. New York: Viking Press, 1925, 11–50.

"Preface." *The Second Book of Negro Spirituals.* Ed. James Weldon Johnson. New York: Viking Press, 1926, 11–24.

"Preface to the First Edition." *The Book of American Negro Poetry [1922, 1931].* Rev. edn. Ed. James Weldon Johnson. New York: Harcourt Brace & Co., 1969, 9–48.

"Uncle Tom's Cabin and the Clansman." *The Selected Writings of James Weldon Johnson*, vol. I: *The New York Age Editorials (1914–1923).* Ed. Sondra Kathryn Wilson. New York: Oxford University Press, 1995, 12–13.

Johnson, Samuel. *Dictionary of the English Language.* New York: AMS Press, Inc., 1967.

Jones, Phyllis, Thomas A. LaVeist, and Marsha Lillie-Blanton. "'Race' in the Epidemiologic Literature: An Examination of the *American Journal of Epidemiology*, 1921–1990." *American Journal of Epidemiology* 134:10 (1991): 1,079–84.

Jordan, Winthrop. *White Over Black: American Attitudes Toward the Negro, 1550–1812.* New York: W. W. Norton & Co., 1968.

Joyce, Joyce A. "*Bantu, Nkodi, Ndungu,* and *Nganga*: Language, Politics, Music, and Religion in African American Poetry." *The Furious Flowering of African American Poetry.* Ed. Joanne V. Gabbin. Charlottesville: University Press of Virginia, 1999, 99–117.

Joynes, L. S. "Remarks on the Comparative Mortality of the White and Colored Populations of Richmond." *Virginia Medical Monthly* 2 (1875): 153–67; 212–17.

Kaufmann, David. *The Business of Common Life.* Baltimore: Johns Hopkins University Press, 1995.

Kerr, Andrew William. *History of Banking in Scotland.* 3rd edn. London: A. & C. Black, 1918.

Kibler, Jr., James E. *The Poetry of William Gilmore Simms: An Introduction and Bibliography*. Spartanburg, SC: Reprint Company, 1979.

"Stewardship and Patria in Simms's Frontier Poetry." *William Gilmore Simms and the American Frontier.* Ed. John Caldwell Guilds and Caroline Collins. Athens: University of Georgia Press, 1997, 209–20.

Kiple, Kenneth F. and Virginia Himmelsteib King. *Another Dimension to the Black Diaspora: Diet, Disease, and Racism.* New York: Cambridge University Pres, 1981.

Knapp, Steven. *Literary Interest: The Limits of Anti-Formalism.* Cambridge, MA: Harvard University Press, 1993.

Kraus, Joe. "How *The Melting Pot* Stirred America: The Reception of Zangwill's Play and Theater's Role in the American Assimilation Experience." *MELUS* 24:3 (Fall 1999): 3–19.

Krehbiel, Henry. *Afro-American Folksongs: A Study in Racial and National Music.* New York: G. Schirmer, 1914.

"Dr. Dvořaks American Symphony." Reprinted in "Henry Krehbiel, Antonín Dvořák, and the Symphony 'From the New World.'" By Michael Beckerman. *Notes* 49:2 (December 1992): 447–73.

Kreiger, Nancy. "Shades of Difference: Theoretical Underpinnings of the Medical Controversy on Black/White Differences in the United States, 1830–70." *International Journal of Health Services* 17:2 (1987): 259–78.

Lanier, Sidney. *The English Novel.* In *"The English Novel" and Essays on Literature.* Ed. Clarence Gohdes and Kemp Malone. Vol. IV of *The Centennial Edition of the Works of Sidney Lanier.* Ed. Charles R. Anderson. Baltimore, Johns Hopkins University Press, 1945, 3–251.

Letters 1874–1877. Ed. Charles R. Anderson and Aubrey H. Starke. Vol. IX of *The Centennial Edition of the Works of Sidney Lanier.* Ed. Charles R. Anderson. Baltimore: Johns Hopkins University Press, 1945.

Letters 1878–1881. Ed. Charles R. Anderson and Aubrey H. Starke. Vol. X of *The Centennial Edition of the Works of Sidney Lanier.* Ed. Charles R. Anderson. Baltimore: Johns Hopkins University Press, 1945.

Music and Poetry. [1898] (New York: Haskell House Publishers, 1969).

Poems and Poem Outlines. Ed. Charles R. Anderson. Vol. I of *The Centennial Edition of the Works of Sidney Lanier.* Ed. Charles R. Anderson. Baltimore: Johns Hopkins University Press, 1945.

The Science of English Verse. In *"The Science of English Verse" and Essays on Music.* Ed. Paull Franklin Baum. Vol. II of *The Centennial Edition of the Works of Sidney Lanier.* Ed. Charles R. Anderson. Baltimore: Johns Hopkins University Press, 1945, 21–244.

Shakespere and His Forerunners: The Peabody Lectures. In *Shakespere and His Forerunners.* Ed. Kemp Malone. Vol. III of *The Centennial Edition of the Works of Sidney Lanier.* Ed. Charles R. Anderson. Baltimore: Johns Hopkins University Press, 1945, 3–310.

"Tiger-Lilies" and Southern Prose. Ed. Garland Greever. Vol. v of *The Centennial Edition of the Works of Sidney Lanier.* Ed. Charles R. Anderson. Baltimore: Johns Hopkins University Press, 1945.

"The Centennial Cantata." In *"The Science of English Verse" and Essays on Music.* Ed. Paull Franklin Baum. Vol. II of *The Centennial Edition of the Works of Sidney Lanier.* Ed. Charles R. Anderson. Baltimore: Johns Hopkins University Press, 1945, 266–73.

"The Death of Byrhtnoth: A Study in Anglo-Saxon Poetry." In *"The English Novel" and Essays on Literature.* Ed. Clarence Gohdes and Kemp Malone. Vol. IV of *The Centennial Edition of The Works of Sidney Lanier.* Ed. Charles R. Anderson. Baltimore: Johns Hopkins University Press, 1945, 290–303.

"From Bacon to Beethoven." In *"The Science of English Verse" and Essays on Music.* Ed. Paull Franklin Baum. Vol. II of *The Centennial Edition of the Works of Sidney Lanier.* Ed. Charles R. Anderson. Baltimore: Johns Hopkins University Press, 1945, 274–90.

"Introduction to the Boy's Froissart." In *"The English Novel" and Essays on Literature.* Ed. Clarence Gohdes and Kemp Malone. Vol. IV of *The Centennial Edition of the Works of Sidney Lanier.* Ed. Charles R. Anderson. Baltimore: Johns Hopkins University Press, 1945, 346–54.

"Introduction to the Boy's King Arthur." In *"The English Novel" and Essays on Literature.* Ed. Clarence Gohdes and Kemp Malone. Vol. IV of *The Centennial Edition of the Works of Sidney Lanier.* Ed. Charles R. Anderson. Baltimore: Johns Hopkins University Press, 1945, 355–69.

"The Physics of Music." In *"The Science of English Verse" and Essays on Music.* Ed. Paull Franklin Baum. Vol. II of *The Centennial Edition of the Works of Sidney Lanier.* Ed. Charles R. Anderson. Baltimore: Johns Hopkins University Press, 1945, 251–65.

LaVeist, Thomas A. "Why We Should Continue to Study Race . . . But Do a Better Job: An Essay on Race, Racism and Health." *Ethnicity & Disease* 6 (1996): 21–29.

Levander, Caroline. *Voices of the Nation: Women and Public Speech in Nineteenth-Century Literature and Culture.* New York: Cambridge University Press, 1998.

Lester, J. C. and D. L. Wilson. *Ku Klux Klan: Its Origin, Growth and Disbandment.* Ed. Walter L. Fleming. 1905; New York: AMS Press, 1971.

Lewis, David Levering. *W. E. B. Du Bois: Biography of a Race, 1868–1919.* New York: Henry Holt, 1993.

Lillie-Blanton, Marsha and Thomas LaVeist. "Race/Ethnicity, the Social Environment, and Health." *Social Sciences and Medicine* 43:1 (1996): 83–91.

Lindsay, Vachel. *The Art of the Moving Picture.* New York: Liveright Publishing Corporation, 1970.

"The Congo: A Study of the Negro Race." *The Poetry of Vachel Lindsay.* Vol. 1. Ed. Dennis Camp. Peoria, IL: Spoon River Poetry Press, 1984, 174–78.

Liszka, James Jakób. *A General Introduction to the Semeiotic of Charles Sanders Peirce.* Bloomington: Indiana University Press, 1996.

Livingston, Robert Eric. "Glocal Knowledges: Agency and Place in Literary Studies." *PMLA* 116:1 (January 2001): 145–57.

Livingstone, David N. *Nathaniel Southgate Shaler and the Culture of American Science.* Tuscaloosa: University of Alabama Press, 1987.

Locke, Alain. *The Negro and His Music.* Port Washington, NY: Kennikat Press, Inc., 1968.

Lovell, Jr., John. *Black Song: The Forge and the Flame; The Story of How the Afro-American Spiritual was Hammered Out.* New York: Macmillan, 1972.

Lueck, Beth L. *American Writers and the Picturesque Tour: The Search for National Identity, 1790–1860.* New York: Garland Publishing, 1997.

Lukács, Georg. *The Historical Novel.* New York: Humanities Press, 1965.

Lutwack, Leonard. *The Role of Place in Literature.* Syracuse University Press, 1984.

Lydston, Frank G. and Hunter McGuire "Sexual Crimes Among the Southern Negroes – Scientifically Considered." *Virginia Medical Monthly* 20 (1893): 105–25.

MacDougall, Hugh B. *Racial Myth in English History: Trojans, Teutons, and Anglo-Saxons.* Montreal: Harvest House, 1982.

MacKay, John. *History of the Burgh of Canongate with Notices of the Abbey and Palace of Holyrood.* Edinburgh: Oliphant Anderson & Ferrier, 1900.

Magee, Bryan. *The Philosophy of Schopenhauer.* New York: Oxford University Press, 1997.

Malof, Joseph. "The Native Rhythm of English Meters." *Texas Studies in Literature and Language* 5:4 (Winter 1964): 580–94.

Mann, Arthur. *The One and the Many: Reflections on the American Identity.* University of Chicago Press, 1979.

"The Melting Pot." *Uprooted Americans: Essays to Honor Oscar Handlin.* Boston: Little, Brown and Company, 1979, 289–318.

Manning, Susan. *The Puritan-Provincial Vision.* Cambridge University Press, 1990.

"Ossian, Scott, and Nineteenth-Century Scottish Literary Nationalism." *Studies in Scottish Literature* 17 (1982): 39–54.

"'This Philosophical Melancholy': Style and Self in Boswell and Hume." *New Light on Boswell.* Ed. Greg Clingham. Cambridge University Press, 1991, 126–40.

Marks, Martin Miller. *Music and the Silent Film: Contexts and Case Studies, 1895–1924.* New York: Oxford University Press, 1997.

Marsh, J. B. T. *The Story of the Jubilee Singers: With their Songs. With Supplement Containing an Account of their Six Years' Tour Around the World, and Many New Songs, by F. J. Loudin.* New edn. Cleveland Printing & Publishing Co., 1892.

Martin, Jeffrey B. "Film out of Theatre: D.W. Griffith, *Birth of a Nation* and the Melodrama *The Clansman.*" *Literature/Film Quarterly* 18:2 (1990): 87–95.

Marx, Anthony W. *Making Race and Nation: A Comparison of South Africa, The United States, and Brazil.* New York: Cambridge University Press, 1998.

Mason, James O. "Understanding the Disparities in Morbidity and Mortality Among Racial and Ethnic Groups in the United States." *Annals of Epidemiology* 3:2 (March 1993): 120–24.

Mason, William. *Caractacus. The Works of William Mason.* Vol. II. London: T. Cadell and W. Davies, 1811, 77–174.

Matas, Rudolph. "The Surgical Peculiarities of the Negro: A Statistical Inquiry Based Upon the Records of the Charity Hospital of New Orleans (Decennium 1884–94)." *Transactions of the American Surgical Association* 4 (1896): 483–610.

McDaniel, Linda E. "American Gods and Devils in Simms's *Paddy McGann.*" *Long Years of Neglect: The Work and Reputation of William Gilmore Simms.* Ed. John Caldwell Guilds. Fayetteville: University of Arkansas Press, 1988, 60–75.

McDiarmid, Lucy. "Joyce, Heaney, and 'That Subject People Stuff.'" *James Joyce and his Contemporaries.* Ed. Diana A. Ben-Merre and Maureen Murphy. New York: Greenwood Press, 1989, 131–39.

McGann, Jerome J. *The Romantic Ideology.* University of Chicago Press, 1983.

McGee, Daniel T. "Post-Marxism: The Opiate of the Intellectuals." *MLQ* 58:2 (June 1997): 201–25.

McKusick, James C. "Symbol." *The Cambridge Companion to Coleridge.* Ed. Lucy Newlyn. Cambridge University Press, 2002, 217–30.

McMaster, Graham. *Scott and Society.* Cambridge University Press, 1981.

Merrell, Floyd. *Peirce, Signs, and Meaning.* University of Toronto Press, 1997.

Merritt, Russell. "Dixon, Griffith, and the Southern Legend: A Cultural Analysis of *The Birth of a Nation.*" *Cinema Examined: Selections from* Cinema Journal. Ed. Richard Dyer MacCann and Jack C. Ellis. New York: E. P. Duton, Inc., 1982, 165–84.

Métraux, Alfred. *Voodoo in Haiti.* Trans. Hugo Charteris. New York: Schocken Books, 1972.

Michaels, Walter Benn. *Our America: Nativism, Modernism, and Pluralism.* Durham, NC: Duke University Press, 1995.

"Autobiography of an Ex-White Man: Why Race is Not a Social Construction." *Transition* 73:1 (1998): 122–43.

"Jim Crow Henry James?" *The Henry James Review* 16:3 (Fall 1995): 286–91.

"The No-Drop Rule." *Critical Inquiry* 20 (Summer 1994): 758–69.

"Posthistoricism." *Transition* 70 (1998): 4–19.

"The Souls of White Folk." *Literature and the Body: Essays on Populations and Persons.* Ed. Elaine Scarry. Baltimore: Johns Hopkins University Press, 1988, 185–209.

"'You Who Never Was There': Slavery and the New Historicism, Deconstruction and the Holocaust." *Narrative* 4:1 (January 1996): 1–16.

Michel, Middleton. "Carcinoma Uteri in the Negro." *Medical News* (October 8, 1892): 400–03.

"Plica Circularis Congunctivæ in the Negro." *Medical News* (October 22, 1892): 461–63.

Miller, Perry. *The Raven and the Whale: The War of Words and Wits in the Era of Poe and Melville.* New York: Harcourt, Brace and Company, 1956.

Mills, Charles W. *Blackness Visible: Essays on Philosophy and Race.* Ithaca, NY: Cornell University Press, 1998.

The Racial Contract. Ithaca, NY: Cornell University Press, 1997.

Misak, C. J. *Truth and the End of Inquiry: A Peircean Account of Truth.* New York: Oxford University Press, 1991.

Molino, Michael R. *Questioning Tradition, Language, and Myth: The Poetry of Seamus Heaney.* Washington DC: Catholic University of America Press, 1994.

Monod, Paul Kléber. *Jacobitism and the English People, 1688–1788.* New York: Cambridge University Press, 1989.

Morrison, Toni. *Conversations with Toni Morrison.* Ed. Danille Taylor-Guthrie. Jackson: University Press of Mississippi, 1994.

Jazz. New York: Penguin, 1993.

Playing in the Dark: Whiteness and the Literary Imagination. New York: Vintage Books, 1992.

"From 'Rootedness: The Ancestor as Foundation' (1984)." *African American Literary Criticism, 1773–2000.* Ed. Hazel Arnett Ervin. New York: Twayne 1999, 198–202.

"Home." *The House that Race Built: Black Americans, U.S. Terrain.* Ed. Wahneema Lubiano. New York: Pantheon Books, 1997, 3–12.

"Interview [With Angels Carabi]." *Belles Lettres* 10.2 (Spring 1995): 40–43.

"Living Memory: A Meeting with Toni Morrison." In Paul Gilroy, *Small Acts: Thoughts on the Politics of Black Cultures* (London: Serpent's Tail, 1993), 175–82.

"Unspeakable Things Unspoken: The Afro-American Presence in American Literature." *Within the Circle: An Anthology of African American Literary Criticism from the Harlem Renaissance to the Present.* Ed. Angelyn Mitchell. Durham, NC: Duke University Press, 1994, 368–98.

Moss, Nancy. "What are the Underlying Sources of Racial Differences in Health?" *Annals of Epidemiology* 7 (1997): 320–21.

Munton, Alan. "Misreading Morrison, Mishearing Jazz: A Response to Toni Morrison's Jazz Critics." *Journal of American Studies* 31:2 (August 1997): 235–51.

Murphy, Peter. *Poetry as an Occupation and an Art in Britain, 1760–1830.* New York: Cambridge University Press, 1993.

"Fool's Gold: The Highland Treasures of MacPherson's Ossian." *ELH* 53:3 (Fall 1986): 567–91.

Nairn, Tom. *The Break-Up of Britain.* London: NLB, 1977.

"Natural and Artificial 'Singing' Sands." *Nature* 386:6620 (March 6, 1997): 29.

Negus, Keith and Patria Román Velázquez. "Belonging and Detachment: Musical Experience and the Limits of Identity." *Poetics 30* (2002): 133–45.

The New Negro: An Interpretation. Ed. Alain Locke. New York: Albert and Charles Boni, 1925.

The New Oxford Annotated Bible. New rev. standard version. New York: Oxford University Press, 1991.

The New Princeton Encyclopedia of Poetry and Poetics. Ed. Alex Preminger and T. V. F. Brogan. Princeton University Press, 1993.

Nicholls, David. *From Dessalines to Duvalier: Race, Colour and National Independence in Haiti*. New York: Cambridge University Press, 1979.

North, Michael. *The Dialect of Modernism: Race, Language, and Twentieth-Century Literature*. New York: Oxford University Press, 1994.

Nowlin, Michael. "Toni Morrison's *Jazz* and the Racial Dreams of the American Writer." *American Literature* 71:1 (March 1999): 151–74.

Nussbaum, Martha. *Poetic Justice: The Literary Imagination and Public Life*. Boston: Beacon Press, 1995.

O'Brien, Eugene. *Seamus Heaney and the Place of Writing*. Gainesville: University Press of Florida, 2002.

O'Donnell, Brennan. *The Passion of Meter: A Study of Wordsworth's Metrical Art*. Kent State University Press, 1995.

O'Malley, Michael. "Specie and Species: Race and the Money Question in Nineteenth-Century America." *The American Historical Review* 99:2 (April 1994): 369–408.

O'Sullivan, John L. '"Introduction." *United States Magazine and Democratic Review* 1:1 (October 1837): 1–15.

Osborne, Newton G. and Marvin D. Feit. "The Use of Race in Medical Research." *Journal of the American Medical Association* 267 (1992): 275–79.

Osmond, T. S. *English Metrists*. New York: Phaeton Press, 1968.

Outlaw, Lucius T. *On Race and Philosophy*. New York: Routledge, 1996.

Peirce, Charles Sanders. *The Collected Papers of Charles Sanders Peirce*. 8 volumes. Ed. Paul Hartshorne and Paul Weiss. Cambridge, MA: Harvard University Press, 1931–58.

Elements of Logic. Vol. II of *Collected Papers of Charles Sanders Peirce*. Ed. Charles Hartshorne and Paul Weiss. Cambridge, MA: Harvard University Press, 1965.

Pragmatism and Pragmaticism. Vol. V of *Collected Papers of Charles Sanders Peirce*. Ed. Charles Hartshorne and Paul Weiss. Cambridge, MA: Harvard University Press, 1965.

Reviews, Correspondence, and Bibliography. Vol. VIII of *Collected Papers of Charles Sanders Peirce*. Ed. Arthur W. Burks. Cambridge, MA: Harvard University Press, 1966.

Science and Philosophy. Vol. VII of *Collected Papers of Charles Sanders Peirce*. Ed. Arthur W. Burks. Cambridge, MA: Harvard University Press, 1966.

Peach, Linden. *Toni Morrison*. New York: St. Martin's Press, 1995.

Pels, Peter. "Occult Truths: Race, Conjecture, and Theosophy in Victorian Anthropology." *Excluded Ancestors, Inventible Traditions: Essays Toward a More Inclusive History of Anthropology*. Ed. Richard Handler. Madison: University of Wisconsin Press, 2000, 11–41.

Persaud, T. V. N. *A History of Anatomy: The Post-Vesalian Era.* Springfield, IL: Charles C. Thomas, 1997.

Phillips, Dana. "Nineteenth-Century Racial Thought and Whitman's 'Democratic Ethnology of the Future.'" *Nineteenth-Century Literature* 49:3 (December 1994): 289–320.

Pike, G. D. *The Jubilee Singers, and Their Campaign for Twenty Thousand Dollars.* Boston: Lee and Shepard, 1873.

Pinch, Adela. "Female Chatter: Meter, Masochism, and the *Lyrical Ballads.*" *ELH* 55 (1988): 835–52.

Pipes, William H. *Say Amen, Brother!: Old-Time Negro Preaching: A Study in American Frustration.* 1951; reprint. Westport, CT: Negro Universities Press, 1992.

Plessy v. Ferguson; A Brief History with Documents. Ed. Brook Thomas. Boston: Bedford Books, 1997.

Poe, Edgar Allan. "The Raven." *The Norton Anthology of American Literature.* 4th edn., Vol. 1. New York: W. W. Norton & Company, 1994, 1447–50.

Posnock, Ross. *Color and Culture: Black Writers and the Making of the Modern Intellectual.* Cambridge, MA: Harvard University Press, 1998.

Post, C. Gordon. "Introduction." In John C. Calhoun, *A Disquisition on Government and Selections from the Discourse.* Ed. C. Gordon Post. New York: Macmillan, 1953, vii–xxx.

"Predisposition to Disease in the Negro." *Medical News* (July 11, 1891): 52–53.

Quayle, Eric. *The Ruin of Sir Walter Scott.* New York: C. N. Potter, 1969.

Raboteau, Albert J. *A Fire in the Bones: Reflections on African-American Religious History.* Boston: Beacon Press, 1995.

"Race," Writing, and Difference. Ed. Henry Louis Gates Jr. University of Chicago Press, 1985.

Radano, Ronald. "Black Noise/White Mastery." *Decomposition: Post-Disciplinary Performance.* Ed. Sue-Ellen Case, Philip Brett, and Susan Leigh Foster. Bloomington: Indiana University Press, 2000, 39–49.

"Soul Texts and the Blackness of Folk." *Modernism/Modernity* 2:1 (January 1995): 71–95.

Radano, Ronald and Philip V. Bohlman. "Introduction: Music and Race, Their Past, Their Presence." *Music and the Racial Imagination.* Ed. Ronald Radano and Philip V. Bohlman. University of Chicago Press, 2000, 1–53.

Ragussis, Michael. *Figures of Conversion: "The Jewish Question" & English National Identity.* Durham, NC: Duke University Press, 1995.

Rampersad, Arnold. *The Art and Imagination of W. E. B. Du Bois.* Cambridge, MA: Harvard University Press, 1976.

Randel, William Pierce. *Centennial: American Life in 1876.* New York: Chilton Book Company, 1969.

Ray, J. Morrison. "Observations Upon Eye Diseases and Blindness in the Colored Race." *New York Medical Journal* 64 (July 18, 1896): 86–88.

Reed, Adolph. *Class Notes: Posing as Politics and Other Thoughts on the American Scene.* New York: The New Press, 2000.

W. E. B. Du Bois and American Political Thought: Fabianism and the Color Line. New York: Oxford University Press, 1997.

Reed, James. *Sir Walter Scott: Landscape and Locality.* London: The Athlone Press, 1980.

Reid, Thomas. *Essays on the Active Powers of Man.* In *Thomas Reid: Philosophical Works.* New York: Georg Olms Verlag, 1983, 509–679.

Reyburn, Robert. "Type of Disease Among the Freed People (Mixed Negro Races) of the United States." *Medical News* 63 (December 2, 1893): 623– 27.

Reynolds, David S. *Walt Whitman's America: A Cultural Biography.* New York: Knopf, 1995.

Rice, Alan J. "Jazzing it up a Storm: The Execution and Meaning of Toni Morrison's Jazzy Prose Style." *Journal of American Studies* 28 (1994): 423–32.

Riis, Thomas L. "Dvořák and his Black Students." *Rethinking Dvořák: Views From Five Countries.* Ed. David R. Beveridge. New York: Oxford University Press, 1996, 265–73.

Robertson, T. L. "The Color of Negro Children When Born." *Alabama Medical and Surgical Age* 10 (1897–98): 413–14.

Robinson, Amy, "It Takes One to Know One: Passing and Communities of Common Interest." *Critical Inquiry* 20 (Summer 1994): 715–36.

Robinson, Cedric J. "In the Year 1915: D.W. Griffith and the Whitening of America." *Social Identities* 3:2 (1997): 161–92.

Rodrigues, Eusebio L. "Experiencing *Jazz.*" *Modern Fiction Studies* 39:3–4 (Fall-Winter 1993): 733–54.

Rogin, Michael. *Subversive Genealogy: The Politics and Art of Herman Melville.* Berkeley: University of California Press, 1983.

"'The Sword Became a Flashing Vision': D. W. Griffith's *The Birth of a Nation.*" *The Birth of a Nation: D. W. Griffith, Director.* Ed. Robert Lang. New Brunswick, NJ: Rutgers University Press, 1994, 250–93.

Rose, Paul Lawrence. *Wagner: Race and Revolution.* New Haven: Yale University Press, 1992.

Ross, Marlon B. "Commentary: Pleasuring Identity, or the Delicious Politics of Belonging." *New Literary History* 31 (2000): 827–50.

Roy, Philip S. "A Case of Chorea in a Negro." *Medical Record* (August 20, 1892): 215.

Ruotolo Christina L. "James Weldon Johnson and the Autobiography of an Ex-Colored Musician." *American Literature* 72:2 (June 2000): 249–74.

Russett, Margaret. *De Quincey's Romanticism: Canonical Minority and the Forms of Transmission.* Cambridge University Press, 1997.

Saussure, Ferdinand de. *Course in General Linguistics.* Trans. Wade Baskin. New York: Philosophical Library, 1959.

Saxton, Alexander. *The Rise and Fall of the White Republic: Class Politics and Mass Culture in Nineteenth-Century America.* London: Verso, 1990.

Scholes, Percy A. *The Oxford Companion to Music.* 10th edn. London: Oxford University Press, 1970.

Schrager, Cynthia D. "Both Sides of the Veil: Race, Science, and Mysticism in W. E. B. Du Bois." *American Quarterly* 48:4 (1996): 551–86.

Scott, Paul Henderson. "The Malachi Episode." *Blackwood's Magazine* 320 (1976): 247–61.

Scott, Sir Walter. *Chronicles of the Canongate.* Vol. 1. Philadelphia: Henry T. Coates & Co., 1900.

The Highland Widow. In *Chronicles of the Canongate.* Vol. 1. Philadelphia: Henry T. Coates & Co., 1900, 91–164.

Ivanhoe. Ed. A. N. Wilson. New York: Penguin Books, 1984.

The Journal of Sir Walter Scott. Ed. W. E. K. Anderson. Oxford: The Clarendon Press, 1972.

The Letters of Sir Walter Scott. Vol. IX. Ed. H. J. C. Grierson. London: Constable & Co. Ltd., 1935.

Letters on Demonology and Witchcraft. London: John Murray, 1831.

Letters from Malachi Malagrowther, Esq. on the Proposed Change of Currency. In *The Miscellaneous Prose Works of Sir Walter Scott.* Edinburgh: R. Cadell, 1847. Vol. 1, 725–55.

The Surgeon's Daughter. In *Chronicles of the Canongate.* Vol. 1. Philadelphia: Henry T. Coates & Co., 1900, 18–191.

"Culloden Papers." *Quarterly Review* 14:28 (January 1816): 283–333.

"Essay on Imitations of the Ancient Ballad." *The Poetical Works of Sir Walter Scott.* Boston: Phillips, Sampson, and Company, 1856, 555–73.

"Introduction to Edition 1830 [of *The Lay of the Last Minstrel*]." *The Poetical Works of Sir Walter Scott.* Boston: Phillips, Sampson, and Company, 1856, 9–15.

"Introductory Remarks on Popular Poetry, and on the Various Collections of Ballads of Britain, Particularly Those of Scotland." *The Poetical Works of Sir Walter Scott.* Boston: Phillips, Sampson, and Company, 1856, 537–54.

"Sir Walter Scott on the Scottish Metrical Psalms." *Life and Work* (February 1884): 17–19.

Scottish National Dictionary, Designed Partly on Regional Lines and Partly on Historical Principles, and Containing All the Scottish Words Known to Be in Use or to Have Been in Use Since C. 1700. 10 Vols. Ed. William Grant. Edinburgh: Scottish National Dictionary Association, Ltd., 1931–75.

Scruton, Roger. *The Aesthetics of Music.* New York: Oxford University Press, 1997.

Sebeok, Thomas A. "Indexicality." *Peirce and Contemporary Thought.* Ed. Kenneth Laine Ketner. New York: Fordham University Press, 1995, 322–42.

Seward, Theodore F. "Preface to the Music." In J. B. T. Marsh, *The Story of the Jubilee Singers: With their Songs. With Supplement Containing an Account of their Six Years' Tour Around the World, and Many New Songs, by F. J. Loudin.* New edn. Cleveland Printing & Publishing Co., 1892, 155–56.

Shakespeare, William. *The Tempest.* Ed. Stephen Orgel. New York: Oxford University Press, 1987.

Shaler, Nathaniel S. *The Neighbor; a Natural History of Human Contacts.* Boston: Houghton Mifflin Company, 1904.

"European Peasants as Immigrants." *The Atlantic Monthly* 71 (May 1893): 646–55.

"The Negro Problem." *The Atlantic Monthly* 54 (November 1884): 696–709.

"Science and the African Problem." *The Atlantic Monthly* 66 (July 1890): 36–45.

Shillingsburg, Miriam J. "William Gilmore Simms and the Myth of Appalachia." *Appalachian Journal* 6 (Winter 1979): 110–19.

Sholl, E. H. "The Negro and his Death Rate." *Alabama Medical and Surgical Age* 3 (1890–91): 377–41.

Shufeldt, R. W. "Comparative Anatomical Characters of the Negro." *Medical Brief* 32 (1904): 26–28.

Shute, D. K. "Racial Anatomical Peculiarities." *American Anthropologist* 9 (1896): 123–32.

Silveri, Louis D. "The Singing Tours of the Fisk Jubilee Singers: 1871–1874." *Feel the Spirit: Studies in Nineteenth-Century Afro-American Music.* Ed. George R. Keck and Sherrill V. Martin. New York: Greenwood, 1988, 105–16.

Simms, William Gilmore. *Carl Werner, An Imaginative Story; With Other Tales of Imagination.* New York: George Adlard, 1838.

Father Abbot, or, The Home Tourist. Charleston, SC: Miller & Browne, 1849.

Geography of South Carolina: Being a Companion to the History of that State. Charleston, SC: Babcock & Co., 1843.

History of South Carolina. New and rev. edn. New York: Redfield, 1860.

The Letters of William Gilmore Simms. 6 vols. Ed. Mary C. Simms Oliphant *et al.* Columbia: University of South Carolina Press, 1952.

Paddy McGann; Or, The Demon of the Stump. Vol. III of *The Writings of William Gilmore Simms, Centennial Edition.* Columbia: University of South Carolina Press, 1972.

Poems Descriptive, Dramatic, Legendary and Contemplative. 2 vols. New York: Redfield, 1853.

Selected Poems of William Gilmore Simms. Ed. James Everett Kibler, Jr. Athens: University of Georgia Press, 1990.

Southward Ho! New York: Redfield, 1856.

Views and Reviews in American Literature, History and Fiction, First Series. Ed. C. Hugh Holman. Cambridge, MA: Harvard University Press, 1962.

The Yemassee: A Romance of Carolina. Rev. edn. New York: W. J. Widdleton, 1856.

"The Apalachian, a Southern Idyll: In Two Lectures." Ed. Miriam J. Shillingsburg. *Appalachian Journal* 1 (Autumn 1972): 2–11; (Spring, 1972): 147–60.

"Charleston: The Palmetto City." *Harper's New Monthly Magazine* 15:65 (June 1857): 1–22.

"Jocassée, A Cherokee Legend." *The Wigwam and the Cabin.* New York: Redfield, 1856, 209–17.

"The Legend of the Happy Valley, and the Beautiful Fawn." *Southern Literary Messenger* 20 (July 1854): 396–403.

"The Morals of Slavery." *The Pro-Slavery Argument; As Maintained by the Most Distinguished Writers of the Southern States.* New York: Negro Universities Press, 1968, 175–285.

"Poetical Works of Wordsworth." *Southern Quarterly Review* 18 (September 1850): 1–23.

"Preface." *War Poetry of the South.* Ed. William Gilmore Simms. New York: Richardson & Company, 1867.

"Sectional Literature." *The Magnolia* (April 1842): 251–52.

"Southern Literature." *The Magnolia* (1841): 1–6; 69–74.

"Summer Travel in the South." *The Southern Quarterly Review* ns 2 (September, 1850): 24–65.

Small-McCarthy, Robin. "The Jazz Aesthetic in the Novels of Toni Morrison." *Cultural Studies* 9:2 (1995): 293–300.

Smith, Geoffrey D. "The Reluctant Democrat and the Amiable Whig: Nathaniel Hawthorne, Edmund Quincy and the Politics of History." *Nathaniel Hawthorne Review* 18:2 (1992): 9–14.

Smith, Julian. "Hawthorne's *Legends of the Province-House.*" *Nineteenth-Century Fiction* 24:1 (June 1969): 31–44.

Smith, William Benjamin. *The Color Line: A Brief in Behalf of the Unborn* (1905). Reprinted in *Racial Determinism and the Fear of Miscegenation, Post-1900.* Series: Anti-Black Thought, 1863–1925 Vol. VIII. Ed. John David Smith. New York: Garland Publishing, Inc., 1993, 45–315.

Smythe, A. G. "The Position of the Hymen in the Negro Race." *American Journal of Obstetrics* 10 (1877): 638–39.

Sollors, Werner. *Beyond Ethnicity: Consent and Descent in American Culture.* New York: Oxford University Press, 1986.

Neither Black nor White yet Both: Thematic Explorations of Interracial Literature. New York: Oxford University Press, 1997.

Spencer, Jon Michael. *The New Negroes and Their Music: The Success of the Harlem Renaissance.* Knoxville: University of Tennessee Press, 1997.

Re-Searching Black Music. Knoxville: University of Tennessee Press, 1996.

Sacred Symphony: The Chanted Sermon of the Black Preacher. New York: Greenwood Press, 1987.

St. John, Sir Spenser. *Hayti; or the Black Republic.* 2nd edn. London: Frank Cass and Company Limited, 1971.

Stanton, William. *The Leopard's Spots: Scientific Attitudes Toward Race in America, 1815–59.* University of Chicago Press, 1960.

Starke, Aubrey Harrison. *Sidney Lanier: A Biographical and Critical Study.* Chapel Hill: University of North Carolina Press, 1933.

Starke, Aubrey. "Lanier's Appreciation of Whitman." *The American Scholar* 2 (October 1933): 398–408.

Stepan, Nancy. *The Idea of Race in Science: Great Britain, 1800–1960.* Hamden, CT: Archon Books, 1982.

Stepan, Nancy Leys and Sander L. Gilman. "Appropriating the Idioms of Science: The Rejection of Scientific Racism." *The "Racial" Economy of Science: Toward a Democratic Future.* Ed. Sandra Harding. Bloomington: Indiana University Press, 1993, 170–93.

Stepto, Robert B. *From Behind the Veil: A Study of Afro-American Narrative.* 2nd edn. Chicago: University of Illinois Press, 1991.

Stern, Julia. "Spanish Masquerade and the Drama of Racial Identity in *Uncle Tom's Cabin.*" *Passing and the Fictions of Identity.* Ed. Elaine K. Ginsberg. Durham, NC: Duke University Press, 1996, 103–30.

Stewart, Dugald. *Elements of the Philosophy of the Human Mind.* Philadelphia: William Young, 1793.

Stewart, Randall. "Hawthorne's Contributions to *The Salem Advertiser.*" *American Literature* 5 (1934): 327–41.

Stocking, George W. "The Turn-of-the-Century Concept of Race." *Modernism/Modernity* 1:1 (1994): 4–16.

Stolley, Paul D. "Race in Epidemiology." *International Journal of Health Services* 29:4 (1999): 905–09.

Sundquist, Eric J. *The Hammers of Creation: Folk Culture in Modern African-American Fiction.* Athens: University of Georgia Press, 1992.

To Wake the Nations: Race in the Making of American Literature. Cambridge, MA: Harvard University Press, 1993.

Sutherland, John. *The Life of Walter Scott.* Cambridge, MA: Blackwell, 1995.

Swann, Karen. "'Christabel': The Wandering Mother and the Enigma of Form." *Studies in Romanticism* 23 (Winter 1984): 533–53.

Thompson, Robert Farris. "From the Isle Beneath the Sea: Haiti's Africanizing Vodou Art." *The Sacred Arts of Haitian Vodou.* Ed. Donald J. Cosentino. Los Angeles: Fowler Museum of Cultural History, 1995, 91–119.

Tiffany, Louis McLane. "Comparison Between the Surgical Diseases of the White and Colored Races." *Transactions of the American Surgical Association* 5 (1887): 261–73.

Tipton, F. "The Negro Problem from a Medical Standpoint." *New York Medical Journal* 63 (May 22, 1886): 569–72.

Trevor-Roper, Hugh. "The Invention of Tradition: The Highland Tradition of Scotland." *The Invention of Tradition.* Ed. Eric Hobsbawm and Terence Ranger. Cambridge University Press, 1983, 15–41.

Trumpener, Katie. *Bardic Nationalism: The Romantic Novel and the British Empire.* Princeton University Press, 1997.

Tucker, William H. *The Science and Politics of Racial Research.* Chicago: University of Illinois Press, 1994.

Turner, Frederick. *Spirit of Place: The Making of an American Literary Landscape.* San Francisco: Sierra Club Books, 1989.

Turner, William C. "Foreword." In Jon Michael Spencer. *Sacred Symphony: The Chanted Sermon of the Black Preacher.* New York: Greenwood Press, 1988, ix–xii.

Turnipseed, E. B. "Letter from South Carolina." *Richmond and Louisville Medical Journal* 6 (1868): 194–95.

Turnipseed, Edward B. "Some Facts in Regard to the Anatomical Differences Between the Negro and White Races." *American Journal of Obstetrics* 10 (1877): 32–33.

Udelson, Joseph H. *Dreamer of the Ghetto: The Life and Works of Israel Zangwill.* Tuscaloosa: University of Alabama Press, 1990.

VanHoosier-Carey, Gregory A. "Byrhtnoth in Dixie: The Emergence of Anglo-Saxon Studies in the Postbellum South." *Anglo-Saxonism and the Construction of Social Identity.* Ed. Allen J. Frantzen and John D. Niles. Gainesville: University Press of Florida, 1997, 157–72.

W. C. "On the Production of Musical Notes from Non-Musical Sands." *Chemical News* 64:1650 (July 10, 1891): 25.

Wade, Maurice L. "From Eighteenth- to Nineteenth-Century Racial Science: Continuity and Change." *Race and Racism in Theory and Practice.* Ed. Berel Lang. New York: Rowman & Littlefield, 2000, 27–43.

Wagner, Richard. *Beethoven; With a Supplement from the Philosophical Works of Arthur Schopenhauer.* Trans. Ed Dannreuther. London: New Temple Press, 1870.

Wakelyn, Jon L. *The Politics of a Literary Man: William Gilmore Simms.* Westport, CT: Greenwood Press, 1973.

Wald, Gayle. *Crossing the Line: Racial Passing in Twentieth-Century U.S. Literature and Culture.* Durham NC: Duke University Press, 2000.

Wald, Priscilla. *Constituting Americans: Cultural Anxiety and Narrative Form.* Durham NC: Duke University Press, 1995.

Walther, Eric H. "Fire-Eaters and the Riddle of Southern Nationalism." *Southern Studies* 3:1 (Spring 1992): 67–77.

Ward, Andrew. *Dark Midnight When I Rise: The Story of the Jubilee Singers Who Introduced the World to the Music of Black America.* New York: Farrar, Straus, and Giroux, 2000.

Warner, William. *Licensing Entertainment: The Elevation of Novel Reading in Britain, 1684–1750.* Berkeley: University of California Press, 1998.

Warren, James Perrin. *Culture of Eloquence: Oratory and Reform in Antebellum America.* University Park: Pennsylvania State University Press, 1999.

Warren, Kenneth W. *Black and White Strangers: Race and American Literary Realism.* University of Chicago Press, 1993.

"Delimiting America: The Legacy of Du Bois." *American Literary History* 1 (Spring 1989): 172–89.

"The End(s) of African-American Studies." *American Literary History* 12:3 (Fall 2000): 637–55.

Warren, Rueben C. "The Morbidity/Mortality Gap: What is the Problem?" *Annals of Epidemiology* 3:2 (March 1993): 127–29.

Washington, Booker T. "The Atlanta Exposition Address." *Up from Slavery*, in *Three Negro Classics* (New York: Avon Books, 1965), 145–50.

Watson, Charles S. *From Nationalism to Secessionism: The Changing Fiction of William Gilmore Simms.* Westport, CT: Greenwood Press, 1993.

Welch, William L. "Lorenzo Sabine and the Assault on Sumner." *New England Quarterly* 65:2 (June 1992): 298–302.

Welsh, Alexander. *The Hero of the Waverley Novels; with New Essays on Scott.* Rev. edn. Princeton University Press, 1992.

Wheeler, Roxanna. *The Complexion of Race: Categories of Difference in Eighteenth-Century British Culture.* Philadelphia: University of Pennsylvania Press, 2000.

Whitman, Walt. *Prose Works 1892.* 2 vols. Ed. Floyd Stovall. New York University Press, 1964.

"Preface 1876 – *Leaves of Grass* and *Two Rivulets.*" *Leaves of Grass.* Ed. Sculley Bradley and Harold W. Boldgett. New York: W. W. Norton & Company, 1973, 746–56.

"Poetry To-day in America – Shakspere – The Future." *Prose Works 1892.* 2 vols. Ed. Floyd Stovall. New York University Press, 1964. Vol. 2, 474–90.

"Slang in America." *Prose Works 1892.* Vol. II. Ed. Floyd Stovall. New York University Press, 1964, 572–77.

Whitney, William Dwight. *The Life and Growth of Language.* New York: Dover, 1979.

Williamson, Joel. *A Rage for Order: Black/White Relations in the American South Since Emancipation.* New York: Oxford University Press, 1986.

Wimsatt, W. K. and Monroe C. Beardsley. "The Concept of Meter: An Exercise in Abstraction." *PMLA* 74:5 (December 1959): 585–98.

"A Word for Rhythm and a Word for Meter." *PMLA* 76:3 (June 1961): 305–08.

Witzig, Ritchie. "The Medicalization of Race: Scientific Legitimization of a Flawed Social Construct." *Annals of Internal Medicine* 125 (1996): 75–79.

Wordsworth, William. *The Oxford Authors: William Wordsworth.* Oxford University Press, 1990.

"Preface." *Lyrical Ballads.* In *The Oxford Authors: William Wordsworth.* Oxford University Press, 1990, 595–619.

Zack, Naomi. *Philisophy of Race and Science.* New York: Routledge, 2002.

Race and Mixed Race. Philadelphia, PA: Temple University Press, 1993.

Zamir, Shamoon. *Dark Voices: W. E. B. Du Bois and American Thought, 1888–1903.* University of Chicago Press, 1995.

Zangwill, Israel. *The Melting-Pot.* New York: The Macmillan Company, 1932.

"Afterword." *Race and Ethnicity in Modern America.* Ed. Richard J. Meister. Lexington, MA: D. C. Heath and Company, 1974, 22–27.

"Mr Zangwill Criticizes the Klan." In Edward Price Bell. "Creed of the Klansmen and Those Who Debate It." *Chicago Daily News Reprints* 8 (1924): 10–14.

Ziff, Larzer. *Literary Democracy.* New York: Viking Press, 1981.

Index